THE NEW PALGRAVE

TIME SERIES AND STATISTICS

D1637491

THE NEW PALGRAVE

TIME SERIES AND STATISTICS

EDITED BY

JOHN EATWELL · MURRAY MILGATE · PETER NEWMAN

W. W. NORTON & COMPANY

NEW YORK · LONDON

© The Macmillan Press Limited, 1990

First published in
The New Palgrave: A Dictionary of Economics
Edited by John Eatwell, Murray Milgate and Peter Newman
in four volumes, 1987

The New Palgrave is a trademark of
The Macmillan Press Limited

First American Edition, 1990
All rights reserved.

ISBN 0-393-02737-6
ISBN 0-393-95862-0 **PBK**.

W. W. Norton & Company, Inc.
500 Fifth Avenue
New York, NY 10110

W. W. Norton & Company, Ltd.
37 Great Russell Street
London WC1B 3NU

Printed in Hong Kong

1   2   3   4   5   6   7   8   9   0

Contents

Contents

General Preface

The books in this series are the offspring of *The New Palgrave: A Dictionary of Economics*. Published in late 1987, the *Dictionary* has rapidly become a standard reference work in economics. However, its four heavy tomes containing over four million words on the whole range of economic thought is not a form convenient to every potential user. For many students and teachers it is simply too bulky, too comprehensive and too expensive for everyday use.

By developing the present series of compact volumes of reprints from the original work, we hope that some of the intellectual wealth of *The New Palgrave* will become accessible to much wider groups of readers. Each of the volumes is devoted to a particular branch of economics, such as econometrics or general equilibrium or money, with a scope corresponding roughly to a university course on that subject. Apart from correction of misprints, etc. the content of each of its reprinted articles is exactly the same as that of the original. In addition, a few brand new entries have been commissioned especially for the series, either to fill an apparent gap or more commonly to include topics that have risen to prominence since the dictionary was originally commissioned.

As *The New Palgrave* is the sole parent of the present series, it may be helpful to explain that it is the modern successor to the excellent *Dictionary of Political Economy* edited by R.H. Inglis Palgrave and published in three volumes in 1894, 1896 and 1899. A second and slightly modified version, edited by Henry Higgs, appeared during the mid-1920s. These two editions each contained almost 4,000 entries, but many of those were simply brief definitions and many of the others were devoted to peripheral topics such as foreign coinage, maritime commerce, and Scottish law. To make room for the spectacular growth in economics over the last 60 years while keeping still to a manageable length, *The New Palgrave* concentrated instead on economic theory, its originators, and its closely cognate disciplines. Its nearly 2,000 entries (commissioned from over 900 scholars) are all self-contained essays, sometimes brief but never mere definitions.

Apart from its biographical entries, *The New Palgrave* is concerned chiefly with theory rather than fact, doctrine rather than data; and it is not at all clear how theory and doctrine, as distinct from facts and figures, *should* be treated in an encyclopaedia. One way is to treat everything from a particular point of view. Broadly speaking, that was the way of Diderot's classic *Encyclopédie raisonée* (1751–1772), as it was also of Léon Say's *Nouveau dictionnaire d'économie politique* (1891–2). Sometimes, as in articles by Quesnay and Turgot in the *Encyclopédie*, this approach has yielded entries of surpassing brilliance. Too often, however, both the range of subjects covered and the quality of the coverage itself are seriously reduced by such a self-limiting perspective. Thus the entry called '*Méthode*' in the first edition of Say's *Dictionnaire* asserted that the use of mathematics in economics 'will only ever be in the hands of a few', and the dictionary backed up that claim by choosing not to have any entry on Cournot.

Another approach is to have each entry take care to reflect within itself varying points of view. This may help the student temporarily, as when preparing for an examination. But in a subject like economics, the Olympian detachment which this approach requires often places a heavy burden on the author, asking for a scrupulous account of doctrines he or she believes to be at best wrong-headed. Even when an especially able author does produce a judicious survey article, it is surely too much to ask that it also convey just as much enthusiasm for those theories thought misguided as for those found congenial. Lacking an enthusiastic exposition, however, the disfavoured theories may then be studied less closely than they deserve.

The New Palgrave did not ask its authors to treat economic theory from any particular point of view, except in one respect to be discussed below. Nor did it call for surveys. Instead, each author was asked to make clear his or her own views of the subject under discussion, and for the rest to be as fair and accurate as possible, without striving to be 'judicious'. A balanced perspective on each topic was always the aim, the ideal. But it was to be sought not *internally*, within each article, but *externally*, between articles, with the reader rather than the writer handed the task of achieving a personal balance between differing views.

For a controversial topic, a set of several more or less synonymous headwords, matched by a broad diversity of contributors, was designed to produce enough variety of opinion to help form the reader's own synthesis; indeed, such diversity will be found in most of the individual volumes in this series.

This approach was not without its problems. Thus, the prevalence of uncertainty in the process of commissioning entries sometimes produced a less diverse outcome than we had planned. 'I can call spirits from the vasty deep,' said Owen Glendower. 'Why, so can I,' replied Hotspur, 'or so can any man;/ But will they come when you do call for them?' In our experience, not quite as often as we would have liked.

The one point of view we did urge upon every one of *Palgrave*'s authors was to write from an historical perspective. For each subject its contributor was asked to discuss not only present problems but also past growth and future prospects. This request was made in the belief that knowledge of the historical development of any theory enriches our present understanding of it, and so helps to construct better theories for the future. The authors' response to the request was generally so positive that, as the reader of any of these volumes will discover, the resulting contributions amply justified that belief.

John Eatwell
Murray Milgate
Peter Newman

Preface

This volume differs from all its companions in the present series in that its contents do not belong to economics, however broadly that is defined. Just as Holmes had his methods which the long-suffering Watson was supposed to apply, so statisticians have their methods which economists try to apply to help solve their own 'whodunits', such as: Was the Fed really guilty of causing the last recession? Did this year's bumper harvest really help to reduce inflation? Is Opec really to blame for the long-run trend of oil prices? Econometrics is the tool of choice to tackle such problems, and that in turn builds upon economic theory and statistical inference. While the first two disciplines are part of economics, statistics is a resource held and used in common by almost all the sciences, natural and social, and by many of the humanities as well.

Precisely because statistics has such universal application, economists can be proud not only of their many substantial contributions to the subject, but also that several major figures in their discipline, such as Edgeworth, Hotelling and Wald, are numbered among the great names in statistics. This is not entirely surprising. Given that most economic data are non-experimental in origin, it was quite natural that economists should develop ingenious methods for interrogating those data. Those pioneers saw clearly that the lack of controls implied by the absence of experiment must be compensated, as far as possible, by shrewdness and skill in posing just the right questions.

Thus, in his review of Jevons's posthumous *Investigations in Currency and Finance* (1884), Edgeworth said that the several long series of data contained in that book help us

to estimate the probability that the differences in the averages for different weeks and months are not accidental. The question which has just been indicated, one of the most delicate in statistics – namely, under what circumstances does a difference in figures correspond to a difference in fact – comes up often in these pages.

Here Edgeworth was asking, and soon after set out to answer, a basic question of inference that by now is second nature to all statisticians and most economists but which in 1884 was quite novel: How significant is the difference between two sample means? But neither then nor later did Edgeworth perceive another whole class of inferential problems inherent in Jevons's data, which derive from the fact that they constitute a set of *time series*; indeed, the very phrase had not yet been invented.

For example, Jevons's time series on the price of Consols is quite lengthy by the standards of economics, referring to the period 1731–1883 and occupying a fold-out diagram over 1.5 metres long. Valuable as it might be for descriptive economic history, however, in order that it can yield valid statistical inferences the whole century and a half of data needs to be broken up into connected sub-periods, each defined by the property that the probabilistic structure of the stochastic process which generates its observations remains constant. But to demonstrate that property requires, in turn, application of the special tools of time series analysis.

Technical methods of statistical inference and time series analysis are best learn from textbooks, 'sitting bolt upright', as Jimmie Savage once said, 'on a hard chair at a desk'. The present volume, ranging widely as it does over a variety of inductive methods used in economics, is a supplement to rather than a substitute for such textbooks, being more at home in an armchair than a hard chair. It is also complementary (and the relation is symmetric) to its companion volumes *Econometrics* and *Utility and Probability*.

The Editors

Statistical Inference in Time Series

P. WHITTLE

1 TIME STATIONARITY

We shall use t to denote time. In principle the world evolves in *continuous time*, when t may take any value. However, observations will effectively be taken discretely, commonly at regular time intervals (e.g. daily, weekly, monthly, ...). For analysis of observations it is then natural to work in *discrete time* and t may be assumed to take only integer values $\{\ldots, -2, -1, 0, 1, 2, \ldots\}$, if the observation interval is taken as the unit of time.

If x denotes a variable of interest then its value at time t will be denoted x_t. If x is observed then the sequence $\{x_t\}$ is a *time series*. Usually the values actually available will constitute a block of consecutive observations $(x_1, x_2, \ldots, x_T)$. This is the *sample*, of length T.

In a statistical approach one will generally regard the x_t as random variables. If one specifies the joint distribution of these random variables then one has specified a *stochastic process*. Such a specification constitutes a stochastic model. Time series analysis is concerned with observations on the model from the observations. There are also data-processing procedures which appeal to no very definite model.

Suppose that the joint distribution of the x_t is not affected by a time translation. Thus, for example, a sample of T consecutive observations has the same distribution, no matter at what point in time it starts. The process is then said to be *stationary*. Stationarity corresponds to the idea that the process has reached a state of statistical equilibrium.

It is common in expositions of time series analysis to assume the model stationary, and we shall in fact consider non-stationary variations only in Section 13. The reasons for this are that one can say little about an unrestricted class of processes, and stationarity is specific enough a property to imply both

1

structure and concepts. The justification is that the assumption is often realistic, at least after some transformation of the observations.

We shall clarify concepts by discussing initially the case of a single variable (so that x is scalar). However, economic contexts certainly require the joint consideration of several variables, and from Section 14 we generalize to the vector case.

We shall in general work with linear models. This is a very strong assumption, although there are certain linear representations which have a canonical status. For some discussion of nonlinear models, see Tong (1984).

2   THE AUTOCOVARIANCE FUNCTION

For a stationary process of finite mean square one can define the quantities

$$\mu = E(x_t)$$
$$v_s = \text{cov}(x_t, x_{t-s}) = E(x_t x_{t-s}) - \mu^2.$$

Here v_s is the covariance between values of x separated in time by a lag of s, it is consequently termed the *autocovariance* of the series at lag s. The corresponding correlation coefficient is the *autocorrelation* $\rho_s = v_s/v_0$. Note that $v_{-s} = v_s$; a relation with vector analogue (47).

The variation of v_s with s is important, as indicating in some degree how dependence between x_t and x_{t-s} varies with lag s. For a Gaussian process (for which all the variables are jointly normal) knowledge of μ and v_s determines the process completely. If the only stationarity demand made is on these first- and second-order moments, then the process is said to be *second-order stationary*.

Stationarity makes Fourier ideas (i.e. the decomposition of a series into sinusoidal components) natural. We shall consequently find that the power transform

$$g(z) = \sum_{-\infty}^{\infty} v_s z^s \tag{1}$$

and the Fourier transform

$$f(\omega) = g(e^{-i\omega}) = \sum_{-\infty}^{\infty} v_s e^{-i\omega s} \tag{2}$$

of the autocovariance play a central role. These are known respectively as the *autocovariance generating function* (AGF) and the *spectral density function* (SDF). The SDF $f(\omega)$ can be regarded as the density for the distribution of 'power' (quadratic variation) in the series over different frequencies ω.

3   FILTERS

Suppose that a stationary process $\{x_t\}$ is taken as the input to some dynamical system which then produces an output

$$y_t = \sum_j b_j x_{t-j}. \tag{3}$$

In a nomenclature taken from electronics such a system is termed a *filter*, in this case a linear time-invariant filter. The quantity b_j is the response in the output at time $t + j$ to a unit pulse in the input at time t; the *transient response*. Physical *realizability* would require that

$$b_j = 0 \quad (j < 0) \tag{4}$$

although there may be contexts where this is not assumed.

Statisticians would term relation (3) a *moving average* of y in terms of x. It would be termed a *one-sided* moving average if the realizability condition (4) were satisfied. If the b_j are such that the sum (3) is convergent in whatever sense is appropriate (often the mean-square sense) then relation (3) will generate a stationary output from a stationary input. This convergence requirement is essentially a *stability* requirement on the filter, or system. If we use v_s^x to denote the covariance function of x, etc., then relation (3) implies the transformation relation for the autocovariance:

$$v_s^y = \sum_j \sum_k b_j b_k v_{s+k-j}^x. \tag{5}$$

This transformation is expressed more significantly in terms of the AGF (1):

$$g^y(z) = B(z) B(z^{-1}) g^x(z). \tag{6}$$

Here $B(z)$ is the power transform

$$B(z) = \sum_j b_j z^j \tag{7}$$

of the transient response of the filter.

4   SOME STANDARD MODELS

The stationary process which is simplest in one sense is that so frequently assumed by statisticians: a sequence $\{\varepsilon_t\}$ of independent, identically distributed random variables. This is a discrete-time version of the engineers' *white noise*, and we shall consistently use ε to denote such a white noise variable. We shall also consistently make the standardizing assumptions $E(\varepsilon) = 0$ and $E(\varepsilon^2) = v$. Then the autocovariance for this process is

$$v_s = v\delta_s = \begin{bmatrix} v & s = 0 \\ 0 & s \neq 0 \end{bmatrix}.$$

The AGF is constant: $g(z) = 0$. The consequent constancy of $f(\omega)$ is taken as indicating that all frequencies are equally represented in white noise.

A derived process is the *moving average* (abbreviated to MA)

$$x_t = \sum_j b_j \varepsilon_{t-j} \tag{8}$$

which we now see as the output of a filter with a white noise input and transient response b_j. By formulae (5) and (6) x will have autocovariance

$$v_s = v \sum_j b_j b_{j-s}$$

and AGF

$$g(z) = v B(z) B(z^{-1}). \tag{9}$$

An even more natural and important model is the *autoregression* (abbreviated to AR)

$$\sum_{j=0}^{p} a_j x_{t-j} = \varepsilon_t. \tag{10}$$

This is a linear constant-coefficient difference equation driven by white noise. We regard relation (10) as a forward recursion determining x_t in terms of current input ε_t and past x-values. We then assume the normalization $a_0 = 1$, and (10) is an *AR of order p*. Define the generating function of coefficients

$$A(z) = \sum_j a_j z^j$$

a polynomial with factorization $\Pi_{j=1}^{p} (1 - \alpha_j z)$, say. Then for relation (10) to be stable (and so generate a stationary x-process) it is necessary and sufficient that all the α_j should have moduli less than unity, i.e. that all the zeros of $A(z)$ should lie strictly outside the unit circle in the complex plane. We can then legitimately 'solve' relation (10) for x in terms of current and past ε. That is, we can recast the AR to a realizable MA form

$$x_t = \sum_{j=0}^{\infty} b_j \varepsilon_{t-j}$$

with coefficients determined by

$$B(z) = A(z)^{-1}. \tag{11}$$

It then follows from (9), (11) that the output of the AR (10) has AGF

$$g(z) = \frac{v}{A(z)A(z^{-1})} \tag{12}$$

Relations (11) and (12) imply that both b_s and v_s are linear combinations of the powers α_j^s for non-negative s, and converge to zero exponentially with increasing s in fact v_s obeys the difference equation

$$\sum_{k=0}^{p} a_k v_{j-k} = v \delta_j \qquad (j = 0, 1, 2, \ldots). \tag{13}$$

These are the *Yule–Walker* relations, deducible from (12) or directly from (10).

Return for a moment to the MA model (8). One can make the reverse implication from (9): if v_s is zero for $|s| > q$, so that $g(z)$ has a representation (9) with $B(z)$ a polynomial of degree q, then the process could have been generated by an $MA(q)$ model

$$x_t = \sum_{j=0}^{q} b_j \varepsilon_{t-j}. \tag{14}$$

In fact, since there will be 2^q factorizations of type (9), in general distinct, there will be up to 2^q MA models (14) consistent with the specified autocovariance function. If $g(z)$ is such that it has no zeros on the unit circle then there is just one factorization of $g(z)$ for which $B(z)$ has no zeros inside the unit circle. This is spoken of as the *invertible* or *minimum phase* model. The term 'invertible' refers to the fact that the process (14) is in this case legitimately invertible to an autoregression of infinite order, with $A(z) = B(z)^{-1}$.

A hybrid autoregressive/moving-average model of orders p, q is the $ARMA(p, q)$ model

$$\sum_{0}^{p} a_j x_{t-j} = \sum_{0}^{q} b_j \varepsilon_{t-j}. \tag{15}$$

The stability requirement is again that $A(z)$ should have all its zeros outside the unit circle; the AGF is then

$$g(z) = v \frac{B(z)B(z^{-1})}{A(z)A(z^{-1})}.$$

This class of models is important as the class of models with rational AGF, derivable from the so-called state space models (see Section 14).

It is both significant and economical to write a relation such as (15) as

$$A(U)x = B(U)\varepsilon$$

where U is the *backwards translation operator*, having the effect

$$Ux_t = x_{t-1}.$$

We shall sometimes condense this notation even further to

$$Ax = B\varepsilon,$$

A and B then representing the distributed-lag linear operators of (15).

If the ARMA model (15) is normalized so that $B(z)$ has all its zeros outside the unit circle then the model is invertible to the infinite-order AR form

$$A_\infty x = \varepsilon, \tag{16}$$

where

$$A_\infty(z) = \sum_{0}^{\infty} a_\infty z^j = \frac{A(z)}{B(z)}.$$

5

A stationary model of another kind is the simple sinusoid

$$x_t = a \cos(\omega t - \psi) = a_1 \cos \omega t + a_2 \sin \omega t \qquad (17)$$

of amplitude a, frequency ω and phase ψ. This is indeed stationary if one assumes that a (possibly) and ψ (necessarily) are random variables, ψ being distributed independently of a and uniformly over its range of 2π. One has then $\mu = 0$, and, for non-zero ω,

$$v_s = \tfrac{1}{2}E(a^2) \cos \omega s,$$

so that this is an example of a process whose autocovariance does not decay to zero with increasing lag. The conditions on a and ψ imply that a_1, a_2 and $a_1 a_2$ all have zero expectations, and a_1^2 and a_2^2 have equal expectations. These are the conditions for second-order stationarity of process (17). If white noise is the 'elementary' process in the time domain, then the same can be said for process (17) in the frequency domain.

A feature of the AR model, emphasized when it was first introduced by Yule (1927), is that it can manifest quasi-periodicity. That is, it can penetrate the type of variation often observed in economic data: with a component which is somewhat periodic, but not rigidly so. If the system represented by the difference equation $A(U)x = 0$ has oscillatory tendencies, this will be reflected in the fact that $A(z)$ has complex zeros, and the transient response of the system has components which are damped oscillatory. For the stochastically disturbed system (10) these damped oscillatory responses will be continually restimulated by the driving noise ε, leading to a quasi-periodic behaviour of x_t and damped oscillatory components in v_s.

5 SAMPLE STATISTICS: THE CORRELOGRAM AND PERIODOGRAM

The standard sample is the observation block $(x_1, x_2, \ldots, x_T)$, denoted X_T. The sample equivalent of μ is the sample mean

$$\bar{x} = \frac{1}{T} \sum_1^T x_t. \qquad (18)$$

The sample equivalent of v_s for positive s would be the sample covariance between the two relatively lagged observation sets $(x_1, x_2, \ldots, x_{T-s})$ and $(x_{s+2}, \ldots, x_T)$ – based then upon only $T - s$ pairs of observations. If one estimates μ in both subsamples by $\bar{x}$ rather than by the subsample means then one would have an estimate of v_s:

$$C_s = \frac{1}{T - s} \sum_{t=s+1}^T (x_t - \bar{x})(x_{t-s} - \bar{x}) \qquad (s = 0, 1, \ldots). \qquad (19)$$

This is the *sample autocovariance*, corresponding to the *sample autocorrelation* $r_s = C_s/C_0$. Sometimes one, indeed, uses the actual subsample means in (19), rather than the full sample mean $\bar{x}$. It can be shown that, under mild conditions, C_s provides a consistent estimator of v_s as T increases. The graph of r_s against s is the classical *correlogram*. Sometimes we shall use this term loosely also for the graph of C_s, the unnormalized correlogram.

If one knew that μ were zero then there would be no need to correct for the mean, and v_s would be estimated simply by

$$C_s = \frac{1}{T-s} \sum_{t=s+1}^{T} x_t x_{t-s} \qquad (s = 0, 1, \ldots). \qquad (20)$$

It makes for considerable simplification if we assume this to be the case from now on, with the understanding that the deviation $x_t - \bar{x}$ is to be substituted wherever x_t occurs. This approach is justified by a general regression result in Section 12.

A very convenient notation is to use $\langle y_t \rangle$ to denote the *sample average* of the variable y. In this notation (18) and (20) can be compactly written $\bar{x} = \langle x_t \rangle$ and $C_s = \langle x_t x_{t-s} \rangle$.

The other classical statistic is the Schuster *periodogram*: a sample squared Fourier amplitude

$$I(\omega) = T^{-1} \left| \sum_{1}^{T} x_t \, e^{-i\omega t} \right|^2 = T^{-1} \left[\left(\sum x_t \cos \omega t \right)^2 + \left(\sum x_t \sin \omega t \right)^2 \right].$$

This can also be written

$$I(\omega) = \sum_{-T}^{T} (1 - |s|/T) C_s \, e^{-i\omega s}.$$

That is, $I(\omega)$ is related to C_s as the SDF $f(\omega)$ is related to v_s, with a tapering correction $(1 - |s|/T)$ which turns out to be appropriate for the finite-sample case. Indeed, if the SDF f exists at ω then $EI(\omega) \to f(\omega)$ with increasing T for almost all ω, and the non-negativity of I implies that $f(\omega) \geqslant 0$. However, $I(\omega)$ is *not* a consistent estimator of $f(\omega)$, as we shall see.

Historically, the periodogram predates the correlogram, and has a clear statistical significance of its own. Consider a model representing x_t as a sinusoid plus white noise:

$$x_t = a_1 \cos \omega t + a_2 \sin \omega t + \varepsilon_t \qquad (21)$$

Such models were common in the early days, when observations often concerned the motion of the planets, or tide levels. If one fits the a-coefficients by least squares then the diminution in residual sum of squares is just $2I(\omega)$. This equality is exact if

$$\omega = 2\pi j / T \qquad (22)$$

for some integer j (when the sample contains an integral number of periods) and holds to within a term of order T^{-1} otherwise, if one now looks for the frequency ω which fits best, one looks for the value maximizing $I(\omega)$.

This procedure is consistent if model (21) holds and a sinusoid is actually present, i.e. the a-coefficients are not both zero. If there is no sinusoid then the ω-fit is meaningless. In this case the sine and cosine transforms occurring in the definition of $I(\omega)$ are distributed normally and independently with zero means

7

and variances $Tv/2$ (at least at the frequencies (22)). This implies that $I(\omega)/v$ is distributed as a standard exponential variable. Indeed, the quantities I_j/v, where

$$I_j = I(2\pi j/T) \qquad (0 < j < T/2)$$

are distributed *independently* as standard exponential variables.

6 FREQUENCY CONCEPTS

Our derivation of the periodogram reinforces the interpretation that $I(\omega)$ measures the strength of variation in the sample at frequency ω, and so that the SDF $f(\omega)$ does the same for the process. The relation (6) for the action of a filter on the AGF can be written

$$f^y(\omega) = \beta(\omega)\beta(-\omega)f^x(\omega) = |\beta(\omega)|^2 f^x(\omega).$$

Here $\beta(\omega) = B(e^{-i\omega}) = \Sigma\, b_j\, e^{-ij\omega}$ is the *frequency response* of the filter, in that an input $e^{i\omega t}$ produces an output $\beta(\omega)e^{i\omega t}$.

For a process with smooth SDF the result asserted at the end of the last section can be extended: the quantities

$$I_j/f_j = I(2\pi j/T)/f(2\pi j/T) \qquad (0 < j < T/2) \tag{23}$$

are approximately distributed independently as standard exponential variables (Whittle, 1951). This assertion needs a more cautious statement if it is to be rigorous, but its validity in some version is fundamental to the subject. It makes plain that the periodogram does not estimate the SDF consistently; the information in the T observations is spread comparably over the canonical periodogram ordinates I_j.

If the SDF is of direct interest then an estimate $\hat{f}(\omega)$ is formed, either by the fitting of a parametric model, or by a linear smoothing of the periodogram $I(\omega)$. There is a large literature on the choice of smoothing kernels (see e.g. Brillinger, 1975). One tests for the presence of sinusoidal components against a background of noise, not necessarily white, by testing the values of $I(\omega)/\hat{f}(\omega)$.

7 LIKELIHOOD AND ESTIMATION FOR THE SCALAR AUTOREGRESSION

Suppose that x follows the AR(p) model (10), with Gaussian ε. Then the probability density of the sample X_T conditional on the (in fact unobserved) past values $x_0, x_{-1}, \ldots$ is

$$\phi = (2\pi v)e^{-p/2}e^{-S/2v}, \tag{24}$$

where S is the 'residual sum of squares'

$$S = \sum_{t=1}^{I} \varepsilon_t^2 = \sum_t \sum_j \sum_k a_j a_k x_{t-j} x_{t-k}.$$

When regarded as a function of the parameters, which will be v and a in this case, ϕ is the *likelihood*, and an important quantity is

$$L = -2 \log \phi$$

In virtue of the two previous formulae this may be written

$$L \sim \text{const} + T\left[\log v + v^{-1} \sum\sum a_j a_k C_{j-k}\right].$$ (25)

Here we have neglected the end effects deriving from the unknown past values, a term of relative order T^{-1}. The estimates $\hat{v}$ and $\hat{a}$ which minimize expression (25) are approximately the maximum likelihood estimates (MLE). These obey the equations

$$\sum_k \hat{a}_k C_{j-k} = \hat{v}\delta_j \qquad (j = 0, 1, 2, \ldots, p).$$ (26)

just a sample version of the first $p + 1$ Yule–Walker relations (13). Estimation equations of this type will recur, so we shall take advantage of the notation introduced in Section 5 to write (26) in the more compact form

$$\langle(\hat{A}x_t)x_{t-j}\rangle = \hat{v}\delta_j \qquad (j = 0, 1, 2, \ldots, p).$$

The quantity $\hat{v}$ is important, as a characterization of the fit of the model. In fact, we find from (25) amd (26) that the minimized value of L is

$$\hat{L} \sim \text{const} + T \log \hat{v}.$$ (27)

We can write $\hat{v}$ explicitly as

$$\hat{v} = |M_p| / |M_{p-1}|$$ (28)

where $|M_s|$ is the determinant of the matrix

$$M_s = \begin{pmatrix} C_0 & C_1 & C_2 & \ldots & C_s \\ C_{-1} & C_0 & C_1 & \ldots & C_{s-1} \\ . & . & . & . & . \\ C_{-s} & C_{1-s} & C_{2-s} & \ldots & C_0 \end{pmatrix}.$$ (29)

(In fact, we can set $C_{-s} = C_s$ etc., but we take the form (29) which will remain valid in the vector case to be considered in Section 15.)

Standard formulae for the covariances of MLEs (if the model is correct) give these as

$$\text{cov}(\hat{a}) \sim vT^{-1}M_{p-1}^{-1}$$

$$\text{var}(\hat{v}) \sim 2v^2 T^{-1}$$

$$\text{cov}(\hat{a}, \hat{v}) \sim 0.$$

8   TESTS OF FIT: ESTIMATES OF ORDER

Even if one accepts the AR hypothesis, one will wish to experiment with schemes of varying order. Let the quantities $\hat{L}$, $\hat{v}$ and $\hat{a}_j$ of the last section be denoted L_p, D_p and a_{pj}, to emphasize their dependence upon the order p of the fitted scheme. Then the principal result is that, if the true scheme is an AR of order p or less, then the quantity

$$L_p - L_{p+1} \sim T \, \log(D_p/D_{p+1}) \tag{30}$$

is distributed as χ_1^2, i.e. as a χ^2 variable with one degree of freedom. By checking whether the observed value of this quantity is significantly large on this basis one obtains some test of the fit of the $AR(p)$ model.

In general, as one increases p there will always be some improvement in fit (i.e. a diminution in D_p), which in practice will be significant if only T is large enough. One would wish for a more absolute basis on which to balance improvement in fit against increase in model complexity. Arguments based upon economical representations of the sample (see e.g. Rissanen, 1983) lead to the conclusion that one should choose the order p to minimize $T \log D_p + p \log T$. This is the BIC criterion due to Akaike (1977); his sometimes more favoured AIC criterion replaces the log T by a 2.

If one has fitted a model of order p, then, in going on to order $p + 1$, one need not begin the calculations *ab initio*. We know that

$$D_p = \sum_{k=0}^{p} a_{pk} C_{-k} = \langle \varepsilon_{pt}^2 \rangle,$$

where ε_{pt} is the residual from the fitted $AR(p)$. Define also

$$\Delta_p = \sum_{k=0}^{p} a_{pk} C_{p+1-k} = \langle \varepsilon_{pt} X_{t-p-1} \rangle.$$

Then a specialization due to Durbin (1960) of a general algorithm due to Levinson (1946) shows that

$$a_{p+1, p+1} = -\Delta_p/D_p$$

$$a_{p+1, j} = a_{pj} + a_{p+1, p+1} a_{p, p+1-j} \qquad (j = 1, 2, \ldots, p).$$

See p. 218 of Hannan and Deistler (1988) for a determination of D_p which is numerically more stable than that given above.

9 THE LIKELIHOOD FOR THE GENERAL GAUSSIAN MODEL

Suppose the model is such that process is Gaussian and specified to within a parameter vector $\theta = (\theta_j)$. The probability density $\phi(X_T | \theta)$ is then multivariate normal. By an appeal either to an infinite-order autoregressive representation of the process

$$\sum_{j=0}^{\infty} a_{\infty j} X_{t-j} = \varepsilon_t \tag{31}$$

or to the joint distribution of the normalized periodogram ordinates (23) one can deduce that the transformed likelihood $L = -2 \log \phi$ has approximately the form

$$L \sim \text{const.} + (T/2\pi) \int_{-\pi}^{\pi} [\log f(\omega) + I(\omega)/f(\omega)] \, d\omega \qquad (32)$$

(Whittle, 1951). This can alternatively be written in terms of the correlogram

$$L \sim \text{const.} + T \left[\log v + \sum_s v^{(s)} C_s \right]. \qquad (33)$$

where $v^{(s)}$ is defined by the Fourier expansion

$$f(\omega)^{-1} = \sum_s v^{(s)} e^{-i\omega s}$$

and the *prediction variance*

$$v = \exp \left[\frac{1}{2\pi} \int_{-\pi}^{\pi} \log f(\omega) \, d\omega \right]$$

is the variance of the white noise input ε in (31). (We assume that a_0 has been normalized to unity, when ε is known as the *innovation*.)

A useful associated result is the assertion (Whittle, 1953a) that the information matrix

$$\mathscr{I} = \left[-E \frac{\partial^2 \log \phi}{\partial \theta_j \partial \theta_k} \right]$$

has the expression

$$\mathscr{I} = \left[\frac{T}{4\pi} \int_{-\pi}^{\pi} \frac{\partial \log f}{\partial \theta_j} \frac{\partial \log f}{\partial \theta_k} \, d\omega \right]. \qquad (34)$$

The importance of this is that one expects the MLE $\hat{\theta}$ to be asymptotically normal with mean θ and covariance matrix

$$\text{cov}(\hat{\theta}) \sim \mathscr{I}^{-1}. \qquad (35)$$

Suppose the parameters are separated into the *scale parameter* $v = \text{var}(\varepsilon)$ and the *structural parameters* which determine the coefficients $a_{\infty j}$ in the AR representation (31). We shall now use θ to denote this vector of structural parameters alone. Then it is true that $\hat{v}$ and $\hat{\theta}$ are asymptotically independent, and that relations (34) and (35) hold for the vector of structural parameters on its own.

11

Let us write the AR representation (31) as

$$A(\theta, U)x_t = \sum_j a_j(\theta)x_{t-j} = \varepsilon_t$$

to emphasize the dependence of A_∞ upon the structural parameters θ. Then the ML estimation of θ is equivalent to the minimization of the residual sum of squares

$$S(\theta) = \sum_{t=1}^{T} [A(\theta, U)x_t]^2 \tag{36}$$

with respect to θ; the MLE of v is then

$$\hat{v} = \hat{S}/T = \min_\theta S(\theta)/T.$$

It must be confessed that the minimization of either expression (34) or (36) with respect to θ is straightforward only for the case of a finite AR with unconstrained coefficients. However, there are natural and effective algorithms for other cases, which we shall examine in the next two sections.

One can state a general test of fit valid under regularity conditions if T is large. It is also valid for the vector case of Sections 14 to 16 when v is a matrix. Suppose that v and a p-vector θ of structural parameters are estimated freely, and let D_p then be the MLE of v. Then the minimized value of L is

$$L_p \sim \text{const} + T \log|D_p|.$$

Suppose that the true model lies in the class considered, but that one also fits a model with a further q free parameters adjoined. Then

$$L_p - L_{p+q} \sim T \log(|D_p|/|D_{p+q}|)$$

is asymptotically distributed as χ^2 with q degrees of freedom. By testing this statistic as χ_q^2 one tests the adequacy of the p-parameter model.

Our neglect of end-effects can lead to serious biases if the autocovariance decays too slowly. Various improvements have been proposed; see e.g. Dahlhaus (1983).

10   ITERATIVE AND RECURSIVE ESTIMATION METHODS

There is an effective gradient algorithm for the minimization of the residual sum of squares (36). This employs some ideas first proposed by Durbin (1960), but the essential elements were added by Hannan and Rissanen (1982). We shall refer to it as the HR algorithm.

Suppose that at the ith stage of iteration one has an estimate $\theta^{(i)}$ of the structural parameter vector θ. Denote the estimate $A(\theta^{(i)}, U)x_t$ of ε_t at this stage by $\hat{\varepsilon}_t$. (This should also carry an i-superscript, which we leave understood, however, in order to simplify notation.) Define also the $1 \times p$ vector $\tilde{\partial}_t$ (i.e. a *row* vector) with jth element

$$\tilde{\partial}_{jt} = \left[\frac{\partial}{\partial \theta_j} A(\theta, U)x_t \right]_{\theta = \theta^{(i)}}. \tag{37}$$

Note that $\bar{\partial}_{jt}$ is not a parameter nor an estimate but a *sensitivity*, the rate of change of the estimated value of ε_t with respect to change in θ_j, with θ set equal to the current estimate $\theta^{(i)}$.

An application of the Gauss–Newton method to the minimization of the residual sum of squares (36) improves the estimate to

$$\theta^{(i+1)} = \theta^{(i)} - \left(\sum_t \bar{\partial}'_t \bar{\partial}_t \right)^{-1} \left(\sum_t \bar{\partial}'_t \varepsilon_t \right) \tag{39}$$

(the prime denoting transpose). This is the essential step of the DHR algorithm.

The sums in (39) are over the sample range $1 \leqslant t \leqslant T$. For the ARMA case the values of $\hat{\varepsilon}_t$ and $\bar{\partial}_t$ can be determined recursively, as we shall see in the next section. However, under all circumstances these values will depend upon the initial values $x_s (s \leqslant 0)$, which are unknown. However, for a model invertible to AR form this dependence will decline to zero with increasing t, and affect estimates only by a term of order T^{-1}.

Note that $v^{-1} \Sigma_t \bar{\partial}'_t \bar{\partial}_t$ supplies an estimate of the information matrix $\mathscr{I}$, since

$$E \sum_t \bar{\partial}'_t \bar{\partial}_t = v \mathscr{I}$$

if θ is given its true value.

An interesting and important point is that the HR algorithm adapts to on-line operation. We have implicitly taken the problem as one of *block estimation*, in that we make inferences from a given sample X_T. In engineering contexts a more natural and much studied approach is that of on-line *recursive estimation*, in which, given inferences from X_{t-1}, one updates these by some rule as the new observation x_t becomes available (see e.g. Young, 1984; Ljung, 1987; Chen, 1985).

Let $\theta^{(t)}$ be the estimate of θ formed at time t. Then the recursive form of relation (38) is

$$\theta^{(t)} = \theta^{(t-1)} - \left(\sum_i^t \bar{\partial}'_s \bar{\partial}_s \right)^{-1} \bar{\partial}'_t \hat{e}_t. \tag{39}$$

For the ARMA model the calculation can be made wholly recursive, as we shall soon see.

There are many recursive estimation algorithms proposed in the literature, generally of the so-called least-squares character. Algorithm (39) is a genuine ML algorithm (in the recursive sense). It seems to have been suggested first by Astrom and Mayne (1983). It is stable if the current θ estimate is reset within a certain stability region whenever it escapes from this region; with this precaution the estimate converges to a value which is consistent and efficient (Hannan, 1980).

11   THE FITTING OF ARMA MODELS

Consider the ARMA(p, q) model (15) with parameters (a, b, v) and normalization $a_0 = b_0 = 1$. Note that the Yule–Walker relations (13) still hold for $j > q$. Thus, by writing down the sample versions (26) of these relations for $j = q+1, q+2, q+p$,

13

say, we derive estimation equations for a. This approach is a special case of the use of *instrumental variables* (see Young, 1984). It will lead to estimates which are consistent but inefficient.

Consider assumed values (a, b) for the coefficients, with b chosen so that the model is invertible (see Section 4). We can then use the relation

$$B\hat{\varepsilon}_t = Ax_t \tag{40}$$

to determine the estimated residuals $\hat{\varepsilon}_1, \hat{\varepsilon}_2, \ldots, \hat{\varepsilon}_T$ from a knowledge of the sample X_T and of the initial values $x_0, x_{-1} \ldots, x_{1-p}$ and $\varepsilon_0, \varepsilon_{-1}, \ldots, \varepsilon_{1-q}$. As explained in the last section, these initial values are unknown, but if we assign them arbitrary values (zero, say) then this will affect estimates by no more than a term of order T^{-1}.

Proceeding in this way one can calculate a residual sum of squares

$$S(a, b) = \sum_1^T \hat{\varepsilon}_t^2$$

whose value will depend upon the particular (a, b) chosen. One then regards minimization of $S(a, b)$ as an exercise in numerical optimization.

This is the approach taken by Box and Jenkins (1970). However, one can greatly improve the approach by adopting the HR gradient technique described in the last section. With a, b given the current assumed values (now to be regarded as current estimates) we have the sensitivities

$$\tilde{a}_{jt} = B^{-1}x_{t-j}, \qquad \tilde{b}_{jt} = -AB^{-1}x_{t-j}.$$

These can be identified with ξ_{t-j} and η_{t-j}, where the sequences $\{\xi_t\}$ and $\{\eta_t\}$ are calculated recursively from

$$B\xi_t = x_t$$
$$B\eta_t = -\hat{\varepsilon}_t. \tag{41}$$

With these quantities determined, one has determined $\tilde{\partial}_t = (\xi_{t-1}, \xi_{t-2}, \ldots, \xi_{t-p}; \eta_{t-1}, \eta_{t-2}, \ldots, \eta_{t-q})$ and can use the algorithm (38) to determine improved estimates of a and b.

This is the algorithm as developed by Hannan and Rissanen. Actually, the full HR algorithm includes a procedure for obtaining good initial estimates of a and b. One first fits a high-order AR and from this obtains initial estimates $\varepsilon_t^{(1)}$ of the residuals (Stage I). One then fits the ARMA model by a simple least squares fit of x_t on $x_{t-1}, \ldots, x_{t-p}; \varepsilon_{t-1}^{(1)}, \ldots, \varepsilon_{t-q}^{(1)}$ (Stage II). The coefficient estimates thus obtained are then taken as the initial values to which the improvement algorithm (38) is to be applied (Stage III). Hannan shows that in fact a single application of this improvement then yields estimates which are asymptotically efficient. Estimation of *order* at the final stage is also important; see Hannan and Deistler (1988) for details.

If the estimation algorithm is to be used in the recursive manner (39) then relations (40) and (41) complete this to a wholly recursive calculation. In using relations (40) and (41) to determine $\hat{\varepsilon}_t$ and $\tilde{\partial}_t$ one will use the last available estimates of A and B, i.e. $A^{(t-1)}$ and $B^{(t-1)}$.

12 REGRESSIONS: THE ARMAX MODEL

Consider what one might regard as a regression model

$$x_t = du_t + u_t.$$

Here u_t is a variable which, like x_t, is observable at time t, but is assumed *exogenous*, in that the distribution of u_t conditioned on past x and u is in fact conditioned only by past u. The variable u_t is a stationary noise variable, not directly observed.

The least square estimate $\langle x_t u_t \rangle / \langle u_t^2 \rangle$ of d is the value minimizing $\Sigma_t (x_t - du_t)^2$. It seems a crude estimate in that, unlike the MLE (derived under assumption of Gaussian noise) it takes no account of the covariance structure of the noise.

However, one has the remarkable simplifying conclusion (due to Grenander and Rosenblatt (1957) that, if $\{u_t\}$ is stationary, then the LSE and MLE in fact differ only by a term of order T^{-1}. (Some regularity conditions are necessary; see Corollary 1 on p. 436 of Hannan (1970) for an exact statement.) It is this result that justifies the estimation of $\mu = E(x)$ by the sample mean $\bar{x}$, and the application of an analysis assuming $\mu = 0$ to the reduced variables $x_t - \bar{x}$ (see Section 5). In fact, the stationarity required of u is the weakened form, that sample autocorrelation coefficients should have a translation-invariant limit for large T. In this sense, even polynomials in t are stationary.

A model in which the exogenous variable affects the system more dynamically is the *ARMAX model*

$$Ax = Du + B\varepsilon, \tag{42}$$

where

$$Du_t = D(U)u_t = \sum_{j=0}^{r} d_j u_{t-j}$$

say.

If $B(U) = 1$, so that the noise input is white, then the model reduces to what might be termed an *ARX model*. In the case the ML estimation of A and D follows the simple LS pattern of relations (26). The estimates are yielded by the sets of linear equations

$$\langle (\hat{A}x_t - \hat{D}u_t)x'_{t-j} \rangle = \hat{v}\delta_j \qquad (j = 0, 1, \ldots, p)$$

$$\langle (\hat{A}x_t - \hat{D}u_t)u'_{t-j} \rangle = 0 \qquad (j = 0, 1, \ldots, r)$$

(the prime having relevance only in the vector case, considered in Section 15).

For the full ARMAX case we must extend the techniques used in the previous section. For current assumed values (a, b, d) of the coefficients the estimated residuals $\hat{\varepsilon}_t$ are now determined by

$$B\hat{\varepsilon}_t = Ax_t - Bu_t$$

The sensitivity vector $\bar{\theta}_t$ now has elements $(\xi_{t-1}, \ldots, \varepsilon_{t-p}; \eta_{t-1}, \ldots, \eta_{t-q}; \zeta_t, \ldots, \zeta_{t-r})$ where ξ, η are still determined recursively by (41) and ζ by

$$B\zeta_t = -u_t. \tag{43}$$

As in the ARMA case, the full DHR method obtains initial estimates by fitting a high-order ARX model to derive initial residual estimates $\varepsilon^{(1)}$ and then obtains initial estimates of the ARMAX coefficients by a LS fit of x_t on to appropriate $x_{t-j}, \varepsilon^{(1)}_{t-j}, u_{t-j}$.

13 NON-STATIONARITY TREND AND SEASONAL COMPONENTS

It must be accepted that economic series are not stationary. Classically, this was dealt with by decomposing the series into additive components

$$x_t = x_t^{(T)} + x_t^{(S)} + x_t^{(N)} \tag{44}$$

these being respectively the *trend* component, the *seasonal* component (reflecting for example effects induced by the season of the year) and the *stationary* (or *noise*) component.

Let us assume the seasonal component absent for the moment, so that the aim is the estimation (or, equivalently, the elimination) of trend. Note that 'trend' has not been defined mathematically; what may be regarded as trend on a short time scale might be regarded as stationary variation on a longer. Procedures suggested reflect this.

One approach is to estimate the trend by the fitting of some smooth function of time to the observations, say a polynomial in t. One generally has no reason for expecting such representations to have any physical validity (e.g. as predictors of the future course of the series). A related and similarly crude approach is to attempt to eliminate trend by *variate-differencing*, i.e. to form $\Delta^p x_t$ where $\Delta x_t = x_t - x_{t-1}$. This would eliminate trends of degree $p-1$, but would transform the SDF of the noise component by a factor $|1 - e^{-i\omega}|^{2p}$.

Another approach is to estimate trend by passing the observations through a *smoothing filter*

$$\hat{x}_t^{(T)} = \sum_s b_s x_{t-s}. \tag{45}$$

Since this operation is performed on the collected series rather than in real time, the filter need not be realizable, and will indeed in general be symmetric $(b_{-s} = b_s)$.

With the mention above of time scale in mind, one might imagine the ideal filter to be the *low-pass filter*, which faithfully extracts only the components of frequency ω less than ω_0, say. The coefficients for such a filter are

$$b_s = \frac{\sin(\omega_0 s)}{\pi s}. \tag{46}$$

However, these coefficients are so slowly convergent with increasing lead or lag (due to the ideal frequency response required of the filter) that their use in the numerical calculation (45) is scarcely practicable.

A compromise between the fitting and filtering approaches is to fit polynomials in a piecewise fashion. That is, we find the polynomial $P_t(s)$ of degree p in s which minimizes

$$\sum_{s=-q}^{q} (x_{t+s} - P_t(s))^2$$

and then estimate the trend value at time t by $P_t(0)$. This leads in fact to a smoothing filter of form (45) with weights which are now zero for s numerically larger than q. Many of the classic actuarial graduation formulae are derived this way.

The crudest such formula is that for $p = 0$, leading to the simple local average $(2q + 1)^{-1}\Sigma_{-q}^{q} x_{t-s}$ as an estimate of trend at time t. This is too simple, in that its performance as a separator of two ranges of frequency is disastrous. As p and q are increased the weights b_s approach the ideal but impracticable choice (46).

An objection to the additive assumption (44) is that trend, if present, will usually manifest itself in *all* the statistics of the process, rather than just its mean. One way of incorporating the possibility of trend into a true model is that suggested by Box and Jenkins (1970): to assume the validity of an AR, ARMA or ARMAX model, but no longer to require that $A(z)$ be such that the model is stable. If $A(z)$ is allowed to have a $(p + 1)$-fold zero at $z = 1$ then the transient response will have a polynomial component of degree p. The stochastically driven model will then show a 'disturbed' polynomial response; i.e. one in which the coefficients of the polynomial change randomly in time. Correspondingly, if $A(z)$ is allowed to have zeros inside the unit circle then the series generated by the model will show disturbed exponentially-growing components.

If the seasonal term is regarded as a rigidly periodic function of period d then the obvious estimate of this term at time t is the average of all observations in the sample of the form x_{t+jd} for integral j. For example, the 'February factor' is estimated by the mean of all the February figures.

Box and Jenkins allowed for seasonalities by taking an ARMA model in which lags of d occurred, so leading to dependence upon history a time d in the past as well as upon the immediate history. This will give a less rigid form of seasonality.

14 MULTIVARIATE MODELS

The multivariate case is the common one in almost all contexts, and certainly in the economic one. We shall in general refer to it as the *vector* case, in that the variables, x, ε, u etc. can all now be vector. We shall, for example, assume x to be an n-vector, by which we mean that it is a *column* vector of size n.

For stationary x the mean μ is then an n-vector, and autocovariance $v_s = E(x_t - \mu)(x_{t-s} - \mu)'$ is an $n \times n$ matrix for which

$$v - s = v_s'. \tag{47}$$

17

The AGF $g(z)$ is then also an $n \times n$ matrix function of the scalar argument z, and the SDF $f(\omega)$ and $n \times n$ matrix function of frequency ω. The non-negativity of f in the scalar case now has the expression that the matrix f is non-negative definite.

If the filter (3) has an n-vector input and an m-vector output then the transient response b_j is an $m \times n$ matrix, and relation (6) becomes

$$g^y(z) = B(z)g^x(z)B(z^{-1}).$$

If the z-argument is understoood then we can write this more compactly as

$$g^y = Bg^x \bar{B}.$$

Correspondingly for the vector form of the ARMA model (15) the expression for the AGF becomes $g = A^{-1}Bv\bar{B}\bar{A}^{-1}$, where v is the covariance matrix of the vector white noise input ε. Stability and stationarity would require that the determinant $|A(z)|$ have all its zeros outside the unit circle.

If one accepts the notion of a vector variable, then it is natural to think that in a sufficiently full description of a given physical situation the process would be Markov. If we persist with our assumption of linearity then the model would have to be of the AR(1) form, which we shall write in this case as

$$x_t = ax_{t-1} + \varepsilon_t. \tag{48}$$

This constitutes a *state-space model*, and x is then a *state variable*. Being an idealized description, x is in general not fully observable, and the convention is that at time t one observes

$$y_t = cx_{t-1} + \eta_t \tag{49}$$

where (ε_t, η_t) jointly constitute vector white noise.

Let $\mathscr{R}$ be the class of vector processes with rational AGF. Then $\mathscr{R}$ is closed under finite linear operations. In particular, the process (48) belongs to $\mathscr{R}$ if the dimension of x is finite, and so then does the process constituted by any subvector of x_t. This is regarded as demonstrating that the class $\mathscr{R}$ arises naturally, as the class of processes that can be derived linearly from a linear Markov process of some finite order.

For vector processes which are Gaussian and have an autoregressive representation expression (32) for the approximate likelihood becomes

$$L \sim \text{const.} + \frac{1}{2\pi} \int_{-\pi}^{\pi} [\log|f(\omega)| + \text{tr}(I(\omega)f(\omega)^{-1})]d\omega$$

(Whittle, 1953b). Here $I(\omega)$ is the matrix periodogram $T^{-1}(\Sigma_t\, x_t \mathrm{e}^{-i\omega t})(\Sigma_t\, x_t' \mathrm{e}^{i\omega t})$ and tr denotes 'trace'.

The autoregressive representation (31) of the process still plays the same key role in estimation. When the model is an unconstrained AR or ARX model then the estimation and test theory is scarcely more complicated than in the scalar case (see Section 15). Interestingly, in other vector cases one no longer has the complete decoupling of structural parameters θ and scale parameters v. This because v (the covariance matrix of ε) now contains some structural information: the correlation between different components of the input noise.

The sensitivity p-vector defined in (37) now becomes an $n \times p$ matrix, and the estimate-improvement step (38) becomes

$$\theta^{(i+1)} = \theta^{(i)} - \left(\sum_t \tilde{\theta}'_t \hat{v}^{-1} \tilde{\theta}_t \right)^{-1} \left(\sum_t \tilde{\theta}'_t \hat{v}^{-1} \hat{\varepsilon}_t \right). \tag{50}$$

Here $\hat{v}$ is the current estimate $T^{-1} \Sigma_t \, \varepsilon_t \hat{\varepsilon}'_t$ of v. The recursive form (39) of the algorithm becomes

$$\theta^{(t)} = \theta^{(t-1)} - J_t^{-1} \tilde{\theta}'_t v_t^{-1} \hat{\varepsilon}_t \tag{51}$$

where J_t and v_t obey the updating recursions

$$J_t = J_{t-1} + \tilde{\theta}'_t v_t^{-1} \tilde{\theta}_t$$

$$t v_t = (t-1) v_{t-1} + \hat{\varepsilon}_t \hat{\varepsilon}'_t.$$

15   INFERENCE FOR VECTOR AR AND ARX MODELS

A common linear econometric model is of the special ARX form

$$a_0 x_t + a_1 x_{t-1} = d_1 u_t + \varepsilon_t \tag{52}$$

where the variables are vector, and the coefficients correspondingly matrix. If one could divide through by a_0 then one would achieve the economists' *reduced form*. The objection to doing so is that in the form (52) one can use economic insight to set many constraints upon the coefficients, and so reduce the need for estimation. However, to apply maximum likelihood to the form (52) is not simple, because of the constraints and also because of the simultaneities (i.e. the more general form of a_0 may imply that components of x_t exert a mutual influence upon each other). There is a large literature on this subject.

If we consider the AR or ARX model, subject only to the normalizing constraint $a_0 = I$, then the scalar case generalizes immediately, and we have already given the estimation equations in Section 12. Tests of fit follow the pattern outlined in Section 9.

The Durbin version of the Levinson algorithm for the recursive (in order) fitting of autoregressions has an interesting twist to its vector generalization (Whittle, 1963). One finds it necessary to imagine that one is fitting autoregressions into both past and future

$$\sum_{j=0}^{p} a_j x_{t-j} = \varepsilon_t$$

$$\sum_{j=0}^{p} \bar{a}_j x_{t+j} = \hat{\varepsilon}_t.$$

19

Let the fitted coefficients for schemes of order p in the two cases be denoted a_{pj} and $\bar{a}_{pj}$. These are of course $n \times n$ matrices. Define the quantities

$$D_p = \sum_k a_{pk} C_{-k}, \qquad \Delta_p = \sum_k a_{pk} C_{p-k+1}$$

$$\bar{D}_p = \sum_k \bar{a}_{pk} C_k, \qquad \bar{\Delta}_p = \sum_k \bar{a}_{pk} C_{-p+k-1}.$$

Then the relations of Section 8 generalize to

$$a_{p+1,p+1} = -\Delta_p \bar{D}_p^{-1}, \qquad a_{p+1,j} = a_{pj} + a_{p+1,p+1} \bar{a}_{p,p-j+1} \qquad (j = 1, 2, \ldots, p)$$

$$\bar{a}_{p+1,p+1} = -\bar{\Delta}_p D_p^{-1}, \qquad \bar{a}_{p+1,j} = \bar{a}_{pj} + \bar{a}_{p=1,p+1} a_{p,p-j+1} \qquad (j = 1, 2, \ldots, p).$$

16   INFERENCE FOR VECTOR ARMAX MODELS

If we consider the ARMAX model (39) of Section 12 as a vector model subject only to the normalization $a_0 = b_0 = I$ then the material of that section generalizes virtually *en bloc*. The sensitivities are updated by the same recursions (41) and (42), these now being understood as matrix recursions. The principal difference is that the iterative algorithm (50) and recursive algorithm (51) now incorporate also updated estimates of v, as there indicated.

A more natural goal than the fitting of an ARMAX model might be the fitting of a state-space model (48), (49) on the basis of the observed y-values. Since the model is not required to explain the variation of the exogenous variables, one might generalize (48) to

$$x_t = ax_{t-1} + du_{t-1} + \varepsilon_t.$$

One has then to estimate the unobserved aspects of x as well as the model parameters. This is a highly unreduced problem, in that there are an infinite number of models of this type equally consistent with given y-statistics. The problem is in fact a latent variable problem, in which one can only hope to estimate a *dimension* (the required dimension of state-space) rather than a full set of structural relations. Whether economically meaningful coordinates can be found in the indicated state-space is the familiar problem of latent variable analysis.

REFERENCES

Akaike, H. 1977. On entropy maximization principle. In *Applications of Statistics*, ed. P.R. Krishnaiah, 27–41. Amsterdam: North-Holland.

Astrom, K.J. and Mayne, D.Q. 1983. A new algorithm for recursive estimation of controlled ARMA processes. In *Proc. 6th IFAC Symposium on Identification and System Parameter Estimation*, eds G.A. Bekey and G.W. Saridis, 122–6. Oxford: Pergamon.

Box, G.E.P. and Jenkins, G.M. 1970. *Time Series Analysis, Forecasting and Control*. San Francisco: Holden-Day.

Brillinger, D.R. 1975. *Time Series; Data Analysis and Theory*. New York: Holt, Rinehart and Winston.

Chen, H-F. 1985. *Recursive Estimation and Control for Stochastic Systems*. New York: Wiley.

Dahlhaus, R. 1983. Spectral analysis with tapered data. *J. Time Ser. Anal.* 4, 163–75.

Durbin, J. 1960. The fitting of time series models. *Rev. Internat. Inst. Statist.* 28, 233–44.

Grenander, U. and Rosenblatt, M. 1957. *Statistical Analysis of Stationary Time Series.* New York: Wiley.

Hannan, E.J. 1970. *Multiple Time Series.* New York: Wiley.

Hannan, E.J. 1980. The estimation of the order of an ARMA process. *Ann. Statist.* 8, 1071–81.

Hannan, E.J. and Rissanen, J. 1982. Recursive estimation of ARMA order. *Biometrika* 69, 91–4.

Hannan, E.J. and Deistler, M. 1988. *The Statistical Theory of Linear Systems.* New York: Wiley.

Levinson, N. 1946. The Wiener RMS (Root Mean Square) error criterion in filter design and prediction. *J. Math. Phys.* 25, 261–78.

Ljung, L. 1987. *System Identification: Theory for the User.* Englewood Cliffs, New Jersey: Prentice-Hall.

Rissanen, J. 1983. Universal prior for parameters and estimation by minimum description length. *Ann. Statist.* 11, 416–31.

Tong, H. 1984. *Threshold Models in Non-linear Time Series Analysis.* New York: Springer.

Whittle, P. 1951. *Hypothesis Testing in Time Series Analysis.* Uppsala: Almquist and Wicksell.

Whittle, P. 1953a. Estimation and information in stationary time series. *Arkiv for Matematik.* 2(23), 423–34.

Whittle, P. 1953b. The analysis of multiple stationary time series. *J. Roy. Statist. Soc. B.* 15, 125–39.

Whittle, P. 1963. On the fitting of multivariate autoregressions and the approximate canonical factorisation of a spectral density matrix. *Biometrika* 50, 129–34.

Young, P. 1984. *Recursive Estimation and Time Series Analysis.* Berlin: Springer.

Yule, G.U. 1927. On a method of investigating periodicities in disturbed series, with special reference to Wolfer's sunspot numbers. *Phil. Trans. Roy. Soc. A.* 226, 267–98.

ARIMA Models

A.C. HARVEY

Autoregressive integrated moving average (ARIMA) models are models which can be fitted to a single time series and used to make predictions of future observations. They owe their popularity primarily to the work of Box and Jenkins (1970), who defined the class of ARIMA and seasonal ARIMA models and provided a methodology for selecting a suitable model from that class.

The ARIMA class of models emerged as the result of a synthesis between the theory of stationary stochastic processes and certain *ad hoc* forecasting procedures based on the discounting of past observations. From the theoretical point of view the ability of an autoregressive-moving average (ARMA) process to approximate any linear stationary process was well known. On the other hand, it had been shown by Muth (1960) that the forecasts generated by the exponentially weighted moving average (EWMA) procedure, i.e.

$$\hat{y}_{t+1/t} = \lambda y_t + (1 - \lambda)\hat{y}_{t/t-1}, \tag{1}$$

where $\hat{y}_{t+1/t}$ is the prediction of y_{t+1} made at time t and λ is the smoothing constant, are identical to the optimal one step ahead forecasts which result when the differenced observations are modelled by a first order moving average process, i.e.

$$\Delta y_t = \xi_t + \theta \xi_{t-1}, \tag{2}$$

where ξ_t is a random disturbance term, Δ is the first difference operator and the MA parameter, θ, is equal to $\lambda - 1$. This result was extended to show that the forecasts produced by Holt's local linear trend procedure are the same as those given by a model in which second differences follow a second-order moving average process,

$$\Delta^2 y_t = \xi_t + \theta_1 \xi_{t-1} + \theta_2 \xi_{t-2}; \tag{3}$$

see Theil and Wage (1964), Nerlove and Wage (1964) and Harrison (1967). The nature of the synthesis effected by Box and Jenkins was to formulate a class of models in which the dth difference of the observations was taken to be stationary and hence capable of approximation by an ARMA process with p autoregressive parameters, $\phi_1, \ldots, \phi_p$ and q moving average parameters $\theta_1, \ldots, \theta_q$, i.e.

$$\Delta^d y_t = \phi_1 \Delta^d y_{t-1} + \cdots + \phi_p \Delta^d y_{t-p} + \xi_t + \theta_1 \xi_{t-1} + \cdots + \theta_q \xi_{t-q}. \qquad (4)$$

The specification of (4) is denoted by writing it as ARIMA (p, d, q). Thus (2) is ARIMA $(0, 1, 1)$ while (3) is ARIMA $(0, 2, 2)$.

Given the ARIMA class of models, it was necessary to provide a methodology for choosing a suitable model from the class. Box and Jenkins (1970) proposed a model selection cycle based on three stages: identification, estimation and diagnostic checking. In the identification stage tentative choices are made for the values of p, d and q using statistical tools such as the correlogram and the sample partial autocorrelation function. Given a specification of these values, the parameters in the model are estimated by maximum likelihood (ML) or an approximation to maximum likelihood. The residuals from the model are then subject to diagnostic checking to determine if they appear to be approximately random. If the model fails these diagnostic checks the complete cycle is repeated, starting with an attempt to identify a new model. Once a suitable model has been fitted, it can be used to make predictions of future observations, together with estimates of the corresponding mean square errors.

ARIMA models of the form (4) are not, in general, appropriate for modelling monthly and quarterly observations as these typically contain a seasonal pattern. However, Box and Jenkins (1970, ch. 9) observed that taking an EWMA of the observations combined with an EWMA of the observations on the current month in previous years, not only produced a viable forecasting procedure but could also be nationalized by the stochastic process

$$\Delta\Delta_s y_t = (1 + \theta L)(1 + \Theta L^s)\xi_t, \qquad (5)$$

where Δ_s is the seasonal difference operator and θ and Θ are parameters. Generalizing (5) gives the class of multiplicative seasonal ARIMA processes, in which a model of order $(p, d, q) \times (P, D, Q)_s$ is specified as

$$\phi(L)\Phi(L^s)\Delta^d\Delta_s^D y_t = \theta(L)\Theta(L^s)\xi_t, \qquad (6)$$

where $\phi(L)$, $\Phi(L^s)$, $\theta(L)$ and $\Theta(L^s)$ are polynomials in the lag operator of order p, P, q and Q respectively. The methodology for selecting a model for the seasonal ARIMA class is essentially the same as that developed for the ARIMA class.

The application of the model selection methodology advocated by Box and Jenkins (1970) is not without its problems. Unless the sample size is very large, which it rarely is in economics, it is difficult to identify an ARIMA model of any degree of complexity using the correlogram and the sample partial autocorrelation function. These difficulties become even more acute when the observations have been differenced. One way of avoiding these problems is to select models by an automatic procedure, using a measure of goodness of fit such as the Akaike Information Criterion (AIC). This approach is now quite common, although it does move away from the spirit of the work of Box and Jenkins (1970), which emphasized the need for judgement on the part of the statistician.

A more radical criticism of Box–Jenkins methodology concerns the suitability of the ARIMA class itself. There is no overwhelming reason why an economic time series should, after an appropriate amount of differencing, be stationary. Furthermore, even if the stationarity assumption is a reasonable one for a differenced series, it does not follow that appproximating the differenced series by an ARMA (p, q) process will necessarily lead to a model with desirable properties for forecasting. Some illustrations of this point can be found in Harvey and Todd (1983) and Harvey (1985). Thus while the ARIMA class may often be too restrictive because of its reliance on stationarity, it can also be argued that is too general. Given the difficulties which arise in applying the Box–Jenkins methodology, it follows that there is ample scope for selecting an inappropriate model. As the examples cited by Jenkins (1982) show, the use of an automatic model selection procedure is only likely to make matters worse.

Recent work has suggested an alternative to ARIMA models, based on the idea that the components known to exist in economic time series, for example trends, seasonals and perhaps even cycles, are modelled explicitly. These components are unobserved but may be handled statistically by means of the state space form as in, say, Kitagawa (1981) or Harvey and Todd (1983). Thus more *a priori* information is put into the initial specification and the model selection methodology is closer to that of econometrics; see Harvey (1985). Following the terminology of simultaneous equation systems in econometrics, Engle (1978) has termed such models 'structural' models. If the model is linear, the 'reduced form' is an ARIMA process. Within this framework the reduced form provides a valid means of constructing forecasts, but it does not provide any direct information which can be used to describe the nature of the series in terms of components of interest.

BIBLIOGRAPHY

Box, G.E.P. and Jenkins, G.M. 1970. *Time Series Analysis: Forecasting and Control.* San Francisco: Holden-Day.

Engle, R.F. 1978. Estimating structural models of seasonality. In *Seasonal Analysis of Economic Time Series*, ed. A. Zellner, Washington DC, Bureau of the Census, 281–308.

Harrison, P.J. 1967. Exponential smoothing and short-term sales forecasting. *Management Science* 13, 821–42.

Harvey, A.C. 1985. Trends and cycles in macroeconomic time series. *Journal of Business and Economic Statistics* 3, 216–27.

Harvey, A.C. and Todd, P.H.J. 1983. Forecasting economic time series with structural and Box–Jenkins models: a case study (with discussion). *Journal of Business and Economic Statistics* 1, 229–315.

Jenkins, G.M. 1982. Some practical aspects of forecasting in organisations. *Journal of Forecasting* 1, 3–21.

Kitagawa, G. 1981. A nonstationary time series model and its fitting by a recursive filter. *Journal of Time Series Analysis* 2, 103–16.

Muth, J.F. 1960. Optimal properties of exponentially weighted forecasts. *Journal of the American Statistical Association* 55, 299–306.

Nerlove, M. and Wage, S. 1964. On the optimality of adaptive forecasting. *Management Science* 10, 207–24.

Theil, H. and Wage, S. 1964. Some observations on adaptive forecasting. *Management Science* 10, 198–206.

Autoregressive and Moving-average Time-series Processes

MARC NERLOVE AND FRANCIS X. DIEBOLD

Characterization of time series by means of autoregressive (AR) or moving-average (MA) processes or combined autoregressive moving-average (ARMA) processes was suggested, more or less simultaneously, by the Russian statistician and economist, E. Slutsky (1927), and the British statistician G.U. Yule (1921, 1926, 1927). Slutsky and Yule observed that if we begin with a series of purely random numbers and then take sums or differences, weighted or unweighted, of such numbers, the new series so produced has many of the apparent cyclic properties that are thought to characterize economic and other time series. Such sums or differences of purely random numbers are the basis for ARMA models of the processes by which many kinds of economic time series are assumed to be generated, and thus form the basis for recent suggestions for analysis, forecasting and control (e.g. Box and Jenkins, 1970).

Let L be the lag operator such that $L^k x_t = x_{t-k}$. Consider the familiar pth order linear, homogeneous, deterministic difference equation with constant coefficients common in discrete dynamic economic analysis (e.g. Chow, 1975):

$$\psi(L)y_t = 0$$

or

$$y_t - \psi_1 y_{t-1} - \cdots - \psi_p y_{t-p} = 0, \tag{1}$$

Relationships are seldom exact, however, so we introduce a serially uncorrelated random shock ε_t with zero mean and constant variance:

$$E\varepsilon_t = 0.$$

$$E\varepsilon_t \varepsilon_{t'} = \begin{cases} \sigma^2, & t = t' \\ 0, & \text{otherwise.} \end{cases} \tag{2}$$

25

Thus

$$\psi(L)y_t = \varepsilon_t, \qquad (3)$$

which is the pth-order autoregressive process, $\mathrm{AR}(p)$, with constant coefficients studied by Yule (1927).

If the stochastic term in (3) is itself assumed to be a linear combination of past values of a variable such as ε_t, with properties (2), for example,

$$\psi(L)y_t = \mu_t, \qquad (4)$$

where $\mu_t = \phi(L)\varepsilon_t$, and $\phi(\cdot)$ is a polynomial of order q, then the process is a mixed autoregressive moving-average process of order (p, q), ARMA (p, q). The process generating μ_t is simply a moving-average process of order q, MA(q).

Such dynamic processes, under appropriate conditions on the coefficients of ψ, ϕ, and the distribution of ε_t, have found wide application in both theoretical and empirical economics. The ability of such processes to describe the evolution of a series has made ARMA models a powerful tool for forecasting economic time series and other applications, such as seasonal adjustment. Moreover, because the models can capture a wide range of stochastic properties of economic time series, they have been widely used in models involving rational expectations (e.g. Whiteman, 1983).

UNIVARIATE ARMA MODELS. Conditions for weak stationarity and invertibility (i.e. capability of being expressed as a pure, but possibly infinite, AR) are most easily discussed in terms of the so-called z-transform or autocovariance-generating transform of the model. This is obtained for models (3) and (4) by replacing the lag operator by a complex variable z; thus, in general,

$$B(z) = \frac{\phi(z)}{\psi(z)}, \qquad (5)$$

where the expression on the right converges. If the roots of $\psi(z) = 0$ do not lie strictly outside the unit circle (i.e. some lie on or inside), the process described by (3) or (4) will not be stationary, nor will the expression on the right converge outside a circle with radius less than one. (*See* TIME-SERIES ANALYSIS.) In order to find a purely AR representation of MA and ARMA models, we require that $1/\phi(z)$ converge in the same region, so that $\phi(z) = 0$ must have roots outside the unit circle. In this case, $B(z)$ is well-defined everywhere outside the unit circle, and the model defined by (4) is both weakly stationary and invertible; the representation

$$y_t = B(L)\varepsilon_t \qquad (6)$$

is a one-sided, infinite-order MA, with $\Sigma_{j=-\infty}^{\infty} b_j^2 < \infty$.

In Wold (1938) it is shown that every discrete, weakly stationary process may be decomposed into a purely linearly deterministic part (which can be predicted exactly from a sufficient past history) and a part which corresponds to (6) above. (See the discussions of stationarity and ergodicity in TIME-SERIES ANALYSIS.)

Let the autocovariances of a stationary, zero-mean time series, x_t, be given by

$$\gamma(\tau) = E x_t x_{t-\tau}. \tag{7}$$

The function

$$g(z) = \sum_{\tau=-\infty}^{\infty} z^\tau \gamma(\tau) \tag{8}$$

is called the autocovariance generating function. If the function $g(z)$ is known and analytic in a certain region, it is possible to read off the autocovariances of the time series as the coefficients in a Laurent series expansion of the function. For a linearly nondeterministic time series with one-sided MA representation (6) the autocovariance generating transform is given by

$$g_{yy}(z) = \sigma^2 B(z) B(z^{-1}). \tag{9}$$

This function is analytic everywhere in an annulus about the unit circle. If y_t is generated by a stationary ARMA model with invertible MA component then $g_{yy}(z)$ will have no zeros anywhere in this annulus. On the unit circle itself the *spectral density* of the series is proportional by a factor of $(2\pi)^{-1}$ to the autocovariance generating transform:

$$f_{yy}(\lambda) = (1/2\pi) g_{yy}(e^{i\lambda}), \quad -\pi \leqslant \lambda < \pi. \tag{10}$$

Stationary, invertible ARMA processes give rise to time series with spectral densities which are strictly positive in the interval $(-\pi, \pi)$.

Let $1/\beta_j$, $j = 1, \ldots, q$ be the roots, not necessarily distinct, of $\phi(z) = 0$, and let $1/\alpha_j, j = 1, \ldots, p$ be the roots of $\psi(z) = 0$. For a stationary, invertible ARMA model all these roots lie outside the unit circle. The autocovariances of the time series generated by this model are

$$\gamma(\tau) = (1/2\pi i) \oint_{|z|=1} z^{-\tau-1} g(z) \, dz = (\sigma^2/2\pi i) \oint_{|z|=1} z^{p+|\tau|-q-1}$$

$$\times \left\{ \prod_{j=1}^{q} (1-\beta_j z)(z-\beta_j) \Big/ \prod_{k=1}^{p} (1-\alpha_k z)(z-\alpha_k) \right\} dz. \tag{11}$$

By the residue theorem, the integral on the right-hand side of (11) is $2\pi i$ times the sum of the residues enclosed by the unit circle. This fact allows a particularly simple calculaton of the autocovariances of a time series generated by an ARMA model (see Nerlove *et al.* 1979, pp. 78–85). For example, for the general pth-order autoregression, AR(p), with distinct roots, the result is

$$\gamma(\tau) = \sum_{k=1}^{p} \left[\alpha_k^{p+|\tau|-1} \Big/ \left\{ \prod_{j=1}^{p} (1-\alpha_j \alpha_k) \prod_{\substack{j=1 \\ j \neq k}}^{p} (\alpha_j - \alpha_k) \right\} \right], \tag{12}$$

and for the ARMA (1, 1) model, it is

$$\gamma(\tau) = \alpha^{|\tau|}(1-\alpha\beta)(1-\beta/\alpha)/(1-\alpha^2), \quad \tau = \pm 1, \pm 2, \ldots$$

$$= (1 + \beta^2 - 2\alpha\beta)/(1-\alpha^2), \quad \tau = 0. \tag{13}$$

FORMULATION AND ESTIMATION OF UNIVARIATE ARMA MODELS. The problem of *formulating* an ARMA model refers to determination of the orders p and q of the AR and MA components, while the *estimation* problem is that of determining the values of the parameters of the model, for example the roots $1/\alpha_j, j = 1, \ldots, p$, and $1/\beta_k$, $k = 1, \ldots, q$, and the variance σ^2 of ε_t.

Box and Jenkins (1970), among others, have suggested the use of the sample autocorrelation and partial autocorrelation functions as an approach to the problem of formulating an ARMA model. It is known, however, that the estimates of these functions are poorly behaved relative to their theoretical counterparts and thus provide a somewhat dubious basis for model formulation (Nerlove et al., 1979, pp. 57–68, 105–106; Hannan, 1960, p. 41).

More recently, information-theoretic approaches to model formulation, having a rigorous foundation in statistical information theory, have been proposed. These procedures are designated for order determination in general ARMA (p, q) models. The Akaike (1973) Information Criterion (AIC) leads to selection of the model for which the expression

$$\mathrm{AIC}(k) = \ln \hat{\sigma}^2_{\mathrm{ML}} + 2k/T \qquad (14)$$

is minimized, where $\hat{\sigma}^2_{\mathrm{ML}}$ is the maximum likelihood estimate of σ^2_ε, T is sample size, and $k = p + q$. It is well known that the AIC is not consistent, in the sense that it does not lead to selection of the correct model with probability one in large samples (Shibata, 1976; Hannan and Quinn, 1979; Hannan, 1980; Kashyap, 1980). The procedure does, however, have special benefits when selecting the order of an AR model, as shown by Shibata (1980). Specifically, he shows that if the true model can *not* be written as a finite AR, but an AR is fitted anyway, then use of the AIC minimizes asymptotic mean-squared prediction error within the class of AR models.

Schwarz (1978) and Rissanen (1978) develop a consistent modification of the AIC which has become known as the Schwarz Information Criterion (SIC). This criterion selects the model which minimizes

$$\mathrm{SIC}(k) = \ln \hat{\sigma}^2_{\mathrm{ML}} + \frac{\ln T}{T} (k) \qquad (15)$$

and Hannan (1980) shows that this procedure identifies the true model with probability one in large samples, so long as the maximum possible orders of the AR and MA components are known.

Once the orders p and q are determined, the problem of *estimating* the parameters of the ARMA model remains. Various approaches in the time domain are available, such as least squares, approximate maximum likelihood (Box and Jenkins, 1970), or exact maximum likelihood (Newbold, 1974; Harvey and Phillips, 1979; Harvey, 1981). Approximate maximum likelihood in the frequency domain is also possible (Hannan, 1969b; Hannan and Nicholls, 1972; Nerlove et al., 1979, pp. 132–6). The latter is based upon the asymptotic distribution of the sample periodogram ordinates.

Estimation of pure AR models (no MA component) is particularly simple since ordinary least squares yield consistent parameter estimates. The basis of such estimation is the set of Yule–Walker equations (Yule, 1927; Walker, 1931). Consider the AR(p) process:

$$y_t = \sum_{i=1}^{p} \psi_i y_{t-i} + \varepsilon_t. \tag{16}$$

Multiplying (16) by $y_{t-\tau}$, $\tau \geqslant 0$, taking expectations, and recognizing that $\gamma(\tau) = \gamma(-\tau)$ gives

$$\gamma(\tau) = \sum_{i=1}^{p} \psi_i \gamma(\tau - i), \qquad \tau > 0. \tag{17}$$

Dividing (17) by the variance $\gamma(0)$, we obtain the system of Yule–Walker equations:

$$\rho(\tau) = \sum_{i=1}^{p} \psi_i \rho(\tau - i), \qquad \tau > 0, \tag{18}$$

which relate the autocorrelations of the process. This pth-order linear system is easily solved for the ψ_i, $i = 1, \ldots, p$, in terms of the first p autocorrelations. In practice, the theoretical autocorrelations are replaced by their sample counterparts, yielding estimates of the ψ_i, $i = 1, \ldots, p$. These parameter estimates may be conveniently used as start-up values for the more sophisticated, iterative estimation procedures discussed above.

Estimation of MA or mixed models by exact maximum likelihood methods is complicated further by a tendency to obtain a local maximum of the likelihood function at a unit root of the MA component, even when no roots are close to the unit circle (Sargan and Bhargava, 1983; Anderson and Takemura, 1984).

PREDICTION. Optimal linear least squares prediction of time series generated by ARMA processes may be obtained for known parameter values by the Wiener–Kolmogorov approach (Whittle, 1983). If y_t is generated by a stationary, invertible ARMA model with one-sided MA representation (6), a very simple expression may be given for the linear minimum mean-square error (MMSE) prediction of y_{t+v} at time t, y_{t+v}^*, in terms of its own (infinite) past

$$y_{t+v}^* = C(z)y_t, \tag{19}$$

where

$$C(z) = \sum_{j=0}^{\infty} c_j z^j = \frac{1}{B(z)} \left[\frac{B(z)}{z^v} \right]_+.$$

The operator $[.]_+$ eliminates negative powers of z.

Suppose that y_t is AR(1):

$$y_t = \alpha y_{t-1} + \varepsilon_t, \qquad |\alpha| < 1,$$

29

then $y_{t+v}^* = \alpha^v y_t$. If y_t is AR(2):

$$y_t = (\alpha_1 + \alpha_2)y_{t-1} - \alpha_1\alpha_2 y_{t-2} + \varepsilon_t, \quad |\alpha_1|, |\alpha_2| < 1,$$

then $y_{t+1}^* = (\alpha_1 + \alpha_2)y_t - \alpha_1\alpha_2 y_{t-1}$. In general, the result for AR(p) as in (1) is $y_{t+v}^* = \psi_1 y_{t+v-1}^* + \cdots + \psi_p y_{t+v-p}^*$, where $y_{-j}^* = y_{t-j}$, for $j = 0, 1, \ldots$, at time t. Thus for pure autoregressions, the MMSE prediction is a linear combination of only the p most recently observed values.

Suppose that y_t is MA(1):

$$y_t = \varepsilon_t - \beta\varepsilon_{t-1}, \quad |\beta| < 1,$$

then $y_{t+1}^* = -\beta\Sigma_{j=0}^{\infty}\beta^j x_{t-j}$ and $y_{t+v}^* = 0$ for all $v > 1$. For moving-average processes, in general, predictions for a future period greater than the order of the process are zero and those for a period less distant cannot be expressed in terms of a finite number of past observed values.

Finally, suppose that y_t is ARMA (1, 1): $y_t - \alpha y_{t-1} = \varepsilon_t - \beta\varepsilon_{t-1}$, $|\alpha|, |\beta| < 1$, then $y_{t+v}^* = \alpha^{v-1}(\alpha - \beta)\Sigma_{j=0}^{\infty}\beta^j y_{t-j}$. For further examples, see Nerlove et al., 1979, pp. 89–102.

When an infinite past is not available and the parameter values of the process are not known, the problem of optimal prediction is more complicated. The most straightforward approach is via the state-space representation of the process and the Kalman filter (Kalman, 1960; Meinhold and Singpurwalla, 1983).

MULTIVARIATE ARMA PROCESSES.   Let $\Psi(\cdot)$ and $\Phi(\cdot)$ be $K \times K$ matrix polynomials in the lag operator, y_t and ε_t be $K \times 1$ vectors. Then the K-variate ARMA (p, q) process is defined as

$$\Psi(L)y_t = \Phi(L)\varepsilon_t, \quad \varepsilon_t^{iid}(0, \Sigma), \tag{20}$$

where $\Psi(L) = \Psi_0 - \Psi_1 L - \ldots - \Psi_p L^p$ and $\Phi(L) = \Phi_0 - \Phi_1 L - \ldots - \Phi_q L^q$, with each Ψ_j and Φ_j, $y = 0, 1, \ldots$, being a $K \times K$ matrix. The model is weakly stationary if all the zeros of det $|\Psi(z)|$ lie outside the unit circle (Hannan, 1970) and invertible if all the zeros of det$|\Phi(z)|$ also do.

In addition to the issues of formulation, estimation, and prediction, which arise in the univariate case as well, identification (in the usual econometric sense) becomes an important problem. Hannan (1969a) shows that a stationary vector AR process is identified if Φ_0 is an identity matrix (i.e. no instantaneous coupling) and Ψ_p is nonsingular. Hannan (1971) extends the analysis to recursive systems and systems with prescribed zero restrictions.

There are three approaches to the formulation of multivariate ARMA models. Nerlove et al. (1979) and Granger and Newbold (1977) develop an augmented single-equation procedure and Wallis (1977) and Wallis and Chan (1978) develop another procedure which involves preliminary univariate analysis.

A second approach is due to Tiao and Box (1981), who use multivariate analogues of the autocorrelation and partial autocorrelation functions as a guide to model formulation. Their approach is computationally quite simple and usually leads to models with a tractable number of parameters. Identification is achieved by allowing no instantaneous coupling among variables.

Finally, the information-theoretic model formulation procedures which were discussed above generalize to the multivariate ARMA case. Quinn (1980) shows that Schwarz's criterion (SIC) again provides a consistent estimate of the vector AR order. In a large Monte Carlo comparison of criteria for estimating the order of a vector AR process (VAR), Lütkepohl (1985) shows the clear superiority of the SIC in medium-sized samples; the SIC chooses the correct model most often and leads to the best forecasting performance.

As in the case of univariate ARMA models, estimation in the multivariate case may be carried out in the frequency domain (Wilson, 1973; Dunsmuir and Hannan, 1976) or in the time domain (Hillmer and Tiao, 1979). An exact likelihood function in the time domain may also be derived by the Kalman filter by casting the multivariate ARMA model in state space form. Anderson (1980) provides a good survey of estimation in both time and frequency domains.

Prediction in the multivariate case with an infinite past is a straightforward generalization of the results for the univariate case (Judge et al., 1985, pp. 659–60). When only a finite past is available and the parameters of the process must be estimated, the most straightforward approach is again through the Kalman filter (see also Yamamoto, 1981).

APPLICATIONS. In addition to their obvious uses in forecasting, ARMA models, especially multivariate ARMA models, have a wide range of economic and econometric application.

The use of time-series methods in formulating distributed-lag models is discussed at length in Nerlove (1972) and Nerlove et al. (1979, pp. 291–353) and applied in the latter to an analysis of US cattle production. The notion of quasi-rational expectations introduced there is that the expectations on the basis of which economic agents react may, under certain conditions, be assumed to be the statistical expectations of the variables in question, conditional on observations of past history. If these variables are generated by time-series processes, such as those discussed in this article, time-series methods may be used to derive expressions for the MMSE forecasts for any relevant future period; these MMSE forecasts are, by a well-known result, the aforementioned conditional expectations.

An econometric definition of causality based on time-series concepts has been developed by Granger (1969) and extended by Sims (1972). Let (x_t, y_t) be a pair of vectors of observations on some economic time series, and let Ω_{t-1} be the information available up to time t, which includes $\{(x_{t-1}, y_{t-1}), (x_{t-2}, y_{t-2}), \ldots\}$. Granger gives the following definitions in terms of the conditional variances:

Definition 1: x causes y if and only if

$$< \sigma^2(y_t | \Omega_{t-1} - \{x_{t-1}, x_{t-2}, \ldots\}),$$

where $\Omega_{t-1} - \{x_{t-1}, x_{t-2}, \ldots\}$ is the information set omitting the past of the series x_t.

31

Definition 2: x causes y instantaneously if and only if

$$\sigma^2(y_t | \Omega_{t-1}, x_t) < \sigma^2(y_t | \Omega_{t-1}).$$

It may happen that both x causes y, and y causes x; then x and y are related by a feedback system. In applications, (x_t, y_t) is generally assumed to be generated by multivariate ARMA processes, and Ω_t is assumed to consist only of the past history of (x_t, y_t). Since ARMA models are applicable only to weakly stationary time series it must further be assumed that any transformation necessary to achieve stationarity is causality preserving. Granger's (1969) test for causal association is based on a multivariate AR representation, while Sims (1972) bases his on an equivalent MA representation. Sims also introduces a regression-based test related to the above which makes use of both future and past values of the series x_t in relation to the current value of y_t. Pierce and Haugh (1977) show that causality may also be tested in univariate representations of the series. Feige and Pierce (1979) and Lütkepohl (1982) show that the direction of causality so defined may be sensitive to the transformations used to achieve stationarity and to the definition of the information set.

Time series methods have also been applied to the analysis of the efficiency of capital markets (Fama, 1970). The question is whether market prices fully reflect available information, for example, in a securities market. Efficiency requires that the relevant information set be that actually used by the market participants. Since the latter is inherently unobservable, tests of the efficiency of a market can be carried out only within the context of a particular theory of market equilibrium. Various alternatives lead to tests, based on AR or more general models, of the rates of return for different securities over time in the presence of shocks of various sorts which may or may not represent the introduction of new information (Ball and Brown, 1968; Fama et al., 1969; Scholes, 1972).

Finally, an important example of the use of time-series methods in econometrics has been put forth in the controversial revisionist views of Sargent and Sims (1977), and Sims (1980) on appropriate methods of econometric modelling. These views may be traced back to the work of T.C. Liu (1960) who argued that when only reliable *a priori* restrictions were imposed, most econometric models would turn out to be underidentified; furthermore, he argued that most of the exclusion restrictions generally employed and the assumptions about serial correlation made to justify treating certain lagged values of endogenous variables as predetermined, were invalid; he concluded that only unrestricted reduced form estimation could be justified. The revisionist approach treats *all* variables as endogenous and, in general, places no restrictions on the parameters except the choice of variables to be included and lengths of lags. Attention in this approach is focused on the estimation of a general relationship among a relatively short list of variables rather than policy analysis and structural inference, which have been the emphasis of mainstream econometrics. As such, the approach has been mainly useful for data description and forecasting.

BIBLIOGRAPHY

Akaike, H. 1973. Information theory and an extension of the maximum likelihood principle. In *Second International Symposium on Information Theory*, ed. B.N. Petrov and F. Csaki, Budapest: Akademiai Kiado, Budapest, 267–87.

Anderson, T.W. 1980. Maximum likelihood estimation for vector autoregressive moving average models. In *Directions in Time Series*, ed. D.R. Brillinger and G.C. Tiao, Hayward, California: Institute of Mathematical Statistics. 49–59.

Anderson, T.W. and Takemura, A. 1984. Why do noninvertible moving averages occur? Technical Report No. 13, Department of Statistics, Stanford University.

Ball, R. and Brown, P. 1968. An empirical evaluation of accounting income numbers. *Journal of Accounting Research* 6, 159–78.

Box, G.E.P. and Jenkins, G.M. 1970. *Time Series Analysis: Forecasting and Control*. San Francisco: Holden-Day.

Chow, G.C. 1975. *Analysis and Control of Dynamic Economic Systems*. New York: John Wiley.

Dunsmuir, W.T.M. and Hannan, E.J. 1976. Vector linear time series models. *Advances in Applied Probability* 8(2), June, 339–64.

Fama, E.F. 1970. Efficient capital markets: a review of theory and empirical work. *Journal of Finance* 25(2), May, 383–417.

Fama, E.F., Jensen, M., Fisher, L. and Roll, R. 1969. The adjustment of stock market prices to new information. *International Economic Review* 10(1), February, 1–21.

Feige, E.L. and Pierce, D.K. 1979. The casual causal relation between money and income: some caveats for time series analysis. *Review of Economics and Statistics* 61(4), November, 521–33.

Granger, C.W.J. 1969. Investigating causal relationships by econometric models and cross-spectral methods. *Econometrica* 37(3), July, 424–38.

Granger, C.W.J. and Newbold, P. 1977. *Forecasting Economic Time Series*. New York: Academic Press.

Hannan, E.J. 1960. *Time Series Analysis*. London: Methuen.

Hannan, E.J. 1969a. The identification of vector mixed autoregressive-moving average systems. *Biometrika* 56(1), 223–5.

Hannan, E.J. 1969b. The estimation of mixed moving average autoregressive systems. *Biometrika* 56(3), 579–93.

Hannan, E.J. 1970. *Multiple Time Series*. New York: John Wiley & Sons.

Hannan, E.J. 1971. The identification problem for multiple equation systems with moving average errors. *Econometrica* 39(5), September, 751–65.

Hannan, E.J. 1980. The estimation of the order of an ARMA process. *Annals of Statistics* 8(5), September 1071–81.

Hannan, E.J. and Nicholls, D.F. 1972. The estimation of mixed regression, autoregression, moving average and distributed lag models. *Econometrica* 40(3), May, 529–47.

Hannan, E.J. and Quinn, B.G. 1979. The determination of the order of an autoregression. *Journal of the Royal Statistical Society, Series B* 41(2), 190–95.

Harvey, A.C. 1981. *Time Series Models*. Oxford: Philip Allan; New York; Halsted Press.

Harvey, A.C. and Phillips, G.D.A. 1979. The estimation of regression models with ARMA disturbances. *Biometrika* 66(1), 49–58.

Hillmer, S.C. and Tiao, G.C. 1979. Likelihood function of stationary multiple autoregressive moving average models. *Journal of the American Statistical Association* 74(367), September, 652–60.

Judge, G.G., Griffiths, W.E., Hill, R.C., Lütkepohl, H. and Lee, T.C. 1985. *The Theory and Practice of Econometrics.* 2nd edn, New York: John Wiley.

Kalman, R.E. 1960. A new approach to linear filtering and prediction problems. *Journal of Basic Engineering, ASME Transactions* 82D, 35–45.

Kashyap, R.L. 1980. Inconsistency of the AIC rule for estimating the order of AR models. *Transactions on Automatic Control* 25(5), October, 996–8.

Liu, T.C. 1960. Underidentification, structural estimation, and forecasting. *Econometrica* 28(4), October, 855–65.

Lütkepohl, H. 1982. Non-causality due to omitted variables. *Journal of Econometrics* 19, 367–78.

Lütkepohl, H. 1985. Comparison of criteria for estimating the order of a vector autoregressive process. *Journal of Time Series Analysis* 6(1), 35–52.

Meinhold, R.J. and Singpurwalla, N.D. 1983. Understanding the Kalman filter. *American Statistician* 37, 123–7.

Nerlove, M. 1972. Lags in economic behaviour. *Econometrica* 40(2), March, 221–51.

Nerlove, M., Grether, D.M. and Carvalho, J.L. 1979. *Analysis of Economic Time Series: A synthesis.* New York: Academic Press.

Newbold, P. 1974. The exact likelihood function for a mixed autoregressive-moving average process. *Biometrika* 61(3), 423–6.

Pierce, D.A. and Haugh, L.D. 1977. Causality in temporal systems: characterizations and a survey. *Journal of Econometrics* 5(3), 265–93.

Quinn, B.G. 1980. Order determination for a multivariate autoregression. *Journal of the Royal Statistical Society*, Series B 42(2), 182–5.

Rissanen, H. 1978. Modelling by shortest data description. *Automatica* 14(5), September, 465–71.

Sargan, J.D. and Bhargava, A. 1983. Maximum likelihood estimation of regression models with moving average errors when the root lies on the unit circle. *Econometrica* 51(3), May, 799–820.

Sargent, T.J. and Sims, C.A. 1977. Business cycle modeling without pretending to have too much a priori economic theory. In *New Methods of Business Cycle Research*, ed. C.A. Sims, Minneapolis: Federal Reserve Bank of Minneapolis.

Scholes, M. 1972. The market for securities: substitution versus price pressure and the effects of information on share prices. *Journal of Business* 45(2), April, 179–211.

Schwarz, G. 1978. Estimating the dimension of a model. *Annals of Statistics* 6(2), March, 461–4.

Shibata, R. 1976. Selection of the order of an autoregressive model by the AIC. *Biometrika* 63(1), 117–26.

Shibata, R. 1980. Asymptotically efficient estimates of the order of a model for estimating parameters of a linear process. *Annals of Statistics* 8(5), September, 1147–64.

Sims, C.A. 1972. Money income and causality. *American Economic Review* 62(4), September, 540–52.

Sims, C.A. 1980. Macroeconomics and reality. *Econometrica* 48(1), *January* 1–47.

Slutsky, E. 1927. The summation of random causes as the source of cyclic processes. Trans. In *Econometrica* 5, 105–46.

Tiao, G.C. and Box, G.E.P. 1981. Modeling multiple time series with applications. *Journal of the American Statistical Society* 76, 802–816.

Walker, G. 1931. On periodicity in series of related terms. *Proceedings of the Royal Society London*, Series A 131, 518–32.

Wallis, K.F. 1977. Multiple time series analysis and the final form of econometric models. *Econometrica* 45(6), September, 1481–97.

Wallis, K.F. and Chan, W.T. 1978. Multiple time series modeling: another look at the mink–muskrat interaction. *Applied Statistics* 27(2), 168–75.

Whiteman, C.H. 1983. *Linear Rational Expectations Models.* Minneapolis: University of Minnesota Press.

Whittle, P. 1983. *Prediction and Regulation by Linear Least Squares Methods.* 2nd revised, Minneapolis: University of Minnesota Press.

Wilson, G.T. 1973. The estimation of parameters in multivariate time series models. *Journal of the Royal Statistical Society*, Series B 35(1), 76–85.

Wold, H. 1938: *A Study in the Analysis of Stationary Time Series.* Stockholm: Almqvist and Wiksell.

Yamamoto, T. 1981. Prediction of multivariate autoregressive-moving average models. *Biometrika* 68(2), 485–92.

Yule, G.U. 1921. On the time-correlation problem with special reference to the variate-difference correlation method. *Journal of the Royal Statistical Society* 84, July, 497–526.

Yule, G.U. 1926. Why do we sometimes get nonsense correlations between time series? A study in sampling and the nature of time series. *Journal of the Royal Statistical Society* 89, January, 1–64.

Yule, G.U. 1927. On a method for investigating periodicities in disturbed series with special reference to Wolfer's sunspot numbers. *Philosophical Transactions of the Royal Society of London*, Series A 226, 267–98.

Bayesian Inference

ARNOLD ZELLNER

Bayesian inference is a mode of inductive reasoning that has been used in many sciences, including economics. Bayesian inference procedures are available to evaluate economic hypotheses and models, to estimate values of economic parameters and to predict as yet unobserved values of variables. In addition, Bayesian inference procedures are useful in solving many decision problems including economic control and policy problems, firms' and consumers' stochastic optimization problems, portfolio problems, experimental design problems, etc. Many examples of these uses of Bayesian inference procedures are provided in Jeffreys (1967), De Groot (1970), Zellner (1971), Box and Tiao (1973), Leamer (1978), Boyer and Kihlstrom (1984), and Berger (1985).

A distinctive feature of Bayesian inference procedures is that they permit investigators to use both sample and prior information in a logically consistent manner in making inferences. This is important since prior information is widely used by Bayesian and non-Bayesian workers in making inferences. Bayes' Theorem, sometimes referred to as the Principle of Inverse Probability, serves as a fundamental learning model in the Bayesian approach. Initial or prior information is combined with current sample information by use of Bayes' Theorem to produce a 'post-data' or 'posterior distribution' that incorporates both prior and sample information. In this way prior or initial views are transformed by use of Bayes' Theorem to post-data views, a transformation that is a key, operational learning process.

Thomas Bayes, an 18th-century British Presbyterian minister, is usually given credit for solving the famous 'inverse probability problem', stated by Bayes (1763) as follows: '*Given* the number of times in which an unknown event has happened and failed: *Required* the chance that the probability of its happening in a single trial lies somewhere between any two degrees of probability that can be named'. The solution, published two years after Bayes' death, was arrived at by an ingenious geometrical argument. (See Stigler (1983) for further considerations regarding the origins of the solution.) Note that Bayes' inverse problem is fundamentally different from those encountered in games of chance, for example coin flipping, in which the probabilities of outcomes are known and the probabilities of various outcomes must be calculated. These are problems in *direct* probability; for example, calculate the probability of observing five heads in six flips of a fair coin. In Bayes' *inverse* probability problem, five heads in six flips of a coin are observed and what must be calculated or inferred is the chance that the probability of a head on a single flip lies in a given interval, say 0.4 to 0.7. Thus the probability of a head on a single toss is unknown and must be inferred from the outcomes. The modern solution, due to Laplace (see Molina, 1940) will be presented below. It is clear that the inverse problem is typical of scientific problems in which we observe data or outcomes and must infer the probabilistic mechanism or model that probably produced them. Cox (1961) and Jaynes (1984) provide fundamental analysis justifying Bayes' Theorem as a central tool in inductive reasoning.

Since Bayes' essay was published in 1763, Laplace (1820), Edgeworth (1928), Jeffreys (1967, 1973), de Finetti (1970), Wald (1950), Savage (1954), Good (1950, 1965), Lindley (1965, 1971) and many others have contributed to the development of Bayesian analysis and applications of it to many scientific estimation, prediction, testing and other problems. In what follows, an overview of these developments will be presented and illustrated with analyses of selected problems.

I. ESTIMATION PROBLEMS

Bayes' Theorem plays a central role in estimation problems. Let $\mathbf{y}$ denote a vector of observations contained in a sample space R_y and $\boldsymbol{\theta}$ a vector of parameters contained in a parameter space $\boldsymbol{\Theta}$. Given initial information I_0, let $p(\mathbf{y}, \boldsymbol{\theta}|I_0)$ be the joint probability density function (pdf) for $\mathbf{y}$ and $\boldsymbol{\theta}$. Then

$$p(\mathbf{y}, \boldsymbol{\theta}|I_0) = p(\boldsymbol{\theta}|I_0)p(\mathbf{y}|\boldsymbol{\theta}, I_0)$$
$$= p(\mathbf{y}|I_0)p(\boldsymbol{\theta}|\mathbf{y}, I_0), \tag{1.1}$$

where $p(\cdot|\cdot)$ is a generic symbol for a pdf labelled by its argument. Then from (1.1),

$$p(\boldsymbol{\theta}|D) = p(\boldsymbol{\theta}|I_0)p(\mathbf{y}|\boldsymbol{\theta}, I_0)/p(\mathbf{y}|I_0)$$
$$\propto p(\boldsymbol{\theta}|I_0)p(\mathbf{y}|\boldsymbol{\theta}, I_0), \tag{1.2a}$$

where $D \equiv (\mathbf{y}, I_0)$, the sample and prior information and '$\propto$' denotes 'is proportional to'. The result in (1.2a) is Bayes' Theorem where $p(\boldsymbol{\theta}|D)$ is the posterior pdf for $\boldsymbol{\theta}$, $p(\boldsymbol{\theta}|I_0)$ is the prior pdf for $\boldsymbol{\theta}$ and $p(\mathbf{y}|\boldsymbol{\theta}, I_0)$ is the pdf for $\mathbf{y}$ given $\boldsymbol{\theta}$ and I_0, which when viewed as a function of $\boldsymbol{\theta}$ is the likelihood function. Thus Bayes' Theorem can be stated as

$$\text{Posterior pdf} \propto (\text{Prior pdf}) \times (\text{Likelihood function}) \tag{1.2b}$$

with the factor of proportionality being a normalizing constant.

In (1.2), $p(\boldsymbol{\theta}|I_0)$, the prior pdf, represents information about possible values for $\boldsymbol{\theta}$ *prior to observing* $\mathbf{y}$. The information in the observations $\mathbf{y}$ is incorporated in the likelihood function and (1.2) transforms the information in the prior pdf and the likelihood function into a posterial pdf for θ, $p(\theta|D)$, that is used to make inferences about the possible values of the elements of θ.

It is seen from (1.2) that the likelihood function plays an important role in Bayes' Theorem in summarizing the sample information. According to the likelihood principle, the likelihood function contains all the sample information and thus no sample information is disregarded when the likelihood function is employed. If there is uncertainty regarding the likelihood function's form, various forms can be considered, as explained below and the sample and prior information can be employed in a Bayesian fashion to help resolve the uncertainty.

In the Bayesian approach to inference prior information about the possible values of θ is formally and explicitly introduced by use of a prior pdf, $p(\theta|I_0)$ in (1.2). If little prior information is available, a 'diffuse' or 'non-informative' prior pdf is employed, that is one that contains little information about the possible values of θ. On the other hand, if prior information about the possible values of θ is available, an 'informative' prior pdf would be employed. Prior information may be derived from past studies, economic theory, etc. For example, subject matter considerations and past studies may indicate that a parameter's value falls between zero and one and a prior pdf reflecting this restriction on the range of the parameter would be employed. This is but one type of prior information that may be available and can be incorporated in analyses by use of Bayes' Theorem.

To illustrate the use of Bayes' Theorem in estimation, several simple, important problems will be analysed.

Example 1: Normal mean with normal prior.   Assume that the observations y_i, $i = 1, 2, \ldots, n$ have been independently drawn from a normal distribution with unknown mean θ, $-\infty < \theta < \infty$, and known variance, $\sigma^2 = \sigma_0^2$. The likelihood function is

$$p(y|\theta, \sigma^2 = \sigma_0^2) = (2\pi\sigma_0^2)^{-n/2} \exp\left\{ -\sum_{i=1}^{n} (y_i - \theta)^2 \right\} \propto \exp\{-n(\theta - \bar{y})^2/2\sigma_0^2\},$$

where

$$\bar{y} = \sum_{i=1}^{n} y_i/n$$

is the sample mean and

$$\sum_{i=1}^{n} (y_i - \theta)^2 = \sum_{i=1}^{n} (y_i - \bar{y})^2 + n(\theta - \bar{y})^2$$

has been employed. Further, assume that prior information regarding θ's possible values is well represented by a normal prior pdf with mean m and variance v, i.e. $p(\theta|m, v) = (2\pi v)^{-1/2} \exp\{-(\theta - m)^2/2v\}$. Then using Bayes' Theorem in (1.2), the posterior pdf for θ is

$$p(\theta|D) \propto (\text{prior pdf}) \times (\text{likelihood function})$$

$$\propto \exp\{-[(\theta - m)^2/v + n(\theta - \bar{y})^2/\sigma_0^2]/2\}$$

$$\propto \exp\{-(\theta - \bar{\theta})^2/2\tau^2\}, \tag{1.3}$$

a normal pdf with mean $\bar{\theta}$ and variance τ^2 given by

$$\bar{\theta} = (h_0 m + h\bar{y})/(h_0 + h) \tag{1.4}$$

$$\tau^2 = 1/(h_0 + h), \tag{1.5}$$

where $h_0 = 1/v$, the prior precision and $h = n/\sigma_0^2$, the sample precision. It is seen that the posterior mean $\bar{\theta}$ is a weighted average of the prior mean m and the sample mean $\bar{y}$ with the prior precisions, $h_0 = 1/v$ and $h = n/\sigma_0^2$ as weights. As the prior variance $v \to \infty$, that is the prior pdf is very spread out reflecting little information about θ's value, the posterior mean, $\bar{\theta} \to \bar{y}$, the sample mean and the posterior distribution approaches a normal pdf with mean $\bar{y}$ and variance σ_0^2/n. Also, as n grows large, the posterior pdf approaches a normal pdf with mean $\bar{y}$ and variance σ_0^2/n. For finite v and n, the normal distribution in (1.3) can be employed to make probability statements regarding θ's possible value. For example, the posterior probability that $a < \theta < b$ is given by

$$\Pr(a < \theta < b | D) = \int_a^b p(\theta|D) \, d\theta$$

$$= F(b|D) - F(a|D), \tag{1.6}$$

where $F(\cdot|D)$ is the cumulative posterior normal distribution associated with (1.3).

Example 2: Binomial Trials. Assume that θ, $0 \leqslant \theta \leqslant 1$, is the probability of 'success' on a given trial and that n independent trials yield r successes and $n - r$ failures. The likelihood function is given by

$$\binom{n}{r} \theta^r (1 - \theta)^{n-r}.$$

Further assume that prior information regarding θ's possible value is well represented by a beta pdf with parameters a and b, that is $p(\theta|a, b) = \theta^{a-1}(1 - \theta)^{b-1}/B(a, b)$ with $0 \leqslant \theta \leqslant 1$, $a, b > 0$ and where

$$B(a, b) = \int_0^1 \theta^{a-1}(1 - \theta)^{b-1} \, d\theta,$$

the beta function. Then the posterior pdf for θ is

$$p(\theta|D) \propto \theta^{r+a-1}(1 - \theta)^{n-r+b-1} \qquad 0 \leqslant \theta \leqslant 1 \tag{1.7}$$

which is in the beta form with parameters $a' = r + a$ and $b' = n - r + b$. Thus the normalized posterior pdf is $p(\theta \mid D) = \theta^{a'-1}(1-\theta)^{b'-1}/B(a', b')$. With the posterior pdf in (1.7), it is possible to compute the posterior probability that $c_1 < \theta < c_2$, where c_1 and c_2 are any given numbers in the closed interval zero and one, as follows

$$\Pr(c_1 < \theta < c_2 \mid D) = \int_{c_1}^{c_2} p(\theta \mid D)\, d\theta. \qquad (1.8)$$

The integral in (1.8) can be evaluated using tables of the incomplete beta function or by numerical integration and is a solution to Bayes' inverse probability problem stated earlier. Note that if $a = b = 1$, the prior for θ is uniform over the interval zero to one, the Bayes–Laplace rule for representing little prior information about θ's value – see Jeffreys (1967, pp. 123–5) and Geisser (1984) for further discussion of this rule and other rules for representing knowing little about a binomial parameter.

In the two examples analysed above there were sufficient statistics, $\bar{y}$ for the normal mean problem and r for the binomial problem. It was the case that the posterior distributions were functions of these simple sufficient statistics. This is a general property of Bayesian analyses that is simply shown. Let $\mathbf{t}' = (t_1, t_2, \ldots, t_m)$ be a vector of sufficient statistics. Then $p(\mathbf{y} \mid \boldsymbol{\theta}) = h(\mathbf{y})p(\mathbf{t} \mid \boldsymbol{\theta})$, where $h(\mathbf{y})$ is a function of just the data $\mathbf{y}$ and Bayes' Theorem in (1.2) yields

$$p(\boldsymbol{\theta} \mid D) \propto p(\boldsymbol{\theta} \mid I_0)p(\mathbf{y} \mid \boldsymbol{\theta}, I_0)$$

$$\propto p(\boldsymbol{\theta} \mid I_0)p(\mathbf{t} \mid \boldsymbol{\theta}, I_0). \qquad (1.9)$$

Thus $p(\boldsymbol{\theta} \mid D)$ depends on the data just through $\mathbf{t}$, the vector of sufficient statistics.

Further, in both examples analysed above, the prior distributions' forms were in the same form as the likelihood function. When this is the case, the prior distribution is said to have a 'natural conjugate' form – see, e.g. Raiffa and Schlaifer (1961) for further discussion of natural conjugate prior distributions.

Another property of Bayes' Theorem that is quite useful and appealing is that it can be applied sequentially to data sets with results that are identical to what is obtained by an application to an entire data set. To illustrate, consider two independent data vectors, $\mathbf{y}_1$, with pdf $p(\mathbf{y}_1 \mid \boldsymbol{\theta})$ and $\mathbf{y}_2$ with pdf $p(\mathbf{y}_2 \mid \boldsymbol{\theta}, I_0)$. If $p(\boldsymbol{\theta} \mid I_0)$ is the prior pdf, then the posterior pdf is

$$p(\boldsymbol{\theta} \mid D) \propto p(\boldsymbol{\theta} \mid I_0)p(\mathbf{y}_1 \mid \boldsymbol{\theta}, I_0)p(\mathbf{y}_2 \mid \boldsymbol{\theta}, I_0), \qquad (1.10)$$

where $D = (\mathbf{y}_1, \mathbf{y}_2, I_0)$. If we analyse the data sets sequentially, $p_1(\boldsymbol{\theta} \mid D_1) \propto p(\boldsymbol{\theta} \mid I_0)p(\mathbf{y}_1 \mid \boldsymbol{\theta}, I_0)$ is the posterior pdf based on $D_1 = (\mathbf{y}_1, I_0)$. If $p_1(\boldsymbol{\theta} \mid D_1)$ is employed as a prior pdf for the analysis of the data set $\mathbf{y}_2$, the posterior pdf is $p(\boldsymbol{\theta} \mid D) \propto p_1(\boldsymbol{\theta} \mid D_1)p(\mathbf{y}_2 \mid \boldsymbol{\theta}, I_0)$ which is just the same as (1.10). Thus the same posterior pdf is obtained by proceeding sequentially as by proceeding as shown in (1.10).

When a vector of parameters $\boldsymbol{\theta}$ is involved in Bayes' Theorem in (1.2), marginal and conditional posterior pdfs are of interest. Let $\boldsymbol{\theta}$ be partitioned as

$\theta' = (\theta_1', \theta_2')$ and suppose that interest centres on θ_1. For example θ_2 may be a vector of nuisance parameters that are of little interest to an investigator. The following integration can be performed analytically or numerically to obtain the marginal posterior pdf for θ_1, denoted by $p(\theta_1 \mid D)$,

$$p(\theta_1 \mid D) = \int_{\Theta_2} p(\theta_1, \theta_2 \mid D) \, d\theta_2, \qquad (1.11a)$$

where Θ_2 is the region containing θ_2. The capability of integrating out nuisance parameters is an extremely important property of the Bayesian approach. Further, writing $p(\theta_1, \theta_2 \mid D) = p(\theta_1 \mid \theta_2, D) p(\theta_2 \mid D)$ where $p(\theta_1 \mid \theta_2, D)$ is the conditional posterior pdf for θ_1 given θ_2 and $p(\theta_2 \mid D)$ is the marginal posterior pdf for θ_2, the integral in (1.11a) can be expressed as

$$p(\theta_1 \mid D) = \int_{\Theta_2} p(\theta_1 \mid \theta_2, D) p(\theta_2 \mid D) \, d\theta_2. \qquad (1.11b)$$

Thus the marginal pdf, $p(\theta_1 \mid D)$ can be expressed as an average of conditional posterior pdfs, $p(\theta_1 \mid \theta_2, D)$ with the marginal posterior pdf $p(\theta_2 \mid D)$ as the weight function.

The conditional posterior pdf, $p(\theta_1 \mid \theta_2, D)$ is very important in performing sensitivity analyses. That is, $p(\theta_1 \mid \theta_2, D)$ can be computed for various assigned values for θ_2 to determine how sensitive inferences about θ_1 are to what is assumed about θ_2. See Zellner (1971) and Box and Tiao (1973) for many examples of such sensitivity analyses. For example, θ_2 might be an autocorrelation parameter representing a possible departure from independence and θ_1 a vector of regression coefficients. How a departure from independence affects inferences about regression coefficients can be assessed using conditional posterior distributions.

The large sample properties of posterior distributions is also of interest. Under relatively mild conditions, it has been shown in the literature that as the sample size grows, posterior distributions assume a normal shape with mean approximately equal to the maximum likelihood (ML) estimate and covariance matrix equal to the inverse of the matrix of second derivatives of the log-likelihood function with respect to the parameters evaluated at the ML estimates. Jeffreys (1967, p. 193) views this result as a Bayesian justification for the ML estimate in large samples. For proofs of the asymptotic normality of posterior distributions, see Jeffreys (1967), Heyde and Johnstone (1979) and Hartigan (1983). Heyde and Johnstone (1979) show that when the observations are independently and identically distributed, the conditions needed to prove the asymptotic normality of posterior distributions are identical to those needed to prove asymptotic normality of ML estimators. However, when observations are stochastically dependent, as in time series problems, they show that the conditions needed for asymptotic normality of posterior distributions are simpler and more robust than those needed for proving asymptotic normality of ML estimators.

In summary, Bayes' Theorem provides the complete, finite sample posterior pdf for parameters appearing in all kinds of econometric models. These posterior distributions can be employed to make probability statements about parameters' possible values – see e.g. (1.6) above for an example. If nuisance parameters are present, they can be integrated out of the joint posterior pdf to obtain a marginal posterior pdf for parameters of interest as shown in (1.11). Further, if the sample size is large, posterior pdfs assume a normal shape in general with a mean approximately equal to the ML estimate. However, if the sample size is not large, the ML estimate is often not a good approximation to the posterior mean and posterior pdfs' forms are usually non-normal – see Zellner and Rossi (1984) for illustrations of these points using logit models. While the complete posterior pdf is generally available in Bayesian analyses, often interest centres on obtaining an optimal point estimate for a parameter. The Bayesian solution to the problem of point estimation is presented below.

1.1. BAYESIAN POINT ESTIMATION. Given a posterior pdf for $\theta \subset \Theta$, $p(\theta|D)$ derived using Bayes' Theorem in (1.2), an estimate of θ, say $\hat{\theta} = \hat{\theta}(D)$, where $D = (\mathbf{y}, I_0)$, the sample and prior information, is desired. Some measure of central tendency relating to the posterior pdf, say the mean, modal value or median might be used as a point estimate. However, if the posterior pdf is asymmetric, these measures of central tendency will differ and the problem of choice among them remains. When a loss function, $L(\theta, \hat{\theta})$, is available, this problem can be solved by choosing the value of $\hat{\theta}$ that minimizes expected loss and such a value is the Bayesian point estimate. Explicitly, the problem to be solved in Bayesian point estimation is min $EL(\theta, \hat{\theta})$ with respect to $\hat{\theta}$, or

$$\min_{\hat{\theta}} \int_{\Theta} L(\theta, \hat{\theta}) p(\theta|D) \, d\theta. \tag{1.12}$$

The solution to the minimization problem (1.12), denoted by $\hat{\theta}^*$ is the Bayesian point estimate. Note that $-L(\theta, \hat{\theta})$ can be interpreted as a utility function and thus (1.12) is equivalent to choosing a value for $\hat{\theta}$ that maximizes expected utility. Given the form of $L(\theta, \hat{\theta})$, the problem in (1.12) can be solved analytically or by numerical integration techniques. Below, solutions will be presented for some widely used loss functions.

a. *Quadratic loss functions.* Let $L(\theta, \hat{\theta}) = c_1(\hat{\theta} - \theta)^2$, where c_1 is a given positive constant. Then

$$EL = c_1 E(\theta - \hat{\theta})^2 = c_1 E[\theta - \bar{\theta} - (\hat{\theta} - \bar{\theta})]^2$$
$$= c_1 [E(\theta - \bar{\theta})^2 + (\hat{\theta} - \bar{\theta})^2],$$

where $\bar{\theta} = E(\theta|D)$ is the posterior mean of θ. Then the value of $\hat{\theta}$ that minimizes expected loss is $\hat{\theta}^* = \bar{\theta}$, the posterior mean. This is a very general result applicable to all kinds of point estimation problems for which the above 'squared error' loss function is appropriate. For example, in the normal mean problem analysed above, the optimal point estimate relative to the above squared error loss function is the posterior mean given in (1.4). For the Binomial Trials problem with posterior pdf given in (1.7), the optimal point estimate relative to squared error loss is the mean of the posterior pdf, namely, $\hat{\theta}^* = (r+a)/(n+a+b)$.

If θ is a vector of parameters and if the loss function is $L(\theta, \hat{\theta}) = (\hat{\theta} - \theta)'Q(\hat{\theta} - \theta)$, where Q is a given positive definite symmetric matrix, then

$$EL = E(\hat{\theta} - \theta)'Q(\hat{\theta} - \theta)$$

$$= E[\hat{\theta} - \bar{\theta} - (\theta - \bar{\theta})]'Q[\hat{\theta} - \bar{\theta} - (\theta - \bar{\theta})]$$

$$= (\hat{\theta} - \bar{\theta})'Q(\hat{\theta} - \bar{\theta}) + E(\theta - \bar{\theta})'Q(\theta - \bar{\theta}), \qquad (1.13)$$

where $\bar{\theta} = E\theta \,|\, D$ is the posterior mean of θ. From the last line of (1.13), it is clear that the value of $\hat{\theta}$ that minimizes expected loss is $\hat{\theta}^* = \bar{\theta}$, the posterior mean. Thus for multiparameter point estimation problems employing a quadratic loss function, the posterior mean is an optimal point estimate in terms of minimizing posterior expected loss.

b. *Absolute error loss functions.* If the loss function is $L(\theta, \hat{\theta}) = c_2 |\hat{\theta} - \theta|$, where c_2 is a given positive constant, the value of $\hat{\theta}$ that minimizes expected loss is the median of the posterior pdf for θ, $p(\theta \,|\, D)$. With $a \leqslant \theta \leqslant b$, posterior expected loss is:

$$EL(\theta, \theta) = c_2 \int_a^b |\hat{\theta} - \theta| p(\theta \,|\, D) \, d\theta$$

$$= c_2 \left[\int_a^\theta (\hat{\theta} - \theta) p(\theta \,|\, D) \, d\theta + \int_\theta^b (\theta - \hat{\theta}) p(\theta \,|\, D) \, d\theta \right].$$

Then

$$\frac{dEL(\theta, \hat{\theta})}{d\hat{\theta}} = c_2 [F(\hat{\theta} \,|\, D) - 1 + F(\hat{\theta} \,|\, D)], \qquad (1.14)$$

where $F(\hat{\theta} \,|\, D) = \int_a^\theta p(\theta \,|\, D) \, d\theta$ is the cumulative posterior distribution function. The value of $\hat{\theta}$ that sets (1.14) equal to zero is $\hat{\theta} = $ median of the posterior pdf and this is the value that minimizes expected loss since $d^2 EL/d\hat{\theta}^2$, evaluated at the median, is strictly positive. Thus for an absolute error loss function, the posterior median is an optimal point estimate. For the normal mean problem analysed above, the posterior pdf in (1.3) is normal and hence the median is equal to the mean, given in (1.4), since the normal posterior pdf is symmetric. For asymmetric posterior pdfs, such as that shown in (1.7), the median will not be equal to the mean.

c. *Zero-one loss functions.* If loss is equal to zero as $\hat{\theta} - \theta$ approaches zero and is equal to one for $|\hat{\theta} - \theta| \neq 0$, then the modal value of the posterior pdf is the value of $\hat{\theta}$ that minimizes expected loss – for a proof, see, e.g. Blackwell and Girshick (1954). This with a zero-one loss function, the modal value of (1.7), $\hat{\theta}^* = (r+a-1)/(n+a+b-2)$ is optimal. Note that this value differs from the posterior mean $(r+a)/(n+a+b)$ that is optimal for a squared error loss function.

d. *Asymmetrix LINEX loss function.* Let the loss function be given by

$$L(\hat{\theta} - \theta) = b[e^{a(\hat{\theta} - \theta)} - a(\hat{\theta} - \theta) - 1], \quad b > 0$$
$$a \neq 0 \tag{1.15}$$

a class of asymmetric loss functions introduced and used by Varian (1975). For $\hat{\theta} - \theta = 0$, loss is zero and when $a > 0$, loss rises almost exponentially for $\hat{\theta} - \theta > 0$ and approximately linearly when $\hat{\theta} - \theta < 0$. The reverse is true when $a < 0$. Posterior expected loss is given by

$$EL = b[e^{a\hat{\theta}} Ee^{-a\theta} - a(\hat{\theta} - E\theta) - 1]$$

and the value of $\hat{\theta}$ that minimizes expected loss is

$$\hat{\theta}* = -(1/a) \log Ee^{-a\theta}, \tag{1.16}$$

as shown in Zellner (1986). When (1.16) is evaluated using the normal posterior pdf in (1.3), the result is

$$\hat{\theta}* = \bar{\theta} - a\tau^2/2, \tag{1.17}$$

with $\bar{\theta}$ the posterior mean in (1.4) and τ^2 the posterior variance in (1.5). It is seen that the optimal point estimate in (1.17) is less than the posterior mean when $a > 0$ and greater than the posterior mean when $a < 0$ reflecting the asymmetry of the LINEX loss function in (1.15).

As the above examples indicate, the Bayesian point estimate is tailored to be optimal relative to the specific loss function that is deemed appropriate. For other loss functions, the problem of minimizing expected loss, shown in (1.12), can be solved, either analytically or by numerical integration to obtain an optimal Bayesian point estimate. This general procedure is applicable to all estimation problems in econometrics and statistics for which expected loss is finite, that is, for which the integral in (1.12) converges to a finite value.

To appraise the general *sampling properties* of Bayesian estimates, $\hat{\theta} = \hat{\theta}(\mathbf{y}, I_0)$ is regarded as a random estimator. Relative to a specific loss function, $L(\theta, \hat{\theta})$, the risk function is given by

$$r(\theta) = \int_{R_y} L(\theta, \hat{\theta}) p(\mathbf{y} \mid \theta, I_0) \, d\mathbf{y} \tag{1.18}$$

and the Bayesian estimator is, by definition, the one that minimizes average or Bayes risk (BR),

$$BR = \int_{\Theta} r(\theta) p(\theta \mid I_0) \, d\theta, \tag{1.19}$$

where $p(\theta \mid I_0)$ is a given prior pdf for θ that is assumed to be positive over the region Θ.

Upon substituting (1.18) in (1.19),

$$BR = \int_{\Theta} \int_{R_y} L(\theta, \hat{\theta}) p(\mathbf{y} \mid \theta, I_0) p(\theta \mid I_0) \, d\mathbf{y} \, d\theta. \tag{1.20a}$$

Using $p(\mathbf{y}|\theta, I_0)p(\theta|I_0) = p(\theta|D)p(\mathbf{y}|I_0)$, where $D = (\mathbf{y}, I_0)$ and interchanging the order of integration, (1.20a) can be expressed as

$$\text{BR} = \int_{R_y} \left[\int_{\Theta} L(\theta, \hat{\theta})p(\theta|D)\, d\theta \right] p(\mathbf{y}|I_0)\, d\mathbf{y}. \tag{1.20b}$$

If the integral defining BR converges to a finite value and if $p(\mathbf{y}|I_0) > 0$ over the region R_y, then the value of $\hat{\theta}$ that minimizes the integral in square brackets in (1.20b) minimizes BR, i.e. it is the estimator that minimizes Bayes or average risk. Note that the integral in square brackets defines posterior expected loss. Thus the solution to the problem in (1.12), viewed as an estimator is the estimator that minimizes BR and is by definition the Bayesian estimator. The estimator is admissible since if there were another estimator that had lower risk, $r(\theta)$ given in (1.18), over Θ, it would have lower BR, a contradiction since the Bayesian estimator, by construction, minimizes BR. These and other properties of Bayesian estimators are discussed in De Groot (1970), Berger (1985) and other works on decision theory. Thus Bayesian estimators relative to the loss function and prior pdf used to derive them have very good sampling properties under the condition that BR is finite, a sufficient condition for admissibility of the Bayesian estimator.

To illustrate some of the above concepts, consider estimation of a mean θ in the normal mean problem in Example 1 relative to a squared error loss function $L(\theta, \hat{\theta}) = (\theta - \hat{\theta})^2$. As mentioned above, the posterior mean in (1.4) is the Bayesian estimator for this problem that we write as

$$\bar{\theta} = wm + (1 - w)\bar{y} \tag{1.21}$$

with $w = h_0/(h + h_0)$. Since $\bar{y}$ is normally distributed with mean θ and variance σ_0^2/n, the risk of $\bar{\theta}$ relative to a squared error loss function is

$$r(\theta) = E_{\bar{y}}(\theta - \bar{\theta})^2$$

$$= \theta^2 - 2\theta E\bar{\theta} + E\bar{\theta}^2$$

$$= \theta^2 - 2\theta[wm + (1 - w)E\bar{y}] + E[wm + (1 - w)\bar{y}]^2$$

$$r(\theta) = w^2(\theta - m)^2 + (1 - w)^2\sigma_0^2/n. \tag{1.22}$$

It is clear that $r(\theta)$ is smallest when $\theta = m$, the prior mean. To compute BR, we average $r(\theta)$ using the normal prior for θ with mean m and variance $v = 1/h_0$ to obtain

$$\text{BR} = w^2 v + (1 - w)^2\sigma_0^2/n$$

$$= 1/(h_0 + h), \tag{1.23}$$

where $\sigma_0^2/n = 1/h$. For comparison, the risk function for the sample mean, $\bar{y}$, is

$$r(\theta) = E(\theta - \bar{y})^2$$

$$= \sigma_0^2/n. \tag{1.24}$$

45

On comparing (1.24) and (1.22), it is seen that when θ is close to the prior mean, (1.22) is smaller than (1.24). The BR of the sample mean is

$$\mathrm{BR} = \sigma_0^2/n = 1/h, \tag{1.25}$$

which is larger than the BR of the posterior mean in (1.23). This is not surprising since the posterior mean is the estimator that minimizes BR.

Above, proper prior pdfs were employed to obtain Bayesian estimates and estimators. When *improper* prior pdfs are employed to represent vague or little prior information about parameters' values as in Jeffreys (1967) and others' works, posterior pdfs are usually proper and posterior probability statements can be made. Rényi (1970) – see also Hartigan (1983) – has provided an axiom system for probability theory that accommodates improper prior pdfs or unbounded measures and within the context of which Bayes' Theorem remains valid. When such prior pdfs are employed, the solution to the point estimation problem in (1.12) is termed a generalized Bayes estimate (GBE). Often BR is not finite for GB estimators and they need not in general be admissible. To illustrate, a normal mean problem and a regression problem will be analysed employing diffuse, improper prior pdfs.

Example 3: Normal mean with an improper prior. Assume that n observations have been independently drawn from a normal distribution with mean θ and variance σ^2, both of which have unknown values. The likelihood function is given by

$$p(\mathbf{y}\,|\,\theta,\,\sigma) \propto \sigma^{-n} \exp\{-(\mathbf{y}-\imath\theta)'(\mathbf{y}-\imath\theta)/2\sigma^2\}$$

$$\propto \sigma^{-n} \exp\{-[vs^2 + n(\theta-\bar{y})^2]/2\sigma^2\}, \tag{1.26}$$

where $\mathbf{y}' = (y_1, y_2, \ldots, y_n)$, $\imath' = (1, 1, \ldots, 1)$, a $1 \times n$ vector with all elements equal to one,

$$\bar{y} = \sum_{i=1}^{n} y_i/n,$$

the sample mean and

$$vs^2 = \sum_{i=1}^{n} (y_i - \bar{y})^2 \quad \text{and} \quad v = n-1.$$

Jeffreys's (1967) diffuse improper prior pdf for this problem is,

$$p(\theta,\,\sigma) \propto 1/\sigma. \qquad -\infty < \theta < \infty \qquad 0 < \sigma < \infty \tag{1.27}$$

That is θ and $\log \sigma$ are assumed independently and uniformly distributed. Since the integral of $p(\theta, \sigma)$ over the range $-\infty < \theta < \infty$ and $0 < \sigma < \infty$ does not converge to one, the prior pdf is termed 'improper'. See Zellner (1971, 1977) and Berger (1985) for further discussion of (1.27). On combining the likelihood function in (1.26) with the prior in (1.27) by Bayes' Theorem, the result is the joint posterior pdf for θ and σ, namely

$$p(\theta, \sigma \mid D) \propto \sigma^{-(n+1)} \exp\{-[vs^2 + n(\theta - \bar{y})^2]/2\sigma^2\}. \tag{1.28}$$

From (1.28), it is seen that the conditional posterior pdf for θ given σ is normal with mean $\bar{y}$ and variance σ^2/n. Also by integrating (1.28) with respect to σ, 0 to ∞, the marginal posterior pdf for θ is

$$p(\theta \mid D) \propto \{vs^2 + n(\theta - \bar{y})^2\}^{-(v+1)/2} \tag{1.29}$$

which is a proper pdf, given $v > 0$, in the univariate Student-t form. That is $t = \sqrt{n}(\theta - \bar{y})/s$ has a standardised Student-t pdf with v degrees of freedom. Also, on integrating (1.28) with respect to θ, from $-\infty$ to ∞, the result is the marginal posterior for σ,

$$p(\sigma \mid D) \propto \sigma^{-(v+1)} \exp\{-vs^2/2\sigma^2\}, \tag{1.30}$$

a proper pdf in the inverted-gamma form – see, e.g. Zellner (1971) for its properties. Thus even though the improper prior pdf in (1.27) was employed, the posterior pdfs in (1.29) and (1.30) are proper and can be employed to make posterior probability statements about the values of θ and σ.

To obtain an optimal point estimate for θ, assume that a squared error loss function is appropriate, that is $L(\theta, \hat{\theta}) = (\hat{\theta} - \theta)^2$. Relative to this loss function the value of $\hat{\theta}$ that minimizes posterior expected loss is the posterior mean of (1.29) which is $\bar{y}$ for $v > 1$. The risk of $\bar{y}$ relative to the squared error loss function is $E(\bar{y} - \theta)^2 = \sigma^2/n$ since $\bar{y}$ has a normal pdf with mean θ and variance σ^2/n. If we try to compute the BR of $\bar{y}$ relative to the improper prior in (1.27), it is clear that BR is unbounded, that is the integral defining

$$\text{BR} = \int_0^\infty \int_{-\infty}^\infty r(\theta) p(\theta, \sigma \mid I_0) \, d\theta \, d\sigma$$

diverges. Thus $\bar{y}$, the posterior mean does not minimize BR. A different argument must be used to establish the admissibility of $\bar{y}$ – see e.g. Blyth (1951) and Berger (1985) for proofs of the admissibility of $\bar{y}$.

As regards the posterior pdf for σ in (1.30), it can be transformed to a posterior pdf for σ^2 by a simple change of variable from σ to $\phi = \sigma^2$ to yield

$$p(\phi \mid D) \propto \phi^{-(n+2)/2} \exp\{-vs^2/2\phi\}. \qquad 0 < \phi < \infty \tag{1.31}$$

The posterior mean of ϕ is $\bar{\phi} = vs^2/(v - 2)$, for $v > 2$ which is optimal relative to a squared error loss function. Also, with respect to a relative squared error loss function, $L(\hat{\phi}, \phi) = (\hat{\phi} - \phi)^2/\phi^2$, the optimal value of $\hat{\phi}$ is $\hat{\phi}^* = vs^2/(v + 2)$ since $EL = \hat{\phi}^2 E1/\phi^2 - 2\hat{\phi}E1/\phi + 1$ and the minimizing value of $\hat{\phi}$ is $\hat{\phi}^* = E(1/\phi)/E(1/\phi^2) = vs^2/(v + 2)$. Finally the modal value of (1.30) that is optimal relative to a zero-one loss function is $\hat{\phi}_{m0} = vs^2/(v + 2)$. Thus point estimates that are optimal relative to various loss functions are readily obtained. Finally from (1.30), vs^2/ϕ has a χ_v^2 posterior pdf, a fact that is very useful in making posterior probability statements regarding ϕ's values.

Example 4: Normal regression model with a diffuse prior. Assume that the $n \times 1$ observation vector $\mathbf{y}$ is generated by $\mathbf{y} = X\boldsymbol{\beta} + \mathbf{u}$, where X is an $n \times k$ non-stochastic matrix with rank k, $\boldsymbol{\beta}$ is a $k \times 1$ vector of regression coefficients with unknown values and $\mathbf{u}$ is an $n \times 1$ vector of disturbance terms assumed independently drawn from a normal pdf with zero mean and finite variance σ^2 with unknown value. The likelihood function under these assumptions is

$$p(\mathbf{y}|X, \boldsymbol{\beta}, \sigma) \propto \sigma^{-n} \exp\{-(\mathbf{y} - X\boldsymbol{\beta})'(\mathbf{y} - X\boldsymbol{\beta})/2\sigma^2\}$$

$$\propto \sigma^{-n} \exp\{-[vs^2 + (\boldsymbol{\beta} - \hat{\boldsymbol{\beta}})'X'X(\boldsymbol{\beta} - \hat{\boldsymbol{\beta}})]/2\sigma^2\}, \quad (1.32)$$

where $\hat{\boldsymbol{\beta}} = (X'X)^{-1}X'\mathbf{y}$, $vs^2 = (\mathbf{y} - X\hat{\boldsymbol{\beta}})'(\mathbf{y} - X\boldsymbol{\beta})$ and $v = n - k$. The diffuse prior pdf that will be employed is

$$p(\boldsymbol{\beta}, \sigma|I_0) \propto 1/\sigma, \quad -\infty < \beta_i < \infty \quad i = 1, 2, \ldots, k$$

$$0 < \sigma < \infty. \quad (1.33)$$

That is the elements of $\boldsymbol{\beta}$ and $\log \sigma$ are assumed to be uniformly and independently distributed. Since (1.33) does not integrate to a constant, it is an improper pdf. However on combining it with the likelihood function in (1.33) by means of Bayes' Theorem, the resulting joint posterior pdf is,

$$p(\boldsymbol{\beta}, \sigma|D) \propto \sigma^{-(n+1)} \exp\{-[vs^2 + (\boldsymbol{\beta} - \hat{\boldsymbol{\beta}})'X'X(\boldsymbol{\beta} - \hat{\boldsymbol{\beta}})]/2\sigma^2\}. \quad (1.34)$$

From (1.34), it is seen that the conditional posterior pdf for $\boldsymbol{\beta}$ given σ is normal with mean $\hat{\boldsymbol{\beta}}$ and covariance matrix $(X'X)^{-1}\sigma^2$. Since σ's value is unknown, this result is not very useful in practice. To get rid of the nuisance parameter σ, (1.34) is integrated with respect to σ to yield the marginal posterior pdf for β,

$$p(\boldsymbol{\beta}|D) \propto \{vs^2 + (\boldsymbol{\beta} - \hat{\boldsymbol{\beta}})'X'X(\boldsymbol{\beta} - \hat{\boldsymbol{\beta}})\}^{-(v+k)/2} \quad (1.35)$$

a posterior pdf that is the multivariate Student-t form – see, e.g. Raiffa and Schlaifer (1961) and Zellner (1971) for its properties. For $v > 1$, the mean of (1.34) is $E(\boldsymbol{\beta}|D) = \hat{\boldsymbol{\beta}} = (X'X)^{-1}X'\mathbf{y}$, the least squares quantity and ML estimate. This then is another example wherein a non-Bayesian result has been produced by the Bayesian approach. Further, from (1.35), the marginal pdf for an element of $\boldsymbol{\beta}$, say β_i is in the univariate Student-t form; that is, $(\beta_i - \hat{\beta}_i)/s_{\hat{\beta}_i}$ has a univariate Student-t pdf with v degrees of freedom, where $\hat{\beta}_i$ is the ith element of $\hat{\boldsymbol{\beta}}$ and $s_{\hat{\beta}_i}^2 = m^{ii}s^2$, where m^{ii} is the i-ith element of $(X'X)^{-1}$. Thus posterior probability statements about β_i's value, e.g. $\Pr(\beta_i > 0|D)$ can be made using properties of the univariate Student-t pdf.

Further, on integrating (1.34) with respect to the elements of $\boldsymbol{\beta}$, the following marginal posterior pdf for σ is obtained

$$p(\sigma|D) \propto \sigma^{-(v+1)} \exp\{-vs^2/2\sigma^2\} \quad (1.36)$$

a posterior pdf in the 'inverted gamma' form – see, e.g. Raiffa and Schlaifer (1961) and Zellner (1971) for its properties. By a change of variable in (1.36), the posterior pdf for $\phi = \sigma^2$, the variance is

$$p(\phi|D) \propto \phi^{-(v+2)/2} \exp\{-vs^2/2\phi\} \quad (1.37)$$

for which it is the case that vs^2/ϕ has a χ^2_v pdf with $v = n - k$ degrees of freedom. The modal values and moments of (1.36) and (1.37) are readily available. Also, posterior probability statements regarding ϕ's possible values can be evaluated using tables of the χ^2_v pdf; that is the posterior probability that ϕ lies between vs^2/a_2 and vs^2/a_1, given by $\Pr\{vs^2/a_2 < \phi < vs^2/a_1 \mid D\}$, where $a_1, a_2 > 0$ are given constants, can be evaluated by use of χ^2_v tables by noting that the required probability is equal to $\Pr\{a_1 < vs^2/\phi < a_2 \mid D\}$, where vs^2/ϕ has a χ^2_v posterior pdf.

As can be seen from what has been presented above, Bayesian point estimates can be readily computed from posterior pdfs that are optimal relative to loss functions that are deemed appropriate. They reflect both sample and prior information, as little or as much of the latter as is available. As regards sampling properties of point estimates, some properties of Bayesian estimators have been noted above. The relevance of sampling properties for making inferences from a *given* sample of data has been questioned by some – see e.g. Tiao and Box (1975). Indeed, it is difficult to state which sequence of future samples is most relevant for a given problem. Usually the sequence considered is *identical repetitions* of the process giving the sample data. This sequence is often not the most relevant sequence. However, before the sample data are drawn, it appears relevant to consider possible outcomes, particularly with respect to design of experiments, and it is here that sampling properties of procedures, including point estimation procedures, are most relevant. Once the data are drawn, the researcher's task is to make inferences based on the given sample and prior information.

With this said about point estimation, attention will now be given to interval estimation.

1.2 INTERVAL ESTIMATION. Given that a posterior pdf for a parameter θ, $p(\theta \mid D)$ is available that is unimodal, in interval estimation an interval is sought within which the parameter's value lies with a specified posterior probability, say 0.95. Since such intervals are not unique, it is necessary to impose a condition so that a unique interval is obtained. The condition is that of all intervals with posterior probability $1 - \alpha$, the one selected is the shortest. Formally, the length of the interval, say $b - a$ is minimized subject to the condition that $\Pr(a < \theta < b \mid D) = \int_a^b p(\theta \mid D)\, d\theta = 1 - \alpha$, the given posterior probability. The solution for this constrained minimization problem is to take the values of a and b such that $p(a \mid D) = p(b \mid D)$ – see, e.g. Zellner (1971) for a proof. Given that $p(\theta \mid D)$ is unimodal, the posterior interval with probability content $1 - \alpha$ so computed has posterior densities associated with it that are greater than any other interval with posterior probability $1 - \alpha$ and thus has been called a posterior highest density (PHD) interval.

Example 5: PHD interval for a regression coefficient. In Example 4, it was indicated that the posterior pdf for a regression coefficient β_i is in the univariate Student-t form, that is $t_v = (\beta_i - \hat{\beta}_i)/s_{\beta_i}$ has a univariate Student-t posterior pdf with $v = n - k$ degrees of freedom. Then, with given probability $1 - \alpha$, say 0.95,

$\Pr(-c < t_v < c \mid D) = 1 - \alpha$, where $c > 0$ is obtained from t-tables with v degrees of freedom. Note from the symmetry of the Student-t pdf, $p(-c \mid D) = p(c \mid D)$ as required for a PHD interval. Also the event $-c < t_v < c$ is equivalent to $\hat{\beta}_i - cs_\beta < \beta_i < \hat{\beta}_i + cs_\beta$ and thus the posterior probability that β_i is in the given interval $\hat{\beta}_i \pm cs_{\beta_i}$ is 0.95.

Further, a posterior region for the regression coefficient vector can be computed using the following result from (1.35), a property of the multivariate Student-t pdf, namely,

$$F_{k,v} = (\boldsymbol{\beta} - \hat{\boldsymbol{\beta}})' X' X (\boldsymbol{\beta} - \hat{\boldsymbol{\beta}}) / ks^2 \tag{1.38}$$

which has a posterior F distribution with k and v degrees of freedom. When $\boldsymbol{\beta}$ has two elements, (1.38) can be employed to compute a confidence region in the form of an ellipse with a given posterior probability, $1 - \alpha$, such that β_1 and β_2 fall within it by choosing a value of $F_{k,v}$, say F_α such that $\Pr(F_{k,v} \leqslant F_\alpha) = 1 - \alpha$.

II. BAYESIAN PREDICTION PROCEDURES

Let $\mathbf{y}_f$ represent a vector of as yet unobserved variables and assume that the pdf for $\mathbf{y}_f$ is $f(\mathbf{y}_f \mid \boldsymbol{\theta})$, where $\boldsymbol{\theta}$ is a vector of parameters with unknown values. The fact that $\boldsymbol{\theta}$ has an unknown value makes it difficult to use $f(\mathbf{y}_f \mid \boldsymbol{\theta})$ to make probability statements about possible values of $\mathbf{y}_f$. However, if a posterior pdf for $\boldsymbol{\theta}$, $p(\boldsymbol{\theta} \mid D)$ is available, provided by Bayes' Theorem in (1.2), then the joint pdf for $\mathbf{y}_f$ and $\boldsymbol{\theta}$ is given by $f(\mathbf{y}_f \mid \boldsymbol{\theta} \mid D)$, where D represents past data and prior information. Then the marginal or predictive pdf for $\mathbf{y}_f$, $p(\mathbf{y}_f \mid D)$, is given by,

$$p(\mathbf{y}_f \mid D) = \int_\Theta f(\mathbf{y}_f \mid \boldsymbol{\theta}) p(\boldsymbol{\theta} \mid D) \, d\boldsymbol{\theta}. \tag{2.1}$$

From (2.1) it is seen that the predictive pdf can be interpreted as an average of $f(\mathbf{y}_f \mid \boldsymbol{\theta})$ with $p(\boldsymbol{\theta} \mid D)$ serving as the weight function. The result in (2.1) gives the complete predictive pdf for the vector of future values, $\mathbf{y}_f$, from which marginal pdfs for particular elements of $\mathbf{y}_f$ can be obtained by integration. Also, moments of the elements of $\mathbf{y}_f$ can be evaluated. As explained below, the mean of the predictive pdf (2.1) is an optimal point prediction relative to a quadratic loss function. Also, predictive intervals and regions for elements of $\mathbf{y}_f$ can be computed from (2.1).

As regards point prediction, given a predictive loss function, $L(\mathbf{y}_f, \hat{\mathbf{y}}_f)$, where $\hat{\mathbf{y}}_f = \hat{\mathbf{y}}_f(D)$ is some point prediction, an optimal value for $\hat{\mathbf{y}}_f$ is obtained by minimizing expected loss, that is by solving the following problem:

$$\min_{\hat{\mathbf{y}}_f} \int L(\mathbf{y}_f, \hat{\mathbf{y}}_f) p(\mathbf{y}_f \mid D) \, d\mathbf{y}_f. \tag{2.2}$$

The solution, $\hat{\mathbf{y}}_f^*$, is the optimal point prediction. For example, for a quadratic loss function, $L(\mathbf{y}_f, \hat{\mathbf{y}}_f) = (\mathbf{y}_f - \hat{\mathbf{y}}_f)' Q (\mathbf{y}_f - \hat{\mathbf{y}}_f)$, where Q is a given positive definite symmetric matrix, expected loss is given by

$$E(\mathbf{y}_f - \hat{\mathbf{y}}_f)'Q(\mathbf{y}_f - \hat{\mathbf{y}}_f) = E[\mathbf{y}_f - \bar{\mathbf{y}}_f - (\hat{\mathbf{y}}_f - \bar{\mathbf{y}}_f)]'Q[\mathbf{y}_f - \bar{\mathbf{y}}_f - (\hat{\mathbf{y}}_f - \bar{\mathbf{y}}_f)]$$

$$= E(y_f - \bar{y}_f)'Q(y_f - \bar{y}_f) + (\hat{y}_f - \bar{y}_f)'Q(\hat{y} - \bar{y}_f),$$

$$(2.3)$$

where $\bar{\mathbf{y}}_f$ is the mean of the predictive pdf. From (2.3), it is clear that taking $\hat{y}_f = \bar{y}_f$ minimizes expected loss. Thus, in general, the mean of a predictive pdf is an optimal point prediction relative to quadratic loss. As in the case of point estimation, if other loss functions are employed, point predictions that are optimal relative to them can be calculated by solving the problem in (2.2) analytically or numerically. This analysis for absolute error, zero-one and LINEX loss functions is similar to that presented above in connection with point estimation. Also, Bayesian point predictors based on proper prior distributions are admissible and minimize Bayes risk.

To illustrate the calculation of a predictive pdf for the multiple regression model with the posterior pdf for its parameters given in (1.34), let a future scalar observation, y_f, be given by

$$y_f = \mathbf{x}_f'\boldsymbol{\beta} + u_f,$$

$$(2.4)$$

where $\mathbf{x}_f'$ is a $1 \times k$ given vector and u_f is a normal error term with zero mean and variance σ^2. Then noting from (1.34) that the posterior pdf of $\boldsymbol{\beta}$ given σ is $N[\hat{\boldsymbol{\beta}}, (X'X)^{-1}\sigma^2]$, the conditional distribution of y_f given σ is normal with mean $\mathbf{x}_f'\hat{\boldsymbol{\beta}}$ and covariance matrix, $[1 + \mathbf{x}_f'(X'X)^{-1}\mathbf{x}_f]\sigma^2$. On multiplying this conditional predictive pdf for y_f by the posterior pdf for σ, given in (1.36) and integrating over σ, the result is

$$p(y_f|D) \propto \{vs^2 + (y_f - \hat{y})^2/a^2\}^{-(v+1)/2},$$

$$(2.5)$$

where $\hat{y}_f = \mathbf{x}_f'\hat{\boldsymbol{\beta}}$, $a^2 = 1 + \mathbf{x}_f'(X'X)^{-1}\mathbf{x}_f$ and $v = n - k$, a pdf in the univariate Student-t form with v degrees of freedom with mean $\hat{y}_f$. Thus

$$t_v = (y_f - \hat{y}_f)/as$$

$$(2.6)$$

has a univariate Student-t pdf with v degrees of freedom. Using (2.6), a predictive interval for y_f can be computed that has a given probability, say $1 - \alpha$, of including y_f. Such an interval takes the form $\hat{y}_f \pm c_{\alpha/2}as$, where $c_{\alpha/2}$ is a constant obtained from tables of the t-distribution. The probability statement associated with this interval is:

$$\Pr\{\hat{y}_f - c_{\alpha/2}as < y_f < \hat{y}_f + c_{\alpha/2}as|D\} = 1 - \alpha.$$

$$(2.7)$$

Note that y_f is random and the endpoints of the interval are non-random since they depend just on the given data D. A similar analysis can be performed to obtain the predictive pdf for a vector of future values $\mathbf{y}_f$, assumed generated by $\mathbf{y}_f = X_f\boldsymbol{\beta} + \mathbf{u}_f$ when the value of X_f is given.

Above in (2.4), $\mathbf{x}_f$ was assumed given. If $\mathbf{x}_f$'s value is unknown then the predictive pdf for y_f is given by

$$p(y_f \,|\, D) = \int p(y_f \,|\, \mathbf{x}_f, D) p(\mathbf{x}_f \,|\, D_1) \, d\mathbf{x}_f, \tag{2.8}$$

where $p(\mathbf{x}_f \,|\, D_1)$ is the predictive pdf for $\mathbf{x}_f$ given data D_1. The integration in (2.8) may be performed analytically or numerically. Further, predictive pdfs can be computed for linear combinations of future values, say $\mathbf{z} = A\mathbf{y}_f$ where A is a given matrix, for time series models – see Broemeling (1985), Monahan (1983) and Zellner (1971); for simultaneous equation models – see Richard (1973), and for many other models – see Aitchison and Dunsmore (1975).

III. BAYESIAN ANALYSIS OF HYPOTHESES

Bayesian methods are available for analysing hypotheses about parameters' values and for comparing and choosing between alternative hypotheses or models, be they nested or non-nested. Prior probabilities are assigned to hypotheses or models that reflect the degrees of confidence associated with them and Bayes' Theorem is employed to compute posterior probabilities for them that reflect the information in sample data. This approach differs radically from non-Bayesian testing procedures in which one hypothesis, e.g. the null hypothesis, or one of two models is assumed to be 'true' and a test statistics' distribution, derived under an assumed true null hypothesis or model is employed to 'accept' or 'reject' the assumed true hypothesis or model. For further consideration of these issues see Jeffreys (1967), Jaynes (1984), Kruskal (1978), Leamer (1978), and Zellner (1971, 1984).

To illustrate the Bayesian approach for analysing hypotheses, consider first a scalar parameter θ, say a population mean or a regression coefficient with possible values $-\infty < \theta < \infty$. Assume that the following two hypotheses are of interest, $H_1 : \theta > 0$ and $H_2 : \theta \leqslant 0$. Given a prior pdf for the parameter, $p(\theta \,|\, I_0)$, the prior probability that $\theta > 0$ is given by

$$\Pr(\theta > 0 \,|\, I_0) = \int_0^\infty p(\theta \,|\, I_0) \, d\theta \tag{3.1}$$

and the prior probability that $\theta \leqslant 0$ is

$$\Pr(\theta \leqslant 0 \,|\, I_0) = \int_{-\infty}^0 p(\theta \,|\, I_0) \, d\theta = 1 - \Pr(\theta > 0 \,|\, I_0). \tag{3.2}$$

Then the prior odds for H_1 versus H_2, denoted by K_{12}^0 is

$$K_{12}^0 = \Pr(\theta > 0 \,|\, I_0) / \Pr(\theta \leqslant 0 \,|\, I_0). \tag{3.3}$$

These probabilities and K_{12} summarize initial views of the hypotheses H_1 and H_2. If data $\mathbf{y}' = (y_1, y_2, \ldots, y_n)$ are observed relating to θ's possible value, Bayes' Theorem in (1.2) can be employed to compute the posterior pdf for θ, $p(\theta \,|\, D)$, where $D = (\mathbf{y}, I_0)$ represents the sample and prior information. Then

$$\Pr(\theta > 0 \,|\, D) = \int_0^\infty p(\theta \,|\, D) \, d\theta \tag{3.4}$$

and

$$\Pr(\theta \leqslant 0 \mid D) = \int_{-\infty}^{0} p(\theta \mid D) \, \mathrm{d}\theta \qquad (3.5)$$

are the posterior probabilities associated with H_1 and H_2, respectively and their ratio, K_{12}, is the posterior odds. The posterior probabilities in (3.4) and (3.5) differ from (3.1) and (3.2) because the former incorporate the information in the data. This approach can be extended to cases in which θ is a vector, say $\boldsymbol{\theta}' = (\theta_1, \theta_2)$ and hypotheses such as $H_1 : \theta_1 > 0$ and $\theta_2 > 0$; $H_2 : \theta_1 \leqslant 0$ and $\theta_2 > 0$; $H_3 : \theta_1 > 0$ and $\theta_2 \leqslant 0$ and $H_4 : \theta_1 \leqslant 0$ and $\theta_2 \leqslant 0$. In analyses of these four hypotheses, bivariate prior and posterior pdfs for θ_1 and θ_2 can be employed to compute probabilities associated with each of the four hypotheses. These and other hypotheses, involving inequality constraints on parameters' values, are easily analysed. The integrals giving probabilities can be evaluated analytically or numerically – see Zellner (1971, pp. 194–200) for an example of this type of analysis relating to a second order autoregressive process.

Above, various probabilities associated with hypotheses have been computed. Given a loss structure, it is possible to choose a hypothesis so as to minimize expected loss. That is, in considering two hypotheses, a two-action-two-state loss structure is shown in Table 1, where L_{12} is the loss incurred when H_1 is selected and H_2 is appropriate, an error of type II, whereas loss L_{21} is incurred if H_2 is chosen when H_1 is appropriate, an error of type I. Given probabilities, $\Pr(H_1 \mid D)$ and $\Pr(H_2 \mid D)$, say computed from (3.4) and (3.5), respectively, they can be used to compute expected losses shown in the last column of the table. Then H_1 is chosen if $L_{12} \Pr(H_2 \mid D) < L_{21} \Pr(H_1 \mid D)$ and H_2 otherwise. The condition for choosing H_1 is:

$$1 < L_{21} \Pr(H_1 \mid D) / L_{12} \Pr(H_2 \mid D). \qquad (3.6)$$

In the special case of a symmetric loss structure, $L_{12} = L_{21}$, the decision rule in (3.6) reduces to choose H_1 if $\Pr(H_1 \mid D) > \Pr(H_2 \mid D)$. Note that the decision rule in (3.6) reflects prior and sample information as well as the loss structure.

Table 1

	States of world		
Acts	H_1 is appropriate	H_2 is appropriate	Expected loss
Choose H_1	0	L_{12}	$L_{12} \Pr(H_2 \mid D)$
Choose H_2	L_{21}	0	$L_{21} \Pr(H_1 \mid D)$
Probabilities:	$\Pr(H_1 \mid D)$	$\Pr(H_2 \mid D)$	

In the examples considered above, the hypotheses considered did not involve assigning a specific value to a parameter, e.g. $\theta = 0$ or $\theta = 1$. Since hypotheses such as these are frequently encountered in applied work, it is important to be able to appraise them. Jeffreys (1967, Chs V and VI), who is a pioneer in this area, has provided many Bayesian solutions for such testing problems. In this approach, a hypothesis H_1: $\theta = 0$ is considered relative to another hypothesis, H_2: $\theta = \theta_2$, where θ_2 is a given value different from 0. Prior probabilities, Π_1 and Π_2 are assigned to H_1 and H_2, respectively. Assume further that a vector of observations $\mathbf{y}$ is available and that $p(\mathbf{y}|\theta = 0)$ is the likelihood function under hypothesis H_1 and $p(\mathbf{y}|\theta = \theta_2)$ is the likelihood function under hypothesis H_2. Then Bayes' Theorem is employed to obtain the following posterior odds, K_{12} relating to H_1 versus H_2:

$$K_{12} = (\Pi_1/\Pi_2) \times \{p(\mathbf{y}|\theta = 0)/p(\mathbf{y}|\theta = \theta_2)\}$$
$$= (\text{Prior Odds}) \times (\text{Bayes' Factor}). \tag{3.7}$$

In (3.7) Π_1/Π_2 is the prior odds for H_1 versus H_2 while the Bayes' Factor (BF) is the ratio of likelihood functions, $p(\mathbf{y}|\theta = 0)/p(\mathbf{y}|\theta = \theta_2)$. The result in (3.7) can be regarded as a transformation of the prior odds into a posterior odds reflecting both prior and sample information. The following example illustrates use of (3.7).

Example 6: Posterior odds for two simple hypotheses. Let $y_i = \theta + \varepsilon_i$, $i = 1, 2, \ldots,$ n where the ε_i's have been independently drawn from a normal distribution with zero mean and unit variance. Consider two hypotheses about the value of the mean, θ, H_1: $\theta = 0$ and H_2: $\theta = \theta_2 > 0$, with prior odds, $\Pi_1/\Pi_2 = 1$. Then the posterior odds are given by $K_{12} = (\Pi_1/\Pi_2) \cdot p(\mathbf{y}|\theta = 0)/p(\mathbf{y}|\theta = \theta_2)$, or with $\Pi_1/\Pi_2 = 1$,

$$K_{12} = \exp\left\{ -\sum_1^n y_i^2/2 \right\} \Big/ \exp\left\{ -\sum_1^n (y_i - \theta_2)^2/2 \right\}$$
$$= \exp\{n\theta_2(\theta_2/2 - \bar{y})\}. \tag{3.8}$$

It is seen that if $\bar{y} = \theta_2/2$, $K_{12} = 1$ while if $\bar{y} < \theta_2/2$, $K_{12} > 1$, a result favouring H_1 and if $\bar{y} > \theta_2/2$, $K_{12} < 1$, evidence against H_1. If $\bar{y} = 0$, $K_{12} = \exp\{n\theta_2^2/2\} > 1$ with K_{12} larger the larger are n, the sample size and θ_2. Similarly, if $\bar{y} = \theta_2$, $K_{12} = \exp\{-n\theta_2^2/2\} < 1$ with K_{12} smaller the larger are n and θ_2. Note also that $\partial \log K_{12}/\partial \bar{y} = -n\theta_2 < 0$ indicating that K_{12} is a monotonically decreasing function of $\bar{y}$ with $\theta_2 > 0$.

Above two simple hypotheses have been analysed. Posterior odds can also be computed for composite hypotheses which do not involve assigning specific values for all parameters. For example in terms of Example 6, it is possible to compute posterior odds for the two hypotheses, H_1: $\theta = 0$ versus H_2: $\theta \neq 0$ or for pairs of the following three hypotheses, H_1: $\theta = 0$, H_2: $\theta > 0$ and H_3: $\theta < 0$. In these cases, there is a simple hypothesis, $\theta = 0$ and composite hypotheses, $\theta \neq 0$, $\theta > 0$

and $\theta < 0$. In the former case the posterior odds is given by $K_{12} = \Pi_1/\Pi_2 \times BF_{12}$ with the BF given as follows

$$BF_{12} = p(\mathbf{y}\,|\,\theta = 0)\Big/\int_{-\infty}^{\infty} p(\mathbf{y}\,|\,\theta)\pi(\theta)\,\mathrm{d}\theta, \qquad (3.9)$$

where $\pi(\theta)$ is a prior pdf for θ under $H_2: \theta \neq 0$. Since in this case the two hypotheses are exhaustive, $K_{12} = P/(1-P)$, where P is the posterior probability for H_1 and $1-P$ is the posterior probability for H_2. For the three hypotheses, $H_1: \theta = 0$, $H_2: \theta > 0$ and $H_3: \theta < 0$, posterior odds, K_{12}, K_{13} and K_{23} can be computed given that prior probabilities Π_1, Π_2 and Π_3 for the hypotheses and prior pdfs for θ under H_2 and H_3, $\pi_2(\theta)$, $0 < \theta < \infty$, and $\pi_3(\theta)$, $-\infty < \theta < 0$ are available. For example, the posterior odds for H_1 versus H_3 and for H_2 and H_3 are:

$$K_{13} = (\Pi_1/\Pi_3)p(\mathbf{y}\,|\,\theta = 0)\Big/\int_{-\infty}^{0} p(\mathbf{y}\,|\,\theta)\pi_3(\theta)\,\mathrm{d}\theta \qquad (3.10)$$

$$K_{23} = (\Pi_2/\Pi_3)\int_{0}^{\infty} p(\mathbf{y}\,|\,\theta)\,\mathrm{d}\theta \int_{-\infty}^{0} p(\mathbf{y}\,|\,\theta)\pi_3(\theta)\,\mathrm{d}\theta. \qquad (3.11)$$

See Jeffreys (1967), Leamer (1978) and Zellner (1971, 1984) for further analysis of these testing problems. Also treated in these works are regression testing problems, for example computation of posterior odds for the hypotheses $H_1: \boldsymbol{\beta} = \mathbf{0}$ and $H_2: \boldsymbol{\beta} \neq \mathbf{0}$, where $\boldsymbol{\beta}$ is a vector of regression parameters in the usual linear regression model, $\mathbf{y} = X\boldsymbol{\beta} + \mathbf{u}$. Further, hypotheses referring to sub-vectors of $\boldsymbol{\beta}$ are considered in these works as well as non-nested regression models. For testing problems in multivariate regression, see Rossi (1980) and Smith and Spiegelhalter (1980). Also, asymptotic approximations to general posterior odds expressions have been considered by Jeffreys (1967), Lindley (1964), Schwarz (1978), Leamer (1978), and Zellner and Rossi (1984).

Finally, it is the case that posterior probabilities associated with alternative hypotheses can be used to obtain estimates and predictions that reflect uncertainties associated with alternative hypotheses. For example, consider the hypotheses for a regression coefficient vector $\boldsymbol{\beta}$, $H_1: \boldsymbol{\beta} = \boldsymbol{\beta}_1$, a given value, and $H_2: \boldsymbol{\beta} \neq \boldsymbol{\beta}_1$ with posterior probabilities P and $1-P$, respectively, computed from the posterior odds $K_{12} = P/(1-P)$. Using a quadratic loss function, $(\boldsymbol{\beta} - \tilde{\boldsymbol{\beta}})'Q(\boldsymbol{\beta} - \tilde{\boldsymbol{\beta}})$, where Q is a given pds matrix and $\tilde{\boldsymbol{\beta}}$ is an estimate, Zellner and Vandaele (1975) show that the value of $\tilde{\boldsymbol{\beta}}$ that minimizes expected loss is given by

$$\tilde{\boldsymbol{\beta}}^* = P\boldsymbol{\beta}_1 + (1-P)\tilde{\boldsymbol{\beta}}_2$$

$$= \boldsymbol{\beta}_1 + 1/(1 + K_{12})(\tilde{\boldsymbol{\beta}}_2 - \boldsymbol{\beta}_1), \qquad (3.12)$$

where $\tilde{\boldsymbol{\beta}}_2$ is the posterior mean of $\boldsymbol{\beta}$ under H_2. It is seen from (3.12) that the optimal estimate is a simple average of $\boldsymbol{\beta}_1$ and $\tilde{\boldsymbol{\beta}}_2$ and that from the second line of (3.12) the estimate can be viewed as a 'shrinkage' estimate with shrinkage factor $1/(1 + K_{12})$. It is also possible to perform this analysis when more than two hypotheses are considered.

Bayesian posterior odds have also been derived and used for analysing non-nested models, say two different distributions for a set of observations or two completely different economic models, say a Keynesian model versus a monetarist model or a translog production model versus a Fourier series production model. For details, see Dyer (1973), Geisel (1975), Rossi (1980) and Zellner (1971).

In summary, Bayesian procedures for analysing many different kinds of hypotheses are available. They involve a statement of uncertainty about alternative hypotheses in the form of prior probabilities and prior distributions for parameters whose values are not specified by the hypotheses under consideration. Using these prior probabilities, likelihood functions, and Bayes' Theorem, posterior odds and probabilities can be computed, analytically or numerically. The posterior odds so obtained provide a representation of views regarding alternative hypotheses that reflects the information in the data.

The Bayesian approach to analysing hypotheses differs markedly from non-Bayesian approaches. In the latter, one hypothesis, the so-called null hypothesis is assumed to be true. A test statistic is chosen, say a t-statistic and its distribution under the null hypothesis, assumed to be true, is derived. Then the value of the test statistic is computed from the data and compared with what is expected under the null hypothesis. If an unusually large value is obtained, the null hypothesis is rejected. The logic of this procedure seems to parallel that of deductive logic in which a proposition is assumed to be true and then a logical contradiction is deduced which implies that the proposition cannot be true. While this approach is valid in deductive logic, it is not valid in inductive logic wherein all propositions or hypotheses are uncertain and is the reason that Bayesians associate probabilities with hypotheses. Further, as Jaynes (1984) points out, if the null hypothesis is rejected in a non-Bayesian analysis, then so too is the distribution of the test statistic that led to the decision rule for rejection. The fundamental difficulty with the non-Bayesian procedure is that it involves two contradictory assumptions, namely, the null hypothesis is true (with probability one) and the null hypothesis may not be true. In the Bayesian approach, the null hypothesis is not assumed to be true but rather it is assigned a probability between zero and one, a formal representation of an investigator's opinion about the inductive (not deductive) validity of the null hypothesis. As the following quotation from Lehmann (1959) indicates, non-Bayesians frequently have to use such subjective beliefs informally in order to get sensible results:

> Another consideration that frequently enters into the specification of a significance level is the attitude toward the hypothesis before the experiment is performed. If one firmly believes the hypothesis to be true, extremely convincing evidence will be required before one is willing to give up this belief, and the significance level will accordingly be set very low (p. 62).

Thus subjective beliefs are frequently employed in non-Bayesian tests but they are not formally incorporated in the theory of such tests in contrast to Bayesian theory in which they are. Further discussion of the comparative features of

Bayesian and non-Bayesian testing procedures appears in Jeffreys (1967), Zellner (1971, 1984), Leamer (1978) and Berger (1985).

IV. ROBUSTNESS ISSUES IN BAYESIAN INFERENCE

It is desirable that Bayesian inferences and decisions not be overly sensitive to minor departures from assumptions about the forms of (a) prior distributions, (b) likelihood functions and (c) loss functions. Various procedures have been suggested that attempt to deal with this issue which are called robust procedures. Robust procedures provide users of them some protection from the effects of various possible departures from assumptions but there is a price to be paid for such protection in terms of the precision of inferences. To illustrate, if there is some uncertainty about whether data follow a normal distribution, it is possible to consider a class of distributions containing the normal as a special case, say a Student-t distribution. Since the Student-t distribution contains more free parameters than a normal distribution, more parameters have to be estimated. If the data distribution is actually normal, there will be a loss of precision in using the Student-t distribution. However, if the normal distribution is inappropriate, use of the Student-t distribution may produce better results. Further, if there is little information regarding the form of a parametric data distribution, it is possible to use non-parametric methods; see, e.g. Jeffreys (1967, p. 211ff), Ferguson (1967) and Boos and Monahan (1983). In this last reference, 'boot-strapped' likelihood functions are employed in Bayesian analyses of data.

As regards prior distributions' forms, hierarchical prior distributions are often employed to guard against the possibility of assigning incorrect values to prior distributions' parameters. That is, if $p(\theta|\mathbf{a})$ is a prior pdf for θ and $\mathbf{a}$ is a vector of prior parameters and there is uncertainty about the value of $\mathbf{a}$, the prior pdf can be elaborated as follows, $p(\theta|\mathbf{a})f(\mathbf{a}|\mathbf{b})$, where $f(\mathbf{a}|\mathbf{b})$ is a prior pdf for $\mathbf{a}$ with parameter vector $\mathbf{b}$. Then the marginal prior pdf for θ is $p(\theta|\mathbf{b}) = \int p(\theta|\mathbf{a})f(\mathbf{a}|\mathbf{b})\,d\mathbf{a}$, an average of $p(\theta|\mathbf{a})$ using $f(\mathbf{a}|\mathbf{b})$ as the weight function. Such hierarchical priors provide some protection against assigning an incorrect value for $\mathbf{a}$ in $p(\theta|\mathbf{a})$ but at a price of increased complexity of analysis. Also, if several prior pdfs are under consideration, say $p_1(\theta|\mathbf{a}_1), p_2(\theta|\mathbf{a}_2), \ldots, p_m(\theta|\mathbf{a}_m)$, it is possible to compute posterior odds given a likelihood function, $l(\theta|\mathbf{y})$ as follows

$$K_{ij} = (\Pi_i/\Pi_i)\,\frac{\displaystyle\int l(\theta|\mathbf{y})p_i(\theta|\mathbf{a}_i)\,d\theta}{\displaystyle\int l(\theta|\mathbf{y})p_j(\theta|\mathbf{a}_j)\,d\theta}, \tag{3.13}$$

where Π_i and Π_j are the prior probabilities associated with prior pdfs i and j, respectively. Assuming that $\Sigma_{i=1}^{m}\,\Pi_i = 1$, posterior probabilities, $P_1, P_2, \ldots, P_m$, with $\Sigma_{i=1}^{m} P_i = 1$, can be computed. These posterior probabilities can be employed to average results across different priors, as shown explicitly in (3.12), and thus to have some protection against using the 'wrong' prior. Also, Berger (1984) suggests using a particular class of prior distributions and checking to determine that inferences are not sensitive to the choice of prior pdf in the particular class. See Kadane (1984) for further discussion of these issues and for suggested measures of robustness.

Last, point estimates and other inference results are often sensitive to the form of the loss function employed. Thus it is important that the effects of possible errors in formulating loss functions be appraised; see Zellner and Geisel (1968), Varian (1975) and Zellner (1984, 1986) for some results relating to this problem area.

V. CONCLUDING REMARKS

An overview of Bayesian inference has indicated that Bayesian inference techniques are available for analysing many basic problems in science. These techniques are noteworthy for their conceptual simplicity and ability to combine prior and sample information in the solution of many scientific inference problems in a coherent manner. Perhaps the most commonly expressed criticism of the Bayesian aproach is that it is 'subjective', the implication being that non-Bayesian procedures are 'objective'. In this connection, it is the case that non-Bayesians employ non-sample, subjective information informally in their analyses in choosing significance levels, functional forms for relations, appraising inference results, etc. The eminent non-Bayesian statistician Freedman (1986) has written:

> When drawing inferences from data, even the most hard-bitten objectivist usually has to introduce assumptions and use prior information. The serious question is how to integrate that information into the inferential process and how to test the assumptions underlying the analysis (p. 127).

In a similar vein, the famous non-Bayesian statistician Tukey (1978) expressed the following views:

> It is my impression that rather generally, not just in econometrics, it is considered decent to use judgment in choosing a functional form, but indecent to use judgment in choosing a coefficient. If judgment about important things is quite all right, why should it not be used for less important ones as well? Perhaps the real purpose of Bayesian techniques is to let us do the indecent thing while modestly concealed behind a formal apparatus. If so, this would not be a precedent. When Fisher introduced the formalities of the analysis of variance in the early 1920s, its most important function was to conceal the fact that the data was being adjusted for block means, an important step forward which if openly visible would have been considered by too many wiseacres of the time to be "cooking the data." If so, let us hope that day will soon come when the role of decent concealment can be freely admitted. ... The coefficient may be better estimated from one source or another, or, even best, estimated by economic judgment ...

It seems to me a breach of the statistician's trust not to use judgment when that appears to be better than using data (p. 52).

Thus, as is obvious, scientists use both sample and prior information in making inferences. Bayesian inference techniques provide a means of combining these two types of information. In many problems Bayesian inference techniques provide good solutions. Whether Bayesian inference techniques are superior to other inference techniques is an issue that is the subject of much past and current research.

BIBLIOGRAPHY

Aitchison, J. and Dunsmore, I.R. 1975. *Statistical Prediction Analysis*. Cambridge and New York: Cambridge University Press.

Bayes, T. 1763. An essay toward solving a problem in the doctrine of chances. *Philosophical Transactions of the Royal Society* 53, 370–418.

Berger, J.O. 1984. The robust Bayesian viewpoint. In *Robustness of Bayesian Analysis*, ed. J. Kadane, Amsterdam: North-Holland, 64–144 (with discussion).

Berger, J.O. 1985. *Statistical Decision Theory and Bayesian Analysis*, 2nd edn. New York: Springer-Verlag.

Blackwell, D. and Girshick, M.A. 1954. *Theory of Games and Statistical Decisions*. New York: John Wiley & Sons.

Blyth, C.R. 1951. On minimax statistical decision procedures and their admissibility. *Annals of Mathematical Statistics* 22, 22–42.

Boos, D.D. and Monahan, J.F. 1983. Posterior distributions for boot-strapped likelihoods. Unpublished manuscript, North Carolina State University, December.

Box, G.E.P. and Tiao, G.C. 1973. *Bayesian Inference in Statistical Analysis*. Reading, Mass.: Addison-Wesley.

Boyer, M. and Kihlstrom, R.E. (eds) 1984. *Bayesian Models in Economic Theory*. Amsterdam: North-Holland.

Broemeling, L.D. 1985. *Bayesian Analysis of Linear Models*. New York: Marcel Dekker.

Cox, R.T. 1961. *The Algebra of Probable Inference*. Baltimore: Johns Hopkins University Press.

de Finetti, B. 1970. *The Theory of Probability*, Vol. 2. English trans., New York: John Wiley, 1974.

De Groot, M.H. 1970. *Optimal Statistical Decisions*. New York: McGraw-Hill.

Dyer, A.R. 1973. Discrimination procedures for separate families of hypotheses. *Journal of the American Statistical Association* 68, 970–74.

Edgeworth, F.Y. 1928. *Contributions to Mathematical Statistics*, ed. A.L. Bowley, London: Royal Statistical Society. Reprinted, Clifton, NJ: Augustus M. Kelley, 1972.

Ferguson, T.S. 1967. *Mathematical Statistics: A Decision Theoretic Approach*. New York: Academic Press.

Freedman, D.A. 1986. Reply. *Journal of Business and Economic Statistics*, January, 126–7.

Geisel, M.S. 1975. Bayesian comparisons of simple macroeconomic models, In *Studies in Bayesian Econometrics and Statistics in Honor of Leonard J. Savage*, ed. S.E. Fienberg and A. Zellner, Amsterdam: North-Holland, 227–56.

Geisser, S. 1984. On prior distributions for binary trials. *The American Statistician* 38, 244–7.

Good, I.J. 1950. *Probability and the Weighing of Evidence*. London: Griffin.

Good, I.J. 1965. *The Estimation of Probabilities*. Cambridge, Mass.: MIT Press.

Hartigan, J. 1983. *Bayes Theory.* New York: Springer-Verlag.

Heyde, C.C. and Johnstone, I.M. 1979. On asymptotic posterior normality for stochastic processes. *Journal of the Royal Statistical Society,* Series B 41, 184–89.

Jaynes, E.T. 1984. The intuitive inadequacy of classical statistics. *Epistemologia* 7, Special Issue on Probability, Statistics and Inductive Logic, 43–74.

Jeffreys, H. 1967. *Theory of Probability.* London: Oxford University Press, 3rd edn (1st edn, 1939).

Jeffreys, H. 1973. *Scientific Inference.* 3rd edn, Cambridge and New York: Cambridge University Press (1st edn, 1931).

Kadane, J.B. (ed.) 1984. *Robustness of Bayesian Analysis.* Amsterdam: North-Holland Publishing Co.

Kruskal, W.H. 1978. Tests of significance. In *International Encyclopedia of Statistics,* ed. W.H. Kruskal and J.M. Tanur, Vol. 2, New York: The Free Press, 944–58.

Laplace, P.S. 1820. *Essai philosophique sur les probabilités.* English translation as *A Philosophical Essay on Probabilities,* New York: Dover, 1951.

Leamer, E.E. 1978. *Specification Searches.* New York: John Wiley & Sons.

Lehmann, E. 1959. *Testing Statistical Hypotheses.* New York: John Wiley & Sons.

Lindley, D.V. 1964. The use of prior probability distributions in statistical inference and decisions. In *Proceedings of the Fourth Berkeley Symposium on Mathematical Statistics and Probability,* ed. J. Neyman, Berkeley: University of California Press, Vol. I, 453–68.

Lindley, D.V. 1965. *Introduction to Probability and Statistics from a Bayesian Viewpoint.* 2 vols. Cambridge: Cambridge University Press.

Lindley, D.V. 1971. *Bayesian Statistics: A Review.* Philadelphia: Society for Industrial and Applied Mathematics.

Molina, E.C. 1940. Some comments on Bayes' essay. In *Facsimiles of Two Papers by Bayes,* ed. W.E. Deming, Washington, DC: Graduate School, US Dept. of Agriculture, vii–xii.

Monahan, J. 1983. Fully Bayesian analysis of ARMA time series models. *Journal of Econometrics* 21, 307–31.

Raiffa, H. and Schlaifer, R. 1961. *Applied Statistical Decision Theory.* Boston: Graduate School of Business Administration, Harvard University.

Rényi, A. 1970. *Foundations of Probability.* San Francisco: Holden-Day.

Richard, J.F. 1973. *Posterior and Predictive Densities for Simultaneous Equation Models.* Berlin: Springer-Verlag.

Rossi, P.E. 1980. Testing hypotheses in mulivariate regression: Bayes vs. non-Bayes procedures. H.G.B. Alexander Research Foundation Graduate School of Business University of Chicago. Paper presented at Econometric Society Meeting, September 1980, Denver.

Savage, L.J. 1954. *The Foundations of Statistics.* New York: John Wiley & Sons.

Schwarz, G. 1978. Estimating the dimension of a model. *Annals of Statistics* 6, 461–4.

Smith, A.F.M. and Spiegelhalter, D.J. 1980. Bayes factors and choice criteria for linear models. *Journal of the Royal Statistical Society,* Series B 42, 213–20.

Stigler, S.M. 1983. Who discovered Bayes's Theorem. *The American Statistician* 37, 290–96.

Tiao, G.C. and Box, G.E.P. 1975. Some comments on 'Bayes' estimators. In *Studies in Bayesian Econometrics and Statistics in Honor of Leonard J. Savage,* ed. S.E. Fienberg and A. Zellner, Amsterdam: North-Holland, 619–26.

Tukey, J.W. 1978. Discussion of Granger on seasonality. In *Seasonal Analysis of Economic Time Series,* ed. A. Zellner, Washington, DC: US Government Printing Office, 50–53.

Varian, H.R. 1975. A Bayesian approach to real estate assessment. In *Studies in Bayesian Econometrics and Statistics in Honor of Leonard J. Savage*, ed. S.E. Fienberg and A. Zellner, Amsterdam: North-Holland Publishing Co., 195–208.

Wald, A. 1950. *Statistical Decision Functions.* New York: John Wiley & Sons, Inc.

Zellner, A. 1971. *An Introduction to Bayesian Inference in Econometrics.* New York: John Wiley & Sons.

Zellner, A. 1977. Maximal data information prior distributions. In *New Developments in the Applications of Bayesian Methods*, ed. A. Aykac and C. Brumat, Amsterdam: North-Holland Publishing Co., 211–232.

Zellner, A. 1984. *Basic Issues in Econometrics.* Chicago: University of Chicago Press.

Zellner, A. 1986. Bayesian estimation and prediction using asymmetric loss functions. *Journal of the American Statistical Association* 81, 446–51.

Zellner, A. and Geisel, M.S. 1968. Sensitivity of control to uncertainty and form of the criterion function. In *The Future of Statistics*, ed. D.G. Watts. New York: Academic Press. 269–89.

Zellner, A. and Rossi, P.E. 1984. Bayesian analysis of dichotomous quantal response models. *Journal of Econometrics* 25, 365–93.

Zellner, A. and Vandaele, W. 1975. Bayes–Stein estimators for k-means, regression and simultaneous equation models. In *Studies in Bayesian Econometrics and Statistics in Honor of Leonard J. Savage*, ed. S.E. Fienberg and A. Zellner, Amsterdam: North-Holland, 317–43.

Continuous and Discrete Time Models

CHRISTOPHER A. SIMS

Most economists recognize that the use of discrete time is only an approximation, but assume (usually implicitly) that the error of approximation involved is trivially small relative to the other sorts of simplification and approximation inherent in economic theorizing. We consider below first the conditions under which this convenient assumption may be seriously misleading. We discuss briefly how to proceed when the assumption fails, and the state of continuous time economic theory.

APPROXIMATION THEORY. Some economic behaviour does involve discrete delays, and most calculated adjustments in individual patterns of behaviour seem to occur following isolated periods of reflection, rather than continually. These notions are sometimes invoked to justify economic theories built on a discrete time scale. But to say there are elements of discrete delay or time-discontinuity in behaviour does not imply that discrete time models are appropriate. A model built in continuous time can include discrete delays and discontinuities. Only if delays were discrete, multiples of a single underlying time unit and synchronized across agents in the economy would modelling with a discrete time unit be appropriate.

None the less sometimes discrete models can avoid extraneous mathematical complexity at little cost in approximation error. It is easy enough to argue that time is in fact continuous and to show that there are in principle cases where use of discrete time models can lead to error. But it is also true in practice that more often than not discrete time models, translated intuitively and informally to give implications for the real continuous time world, are not seriously misleading. The analytical task, still not fully executed in the literature, is to understand why discrete modelling usually is adequate and thereby to understand the special circumstances under which it can be misleading.

62

The basis for the usual presumption is that, when the time unit is small relative to the rate at which variables in a model vary, discrete time models can ordinarily provide good approximations to continuous time models. Consider the case examined in detail in Geweke (1978), of a dynamic multivariate distributed lag regression model, in discrete time.

$$Y(t) = A * X(t) + U(t), \tag{1}$$

where $*$ stands for convolution, so that

$$A * X(t) = \sum_{s=-\infty}^{\infty} A(s)X(t-s). \tag{2}$$

We specify that the disturbances are uncorrelated with the independent variable vector X, i.e. $\mathrm{cov}[X(t), U(s)] = 0$, all t, s. The natural assumption is that, if approximation error from use of discrete time is to be small, $A(s)$ must be smooth as a function of s, and that in this case (1) is a good approximation to a model of the form

$$y(t) = a * x(t) + u(t) \tag{3}$$

where

$$a * x(t) = \int_{-\infty}^{\infty} a(s)x(t-s)\,\mathrm{d}s \tag{4}$$

and y, a and x are functions of a continuous time parameter and satisfy $y(t) = Y(t)$, $x(t) = X(t)$ and $a(t) = A(t)$ at integer t. In this continuous time model we specify, parallelling the stochastic identifying assumption is discrete time, $\mathrm{cov}[x(t), u(s)] = 0$, all t, s. If the discrete model (1) corresponds in this way to a continuous time model, the distributed lag coefficient matrices $A(s)$ are uniquely determined by a and the serial correlation properties of x.

(We should note here that, though this framework seems to apply only to the case where X is a simple discrete sampling of x, not to the time-averaged case where $X(t)$ is the integral of $x(s)$ from $t - 1$ to t, in fact both cases are covered. We can simply redefine the x process to be the continuously unit-averaged version of the original x process. This redefinition does have some effect on the nature of limiting results as the time unit goes to zero (since the unit-averaging transformation is different at each time unit) but turns out to be qualitatively of minor importance. Roughly speaking, sampling a unit-averaged process is like sampling a process whose paths have derivatives of one higher order than the unaveraged process.)

Geweke shows that under rather general conditions

$$\sum_{s=-\infty}^{\infty} \| A(s) - \tau a(s\tau) \|^2 \to 0 \tag{5}$$

as the time unit τ goes to zero, where ' $\| \ \|$ ' is the usual root-sum-of-squared-elements norm. In this result, the continuous time process x and lag distribution

63

a are held fixed while the time interval corresponding to the unit in the discrete time model shrinks.

This is the precise sense in which the intuition that discrete approximation does not matter much is correct. But there are important limitations on the result. Most obviously, the result depends on *a* in (3) being an ordinary function. In continuous time, well-behaved distributed lag relations like (3) are not the only possible dynamic relation between two series. For example, if one replaces (3) by

$$y(t) = \alpha(d/dt)x(t) + u(t) \tag{6}$$

then the limit of *A* in (1) is different for different continuous *x* processes. In a univariate model with second-order Markov *x* (i.e. with $\text{cov}[x(t), x(t-s)] = (1 + \theta|s|)e^{-\theta|s|}\text{var}[x(t)]$), the limiting discrete time model, as τ goes to zero, is

$$Y(t) = a\{-0.02X(t+4) + 0.06X(t+3) - 0.22X(t+2)$$

$$+ 0.80X(t+1) - 0.80X(t-1) + 0.22X(t-2)$$

$$- 0.06X(t-3) + 0.02X(t-4)\} + U(t), \tag{7}$$

(see Sims, 1971).

This result is not as strange as it may look. The coefficients on *X* sum to zero and are anti-symmetric about zero. None the less (7) is far from the naive approximation which simply replaces the derivative operator with the first difference operator. In fact, if the estimation equation were constrained to involve only positive lags of *X*, the limiting form would be

$$Y(t) = \alpha\{1.27X(t) - 1.61X(t-1) + 0.43X(t-2)$$

$$- 0.12X(t-3) + 0.03X(t-4) - 0.01X(t-5)\} + U(t). \tag{8}$$

The naive approximation of (6) by $Y(t) = \alpha[X(t) - X(t) - 1] + U(t)$ is valid only in the sense that if this form is imposed on the discrete model a priori, the least squares estimate of α will converge to its true value. If the resulting estimated model is tested for fit against (7) or (8), it will be rejected.

Despite the fact that the underlying model involves only the contemporaneous derivative of *x*, (7) and (8) both involve fairly long lags in *X*. If *x* paths have higher than first order derivatives (e.g. if they are generated by a third order stochastic differential equation) the lag distributions in (7) and (8) are replaced by still higher order limiting forms. Thus different continuous time processes for *x* which all imply differentiable time paths produce different limiting discrete *A*. Here the fact that the time unit becomes small relative to the rate of variation in *x* does not justify the assumption that approximation of continuous by discrete models is innocuous. In particular, the notion that discrete differencing can approximate derivatives is potentially misleading.

It should not be surprising that the discrete time models may not do well in approximating a continuous time model in which derivatives appear. None the less empirical and theoretical work which ignores this point is surprisingly common.

If a is an ordinary function, there is still chance for error despite Geweke's result. His result implies only that the mean square deviation of a from A is small. This does not require that individual $A(t/\tau)$'s converge to the corresponding $a(t)$ values. For example, in a model where x is univariate and $a(t) = 0$, $t < 0$, $a(0) = 1$, $a(s)$ continuous on $[0, \infty)$, the limiting value for $A(0)$ is 0.5, not 1.0. Thus if $a(t) = e^{-\theta t}$ on $[0, \infty)$, making a a monotone decreasing over that range, $A(t)$ will not be monotone decreasing. It will instead rise between $t = 0$ and $t = 1$. This is not unreasonable on reflection: the discrete lag distribution gives a value at $t = 0$ which averages the continuous time distribution's behaviour on either side of $t = 0$. It should therefore not be surprising that monotonicity of a does not necessarily imply monotonicity of A, but the point is ignored in some economic research.

Another example of possible confusion arises from the fact that if the x process has differentiable paths, $a(t) = 0$ for $t < 0$ does not imply $A(t) = 0$ for $t < 0$. The mean-square approximation result implies that when the time unit is small the sum of squares of coefficients on $X(t - s)$ for negative s must be small relative to the sum of squares on $X(t - s)$ for positive s, but the first few lead coefficients will generally be nonzero and will not go to zero as the time interval goes to zero. This would lead to mistaken conclusions about Granger causal priority in large samples, if significance tests were applied naively.

Geweke's exploration of multivariate models shows that the possibilities for confusing results are more numerous and subtle in that case. In particular, there are ways by which poor approximation of $\alpha_j(s)$ by $A_j(s/\tau)$ in some s interval (e.g. around $s = 0$) can lead to contamination of the estimates of other elements of the A matrix, even though they correspond to x_j's and a_j's which in a univariate model would not raise difficulties.

Since Geweke and I wrote on this subject, the amount of dynamic modelling involving least squares projection of one stochastic process (or vector of processes) y on another x has declined relative to the amount of work structured as estimation of a dynamic prediction model for a single vector y. Here the question becomes whether the continuous time dynamics for y, summarized in a Wold moving average representation

$$y(t) = a * u(t) \tag{9}$$

has an intuitively transparented connection to the corresponding discrete time Wold representation

$$Y(t) = A * U(t). \tag{10}$$

In discrete time the $U(t)$ of the Wold representation is the one-step-ahead prediction error, and in continuous time $u(t)$ also represents new information about y arriving at t. There are two related subquestions: Is the A function the same shape as the a function; and is the U vector related in a natural way to the u vector? The u vector is a continuous time white noise, so that U cannot

65

possibly be a simple discrete sampling of u. None the less one might hope that U would be related to u by

$$U(t) = c * u(t), \tag{11}$$

with $c(t)$ damping rapidly as t increases beyond 1.

Results analogous to those of Geweke for the distributed lag regressive model, displaying the limiting behaviour of the approximation as the time unit shrinks, are not yet available for this model. Some comforting results are clearly obtainable. For example, it is clear that if $a(0)$ is diagonal with all diagonal elements positive and a is continuous on $[0, \infty)$, then as the time interval shrinks to zero, $A(0)$ converges to a diagonal matrix and (11) makes

$$U_i(t) = \int_0^1 u_i(t - s)\, ds. \tag{12}$$

This result is intuitively natural and appealing. However, the requirement that $a(0)$ be diagonal and full rank is restrictive. It implies that none of the elements of the y vector have differentiable paths. If $a(0) = 0$, but the kth right derivative of a at 0 is diagonal and full rank, then $A(0)$ will tend to diagonal form, but (12) will be replaced by a more complicated relation in which values of u_i lagged by more than 1 appear. If $a(0)$ is diagonal and less than full rank, $A(0)$ will not generally converge to diagonal form. It should be clear that the implications for dynamic multiple equation models which obtain identification by asserting serial and cross-serial correlation properties of disturbances could be far-reaching.

ESTIMATION AND CONTINUOUS TIME MODELLING. How can one proceed if one has a model like, say, (6), to which a discrete time model is clearly not a good approximation? The only possibility is to introduce explicitly a model for how x behaves between discrete time intervals, estimating this jointly with (6) from the available data. Doing so converts (6) from a single-equation to a multiple-equation model. That is, the device of treating x as 'given' and non-stochastic cannot work because an important part of the error term in the discrete model arises from the error in approximating $a * x$ by $A * X$. Furthermore, because separating the approximation error component of U from the component due to u is essential, one would have to model serial correlation in u explicitly. The model could take the form

$$\begin{bmatrix} y(t) \\ x(t) \end{bmatrix} = \begin{bmatrix} c(s) & a*b(s) \\ 0 & b(s) \end{bmatrix} * \begin{bmatrix} w(t) \\ v(t) \end{bmatrix}, \tag{13}$$

where w and v are white noise processes fundamental (in the terminology of Rosanov, 1967) for y and x. To give b and c a convenient parametric form, one might suppose them rational, so that (13) can be written as a differential equation, i.e.

$$P(D)y(t) = P^{-1}(D)a * x(t) + w(t)$$

$$Q(D)x(t) = v(t), \tag{14}$$

where P and Q are finite-order polynomials in the derivative operator, $Q^{-1}(D)v = b * v$, and $P^{-1}(D)w = c * w$.

A discrete time model derived explicitly from a continuous time model is likely to be nonlinear at least in parameters and therefore to be more difficult to handle than a more naive discrete model. None the less with modern computing power, such models are usable. Bergstrom (1983) provides a discussion of estimating continuous time constant coefficient linear stochastic differential equation systems from discrete data, the papers in the book (1976) he edited provide related discussions, and Hansen and Sargent (1981) discuss estimation of continuous time rational expectations models from discrete data.

CONTINUOUS TIME THEORY. Modelling in continuous time does not avoid the complexities of connecting discrete time data to continuous time reality – it only allows us to confront them directly. One reason this is so seldom done despite its technical feasibility is that it forces us to confront the weakness of economic theory in continuous time. A model like (14) makes an assertion about how many times y and x are differentiable, and a mistake in that assertion can result in error as bad as the mistake of ignoring the time aggregation problem. Economic theory does not have much to say about the degree of differentiability of most economic time series.

When, as in the case of most macroeconometric models for example, the theory underlying the model has no believable restrictions to place on fine-grained dynamics, it may be better to begin the modelling effort in discrete time. As is often true when models are in some respect under-identified, it is likely to be easier to begin from a normalized reduced form (in this case the discrete time model) in exploring the range of possible interpretations generated by different potential identifying assumptions.

Recent developments in financial economics have produced one area where there are continuous time economic theories with a solid foundation. No theory even in this area delivers continuous time white noise residuals from first principles.

Nevertheless, it is at least clear that stochastic differential equations provide a convenient and practically useful framework for modelling asset prices. For example, Harrison et al. (1984) show that differentiable paths for asset prices imply arbitrage opportunities. However, a process can have nondifferentiable paths without producing white noise residuals at any integer order of differentiation: e.g. a model satisfying (3) with $a(s) = s^{0.5} e^{-s}$. Such a process has continuous paths with unbounded variation and is not a semimartingale. That is, it is not the sum of a martingale and a process with bounded variation. Much of the theoretical literature in financial economics assumes such processes away at the start. As economists begin to connect financial sectors to the rest of the economy (see e.g. Grossman et al., 1985), more attention to time aggregation and continuous time modelling is likely to develop.

BIBLIOGRAPHY

Bergstrom, A.R. (ed.) 1976. *Statistical Inference in Continuous Time Economic Models.* Amsterdam: North-Holland.

Bergstrom, A.R. 1983. Gaussian estimation of structural parameters in higher order continuous time dynamic models. *Econometrica* 51, 117–52.

Geweke, J. 1978. Temporal aggregation in the multiple regression model. *Econometrica* 46, 643–62.

Grossman, S., Melino, A. and Shiller, R. 1985. Estimating the continuous time consumption based capital asset pricing model. National Bureau of Economic Research Working Paper No. 1643.

Hansen, L.P. and Sargent, T.J. 1981. Formulating and estimating continuous time rational expectations models. Federal Reserve Bank of Minneapolis Staff Report No. 75.

Harrison, J.M., Pitbladdo, R. and Schaefer, S.M. 1984. Continuous price processes in frictionless markets have infinite variation. *Journal of Business* 57, 353–65.

Rosanov, Y.A. 1967. *Stationary Random Processes.* San Francisco: Holden-Day.

Sims, C.A. 1971. Approximate specifications in distributed lag models. In Proceedings of the 38th Session, *Bulletin of the International Statistical Institute* 44, Book I, 285–94.

Edgeworth as a Statistician

STEPHEN M. STIGLER

Francis Edgeworth was the leading theorist of mathematical statistics of the latter half of the 19th century, though his influence was diminished by the difficulty of his exposition. He is most frequently remembered today for his work on the Edgeworth Series, but in fact he touched on nearly every sphere of modern statistics, from the analysis of variance to stochastic models, to multivariate analysis, to the asymptotic theory of maximum likelihood estimates, to inventory theory. In some areas such as correlation, his work was decisive in the development of all that followed.

Edgeworth's first purely statistical work was published in 1883, when he began a series of papers examining the methods, rationale and philosophical foundations of probability and its application to the analysis of observational data. Most of this work appeared in the *Philosophical Magazine, Mind,* or the *Journal* of the London (later the Royal) Statistical Society. Between 1883 and 1890 he published over 30 separate papers on a wide selection of statistical topics; these works are best viewed as the tracks left by a first-rate mind as it took an excursion through territory that had already been explored. He found much that was new, but his principal occupation re-examining past works, particularly those of Laplace, to see how they might be used in social science. A major (and under appreciated) accomplishment of this period was Edgeworth's explanation of how simple significance tests could be used to compare averages. The mathematical technique was not new, but the conceptual framework was subtly different from that of the early astronomers, and while Edgeworth's (1885b) explanation may today seem elementary, it had a lasting widespread impact. In subsequent work (Edgeworth, 1885c; Stigler, 1978) he developed what might now be viewed as an analysis for an additive effects model for a two-way classification, and he was sensitive to the effect non-normality or serial dependence could have upon the procedures.

Edgeworth's main orientation in his inferential work was Bayesian, and he presented both philosophical and mathematical investigations of this approach.

To Edgeworth, a prior distribution was based in a rough way upon experience. A uniform prior was often justified because, Edgeworth observed, we do not find a pattern in nature that tends to favour one set of values for its constants over another set. Edgeworth tempered this with a realization that inferences would frequently not be very sensitive to the prior specification (Edgeworth, 1885a). When evaluating the significance of differences, however, Edgeworth reverted to a sampling theory viewpoint. One of his 1883 works includes a derivation of Student's t-distribution as the posterior distribution for a normal mean. From 1890 to 1893 Edgeworth, reacting to work by Galton, gave the first fully developed mathematical examination of correlation and its relation to the multivariate normal distribution (Edgeworth, 1892a, b). Edgeworth showed how the constants of a multivariate normal distribution could be expressed in terms of pairwise correlation coefficients (and hence how the conditional expectation of one variable given others could be expressed in terms of correlation coefficients), and he investigated how a correlation coefficient could be estimated from data. His work gave what may be the earliest version of what has come to be called Pearson's product moment estimate (or Pearson's r). Incidentally, it was Edgeworth who coined the term 'coefficient of correlation', as Galton had used 'index'.

Edgeworth's work on correlation had an immense influence upon Karl Pearson, and through him upon all 20th-century work on this topic. In the 1890s, Edgeworth's statistical work became increasingly occupied by a competition with Karl Pearson as to who could best model skew data. Pearson, with his family of skew curves that included gamma distributions and a scheme (the method of moments) for selecting a curve within this family, is generally conceded to have won the contest. Edgeworth at one time or another tried three different approaches. One of these (the 'method of translation', or fitting a normal curve to transformed data) has become popular in more recent times. Another (fitting separate half-normal curves to the left and right sides of the distribution) has been largely forgotten. The third was based upon what we now call the Edgeworth Series. The essence of Edgeworth's approach was to generalize the central limit theorem by the inclusion of correction terms, terms that appeared in the derivation of the distribution of sums but which became negligible if the number of terms in the sum was large. The idea was that skew distributions found in nature were skew because they were aggregates of relatively small numbers of non-normal components. Edgeworth was thus taking a theoretical approach, one that he felt was more appealing than Pearson's more ad hoc approach. The Edgeworth Series was foreshadowed in his work as early as 1883 (when he found it as a series solution to the heat equation), but the full development came later (Edgeworth, 1905), and the labour he put into it after 1895 was immense, and largely unrewarded. His attempts to provide a methodology for fitting the series to data attracted few followers, Arthur Bowley being the only important one. Bowley's brave attempt to explain the method in his assessment of Edgeworth's work (Bowley, 1928) was only marginally more readable than Edgeworth's own many efforts on this. Ironically, later statisticians (notably Harold Cramér, see Cramér, 1972) have found that Edgeworth's mode of arranging correction terms

70

was far superior to alternatives proposed by Bruns, Gram and Charlier, and the Edgeworth Series has become an important technique for approximating sampling distributions (rahter than data distributions, as Edgeworth has intended).

In addition to these major themes, Edgeworth's work abounds in minor nuggets. The largest of these may be a series of papers in 1908–9 that we can now recognize as containing the germ of a proof of the asymptotic efficiency of maximum likelihood estimates. In a contentious 1935 meeting of the Royal Statistical Society this work was pointed out to R.A. Fisher by Bowley as an unacknowledged predecessor, although it seems doubtful that it had any influence on Fisher (see Pratt, 1976). Of more importance was Edgeworth's work on index numbers and on the theory of banking. While his work on index numbers is more properly treated with his economic work, it is worth noting here that he was a pioneer in the application of probability to the analysis and choice of index numbers. In regard to banking, based upon statistical considerations, he promulgated in 1888 the rule that the reserves of a bank need only be proportional to the square root of its liabilities (Edgeworth, 1888).

In all Edgeworth's work one is constantly coming upon minor, often paradoxical observations (see for example, Stigler, 1980) that reveal the depth of his understanding, the subtlety of his thoughts, and a grasp of mathematics that seems quite at odds with his lack of formal training in the subject. Edgeworth was an independent thinker upon statistical matters, though he was perhaps the earliest to appreciate and follow up on Galton's innovative concepts of regression and correlation. Edgeworth's most important influence was upon Karl Pearson, though Pearson was chary in his recognition of this influence. Taken together, Galton, Edgeworth and Pearson shaped modern statistics to a greater degree than any other individual or group before R.A. Fisher. Edgeworth's works on statistics number at least 75, and it is rare to find one that is self-contained. Bowley (1928) made an attempt to summarize all of Edgeworth's statistical work, and he gave a bibliography of most of it. Stigler (1978, 1986) gives a more recent assessment, and comments upon different aspects of Edgeworth's work can be found in papers by Kendall (1968, 1969) and Pratt (1976).

BIBLIOGRAPHY

Bowley, A.L. 1928. *F.Y. Edgeworth's Contributions to Mathematical Statistics.* London: Royal Statistical Society. Reprinted, New York: Augustus M. Kelley, 1972.

Cramér, H. 1972. On the history of certain expansions used in mathematical statistics. *Biometrika* 59, 205–7.

Edgeworth, F.Y. 1885a. Observations and statistics. An essay on the theory of errors of observation and the first principles of statistics. *Transactions of the Cambridge Philosophical Society* 14, 138–69.

Edgeworth, F.Y. 1885b. Methods of statistics. *Jubilee Volume of the Statistical Society*, 181–217.

Edgeworth, F.Y. 1885c. On methods of ascertaining variations in the rate of births, deaths, and marriages. *Journal of the Royal Statistical Society* 48, 628–49.

Edgeworth, F.Y. 1888. The mathematical theory of banking. *Journal of the Royal Statistical Society* 51, 113–27.

Edgeworth, F.Y. 1892a. Correlated averages. *Philosophical Magazine* (Fifth Series) 34, 190–204.

Edgeworth, F.Y. 1892b. The law of error and correlated averages. *Philosophical Magazine* (Fifth Series) 34, 429–38, 518–26.

Edgeworth, F.Y. 1905. The law of error. *Transactions of the Cambridge Philosophical Society* 20, 36–65, 113–41.

Edgeworth, F.Y. 1908–9. On the probable errors of frequency-constants. *Journal of the Royal Statistical Society* 71, 381–97, 499–512, 651–78; 72, 81–90.

Kendall, M.G. 1968. Francis Ysidro Edgeworth, 1845–1926. *Biometrika* 55, 269–75.

Kendall, M.G. 1969. The early history of index numbers. *Review of the International Statistical Institute* 37, 1–12.

Pratt, J. 1976. F.Y. Edgeworth and R.A. Fisher on the efficiency of maximum likelihood estimation. *Annals of Statistics* 4, 501–14.

Stigler, S.M. 1978. Francis Ysidro Edgeworth, statistician (with discussion). *Journal of the Royal Statistical Society*, Series A 141, 287–322.

Stigler, S.M. 1980. An Edgeworth curiosum. *Annals of Statistics* 8, 931–4.

Stigler, S.M. 1986. *The History of Statistics: The Measurement of Uncertainty before 1900.* Cambridge, Mass.: Belknap Press of the Harvard University Press.

Ergodic Theory

WILLIAM PARRY

To begin in the middle; for that is where ergodic theory started, in the middle of the development of statistical mechanics, with the solution, by von Neumann and Birkhoff, of the problem of identifying space averages with time averages. This problem can be formulated as follows: If $x_t(-\infty < t < \infty)$ represents the trajectory (orbit) passing through the point $x = x_0$ at time $t = 0$ of a *conservative dynamical system*, when can one make the identification

$$(*) \quad \lim_{T \to \infty} (1/T) \int_0^T f(x_t)\, dt = \int_\Omega f\, dm/m(\Omega)$$

for suitable functions defined on the *phase space* Ω of the system?

There are many things to be explained here. For example one might imagine a 'large' number of particles contained in a box, which collide with one another and with the sides of the box according to the usual laws of elastic collision. Each of these particles has three coordinates of position and three coordinates of velocity so that the state of the system is describable by $6n$ coordinates if n is the number of particles. Newtonian laws, of course, provide a history and future for each of these points in $6n$ dimensional space. The same laws imply the law of conservation of energy, so that in principle dynamical systems may be studied with the assumption that energy is constant for each trajectory of a conservative system. Thus in $(*)$ we take the phase space Ω to be that hypersurface of $6n$ dimensional space where the total energy has a given (constant) value, and m is the hypersurface volume (measure) associated with the Liouville invariant volume whose existence is guaranteed by the conservativity of the system. In general $m(\Omega)$ is a finite quantity.

The left-hand side of $(*)$ is the time average along a trajectory for a function (observable) f and the right-hand side is the phase or space average.

Von Neumann proved a mean convergence version of $(*)$ and shortly after, G.D. Birkhoff proved $(*)$ as stated, for *almost all* states, in both cases under the assumption that the system (restricted to Ω) is *ergodic*, a notion, we shall explain presently. (Cf. von Neumann, 1932a and Birkhoff, 1931.) It was soon realized that both versions of (*) (the ergodic theorems) could be formulated and proved in a more abstract setting and indeed one can say that this abstraction and the subsequent mathematics thereby generated is ergodic theory proper.

Let (Ω, m) represent an abstract space with a finite measure. (There is no loss in generality in assuming $m(\Omega) = 1$, as we shall do.) Let T_t represent a family of transformations indexed by time (in various contexts, the real numbers, the integers) such that $T_{t+s} = T_t \circ T_s$. Assume that this family is measure-preserving ($mT_tB = mB$, for all 'measurable' sets). The study of T_t as t varies through its index set, provides a model for an evolutionary system, such as the dynamics in phase space described earlier, in which meaure (volume) is preserved. The system is said to be *ergodic* if Ω cannot be decomposed into two disjoint invariant measurable sets

$$A, B(A \cup B = \Omega, A \cap B = \varnothing, T_tA = A, T_tB = B \text{ all } t)$$

of positive measure.

In a strict sense, the time-average space-average problem was not *solved* by von Neumann and Birkhoff, as far as the classical dynamical system given at the outset is concerned, for the question of whether this system *is* ergodic was left open and it is only recently (Sinai, 1963) that progress has been made in this direction.

Most workers in ergodic theory concern themselves with measure-preserving transformations T_t indexed by the integers, so that with $T_1 = T$, T_t is the iteration of T repeated t times. Results in this context invariably lead to results for real continuous time.

Having freed itself from a particular (albeit important) dynamical system, ergodic theory or more particularly the theory of measure-preserving transformations began to encounter a rich diversity of problems:

(i) When does a measurable transformation, non-singular with respect to a given measure, preserve an equivalent finite (or even σ-finite) measure?

(ii) Are there analogues of the ergodic theorems for Markov processes?

(iii) Where do we find examples of measure-preserving (or non-singular) transformations in other branches? If they are non-singular answer question (i). If they are measure-preserving are they ergodic? If so, interpret the ergodic theorems for them.

(iv) Is it possible to (at least partially) classify the myriad examples coming from other branches of mathematics?

One should notice that in posing these problems ergodic theory became a *global* analysis in two senses: The phase space dynamical system described at the beginning of this article is global in that *all* solutions of a differential equation are involved. Ergodic theory then moves on to treat all other problems having a dynamical character in which an invariant measure appears.

Concerning (ii) one should note that a measure-preserving transformation T gives rise to an isometric operator $Lf = f \circ T$ on various Banach spaces, the most important being $L^1(m)$. In a similar way a Markov process gives rise to a semi-group of positive contractions. For such operators there is a variety of ergodic theorems generalizing the classical results of Birkhoff and von Neumann. As an example there is the powerful general ergodic theorem (Chacon and Ornstein, 1960): If L is a positive contraction on $L^1(m)$ and $f, g \in L^1(m)$ then

$$\sum_{k=0}^{n} L^n f \bigg/ \sum_{k=0}^{n} L^n g$$

converges almost everywhere on the set where the denominator is persistently positive.

Here we have an instance of ergodic theory providing a powerful tool for statistics. This should hardly be surprising, however, as even the classical Birkhoff ergodic theorem has an immediate impact on stochastic processes, for one can always associate a measure-preserving transformation with, say, a sequence of independent and identically distributed random variables in such a way that the strong law of large numbers is an easy corollary of Birkhoff's theorem.

Markov and other stochastic processes have played and continue to play a central role in the development of ergodic theory. In recent years a modelling procedure for understanding hyperbolic dynamical systems based on Markov chains has led to profound results in the area of differentiable statistical mechanics. Thus statistical ideas are exchanged, measure for measure, with those of ergodic theory.

Concerning (iii) here are some examples:

(a) *An 'irrational flow'*. Here $\Omega = \{(z, w): z, w \text{ complex } |z| = |w| = 1\}$, $T_t(z, w) = (e^{2\pi i \alpha t}z, e^{2\pi i \beta t}w)$, α, β are real with α/β irrational. m is an ordinary Lebesgue measure.

(b) *A skew product*. Here (Ω, m) is the same as in (a).

$$T(z, w) = (e^{2\pi i \alpha}z, zw), \qquad \alpha \text{ irrational}.$$

(c) *An automorphism of a torus*. Again (Ω, m) is the same as in (a).

$$T(z, w) = (z^2 w, zx).$$

(d) *A translation of a homogeneous space*. G is a locally compact Lie group and H is a closed subgroup such that the homogeneous space $G/H = \{gH : g \in G\}$ is compact. $\Omega = G/H$ and m is a Haar measure. The transformation T is defined as a translation.

$$T(g, H) = agH$$

for a given element $a \in G$.

(e) *A geodesic flow*. Here we consider an n-dimensional Riemannian manifold M with unit length tangent vectors v located at points of M. Such a vector v defines a unique geodesic curve on M. Ω is the totality of such v and $T_t v$ is the unit tangent vector obtained by allowing v to flow along its geodesic at unit speed after time t. The measure m may be taken to be the natural one associated with Liouville's measure.

(f) *A Hamiltonian dynamical system.* Instead of defining this we mention that (e) above and the n particle phase space system at the beginning of this article are both examples of such a system.

(g) *The evolutionary shift associated with a Markov chain or more particularly of a Bernoulli (independent) sequence of trials.*

For the Bernoulli case Ω consists of points $w = \{w_n\}_{-\infty}^{\infty}$ where w_n represents the outcome of an experiment (heads or tails, for example, in the tossing of a coin) at time n. m is the probability which guarantees the independence of these trials, and T is the shift in time $Tw = w'$ where $w'_n = w_{n+1}$.

(h) *A stationary Gaussian (normal process).*

(i) *The continued fraction transformation.* Here Ω consists of the irrational numbers between 0 and 1. m is 'Gauss's' measure whose density is $1/\log 2(1 + x)$ and $Tx = 1/x$ mod 1.

An alternative account of ergodic theory, which admittedly ignores the history of the subject, could be given which is based on the above examples (and many others). It would motivate the subject by the questions: What do these examples have in common? What concepts underlie them? However, only a posteriori would these questions lose their artificiality.

The first four examples (a), (b), (c) and (d), all arise from algebraic or homogeneous space structures and even (e) falls into this category under certain conditions on the curvature of the manifold. In general, (e) arises from differential geometry. The Bernoulli example (g) (or more generally a Markov chain) arises from probability theory as does (h). The example (i) occurs in the study of continued fractions.

These examples (under suitable conditions) are flows and transformations which display varying degrees of ergodicity or *mixing* and ergodic theoretical techniques reveal important information about them. For example, in Furstenberg, (1961) (b) was used to give a proof of the famous theorem of Weyl that $\alpha n^2 + \beta n + \gamma$ mod 1 is uniformly distributed in the unit interval $[0, 1)$ as n varies (as long as α or β is irrational). The example (c) was closely analysed as a prototype of *hyperbolicity* prior to the development of Anosov and Axiom A dynamical systems. The examples covered by (e) (and the related *horocycle flows*) are central to the study of hyperbolic geometry and to the theory of unitary representations of semi-simple Lie groups. The examples (g), (h) provide the most important classes of stationary stochastic processes and are intimately related to Brownian motion. Example (i) is of vital importance in number theory.

Question (iv) was first approached (von Neumann, 1932b; Halmos and von Neumann, 1942) using spectral techniques. Two measure-preserving transformations S, T are said to be (spatially) *isomorphic* if there is an invertible measure-preserving transformation ϕ between their respective spaces such that $\phi S = T\phi$ a.e. (almost everywhere). Isomorphism implies that the unitary spectral characteristics are indistinguishable (i.e. *spectral* equivalence), but not vice versa. The main result obtained characterized all ergodic measure-preserving transformations with a pure point spectrum. For such transformations S, T identity of point spectrum implies spatial isomorphism and such transformations are (isomorphically) precisely the ergodic translations of compact metric abelian groups.

A similar theory was developed in Abramov (1962) for so-called transformations with quasi-discrete spectrum. Example (b) provides an example of this type of transformation. They had been studied earlier by Anzai. The works of Auslander, Green and Hahn (1963) and Parry (1971) provide further developments in this direction. A completely analogous theory is modelled on the 'rigid' examples of *nilflows* and *unipotent affines* on nil manifolds. The rigidity here refers to the phenomenon of measure isomorphisms *necessarily* being algebraic in character. The most recent work concerning rigidity in ergodic theory (Ratner, 1982) finds this, and related phenomena, in horocycle flows.

So far we have given a condensed account of only one strand in isomorphism theory. The most active work has occurred in connection with examples of an entirely different and *random* character.

This work began with the problem of deciding whether two Bernoulli shifts (which are necessarily spectrally isomorphic) are spatially isomorphic. The first breakthrough occurred with Kolmogorov's introduction of entropy theory into the subject (Kolmogorov, 1958). As modified in Sinai (1959) entropy is a numerical invariant of isomorphism (i.e. if S, T are isomorphic then their entropies $h(S)$, $h(T)$ coincide). This fact provides a multitude of Bernoulli transformations which are not isomorphic. The basic ideas originate with Shannon and McMillan, but they required significant adaptation before they could be used in ergodic theory. The new entropy theory developed apace in the hands of, principally, Russian mathematicians in the 1960s and received its biggest impetus from the American mathematician Ornstein, who in 1968 proved that two Bernoulli transformations with the same entropy are isomorphic (cf. Ornstein, 1970). From that time the subject has grown exponentially, with ever more transformations shown to be (isomorphic to) Bernoulli transformations. Such transformations have to have (to say the least) positive entropy and their *intrinsic* random character is in marked contrast to the rigid examples referred to earlier which are *deterministic* (with zero entropy).

Entropy plays very little role in the looser classification theory which allows velocities (along trajectories) to vary. There are continuous (real) time and discrete versions of this theory and as early as 1943 Kakutani had conjectured that all ergodic systems are *Kakutani equivalent*, using the current nomenclature for this loose equivalence (Kakutani, 1943). Although this conjecture turned out to be false (in fact entropy ensures the existence of at least three Kakutani inequivalent systems), Feldman (1976) and Katok (1977) showed that remarkably dissimilar systems are equivalent according to this notion. In Ornstein and Weiss (1984) it is shown that a modification of Kakutani's conjecture is true. In this connection a grand theory of equivalence relations in ergodic theory has been developed in Rudolph (1984). This is ergodic theory with its head in the clouds.

From a more earthly point of view ergodic theory in the 1960s, through the developments of entropy theory and stimulated by Anosov (1967) and Smale

(1967), began to connect with the newly flourishing field of differentiable dynamical systems.

Examples (c) and (f) are, respectively, prototypes of Anosov diffeomorphisms and flows. Their principal feature here is their global hyperbolic structure. Dynamicists are particularly interested in such systems as they are *structurally stable*, a concept which became something of a dogma in the 1960s and 1970s, as some mathematicians went so far as to assert that any real and persistent system must be structurally stable. (A structurally stable system is, roughly speaking, one which retains its principal features after a small perturbation.) This important concept was modified by Smale when he introduced Axiom A systems and proved that the latter are Ω-stable (structural stability relative to non-wandering sets). Smale thereby axiomatized a vast category of new dynamical systems and presented us with an approach which unified Anosov systems, gradient like dynamical systems and his so-called 'horse shoes'. For these systems Smale proved his spectral decomposition theorem, which describes the non-wandering set of an Axiom A system in much the same way as one describes the irreducible block behaviour of a non-negative matrix, in the theory of Markov chains (Smale, 1967). The *basic* sets of an Axiom A system received further scrutiny in terms of Markov partitions by Sinai (Anosov case) and Bowen (Axiom A case).

Bowen was a key figure in the fruitful convergence of ergodic theory and differentiable dynamical systems because of his profound expertise in both subjects. In a series of papers he provided deep analyses of Axiom A diffeomorphisms and flows (roughly speaking, hyperbolic dynamics) from the point of view of symbolic dynamics and periodic orbits (Bowen, 1977). His work connected happily with the direction Ruelle and Sinai were taking in statistical mechanics (Sinai, 1972; Ruelle, 1978). Together they laid the foundations for statistical mechanics on manifolds.

The subject then has gone full circle to its origins, but on the way it encountered a dazzling variety of iteration problems from other areas, viz. maps of the unit interval (Collet and Eckmann, 1980), boundary measures associated with Fuchsian groups (Patterson, 1976; Sullivan, 1979), analytic maps of the Riemann sphere or complex plane (Rees, 1982), to name but three.

As to recent developments in statistical mechanics the one-dimensional lattice gas has received the most attention. Here one considers a shift transformation (as in the case of a Markov chain) initially in the absence of any probability but supplemented with a natural topology which reflects the connectivity of the transformation. Such a shift is called a *topological Markov chain* (or *shift of finite type*).

Then one considers an action potential describable in terms of a continuous function. Under a stronger (Lipschitz) condition it turns out that there is always a unique shift invariant probability (called an *equilibrium state*) given by a variational principle involving the *pressure* of the potential.

A key tool in this theory is the *transfer* matrix or operator associated with the potential and under suitable (aperiodic and irreducible) conditions, iterations of this operator will force arbitrary probabilities to converge to the equilibrium state.

The one-dimensional lattice gases provide models for simple gases and also for statistical mechanics on manifolds. The results above have analogues (when appropriate conditions are imposed) for differential or even topological dynamical systems (Pesin, 1977). Moreover, at least for hyperbolic systems, one can view topological Markov chains with their potentials, equilibrium states, closed orbits, transfer operators and pressures as (in a technical sense) building schemes for these systems.

A recent new area of ergodic theory which stands outside the developments just sketched is concerned with the application of ergodic theory and topological dynamics to combinatorial number theory. The motivation for this recent work was Szemeredi's proof of a conjecture of Erdos and Turan. The conjecture, which emanated from a result of van der Waerden's states that if $a_1 < a_2 < \cdots$ is an increasing sequence of positive integers and if θ_N denotes the number of these integers less than N, then for every $k > 0$ there is an arithmetic progression in the sequence of length k, as long as $\theta_N / N > \varepsilon$ infinitely often (for some $\varepsilon > 0$).

Furstenberg (1977) provided an ergodic theoretical proof of this result and of many other results with the same 'flavour'. His technique involved building a sequence $\{x_n\}$ of zeros and ones ($x_n = 1$ when and only when n is in the sequence), and embedding this sequence in a shift space. The details, which are quite intricate, involve the proof of a multiple recurrence theorem:

If T is a measure-preserving transformation on (X, m) and if $m(A) > 0$ then for every positive integer k

$$m(A \cap T^n A \cap T^{2n} A \cap \cdots \cap T^{kn} A) > 0$$

for infinitely many integers n.

Although this area is somewhat askew to the other developments outlined above, it needs to be mentioned because of the great research potential it possesses.

Where are the likely growing points for the subject? Here is a list of guesses. Some of them are wild; others are safe; and they are not all of equal weight:

(1) Applications to combinatorial number theory (Furstenberg, 1977);

(2) Problems involving a mixture of prime number theory and ergodic theory inspired perhaps by Vinogradov's theorem that $p\alpha$ mod 1 is uniformly distributed when p runs through the primes and α is irrational;

(3) Greater understanding of the connections between the prime number theorem and the prime orbit theorem (Hejhal, 1976; Parry and Pollicott, 1983);

(4) Further developments of cohomology theory in ergodic theory (Schmidt, 1977);

(5) Developments in *restricted* classification theories of processes; in particular a solution of Williams's problem (Williams, 1973); in particular a solution of the stochastic version of the theory of Adler and Marcus (1979);

(6) Developments from Ornstein's and Weiss's modified Kakutani problem in the theory of von Neumann algebras;

(7) Which ergodic translations, affines and flows are rigid?

(8) A greater understanding of turbulence (Ruelle and Takens, 1971).

BIBLIOGRAPHY

Abramov, L.M. 1962. Metric automorphisms with quasi-discrete spectrum. *Izvestiya Akademii Nauk Ser. Mat.* 26, 513–30; *American Mathematical Society Translations* 2(39), 37–56.

Adler, R.L. and Marcus, B. 1979. Topological entropy and equivalence of dynamical systems. *Memoirs of the American Mathematical Society* 219, 1–84.

Anosov, D.V. 1967. Geodesic flows on closed Riemannian manifolds with negative curvature. *Trudy. Mat. Inst. Steklova* 90, 1–209; *Proceedings of the Steklov Institute of Mathematics (American Mathematical Society Translations)*, 1969, 1–235.

Auslander, L., Green, L. and Hahn, F. 1963. Flows on homogeneous spaces. *Annals of Mathematics Studies* 53, Princeton.

Birkhoff, G.D. 1931. Proof of the ergodic theorem. *Proceedings of the National Academy of Sciences of the USA* 17, 656–60.

Bowen, R. 1977. On Axiom A diffeomorphisms. *American Mathematical Society Regional Conference Series* 35, 1–45.

Chacon, R.V. and Ornstein, D.S. 1960, A general ergodic theorem. *Illinois Journal of Mathematics* 4, 153–60.

Collet, P. and Eckmann, J.P. 1980. *Iterated Maps on the Interval as Dynamical Systems. Progress in Physics*, Vol. 1, Boston: Birkhauser.

Feldman, J. 1976. Non-Bernoulli K-automorphisms and a problem of Kakutani. *Israel Journal of Mathematics* 24, 16–37.

Furstenberg, H. 1961. Strict ergodicity and transformations of the torus. *American Journal of Mathematics* 83, 573–601.

Furstenberg, H. 1977. Ergodic behaviour of diagonal measures and a theorem of Szemeredi on arithmetic progressions. *Journal d'analyse mathématique* 31, 2204–56.

Halmos, P.R. and von Neumann, J. 1942. Operator methods in classical mechanics II. *Annals of Mathematics* 43, 332–50.

Hejhal, D.A. 1976. The Selberg trace formula and the Riemann zeta function. *Duke Mathematical Journal* 43, 441–82.

Kakutani, S. 1943. Induced measure-preserving transformations. *Proceedings of the Imperial Academy of Tokyo* 19, 635–41.

Katok, A. 1977. Monotone equivalence in ergodic theory. *Izvestiya Akademii Nauk Ser. Mat.* 41, 104–157.

Kolmogorov, A.N. 1958. A new metric invariant of transient dynamical systems and automorphisms of Lebesgue spaces. *Doklady Akademii Nauk SSSR* 119, 8561–864 (Russian).

Ornstein, D.S. 1970. Bernoulli shifts with the same entropy are isomorphic. *Advances in Mathematics* 4, 337–52.

Ornstein, D.S. and Weiss 1984. Any flow is the orbit factor of any other. *Ergodic Theory and Dynamical Systems* 4, 105–16.

Parry, W. 1971. Metric classifications of ergodic nil flows and unipotent affines. *American Journal of Mathematics* 93, 819–28.

Parry, W. and Pollicott, M. 1983. An analogue of the prime number theorem for closed orbits of Axiom A flows. *Annals of Mathematics* 118, 573–91.

Patterson, S.J. 1976. The limit set of a Fuchsian group. *Acta Mathematica* 136, 241–73.

Pesin, J. 1977. Characteristic Lyapunov exponents and smooth ergodic theory. *Russian Mathematical Surveys* 32(4), 55–114.

Ratner, M. 1982. Rigidity of horocycle flows. *Annals of Mathematics* 115, 597–614.

Rees, M. 1982. Positive measure sets of ergodic rational maps. University of Minnesota Mathematics Report.

Rudolph, D. 1984. *Restricted Orbit Equivalence*. Reprinted, Baltimore University of Maryland.

Ruelle, D. 1978. *Thermodynamic Formalism*. Reading, Mass.: Addison-Wesley.

Ruelle, D. and Takens, F. 1971. On the nature of turbulence. *Communications in Mathematical Physics* 20, 167–92.

Schmidt, K. 1977. *Cocycles on Ergodic Transformation Groups*. London: Macmillan.

Sinai, J.G. 1959. On the concept of entropy of a dynamical system. *Doklady Akademii Nauk SSSR* 124, 768–71.

Sinai, J.G. 1963. On the foundations of the ergodic hypothesis for a dynamical system of statistical mechanics. *Doklady Akademii SSSR* 153, 1261–4; *Sov. Math. Dokl.* 4 (1963), 1818–22.

Sinai, J.G. 1972. Gibbsian measures in ergodic theory. *Usphehi Matematiceskich Nauk* 27, No. 4, 21–64; *Russian Mathematical Surveys* 27(4), 21–69.

Smale, S. 1967. Differentiable dynamical systems. *Bulletin of the American Mathematical Society* 73, 747–817.

Sullivan, D. 1979. The density at infinity of a discrete group of hyperbolic motions. *Publications mathématiques* 50, 419–450.

Von Neumann, J. 1932a. Proof of the quasi-ergodic hypothesis. *Proceedings of the National Academy of Sciences of the USA* 18, 70–82.

Von Neumann, J. 1932b. Zur operatoren Methode in der klassischen Mechanik. *Annals of Mathematics* 33, 587–642.

Walters, P. 1973. A variational principle for the pressure of continuous transformations. *American Journal of Mathematics* 97, 937–71.

Williams, R.F. 1973. Classification of subshifts of finite type. *Annals of Mathematics* 88, 120–93.

Estimation

MARC NERLOVE AND FRANCIS X. DIEBOLD

Point estimation concerns making inferences about a quantity that is unknown but about which some information is available, e.g., a fixed quantity θ for which we have n imperfect measurements $x_1, \ldots, x_n$. The theory of estimation deals with how best to use the information (combine the values $x_1, \ldots, x_n$) to obtain a single number, estimate, for θ, say $\hat{\theta}$. Interval estimation does not reduce the available information to a single number and is a special case of hypothesis testing. This article deals only with point estimation.

Justification for any particular way of combining the available information can be given only in terms of a *model* connecting the x's to θ. For example, in the case of imperfect measurements $x_1, \ldots, x_n$, we could regard the *errors*, $x_i - \theta$, $i = 1, \ldots, n$ as independent outcomes of a random process so that the joint distribution of the x's depends on θ:

$$p(x_1, \ldots, x_n \mid \theta) = \prod_1^n f(x_i - \theta).$$

In general, a *statistical model* represents the data, observations $x_1, \ldots, x_n$, where the x's may be vectors of quantities, as having arisen as a drawing from a joint distribution depending on some unknown parameters $\theta = (\theta_1, \ldots, \theta_k)'$. For example, consider $x_1, \ldots, x_t$, where x_t is identically and independently distributed according to a univariate normal distribution with mean μ and variance σ^2 (Cramer, 1946). The 'location parameter,' μ, and the 'scale parameter,' σ^2, are unknown but, because they determine the distribution from which the data are supposed to arise, the latter may be used to form a point estimate of the vector $\theta = (\mu, \sigma^2)'$, e.g., $\hat{\theta} = (\bar{x} \Sigma_1^T x_i / T, s^2 = \Sigma_1^T (x_i - \bar{x})^2 / T)'$, the properties of which may be discussed in terms of various criteria and the properties of the family of probability distributions $p(x \mid \theta)$ from which the data are assumed to come. An *estimator* is a *function* of the observations; an *estimate* is the value of such a function for a particular set of observations. The theory of point estimation concerns the justification for estimators in terms of the properties of the estimates which they yield relative to specified criteria.

General treatments of the theory of point estimation may be found in Lehmann (1983), Cox and Hinkley (1974), Rao (1973) and Zellner (1971), *inter alia*.

Econometric estimation problems usually concern inferences about the parameters of conditional rather than unconditional distributions. For example, if the observations $(y_1, x_1), \ldots, (y_n, x_n)$ are assumed to represent a drawing from a multivariate normal distribution with mean vector μ and variance-covariance matrix Σ, then the *conditional* distribution of y given x, $p(y \mid x, \theta)$, is univariate normal with mean $\theta_1 = \mu_1 + \sigma_{12}\sigma_{22}^{-1}(x - \mu_2)$ and variance $\theta_2 = \sigma_{11} - \sigma_{12}\sigma_{22}^{-1}\sigma_{21}$, where

$$\mu = (\mu_1, \mu_2) \quad \text{and} \quad \Sigma = \begin{bmatrix} \sigma_{11} & \sigma_{12} \\ \sigma_{21} & \sigma_{22} \end{bmatrix}.$$

Note that θ_1 is a linear function of x which depends upon the parameters of the originally assumed joint distribution; this function is called the *regression* of y on x. *Regression analysis* deals with the general problem of estimating such functions which characterize conditional distributions, usually those derived from normal distributions.

A standard method, and the one most common in econometrics, for obtaining estimators is the method of *maximum likelihood*. Consideration of this method provides a good introduction to alternative principles of estimation. Let the data $x = (x_1, \ldots, x_n)'$ be fixed and regard $p(x \mid \theta)$ as a function of θ; it is then called the *likelihood*. The value of $\hat{\theta} = \hat{\theta}(x_1, \ldots, x_n)$ which maximizes $p(x \mid \theta)$, if it exists and is unique, is called the maximum-likelihood estimator, or estimate (MLE). (For a general survey, see Norden, 1972–73, or Lehmann, 1983.) The MLE of a continuous function $g(\theta)$ is $g(\hat{\theta})$ where $\hat{\theta}$ is the MLE of θ. Other desirable properties of the MLE are asymptotic as $n \to \infty$. Under regularity conditions: (1) The MLE is weakly *consistent*, i.e., $\lim n \to \infty \Pr(|\hat{\theta}_n - \theta| < \varepsilon) = 1$ for all $\varepsilon > 0$. (2) The MLE is *asymptotically normal*, i.e. the distribution of $\hat{\theta}$ appropriately normalized, $\sqrt{n}(\hat{\theta}_n - \theta)$, tends to the normal distribution, with mean 0 and variance-covariance matrix $[I(\theta)]^{-1}$ where

$$I(\theta) = -E[\partial^2 \log p(x \mid \theta)/\partial\theta \, \partial\theta'].$$

$I(\theta)$ is called the information matrix and shows the information a single observation contains about the parameter θ. (3) The MLE is *asymptotically efficient* in the sense that if θ^* is any other estimator such that $\sqrt{n}(\theta_n^* - \theta)$ tends in distribution to the normal with mean zero and variance-covariance matrix $\Sigma(\theta)$, the matrix $[\Sigma(\theta) - I^{-1}(\theta)]$ is positive semi-definite. For example, in the case of one parameter this means that no other asymptotically normal estimator has, as $n \to \infty$, a smaller variance than the MLE. The conditions for asymptotic normality do ensure, with probability tending to one, a solution to the *likelihood equation* $\partial \log p(x \mid \theta)/\partial\theta = 0$, which is consistent and asymptotically normal and efficient. The problem is that there may be more than one solution, but only one can be the MLE. When the number of parameters to be estimated (elements of the vector θ) tends to infinity with n, the MLEs for some may exist but may not be consistent (Neyman and Scott, 1948).

Solutions to the likelihood equation are not the only estimators which may be consistent, asymptotically normal and efficient, but comparison with the MLE, assuming correct specification of $p(x \mid \theta)$, is facilitated by the fact that all have a normal distribution as $n \to \infty$. For fixed n, the distributions of different estimators are difficult to determine and may, indeed, be quite different. Moreover, when the distributions underlying the data are misspecified, the MLEs generally no longer have these optimal properties (White, 1982; Gourieroux, Monfort and Trognon, 1984), although other, weaker, optimality properties remain. Apart from specification problems, however, the likelihood function provides an important and useful summary of the data, and it and point estimates and hypothesis testing procedures based on it are often justified in this way (Fisher, 1925; Barnard, Jenkins, and Winsten, 1962; Edwards, 1972).

The 'accuracy' of an estimator $\hat{\theta}$ of a scalar parameter θ may be measured (defined) in a variety of ways: by its expected squared or absolute error, relative error, or by $\Pr\{|\hat{\theta} - \theta| \leq \alpha\}$ for some α. Any choice is arbitrary; for convenience expected squared error is the usual choice. Some justification for a particular choice may be provided in terms of a *loss function* $L(\theta, \hat{\theta})$ or the expected loss $EL(\theta, \hat{\theta})$ or *risk function* of *statistical decision theory*. Choice of estimators may be justified in terms of the extent to which the choice minimizes risk or some aspect thereof. Both the *sampling theory* and *Bayesian* approaches to estimation can be interpreted in these terms.

A very weak property that any estimator should have is that no other estimator exists which dominates it in the sense that the latter leads to estimates having uniformly lower expected loss irrespective of θ. Estimators satisfying this criteria are called *admissible*.

In the sampling theoretic approach, emphasis is placed on finding estimators which have desirable properties in terms of relative frequencies in hypothetically repeated samples. For example, we might require that the distribution of an estimator be centred on the true parameter value, i.e., $E(\hat{\theta} - \theta) = 0$. Such estimators are called *unbiased*. Among all unbiased estimators we presumably would prefer one yielding estimates with a distribution concentrated about the mean. Such minimum variance unbiased estimators (MVU) play a key role in the theory of estimation. Specifically, the famous Rao–Blackwell Theorem states that if an unbiased estimator $\hat{\theta}$ is a function of a complete sufficient statistic for θ then it is MVU. A statistic, say Y, is said to be sufficient for θ if the conditional distribution of the observations given T is independent of θ. Completeness is also a property of the distribution functions for the observations; (a family P of distributions (of T) indexed by a parameter θ is said to be complete if there is no 'unbiased estimator of zero' other than $\phi(x) \equiv 0$.) Note that choosing an estimator so as to minimize the expected squared error of the estimate it yields is equivalent to minimizing the unweighted sum of the variance and the squared bias. From a decision theoretic point of view, it may be better to accept an estimator with a small bias if such an estimator has a smaller risk.

In the sampling theoretic approach, emphasis is given to the distribution of estimates yielded by a specified estimator. The likelihood approach, on the other hand, emphasizes the distribution of the observations, given a parametrically specified distribution, under alternative values of these parameters. Concern is primarily with the maximum value of the likelihood function with respect to the parameters and its curvature near the point at which the global maximum occurs, but some approaches stress the relevance of the likelihood function in other neighbourhoods (Barnard et al., 1962; Edwards, 1972). The Bayesian approach carries concern with the entire likelihood function further: estimation and inference are based on the posterior density of the unknown parameters of the distribution generating the observations. This posterior density is proportional to the likelihood function multiplied by a prior density of the parameters, i.e., a weighted average of likelihoods for different parameter values where the weights are determined by prior (subjective) beliefs (See BAYESIAN INFERENCE.)

In the Bayesian approach, both observations and parameters are taken to be stochastic. Let $p(x_1, \theta)$ be the joint probability density function for an observation vector, x, and a parameter vector θ; then $p(x_1, \theta) = p(x|\theta)p(\theta) = p(\theta|x)p(x)$, where $p(\xi|\eta)$ denotes the conditional density of ξ given η and $p(\xi)$ denotes the marginal density of ξ. Thus $p(\theta|x)$ is proportional to $p(\theta)p(x|\theta)$ by the factor

$$p(x) = \int p(\theta)p(x|\theta)\, d\theta.$$

$p(\theta|x)$ is the *posterior* distribution of θ, after having observed the data; $p(\theta)$ is the *prior* distribution of θ; and $p(x|\theta)$ is the *likelihood*. Alternatively, consider the weighted average risk (as defined above):

$$\int EL(\theta, \hat{\theta})w(\theta)\, d\theta,$$

with weights $w(\theta)$ such that

$$\int w(\theta)\, d\theta = 1.$$

When $L(\theta, \hat{\theta}) = (\hat{\theta} - \theta)^2$, the estimator which minimizes such a weighted average risk is

$$\hat{\theta}(x) = \int \theta w(\theta)p(x|\theta)\, d\theta \Big/ \int w(\theta)p(x|\theta)\, d\theta.$$

If the weights $w(\theta)$ are taken to be the values of the marginal density $p(\theta)$, the mean of the posterior Bayes distribution minimizes the expected squared error of the estimates when both the variation of data and the uncertainty with respect to θ are taken into account: $\hat{\theta}$ is the expected value of θ based on the *posterior* distribution of θ. As $n \to \theta$, it may be shown that the influence of the prior distribution diminishes until in the limit it disappears; then, under general circumstances, the minimization of mean square error in the Bayesian framework yields the MLE. The principal difficulty in the Bayesian approach is the choice of a reasonable prior for θ, $p(\theta)$. (For a comprehensive discussion, see Zellner, 1971.)

Instead of minimizing the expected loss, one may minimize the maximum loss. Estimators which do are called *minimax*; the theory is developed in Wald (1950).

There are three general approaches to choice of a prior in Bayesian analysis. First, the prior may be obtained empirically (Maritz, 1970). For example, suppose that the problem is to estimate the percentage of defective items in a particular batch. Assuming such batches were produced in the past suggests a prior based on the proportion of defective items observed in previous batches. This kind of 'updating' forms the basis for the celebrated Kalman filter. Second, the prior may be viewed as representing a 'rational degree of belief' (Jeffreys, 1961). What represents a 'rational degree' is not specified, but the idea leads directly to the use of priors that represent knowing little or nothing, so-called *non-informative priors*. However, total ignorance has proved difficult to capture in many cases. A third approach is that the prior represents a subjective degree of belief (Savage, 1954; Raiffa and Schlaifer, 1961). But of whom? and how arrived at? Minimax-estimation theory offers one possible approach for it leads to the minimum mean-square-error Bayes estimator, i.e., the mean of the posterior distribution of the parameters, when the prior is least favourable in the sense of making expected loss the largest for whatever class of priors is chosen.

Related to this problem is the more general question of *robust estimation*. In order to make sense of any data, it is necessary to assume something. For example, the justification for using the sample mean to estimate the mean of the distribution generating the data is often the assumption that that distribution is normal or nearly so. In that case, the sample mean is not only asymptotically efficient but uniformly MVU, minimax, admissible, etc. But suppose that the distribution is Cauchy (having roughly the same shape as the normal but with very thick tails); then, the sample mean has the same distribution as any individual observation, its accuracy does not improve with n and it is not even a consistent estimator. At least, within the class of distributions which include the Cauchy, the properties of the sample mean, and similarly ordinary least squares, are quite sensitive to the true nature of the underlying distribution of the data. We say that such estimators are not *robust*. Complete discussions are contained in Huber (1981) and Hampel, Ronchetti, Rousseeuw and Stahel (1985).

To conclude, three estimation problems of special concern in economics are discussed: (1) classical linear regression; (2) non-linear regression, and (3) estimation of simultaneous structural equations.

The classical theory of linear regression deals with the following problem: Let X be an $n \times k$ matrix of nonstochastic observations (n for each variable $(x_1, \ldots, x_k)$, β be a $k \times 1$ vector of parameters (one of which becomes an intercept if $x_1 \equiv 1$, say), and y be an $n \times 1$ vector of stochastic variables such that $y - x\beta = \varepsilon \sim N(0, \Sigma)$. The *ordinary least-squares estimates* (OLS), $\hat{\beta} = (X'X)^{-1}X'y$ are MLE and MVU when $\Sigma = \sigma^2 I$. When this is not true, although the OLS estimates are unbiased and consistent, they are not asymptotically efficient or minimum variance. The *generalized least squares estimates* (GLS), $\hat{\beta} = (X'\Sigma^{-1}X)^{-1}X'\Sigma^{-1}$ are efficient, but of course Σ, and therefore Σ^{-1}, is generally unknown. Often, however, a consistent estimate of Σ is available, leading to *feasible*, or *estimated*, GLS estimates.

Many problems in economics lead to non-linear relationships. Linear regression may be a good (local) approximation to such relationships if the data do not vary too widely. Moreover, many non-linear relationships may be transformed into linear ones (e.g., the Cobb–Douglas production function). Often, however, the data are sufficiently variable to make a linear relationship a poor approximation and no linearizing transformation exists. The general non-linear regression model is $y = f(X, \beta, \varepsilon)$ or more frequently $y = f(X, \beta) + \varepsilon$. Least-squares or maximum-likelihood estimates may still be obtained, but the first-order conditions for a minimum or a maximum will generally be non-linear, frequently ruling out analytic expressions for the estimates. Consider the problem of minimizing the sum of squared residuals, $(y - f(X, \beta))'(y - f(X, \beta))$, with respect to β (non-linear least squares); numerical methods for solving this problem are of the general form: $\hat{\beta}_{i+1} = \hat{\beta}_i - s_i P_i V_i$, where $\hat{\beta}_i$ = the value of the estimator parameter vector at iteration i, s_i = the step size at iteration i, P_i = the direction matrix at iteration i, and V_i = the gradient of the objective function at iteration i. The matrix P_i determines the direction in which the parameter vector is changed at each iteration; it is generally taken to be the Hessian matrix evaluated at the current value of the parameter vector or some approximation to it. Let $g(\beta)$ be the objective function; then

$$P_i = [\partial^2 g(\beta)/\partial\beta\partial\beta' \,|\, \beta = \hat{\beta}_i]^{-1}$$

is the Hessian. A justification for this choice is obtained from the second-order (quadratic) approximation to the objective function in the neighbourhood of the current estimate. For a detailed treatment of this problem as well as constrained non-linear estimation see Quandt (1983). The statistical properties of non-linear estimators are discussed by Amemiya (1983).

Economic theory teaches us that the values of many economic variables are often determined simultaneously by the joint operation of several economic relationships, for example, supply and demand determine price and quantity. This leads to a representation in terms of a system of simultaneous structural equations (simultaneous equations model, or SEM). The problem of how to estimate the parameters of a SEM has occupied a central place in econometrics since Haavelmo (1944). A linear SEM is given by, $By_i \times \Gamma x_t = u_t$, $t = 1, \ldots, T$ where B is $G \times G$, Γ is $G \times K$, y_t is $G \times 1$, x_t is $K \times 1$, and u_t is $G \times 1$. u_t is assumed to be zero mean with variance-covariance matrix Σ, often normally distributed, independently and identically for each t. Thus the u_t are serially independent. It is also assumed that plim $\Sigma_1^T x_{it} u_{jt}/T = 0$ all $i = 1, \ldots, K$ and $j = 1, \ldots, G$ and plim $X'X \,|\, T$ is a positive definite matrix, where $X = (x_1, \ldots, x_T)'$. If B is non-singular this system of *structural equations*, as they are called, may be solved for the so called 'endogenous' variables, y_t, in terms of the 'exogenous' variables x_t: $y_t = \Pi x_t + v_t$ where $\Pi = -B^{-1}\Gamma$, $v_t = B^{-1}u_t$, so that $Ev_t = 0$ and $Ev_t v_t' = B^{-1}\Sigma(B^{-1})' = \Omega$. It is, in general not possible to determine B, Γ and Σ from knowledge of the *reduced form* (*RF*) parameters Π and Ω; there are, in principle, many structural systems compatible with the same RF. Given sufficient restrictions on the structural system, however, knowledge of the RF parameters can be used, together with the assumed restrictions, to determine the structural parameters. The SEM is then said to be *identified*.

For *linear* structural equations with *normally distributed* disturbances, the conditions for identification may be derived from the condition that for any system $B^*y_t + \Gamma^*x_t = u_t^*$ for which u_t^* and u_t are identically distributed, where $B^* = FB$, $\Gamma^* = F\Gamma$ and $u_t^* = Fu_t$, then $F \equiv fI$ is implied by the restrictions, where f is any positive scalar (Hsiao, 1983).

Methods of estimating the parameters of SEMs may be put into two categories: (1) *limited-information* methods which estimate parameters of a subset of the equations, usually a subset consisting of a single equation, taking into account only the identifying restrictions on the parameters of equations in that subset, and (2) *full-information* methods which estimate all of the identifiable parameters in the system simultaneously and therefore take into account all identifying restrictions. Full- or limited-information methods may be based on either least-squares or maximum-likelihood principles. ML-based methods yield estimates which are invariant according to the normalization rule (choice of f).

For systems or single equations in SEMs for which there are restrictions just sufficient to identify the parameters of interest, estimates may be based on *indirect least squares*, that is derived directly from the reduced form parameters estimated by applying OLS to each equation of the RF; such estimates are ML. If the restrictions are just sufficient to identify the parameters of each equation, the resulting estimates are *full-information maximum-likelihood* (FIML) estimates. When an equation is over-identified, in the sense that there are more than enough restrictions to identify it, *two-stage least squares* (2SLS) or *limited-information maximum likelihood* (LIML) may be applied equation by equation to each equation which is identified. Provided the model is correctly specified, such estimates are consistent and asymptotically unbiased but not asymptotically efficient, because some restrictions are neglected in the estimation of some parameters. An analog of 2SLS, *three-stage least squares* (3SLS), yields estimates which are asymptotically equivalent to FIML and therefore efficient.

Amemiya (1983) extends all of these methods to non-linear systems. Sargan (1980) discusses identification in non-linear systems.

BIBLIOGRAPHY

Amemiya, T. 1983. Nonlinear regression models. In *Handbook of Econometrics*, Vol. 1, ed. Z. Griliches and M.D. Intriligator, Amsterdam: North-Holland.

Barnard, G.A., Jenkins, G.M. and Winsten, C.B. 1962. Likelihood inference and time series (with discussion). *Journal of the Royal Statistical Society*, Series A, 125, 321–72.

Cox, D.R. and Hinkley, D.V. 1974. *Theoretical Statistics*. London: Chapman & Hall. Distributed in USA by Halsted Press.

Cramer, H. 1946. *Mathematical Methods of Statistics.* Princeton: Princeton University Press.

Edwards, A.W.F. 1972. *Likelihood.* Cambridge and New York: Cambridge University Press.

Fisher, R.J. 1925. Theory of statistical estimation. *Proceedings of the Cambridge Philosophical Society* 22, 700–25.

Gourieroux, C., Monfort, A. and Trognon, A. 1984. Pseudo maximum likelihood methods: theory. *Econometrica* 52, 681–700.

Haavelmo, T. 1944. The probability approach in econometrics. *Econometrica* 12, Supplement, July, 1–115.

Hampel, F.R., Ronchetti, E.M., Rousseeuw, P.J. and Stahel, W.A. 1985. *Robust Statistics.* New York: John Wiley.

Hsiao, C. 1983. Identification. In *Handbook of Econometrics*, Vol. 1, ed. Z. Griliches and M. Intriligator, Amsterdam: North-Holland, 223–83.

Huber, P.J. 1981. *Robust Statistics.* New York: John Wiley.

Jeffreys, H. 1961. *Theory of Probability.* 3rd edn, Oxford: Clarendon Press.

Lehmann, E.L. 1983. *The Theory of Point Estimation.* New York: John Wiley.

Maritz, J.S. 1970. *Empirical Bayes Analysis.* London: Methuen.

Neyman, J. and Scott, E.L. 1948. Consistent estimates based on partially consistent observations. *Econometrica* 16, 1–32.

Norden, R.H. 1972–3. A survey of maximum-likelihood estimation. *Review of the International Institute of Statistics* 40, 329–54; 41, 39–58.

Quandt, R.E. 1983. Computational problems and methods. In *Handbook of Econometrics*, Vol. 1, ed. Z. Griliches and M. Intriligator, Amsterdam: North-Holland, 699–764.

Raiffa, H. and Schlaifer, R. 1961. *Applied Statistical Decision Theory.* Boston: Harvard Business School.

Rao, C.R. 1973. *Linear Statistical Inference and its Applications.* 2nd edn, New York: John Wiley.

Sargan, J.D. 1980. Identification and lack of identification. Paper presented to 4th World Congress of the Econometric Society, 28 August–2 September 1980, Aix-en-Provence, France.

Savage, L.J. 1954. *The Foundations of Statistics.* New York: John Wiley.

Wald, A. 1950. *Statistical Decision Functions.* New York: John Wiley.

White, H. 1982. Maximum-likelihood estimation of misspecified models. *Econometrica* 50, 1–25.

Zellner, A. 1971. *An Introduction to Bayesian Inference in Econometrics.* New York: John Wiley.

Factor Analysis

IRMA ADELMAN

Factor analysis is a branch of analysis of variance used to investigate the structure of a data set. Consider a data set x_{ij} resulting from the observation of several variables j on several objects i. If the data set rises from a complex multidimensional process about which little is known a priori statistical analysis of the data itself might profitably be used to gain insights into various characteristics of the processes which generated the data set. In particular, statistical techniques can be used to: (1) search for a simpler representation of the underlying processes which generated the data by reducing the dimension of the variable space in which the objects are represented; (2) look for the interactions among the variables by forming linear clusters of variables; and (3) seek characterizations of the clusters of variables which relate them to the underlying processes which generated the data set being analysed. Factor analysis performs all three functions.

A variety of factor analytic methods has been introduced. They differ in estimation procedures (least squares or maximum likelihood); fitting equation (original data matrix, covariance or correlation matrix); scaling assumption (original or normalized data, type of normalization and in whether the scaling is performed prior to the estimation or as part of the estimation procedure); and in the normalization principles applied to a factor matrix. For a discussion of the relationship between them see Kruskal (1978). Following Kruskal, we start from the original data, derive the covariance matrix and then discuss the procedures applied to it. The basic technical references are Hotelling (1933), Bartlett (1938), Lawley (1940), Lawley and Maxwell (1971), Jøreskog (1967), and Jøreskog and Goldberger (1972).

Let the variables j characterizing the objects i be measured as deviations from their means. Assume further that the data set x_{ij} was generated by an r-dimensional linear process, with r significantly smaller than the original number of variables J. We are then seeking a representation of x of the form

$$x_{ij} = \sum_r a_{ir} b_{rj} + v_{ij} \tag{1}$$

which, in some sense, comes closest to representing the original data set. In (1) the a_{ir} represent the coefficients, known as 'factor scores', which indicate the 'regression coefficients' of the objects upon each of the r clusters of variables; the b_{rj} represent the coefficients of the variables in each of the r clusters, known as 'factor loadings' or 'factor patterns'. The r clusters of variables are known as factors or components, and represent the coordinates of the lower-dimensional space onto which the data matrix is mapped. In matrix notation, we can write (1) as (2)

$$X = AB + \Sigma, \tag{2}$$

where A is the matrix of a_{ir}, B is the matrix of b_{rj} and Σ is a diagonal disturbance matrix with typical element σ_j^2.

One can fit (2) directly, by least squares or by maximum likelihood, or one can form the sample covariance matrix $C = X'X/N$, where N is the number of objects, and fit it instead. If one assumes that: (1) the a_{ij} are random, identically distributed, with mean 0, and independent both of each other and of the disturbances and (2) applies the normalization T that sets

$$\frac{N-1}{N}(AT^{-1})'(AT^{-1}) = I \tag{3}$$

then the expected value of the sample covariance matrix C is

$$E(C) = B'B + \Sigma^2. \tag{4}$$

This equation can be fitted either by least squares (Hotelling, 1933; Anderson, 1958; Harman, 1960; Jøreskog and Goldberger, 1972) or by maximum likelihood methods (Lawley, 1940; Jøreskog, 1967), to obtain estimates for b_{rj} and σ_j^2. Once these estimates have been obtained, a_{ir} can be estimated by regression methods from eqn (2) keeping B fixed.

In the least squares approach the matrix B is estimated by extracting the successive eigenvectors of

$$(C - \lambda_r I)b_r = 0, \tag{5}$$

where λ_r is the tth characteristic root and b_r is the rth eigenvector. The rth column of B, b_r, represents the makeup of the rth component in terms of the original, observable variables. Goodness of prediction measures analogous to significance intervals can be derived for the estimates of B by using Stone–Geisser or Tukey-jack-knife methods (Wold, 1982).

In the maximum likelihood approach, we form the likelihood function,

$$L = \tfrac{1}{2}(N-1)\ln|C| - \tfrac{1}{2}(N-1)\sum_{i,j} x_{ji}x_{ij}C^{ij}/N - 1, \tag{6}$$

where $|C|$ is the determinant of C, and C^{ij} is the ijth element of C^{-1}. To find the maximum likelihood estimators of B and Σ, we differentiate (6) with respect to the elements of B and Σ and set the resulting equations equal to zero. The maximum equations are then solved simultaneously for B and Σ by applying techniques such as Fletcher–Powell (1963) for the simultaneous optimization of nonlinear equation systems. The maximum likelihood aproach was first developed by Lawley (1940); practical estimation techniques for it were developed by Jøreskog (1967). The use of maximum likelihood has both advantages and disadvantages: it requires stringent assumptions about the distributions of the parameter set B and the disturbances Σ but it also enables one to estimate confidence intervals on the parameters of B and on the goodness of fit (Lawley and Maxwell, 1971; and Jennrich and Thayer, 1973).

Both the least squares approach and the maximum likelihood approach yield estimates of B which are not unique since a rigid rotation of B yields the same estimating equations. Several approaches have been proposed for deriving unique estimates. These include normalization assumptions on $A'A$ or $B'B$ and rotation assumptions aimed at increasing ease of interpretability such as the varimax rotation (Kaiser, 1958).

The first applications of factor analysis in the social sciences were in psychology, for which the technique was first developed by Spearman (1904), and used to analyse mental abilities (see Bolton et al., 1973 for a survey). In economics, the first application was to demand analysis (Stone, 1945). Stone hypothesized that demand for commodities is explained by three types of influences: national income and own and other prices; social influences affecting tastes and market conditions; and forces peculiar to a particular community. He used a three-factor confluence analysis model, similar to factor analysis, to identify the factors affecting consumer demand. A recent study of market demand employing modern factor analysis is Huang et al. (1980). Stone (1947) and Geary (1948) used factor analysis to study interaction patterns among time series. Using time series representing the components of national income and product in the US, Stone showed that 97.5 per cent of their total variance could be represented by three factors. Banks (1954) used factor analysis in agriculture to predict overall agricultural productivity from crop productivity data on a small number of crops.

The most numerous applications of factor analysis to economics have been in economic development (Adelman and Morris, 1967; Rayner, 1970; Schilderinck, 1969). In a series of studies, Adelman and Morris investigated the interdependence of economic, social and political phenomena in the development process. Their observations were 74 countries; their variables were typologies representing various aspects of economic, social and political structure. Four factors explained most of the covariance: a modernization factor, which includes indicators of economic and social development; a political development factor; a political leadership factor; and a social and political stability factor. They found that the relative importance of these factors in explaining intercountry differences in growth rates changes systematically with country development levels, with social forces declining in importance and political leadership increasing. Other applications have been to the economics of education (Aigner and Goldberger, 1977) and to stock market prices (King, 1966).

Recent uses of factor analysis have been in the estimation of the parameters of unobservable variables, defined as variables whose measurable quantities differ from their theoretical counterparts and to error-in-variables models. Other recent advances have been in nonlinear factor analysis (McDonald, 1967) and in the dynamic analysis of factor structures (Geweke, 1977).

BIBLIOGRAPHY

Adelman, I. and Morris, C.T. 1967. *Society, Politics, and Economic Development: A Quantitative Approach.* Baltimore: Johns Hopkins Press.

Aigner, D.J. and Goldberger, A.S. (eds) 1977. *Latent Variables in Socioeconomic Models.* Amsterdam: North-Holland.

Anderson, T.W. 1958. *An Introduction to Multivariate Statistical Analysis.* New York: Wiley.

Banks, C. 1954. The factorial analysis of crop productivity: a reexamination of professor Kendall's data. *Journal of the Royal Statistical Society*, Series B 16, 100–111.

Bartlett, M.S. 1938. Methods of estimating mental factors. *Nature* 141, 609–10.

Bolton, B., Hinman, S. and Tuft, S. 1973. *Annotated Bibliography: Factor Analytic Studies 1941–1970.* 4 vols, Fayetteville: University of Arkansas, Arkansas Rehabilitation Research and Training Center. (Tuft did not collaborate on vols 3 and 4.)

Fletcher, R. and Powell, M.J.D. 1963. A rapidly convergent descent method for minimization. *Computer Journal* 6, 163–8.

Geary, R.C. 1948. Studies in relation between economic time series. *Journal of the Royal Statistical Society*, Series B 10, 140–58.

Geweke, J. 1977. The dynamic factor analysis of economic time-series models. In *Latent Variables in Socioeconomic Models*, ed. D.J. Aigner and A.S. Goldberger, Amsterdam: North-Holland.

Harman, H.H. 1960. *Modern Factor Analysis.* 3rd edn, revised, Chicago: University of Chicago Press, 1976.

Hotelling, H. 1933. Analysis of a complex of statistical variables into principal components. *Journal of Educational Psychology* 24, 417–41, 498–520.

Huang, C.-L., Raunika, R. and Fletcher, S.M. 1980. Estimation of demand parameters based on factor analysis. Paper presented at the American Agricultural Economics Association Meetings in Urbana, Illinois.

Jennrich, R.I. and Thayer, D.T. 1973. A note on Lawley's formulas for standard errors in maximum likelihood factor analysis. *Psychometrika* 38, 571–80.

Jøreskog, K.G. 1963. *Statistical Estimation in Factor Analysis: A New Technique and its Foundation.* Stockholm: Almqvist & Wiksell.

Jøreskog, K.G. 1967. Some contributions to maximum likelihood factor analysis. *Psychometrika* 32, 443–82.

Jøreskog, K.G. 1984. *Advances in Factor Analysis and Structural Equation Models.* Lanham: University Press of America.

Jøreskog, K.G. and Goldberger, A.S. 1972. Factor analysis by generalized least squares. *Psychometrika* 37, 243–60.

Kaiser, H.F. 1958. The varimax criterion for analytic rotation in factor analysis. *Psychometrika* 23, 187–200.

King, B. 1966. Market and industry factors in stock price behavior. *Journal of Business* 39, Supplement, 139–90.

Kruskal, J.B. 1978. Factor analysis: bilinear methods. In *International Encyclopedia of Statistics*, New York: Macmillan, 307–30.

Lawley, D.N. 1940. The estimation of factor loadings by the method of maximum likelihood. Royal Society of Edinburgh, Section A, *Proceedings* 60, 64–82.

Lawley, D.N. and Maxwell, A.E. 1963. *Factor Analysis as a Statistical Method.* 2nd edn, London: Butterworth, 1971; New York: American Elsevier.

McDonald, R.P. 1967. Factor interaction in nonlinear factor analysis. *British Journal of Mathematical and Statistical Psychology* 20, 205–15.

Rayner, A.C. 1970. The use of multivariate analysis in development theory: a critique of the approach used by Adelman and Morris. *Quarterly Journal of Economics* 84, 639–47.

Schilderinck, J.H.F. 1969. *Factor Analysis Applied to Developed and Developing Countries.* Rotterdam: Rotterdam University Press.

Spearman, C.E. 1904. 'General intelligence' objectively determined and measured. *American Journal of Psychology* 15, 201–293.

Stone, R. 1945. The analysis of market demand. *Journal of the Royal Statistical Society,* Series A 108, 286–382.

Stone, R. 1947. On the interdependence of blocks of transactions. *Journal of Royal Statistical Society,* Series B 9, 1–45.

Thurstone, L.L. 1935. *The Vectors of Mind: Multiple-factor Analysis for the Isolation of Primary Traits.* Chicago: University of Chicago Press.

Wold, H. 1982. Soft modeling and some extensions. In *Systems under Indirect Observation,* ed. K.G. Jöreskog and H. Wold, Amsterdam: North-Holland, II, 1–54.

Ronald Aylmer Fisher

A.W.F. EDWARDS

R.A. Fisher was born in London on 17 February 1890, the son of a fine-art auctioneer. His twin brother was still-born. At Harrow School he distinguished himself in mathematics, despite being handicapped by poor eyesight which prevented him working by artificial light. His teachers used to instruct by ear, and Fisher developed a remarkable capacity for pursuing complex mathematical arguments in his head. This manifested itself in later life in his ability to reach a conclusion whilst forgetting the argument; to handle complex geometrical trains of thought; and to develop and report essentially mathematical arguments in English (only for students to have to reconstruct the mathematics later).

He entered Gonville and Caius College, Cambridge, as a scholar in 1909, graduating BA in mathematics in 1912. Prevented from entering war service in 1914 by his poor eyesight, Fisher held several jobs before being appointed Statistician to Rothamsted Experimental Station in 1919. In 1933 he became Galton Professor of Eugenics at University College, London, and in 1943 Arthur Balfour Professor of genetics in Cambridge and a Fellow of Caius College. He retired in 1957 and spent his last few years in Adelaide, Australia, where he died from a post-operative embolism on 29 July 1962.

He married Ruth Eileen Guiness in 1917 and they had two sons and six daughters. He was elected a Fellow of the Royal Society in 1929 and was knighted in 1952 for services to science.

Fisher made a most profound contribution to applied and theoretical statistics and to genetics. He had been attracted to natural history, and especially the works of Darwin, at school, and he had bought Bateson's *Principles of Genetics*, with its translation of Mendel's paper, in his first term as an undergraduate. Before graduating he had already remarked on the surprisingly good fit of Mendel's data, published a paper introducing the method of maximum likelihood, and given a proof of the distribution of the 't' statistic which Student had only conjectured.

In 1915 Fisher published the distribution of the correlation coefficient; in 1918 the seminal work in biometrical genetics, 'The correlation between relatives on the supposition of Mendelian inheritance', in which he introduced the word 'variance' and foreshadowed his later development of the analysis of variance; and in 1922 'On the mathematical foundations of theoretical statistics', a paper which revolutionized statistical thought.

As Statistician at Rothamsted he founded the subject of experimental design based on randomization, pursued vigorously the development of statistical estimation theory and invented – or, at least, captured – the quixotic notion of fiducial probability. Moving to London the pace did not slacken, for in addition to pioneering genetical work, especially in connection with the human blood groups, Fisher's statistical explorations revealed the likelihood principle, conditional inference and the concept of ancillarity.

World War II found him embattled on many fronts. Unhappy at home, he found his scientific activity disrupted by wartime conditions including the evacuation of his Department from London. The profundity of his work on statistical inference was ill-appreciated in America, where preoccupation with wartime problems encouraged an excessively mathematical and operational view with which Fisher had little sympathy. In mathematical genetics there were similar difficulties as the American school, starting from his 'fundamental theorem of natural selection', developed ideas of 'adaptive topographies' with false analogies to physical systems. It was not until well after his death that in both statistical inference and mathematical genetics the criticisms which he had advanced came to be appreciated.

After the war, from the relative peace of Cambridge, Fisher saw his theoretical work in both subjects suffer further temporary eclipse. He made great, but ultimately unsuccessful, efforts to establish biochemical genetics in his Department and to secure for Cambridge the national laboratories for human blood-group work. When close to retirement, he was amongst the first to realize the significance of Watson and Crick's discovery of the structure of DNA (1953), and to apply the new computers to a biological problem (1950).

Perhaps embittered by his postwar experiences (though he never relaxed his scientific work), he found some consolation in the Presidency of Caius College from 1956 to 1959, a post second to the Master, and further happiness in retirement in Adelaide.

Fisher wrote five books and published a famous set of statistical tables jointly with F. Yates. An extremely informative and admirably objective biography was published by one of his daughters in 1978 (Box, 1978).

In the field of economics Fisher's name would be remembered for his contributions to statistics alone, so fully chronicled in Box's biography, but we may here draw attention to three other areas not emphasized in the biography but which are especially relevant.

First, the 'fundamental theorem of natural selection' (1930). Although this is specifically directed at a genetical problem, it relies on a simpler implicit theorem of widespread relevance wherever discussion centres on differential growth rates, namely 'the rate of change in the growth-rate is proportional to the variance in growth-rates'. This precise theorem, which is easily proved mathematically, captures the notion that the growth rate of the fastest-growing sub-population (or economic sector, etc.) will come to dominate the overall growth-rate.

Secondly, the modern preoccupation with 'socio-biology' has as one of its origins *The Genetical Theory of Natural Selection* (1930), a fact that only surprises those who have not studied the book and Fisher's other writings on human affairs in the two decades before World War II.

Thirdly, Fisher not only introduced the Theory of Games into evolutionary biology (at the suggestion of Dr Cavalli, later Professor Cavalli-Sforza), but he discovered and published the idea of a randomized or 'mixed' strategy as early as 1934, independently of von Neumann. The problem was the card game '*Le Her*', though if Fisher had gone to the primary source (the correspondence between Montmort and Nicholas Bernoulli, published in 1713) rather than relying only on Todhunter's *History of the Mathematical Theory of Probability* (1865), he would have found that his solution had already been given by Waldegrave.

SELECTED WORKS

1915. Frequency distribution of the values of the correlation coefficient in samples from an indefinitely large population. *Biometrika* 10, 507–21.

1918. The correlation between relatives on the supposition of Mendelian inheritance. *Transactions of the Royal Society of Edinburgh* 52, 399–433.

1922. On the mathematical foundations of theoretical statistics. *Philosophical Transactions. Royal Society of London, Series A* 222, 309–68.

1925. *Statistical Methods for Research Workers*. Edinburgh: Oliver and Boyd.

1930. *The Genetical Theory of Natural Selection*. Oxford: Clarendon Press.

1935. *The Design of Experiments*. Edinburgh: Oliver and Boyd.

1938. With F. Yates. *Statistical Tables for Biological, Agricultural and Medical Research*. Edinburgh: Oliver and Boyd.

1949. *The Theory of Inbreeding*. Edinburgh: Oliver and Boyd.

1950. *Contributions to Mathematical Statistics*. New York: Wiley.

1956. *Statistical Methods and Scientific Inference*. Edinburgh: Oliver and Boyd.

1971–4. *Collected Papers of R. A. Fisher*. Ed. J.H. Bennett. Adelaide: University of Adelaide, 5 vols.

BIBLIOGRAPHY

Box, Joan Fisher. 1979. *R. A. Fisher: The Life of a Scientist*. New York: Wiley.

Forecasting

CLIVE W.J. GRANGER

Decisions in the fields of economics and management have to be made in the context of forecasts about the future state of the economy or market. As decisions are so important as a basis for these fields, a great deal of attention has been paid to the question of how best to forecast variables and occurrences of interest. There are several distinct types of forecasting situations including event timing, event outcome, and time-series forecasts. Event timing is concerned with the question of when, if ever, some specific event will occur, such as the introduction of a new tax law, or of a new product by a competitor, or of a turning point in the business cycle. Forecasting of such events is usually attempted by the use of leading indicators, that is, other events that generally precede the one of interest. Event-outcome forecasts try to forecast the outcome of some uncertain event that is fairly sure to occur, such as finding the winner of some election or the level of success of a planned marketing campaign. Forecasts are usually based on data specifically gathered for this purpose, such as a poll of likely voters or of potential consumers. There clearly should be a positive relationship between the amount spent on gathering the extra data and the quality of the forecast achieved.

A time series x_t is a sequence of values gathered at regular intervals of time, such as daily stock market closing prices, interest rates observed weekly, or monthly unemployment levels. Irregularly recorded data, or continuous time sequences may also be considered but are of less practical importance. When at time n (now), a future value of the series, x_{n+h}, is a random variable where h is the forecast horizon. It is usual to ask questions about the conditional distribution of x_{n+h} given some information set I_n, available now from which forecasts will be constructed. Of particular importance are the conditional mean

$$f_{n,h} = E[x_{n+h} | I_n]$$

and variance, $V_{n,h}$. The value of $f_{n,h}$ is a point forecast and represents essentially the best forecast of the most likely value to be taken by the variable x at time

$n + h$. With a normality assumption, the conditional mean and variance can be used together to determine an interval forecast, such as an interval within which $x_{n,h}$ is expected to fall with 95 per cent confidence. An important decision in any forecasting exercise is the choice of the information set I_n. It is generally recommended that I_n include at least the past and present of the individual series being forecast, $x_{n-j, j \geqslant 0}$. Such information sets are called *proper*, and any forecasting models based upon them can be evaluated over the past. An I_n that consists just of x_{n-j}, provides a univariate set so that future x_i are forecast just from its own past. Many simple time-series forecasting methods are based on this information set and have proved to be successful. If I_n includes several explanatory variables, one has a multivariate set. The choice of how much past data to use and which explanatory variables to include is partially a personal one, depending on one's knowledge of the series being forecast, one's levels of belief about the correctness of any economic theory that is available, and on data and computer availability. In general terms, the more useful explanatory variables that are included in I_n, the better the forecast that will result. However, having many series allows for a confusing number of alternative model specifications that are possible so that using too much data could quickly lead to diminishing marginal returns in terms of forecast quality. In practice, the data to be used in I_n will often be partly determined by the length of the forecast horizon. If h is small, a short-run forecast is being made and this may concentrate on frequently varying explanatory variables. Short-term forecasts of savings may be based on interest rates, for example. If h is large so that long-run forecasts are required, then slowly changing, trending explanatory variables may be of particular relevance. A long-run forecast of electricity demand might be largely based on population trends, for example. What is considered short- or long-run will usually depend on the properties of the series being forecast. For very long forecasts, allowances would have to be made for technological change as well as changes in demographics and the economy. A survey of the special and separate field of technological forecasting can be found in Martino (1983).

If decisions are based on forecasts, it follows that an imperfect forecast will result in a cost to the decision maker. For example, if $f_{n,h}$ is a point forecast made at time n, of x_{n+h}, the eventual forecast error will be

$$e_{n,h} = x_{n,h} - f_{n,h}$$

which is observed at time $n + h$. The cost of making an error e might be denoted as $C(e)$, where $C(e)$ is positive with $C(0) = 0$. As there appears to be little prospect of making error-free forecasts in economics, positive costs must be expected, and the quality of a forecast procedure can be measured as the expected or average cost resulting from its use. Several alternative forecasting procedures can be compared by their expected costs and the best one chosen. It is also possible to compare classes of forecasting models, such as all linear models based on a specific, finite information set, and to select the optimum model by minimizing the expected cost. In practice the true form of the cost function is not known for decision sequences, and in the univariate forecasting case a pragmatically useful substitute to the real $C(e)$ is to assume that it is well approximated by ae^2 for some positive a. This enables least-squares statistical techniques to be used when a model is estimated and is the basis of a number of theoretical results including that the optimal forecast of x_{n+h} based on I_n is just the conditional mean of $x_{n,h}$. In the economics literature, optimum forecasts have also been called *rational expectations*, based on a specific cost function and an information set.

When using linear models and a least-square criterion, it is easy to form forecasts under an assumption that the model being used is a plausible generating mechanism for the series of interest. Suppose that a simple model of the form

$$x_t = \alpha x_{t-1} + \beta y_{t-2} + \varepsilon_t$$

is believed to be adequate where ε_t is a zero-mean, white noise (unforecastable) series. When at time n, according to this model, the next value of x will be generated by

$$x_{n+1} = \alpha x_n + \beta y_{n-1} + \varepsilon_{n+1}.$$

The first two terms are known at time n, and the last term is unforecastable. Thus

$$f_{n,1} = \alpha x_n + \beta y_{n-1}$$

and

$$e_{n,1} = \varepsilon_{n+1}.$$

x_{n+2}, the following x, will be generated by

$$x_{n+2} = \alpha x_{n+1} + \beta y_n + \varepsilon_{n+2}.$$

The first of these terms is not known at time n, but a forecast is available for it, αf_n, the second term is known at time n, and the third term is not forecastable, so that

$$f_{n,2} = \alpha f_{n,1} + \beta y_n$$

and

$$e_{n,2} = \varepsilon_{n+2} + \alpha(x_{n+1} - f_{n,1})$$
$$= \varepsilon_{n+2} + \alpha \varepsilon_{n+1}.$$

To continue this process for longer forecast horizons, it is clear that forecasts will be required for y_{n+h-2}. The forecast formation rule is that one uses the model available as though it is true, ask how a future x_{n+h} will be generated, use all known terms as they occur, and replace all other terms by optimal forecasts. For non-linear models this rule can still be used, but with the additional complication that the optimum forecast of a function of x is not the same function of the optimum forecast of x.

The central problem in practical forecasting is chosing the model from which the forecasts are derived. If a univariate information set is used, it is natural to consider the models developed in the field of time-series analysis. A class of models that have proved successful in short-run forecasting are the autoregressive-moving average models (ARMA). If a series is regressed on lagged values of itself up to p lags, and the residual is a weighted sum of a white noise series, up to q lags, the result is an ARMA (p, q) model. There is a tendency to prefer a parsimonious model so that the number of parameters (p, q) is minimized amongst models that perform equally satisfactorily. If the first difference of a series is well modelled as an ARMA process, but the level of the series is not, the basic series is said to be integrated of order one and called an integrated ARMA process, denoted ARIMA. Box and Jenkins (1970) discussed the statistical properties of these series and relevant constraints on the parameters. They suggested three stages of analysis, (i) identification – the choice of a small subset of models for further analysis, (ii) estimation of parameters, and (iii) diagnostic checks on whether the estimated model eventually selected is fitting the data adequately by comparing with other similar models. These techniques can be generalized to modelling vector x_t series, although with some difficulties. For example, vector autoregressive models, with imprecise constraints on parameters, have been found to provide successful short-run forecasts of macroeconomic variables (Doan, Litterman, and Sims, 1984). These models are largely agnostic towards the correctness or otherwise of an economic theory. Their main competitors are the econometrics models which historically were large in that many economic variables were modelled simultaneously, occasionally several hundred to a few thousand variables, but had less emphasis on dynamics and used some economic theory, often an equilibrium theory, as a starting point for specification and analysis. They have become more dynamic in recent years whilst still emphasizing the many important interrelationships that can be expected to hold between economic variables. Both basic approaches seem to have special strengths and relative weaknesses, a good theory effectively expands the information available, but an incorrect or loosely stated theory can mislead the modelling process. Econometric models now often consider the inclusion of rational expectations as explanatory variables, and all models have considered the introduction of non-linear terms and also time-varying parameters, usually by use of the Kalman filter algorithm.

The forecasting process is generally improved by continual evaluation of previously made forecasts. The theory of optimal forecasts provides some helpful evaluation criteria, such as that h-step forecasts errors should be $MA(h-1)$, so that one-step errors from optimal forecasts should be white noise, and that generally forecasts perform less well as the horizon increases. A practical evaluation procedure is to regress the actual x_t on their forecasts, for example

$$x_{t+1} = \alpha + \beta f_{t,1} + \varepsilon_{t+1}.$$

If the one-step forecast is optimal for some information set, it follows that the true values of the parameters should be $\alpha = 0$ and $\beta = 1$ and also that ε_t should be white noise. If any of these properties are not found for the regresssion, the forecasts can be immediately improved. Unfortunately this procedure does not answer the question of whether all the information in I_n is being fully utilized or if a different information set would produce better forecasts. One way that these questions can be approached is by combining forecasts from different sources or based on different information sets so that a regression is run of the form

$$x_{t+1} = \alpha + \beta_1 f_{t,1} + \beta_2 g_{t,1} + \varepsilon_{t+1},$$

where f and g are the two forecasts to provide appropriate weights. This and the other topics mentioned here are discussed in greater detail in Granger and Newbold (1987).

BIBLIOGRAPHY

Box, G. and Jenkins, G. 1970. *Time Series Analysis, Forecasting and Control.* San Francisco: Holden Day.

Doan, T., Litterman, R. and Sims, C. 1984. Forecasting and conditional projection using realistic prior distributions. *Econometric Review* 3, 131–44.

Granger, C.W.J. and Newbold, P. 1987. *Forecasting Economic Time Series.* 2nd edn, New York: Academic Press.

Martino, J. 1983. *Technological Forecasting for Decision Making.* 2nd edn, Amsterdam: North-Holland.

Heteroskedasticity

J. KMENTA

One of the basic assumptions of the classical regression model

$$Y_i = \beta_1 + \beta_2 X_{i2} + \cdots + \beta_K X_{iK} + \varepsilon_i \qquad (i = 1, 2, \ldots, n)$$

is that the variance of the regression disturbance ε_i is constant for all observations, that is, that $\mathrm{Var}(\varepsilon_i) = \sigma^2$ for all i. This feature of ε_i is known as *homoskedasticity* and its absence is called *heteroskedasticity*. The homoskedasticity assumption is quite reasonable for observations on aggregates over time, since the values are of a similar order of magnitude for all observations. It is, however, implausible with respect to observations on microeconomic units such as households or firms included in a survey, since there are likely to be substantial differences in magnitude of the observed values. For example, in the case of survey data on household income and consumption, we would expect less variation in consumption of low-income households, whose average level of consumption is low, than in consumption of high-income households, whose average level of consumption is high. Empirical evidence suggests that this expectation is in accord with actual behaviour. Heteroskedasticity also arises when the data are in the form of group averages and the groups are of unequal size.

Heteroskedasticity has two important consequences for estimation: (1) The least squares estimators of the regression coefficients are no longer efficient or asymptotically efficient. (2) The estimated variances of the least squares estimators are, in general, biased, and the conventionally calculated confidence intervals and tests of significance are invalid. The second of these consequences is more serious than the first since inefficiency of estimation can be compensated for by a large number of observations.

The deficiencies of the least squares estimation can be remedied by adopting a *weighted* (or *generalized*) least squares procedure. This method involves weighting each observation by the reciprocal of the respective standard deviation of the disturbance, and then applying the least squares method to the transformed equation

$$(Y_i/\sigma_i) = \beta_1(1/\sigma_i) + \beta_2(X_{i2}/\sigma_i) + \cdots + \beta_K(X_{iK}/\sigma_i) + u_i,$$

where

$$\sigma_i = \sqrt{\mathrm{Var}(\varepsilon_i)} \quad \text{and} \quad u_i = \varepsilon_i/\sigma_i.$$

The difficulty with the weighted least squares method is that its implementation requires knowledge of σ_i, which is rarely available. This difficulty is usually overcome by making certain assumptions about σ_i or, when possible, by estimating σ_i. The assumptions typically involve associating σ_i with some variable Z_i, normally represented by one of the explanatory variables of the regression equation. For instance, in a microconsumption function the variance of the disturbance is frequently positively associated with income. In general, two forms of association between σ and Z have been proposed in the literature and applied in practice: a *multiplicative* and an *additive* form. Multiplicative heteroskedasticity – which is more common – can be described as

$$\sigma_i^2 = \sigma^2 Z_i^\delta,$$

where σ and δ are parameters to be estimated. A frequent representation of additive heteroskedasticity is

$$\sigma_i^2 = a + bZ_i + cZ_i^2,$$

where a, b, and c are parameters to be estimated. Estimation of the parameters involved in the specification of σ_i can be carried out simultaneously with the estimation of the regression coefficients by using the method of maximum likelihood. No assumptions about the form of heteroskedasticity are necessary where σ_i can be estimated from replicated data which, unfortunately, are rather rare in applied economic research.

The presence or absence of heteroskedasticity may be subjected to a test. Several suitable tests, some developed only recently, are available and are described in recent econometric texts.

The problem of heteroskedasticity and its consequences was brought to the attention of applied economists by two seminal research monographs, Stone (1954) and Prais and Houthakker (1955). The subject has been further developed by a number of econometricians and is now standard fare in all introductory courses of econometrics; see, for example Kmenta (1986).

BIBLIOGRAPHY

Kmenta, J. 1986. *Elements of Econometrics*. 2nd edn, New York: Macmillan Publishing Co.
Prais, S.J. and Houthakker, H.S. 1955. *The Analysis of Family Budgets*. Cambridge: Cambridge University Press.
Stone, J.R.N. 1954. *The Measurements of Consumers' Expenditure and Behaviour in the United Kingdom, 1920–1938*. Vol. 1, Cambridge: Cambridge University Press.

Harold Hotelling

KENNETH J. ARROW

Harold Hotelling, a creative thinker in both mathematical statistics and economics, was born in Fulda, Minnesota, on 29 September 1895 and died in Chapel Hill, North Carolina, on 26 December 1973. His influence on the development of economic theory was deep, though it occupied a relatively small part of a highly productive scientific life devoted primarily to mathematical statistics; only ten of some 87 published papers were devoted to economics, but of these six are landmarks which continue to this day to lead to further developments. His major research, on mathematical statistics, had, further, a generally stimulating effect on the use of statistical methods in different specific fields of application, including econometrics.

His early interests were in journalism; he received his BA in that field from the University of Washington in 1919. Later in classes, he would illustrate the use of dummy variables in regression analysis by a study (apparently never published) of the effect of the opinions of different Seattle newspapers on the outcome of elections and referenda. The mathematician and biographer of mathematicians, Eric T. Bell, discerned talent in Hotelling and encouraged him to switch his field. He received an MA in mathematics at Washington in 1921 and a PhD in the same field from Princeton in 1924; he worked under the topologist, Oswald Veblen (Thorstein Veblen's nephew), and two of his early papers dealt with manifolds of states of motion.

The year of completing his PhD, he joined the staff of the Food Research Institute at Stanford University with the title of Junior Associate. In 1925 he published his first three papers, one of manifolds, one on a derivation of the F-distribution and one on the theory of depreciation. Here, apparently for the first time, he stated the now generally accepted definition of depreciation as the decrease in the discounted value of future returns. This paper was a turning-point both in capital theory proper and in the reorientation of accounting towards more economically meaningful magnitudes.

In subsequent years at Stanford he became Research Associate of the Food

Research Institute and Associate Professor of Mathematics, teaching courses in mathematical statistics and probability (including an examination of Keynes's *Treatise on Probability*) along with others in differential geometry and topology. In 1927, he showed that trend projections of population were statistically inappropriate and introduced the estimation of differential equations subject to error; he returned to the statistical interpretation of trends in a notable joint paper (1929a) with Holbrook Working, largely under the inspiration of the needs of economic analysis.

The same year he published the famous paper on stability in competition (1929b), in which he introduced the notions of locational equilibrium in duopoly. This paper is still anthologized and familiar to every theoretical economist. As part of the paper, he noted that the model could be given a political interpretation, that competing parties will tend to have very similar programmes. Although it took a long time for subsequent models to arise, these few pages have become the source for a large and fruitful literature.

The paper was in fact a study in game theory. In the first stage of the game, the two players each chose a location on a line. In the second, they each chose a price. Hotelling sought what would now be called a subgame perfect equilibrium point. However, there was a subtle error in his analysis of the second stage, as first shown by d'Aspremont, Gabszewicz and Thisse (1979). Hotelling indeed found a local equilibrium, but the payoff functions are not concave; if the locations are sufficiently close to each other, the Hotelling solution is not a global equilibrium. Unfortunately, this is the interesting case, since Hotelling concluded that the locations chosen in the first stage would be arbitrarily close in equilibrium. In fact, the optimal strategies must be mixed (Dasgupta and Maskin, 1986, pp. 30–32).

His paper on the economics of exhaustible resources (1931a) applied the calculus of variations to the problem of allocation of a fixed stock over time. All of the recent literature, inspired by the growing sense of scarcity (natural and artificial), is essentially based on Hotelling's paper. Interestingly enough, according to his later accounts, the *Economic Journal* rejected the paper because its mathematics was too difficult (although it had published Ramsey's papers earlier); it was finally published in the *Journal of Political Economy*.

In 1931, he was appointed Professor of Economics at Columbia University, where he was to remain until 1946. There he began the organization of a systematic curriculum in theoretical statistics, which eventually attained the dignity of a separate listing in the catalogue, though not the desired end of a department or degree-granting entity. Toward the end of the 1930s, he attracted a legendary set of students who represented the bulk of the next generation of theoretical statisticians. His care for and encouragement of his students were extraordinary: the encouragement of the self-doubtful, the quick recognition of talent, the tactfully-made research suggestion at crucial moments created a rare human and scholarly community. He was as proud of his students as he was modest about his own work.

He also gave a course in mathematical economics. The general environment was not too fortunate. The predominant interests of the Columbia Department of Economics were actively anti-theoretical, to the point where no systematic course in neoclassical price theory was even offered, let alone prescribed for the general student. Nevertheless, several current leaders in economic theory had the benefit of his teaching. But his influence was spread more through his papers, particularly those (1932, 1935) on the full development of the second-order implications for optimization by firms and households (contemporaneous with Hicks and Allen) and above all by his classic presidential address (1938) before the Econometric Society on welfare economics. Here we have the first clear understanding of the basic proposition (Hotelling, as always, was meticulous in acknowledging earlier work back to Dupuit), as well as the introduction of extensions from the two-dimensional plane of the typical graphical presentation to the calculation of benefits with many related commodities. He argued that marginal-cost pricing was necessary for Pareto optimality even for decreasing-cost industries, used the concept of potential Pareto improvement, and showed that suitable line integrals were a generalization of consumers' and producers' surplus for many commodities. Here also we have the clearest expression in print of Hotelling's strong social interests which motivated his technical economics. His position was undogmatic but in general it was one of market socialism. He had no respect for acceptance of the *status quo* as such, and the legitimacy of altering property rights to benefit the deprived was axiomatic with him; but at the same time he was keenly aware of the limitations on resources and the importance in any human society of the avoidance of waste.

Important as was his contribution to economics, most of his effort and his influence were felt in the field of mathematical statistics, particularly in the development of multivariate analysis. In a fundamental paper (1931b), he generalized Student's test to the simultaneous test of hypotheses about the means of many variables with a joint normal distribution. In the course of this paper, he gave a correct statement of what were later termed 'confidence intervals'. In two subsequent papers (1933, 1936) he developed the analysis of many statistical variables into their principal components and developed a general approach to the analysis of relations between two sets of variates. The statistical methodologies of these papers and in particular the last contributed significantly to the later development of methods for estimating simultaneous equations in economics.

In 1946, he finally had the long-desired opportunity of creating a department of mathematical statistics, at the University of North Carolina, where he remained until retirement. He continued his active interest in economics there.

Space forbids more than the brief mention of his important work in the foundation of two learned societies, the Econometric Society and the Institute of Mathematical Statistics, both of which he served as President at a formative stage. He received many formal honours during his lifetime, including honorary degrees from Chicago and Rochester; he was the first Distinguished Fellow of the American Economic Association when that honour was created, as well as a member of the National Academy of Sciences and the Accademia Nazionale dei Lincei, Honorary Fellow of the Royal Statistical Society and Fellow of the Royal Economic Society.

SELECTED WORKS

1925. A general mathematical theory of depreciation. *Journal of the American Statistical Association* 20, 340–53.

1927. Differential equations subject to error. *Journal of the American Statistical Association* 22, 283–314.

1929a. (With H. Working). Applications of the theory of error to the interpretation of trends. *Journal of the American Statistical Association* 24, 73–85.

1929b. Stability in competition. *Economic Journal* 39, 41–57.

1931a. The economics of exhaustible resources. *Journal of Political Economy* 39, 137–75.

1931b. The generalization of Student's ratio. *Annals of Mathematical Statistics* 21, 360–78.

1932. Edgeworth's taxation paradox and the nature of supply and demand functions. *Journal of Political Economy* 40, 577–616.

1933. Analysis of a complex of statistical variables with principal components. *Journal of Educational Psychology* 24, 417–41, 498–520.

1935. Demand functions with limited budgets. *Econometrica* 3, 66–78.

1936. Relation between two sets of variates. *Biometrika* 28, 321.

1938. The general welfare in relation to problems of taxation and of railway and utility rates. *Econometrica* 6, 242–69.

BIBLIOGRAPHY

Dasgupta, P. and Maskin, E. 1986. The existence of equilibrium in discontinuous economic games, II: Applications. *Review of Economic Studies* 53, 27–41.

d'Aspremont, C., Gabszewicz, J.-J. and Thisse, J. 1979. On Hotelling's 'Stability in Competition'. *Econometrica* 47, 1145–50.

Hypothesis Testing

GREGORY C. CHOW

1. TESTING RESTRICTIONS ON PARAMETERS. For those who believe that economic hypotheses have to be confirmed by empirical observations, hypotheses testing is an important subject in economics. As a classical example, when an economic relation is represented by a linear regression model:

$$Y = X\beta + \varepsilon, \tag{1}$$

where Y is a column vector of n observations on the dependent variable y, X is an $n \times k$ matrix with each column giving the corresponding n observations on each of k explanatory variables (which typically include a column of ones), β is a column of k regression coefficients and ε is a vector of n independent and identically distributed residuals with mean zero and variance σ^2, it is of interest to test a hypothesis consisting of m linear restrictions on β:

$$R\beta = r, \tag{2}$$

where R is $m \times k$ and r is $m \times 1$. A most common case occurs when there is only one restriction ($m = 1$) and (2) is reduced to $\beta_i = 0$, the hypothesis being that the ith explanatory variable has no effect on y.

Among the statistical tests often employed in economic research are the likelihood ratio (LR) test, the Wald test and the Lagrangian multiplier (LM) test. The LR test, due to Neyman and Pearson (1928), uses as the test statistic the likelihood ratio:

$$\mu = \frac{L(Y, \hat{\theta}^*)}{L(Y, \hat{\theta})},$$

where L is the likelihood function, $\hat{\theta}^*$ is the maximum-likelihood estimator of a parameter vector θ under the null hypothesis to be tested, or subject to a vector $h(\theta) = 0$ of m restrictions such as (2), and $\hat{\theta}$ is the ML estimator of θ without

109

imposing the restrictions. A high value of the likelihood ratio μ favours the null hypothesis. The Wald test, proposed by Wald (1943), uses the test statistic:

$$W = h(\hat{\theta})'[\text{Cov } h(\hat{\theta})]^{-1}h(\hat{\theta}), \tag{4}$$

where Cov denotes covariance matrix. The null hypothesis $h(\theta) = 0$ will be accepted if the vector $h(\hat{\theta})$ is sufficiently close to zero, or if the statistic W is sufficiently small. Wald (1943) has shown that under general conditions, the statistics W and $-2 \ln \mu$ have the same asymptotic distribution.

The LM test, suggested by Silvey (1959), uses the Lagrangian multiplier $\hat{\lambda}$ obtained by maximizing the Lagrangian expression:

$$n^{-1} \ln L(Y, \theta) + \lambda'h(\theta) \tag{5}$$

or by solving the associated first-order conditions for $\hat{\theta}^*$ and $\hat{\lambda}$:

$$n^{-1} \frac{\partial \ln L(Y, \hat{\theta}^*)}{\partial \theta} + H_\theta \hat{\lambda} = 0$$

$$h(\hat{\theta}^*) = 0, \tag{6}$$

where H_θ denotes the $k \times m$ matrix $\partial h'(\theta)/\partial \theta$. The solution of (6) gives the maximum-likelihood estimator $\hat{\theta}^*$ subject to the restriction $h(\theta) = 0$ and the associated Lagrangian multiplier $\hat{\lambda}$. Under the null hypothesis $h(\theta) = 0$, $\sqrt{n}\hat{\lambda}$ has a normal limiting distribution with mean zero and a certain covariance matrix $-R$. Hence the statistic $-\hat{\lambda}'R^{-1}\hat{\lambda}$ is distributed asymptotically as $\chi^2(m)$. This statistic can be rewritten as a score statistic (see Chow, 1983, pp. 286–9):

$$-n\hat{\lambda}'\hat{R}^{-1}\hat{\lambda} = [\partial \ln L(Y, \hat{\theta}^*)/\partial \theta']$$
$$\times [-\partial^2 \ln L(Y, \hat{\theta}^*)/\partial \theta \partial \theta']^{-1}[\partial \ln L(Y, \hat{\theta}^*)/\partial \theta]. \tag{7}$$

As is well known, under the null hypothesis $\partial \ln L(Y, \theta)/\partial \theta$ has mean zero and covariance matrix $-E\partial^2 \ln L/\partial \theta \partial \theta'$. If the vector $\partial \ln L(Y, \hat{\theta}^*)/\partial \theta'$ is very different from zero, as measured by the statistic (7), one would be inclined to reject the null hypothesis. Silvey (1959) has shown that under fairly general assumptions:

$$-p \lim(2 \log \mu) = p \lim W = -p \lim n\hat{\lambda}'R^{-1}\hat{\lambda} \tag{8}$$

and that the LR test, the Wald test and the LM test are asymptotically equivalent in the sense that their test statistics have the same asymptotic distribution. The equivalence for testing the hypothesis (2) in the linear regression case with normal residuals is shown in Chow (1983, pp. 290–1).

An example of (2) often encountered in practice is the hypothesis that certain subsets of coefficients in two linear regressions are equal. The test serves to detect whether certain economic parameters have changed from one sample period to another or whether they are different in two different situations (see Chow, 1960). Let the two samples of n_1 and n_2 observations be represented by:

$$Y_i = X_i\beta_i + \varepsilon_i = Z_i\gamma_i + W_i\delta_i + \varepsilon_i. \qquad (i = 1, 2) \tag{9}$$

We wish to test $H_0: \gamma_1 = \gamma_2$, each with k_1 elements. A linear regression model for both samples can be written as:

$$
\begin{bmatrix} Y_1 \\ Y_2 \end{bmatrix} = \begin{bmatrix} Z_1 & 0 & W_1 & 0 \\ 0 & Z_2 & 0 & W_2 \end{bmatrix} \begin{bmatrix} \gamma_1 \\ \gamma_2 \\ \delta_1 \\ \delta_2 \end{bmatrix} + \begin{bmatrix} \varepsilon_1 \\ \varepsilon_2 \end{bmatrix}.
$$

(10)

The null hypothesis $\gamma_1 = \gamma_2$ can be written as a set of k_1 linear restrictions:

$$
R\beta = \begin{bmatrix} I & -I & 0 & 0 \end{bmatrix} \begin{bmatrix} \gamma_1 \\ \gamma_2 \\ \delta_1 \\ \delta_2 \end{bmatrix} = 0.
$$

(11)

When the elements of ε_1 and ε_2 are normal, the test statistic is:

$$
\frac{(A - B)/k_1}{B/(n_1 + n_2 - 2k)},
$$

(12)

where A is the sum of squared residuals of (10) estimated by imposing the k_1 restrictions (11) and B is the sum of squared residuals estimated without imposing the restrictions. Under H_0, the statistic (12) has an $F(k_1, n_1 + n_2 - 2k)$ distribution.

Much useful information concerning economic relations can be ascertained by testing hypotheses about the parameters of economic models. For example, one question in applying the regression model (1) to time-series data is whether the elements ε_t are serially correlated. One may postulate a first-order autoregressive model $\varepsilon_t = \rho \varepsilon_{t-1} + \eta_t$ for the residuals, where η_t is assumed to be independent and identically distributed. The hypothesis of interest is $\rho = 0$. As another example, one may ask whether the relation between y and a certain explanatory variable x_j is linear. A partial answer is given by introducing powers of x_j in the regression and testing whether their coefficients are significantly different from zero.

2. TESTING NON-NESTED HYPOTHESES. In the last section, the hypothesis to be tested consists of a set of restrictions $g(\theta) = 0$ on the parameter vector θ. Since the null hypothesis states that the parameter θ lies in a subspace of a parameter space, it is nested within a more general hypothesis. Comparing a more general alternative hypothesis with a more restrictive null hypothesis nested within the former is to test a nested hypothesis. When the two hypotheses to be compared are not nested, we are testing *non-nested* hypotheses. One important example of non-nested hypothesis consists of two regression models, (1) and:

$$
Y = Z\gamma + u,
$$

(13)

where Z is an $n \times p$ matrix including a different set of explanatory variables from those included in X of model (1). X and Z may have some variables in common, but neither hypothesis can be derived from restricting the values of the parameter

111

vector permitted by the other hypothesis. In general, one may wish to choose between two non-nested hypotheses represented by two density functions $f_1(y, \theta_1)$ and $f_2(y, \theta_2)$ for generating y.

For the purpose of choosing between two competing density functions, Cox (1961, 1962) suggests combining them in the model:

$$h(y; \theta_1, \theta_2, \lambda) = k f_1(y, \theta_1)^{\lambda} f_2(y, \theta_2)^{1-\lambda}. \tag{14}$$

If the maximum-likelihood estimate of λ is close to 1, choose f_1; if it is close to zero, choose f_2; if neither, the result is inconclusive. Quandt (1974) proposes an alternative way of combining the two density functions, namely:

$$h(y; \theta_1, \theta_2, \lambda) = \lambda f_1(y, \theta_1) + (1-\lambda) f_2(y, \theta_2). \tag{15}$$

For choosing between two normal linear regression models (1) and (13), all parameters in (15) are identifiable, whereas for (14) one cannot separately identify λ, β, γ, $\sigma_1^2 = E\varepsilon_i^2$ and $\sigma_2^2 = Eu_i^2$.

A common approach to choosing between non-nested models is to formulate a more general model nesting them and reduce the problem to one of testing a nested hypothesis, as exemplified by the methods just described. As another example, to choose between linear regression models (1) and (13), one may formulate a more general linear regression model including both sets of explanatory variables X and Z. If this general model is assumed to be the true model, then both (1) and (13) may be false. Nevertheless, one may still ask which has a smaller error in predicting y by testing the null hypothesis that the residual variances of these models are equal. The residual variance of the regression of Y on X is:

$$n^{-1}[E(Y'Y) - (EY)'X(X'X)^{-1}X'(EY)]$$

and similarly for the regression of Y on Z. In the general model, let $EY = [X Z]\alpha$. The equality of these residual variances means:

$$\alpha'[X \quad Z]'[X(X'X)^{-1}X' - Z(Z'Z)^{-1}Z'][X \quad Z]\alpha \equiv \alpha'H\alpha = 0. \tag{16}$$

This is a quadratic restriction on the coefficient vector α in a linear regression model. It can be tested by the methods of (3), (4) and (5). See Chow (1980; 1983, pp. 278–84). Some other works on testing non-nested hypotheses are cited in Chow (1983, pp. 284–6).

3. TESTING MODEL SPECIFICATIONS. When an economist wishes to find out whether a certain model is correctly specified, tests of model specification can be used. The situation here differs from that of section 2 in having no specific model to compete with the model in question. It differs from that of section 1 in not singling out, at least in the first instance, certain parameters as the likely sources of model misspecifications. If one believes that an omitted variable in a regression model may be the culprit, one would test whether its coefficient is significantly different from zero. If one believes that the residuals may be serially correlated,

one might add an autoregressive structure to the residual and test the significance of its coefficients. Likewise, one may drop certain explanatory variables by testing the significance of their coefficients. In tests of model specifications, the alternatives are less specific. The tests aim at detecting misspecifications of a model against a variety of alternatives.

One approach to specification testing, initiated by Wu (1973) and studied by Hausman (1978), is based on comparing two estimators of a parameter vector which are both consistent and asymptotically normal if the model is correctly specified. One estimator $\hat{\gamma}^0$ is asymptotically efficient if the model is correctly specified but is inconsistent if the model is incorrectly specified. The second estimator $\hat{\gamma}$ is consistent even if the model is incorrectly specified. If the difference $\hat{q} = \hat{\gamma} - \hat{\gamma}^0$ is large, one tends to reject the null hypothesis that the model is correctly specified. Let $V(\hat{q})$ be the covariance matrix of the asymptotic distribution of $\sqrt{n}\hat{q}$ and $\hat{V}(\hat{q})$ be a consistent estimate of $V(\hat{q})$. Then under the null hypothesis, which implies $p \lim q = 0$:

$$n\hat{q}'\hat{V}(\hat{q})^{-1}\hat{q} \tag{17}$$

will have $\chi^2(k)$ as its asymptotic distribution, k being the number of elements of $\hat{q}$. As an example, consider testing whether X is correlated with ε in model (1). Under the null hypothesis $p \lim n^{-1}X'\varepsilon = 0$, an asymptotically efficient estimator is the least-squares estimator $\hat{\beta}^0$. Even if the null hypothesis does not hold a consistent estimator is the instrumental variable estimator $\hat{\beta} = (W'X)^{-1}Y$ where we assume $p \lim n^{-1}W'X$ to be a nonsingular matrix and $p \lim n^{-1/2}W'\varepsilon$ to converge in distribution to k-variate normal with zero mean. A $\chi^2(k)$ statistic can be constructed to test the null hypothesis, using the difference $\hat{q} = \hat{\beta} - \hat{\beta}^0$ and its covariance matrix. Another example is to test the correct specification of simultaneous equations by comparing a three-stage least-squares estimator $\hat{\gamma}^0$ and a two-stage least-squares estimator $\hat{\gamma}$.

A convenient framework of Newey (1985) views specification testing as choosing some function $m(y, \theta)$ which satisfies the moment condition:

$$E[m(y, \theta_0)] = 0 \tag{18}$$

if the model $f(y, \theta)$ is correctly specified, and testing this condition by using the sample moment $\Sigma_{t=1}^{n} m(y_t, \hat{\theta})/n$. For example, the information matrix test of White (1982) compares two estimates of the information matrix and uses as elements of the vector function $m(y, \theta)$:

$$m_h(y, \theta) = \frac{\partial \ln f(y, \theta)}{\partial \theta_i} \cdot \frac{\partial \ln f(y, \theta)}{\partial \theta_j} + \frac{\partial^2 \ln f(y, \theta)}{\partial \theta_i \partial \theta_j}, \tag{19}$$

$$(h = i + j - 1; i = 1, \ldots, j; j = 1, \ldots, k)$$

where k is the number of parameters. The Hausman test using (17) is shown by Newey (1985) to be asymptotically equivalent to a particular moment-condition test.

Economists using various specification tests should be reminded that these tests serve the same purpose as the many diagnostic checks for statistical models used in the literature. Examples are the diagnostic checks of Box and Jenkins (1970) for time-series models and those of Belsley, Kuh and Welsch (1980) for regression models.

4. MODEL SELECTION CRITERIA. The statistical tests presented so far are based on the notion that if a model is true (an assumption to be tested), it will be chosen. This notion might be questioned because the true model can be very complicated and in practice one may prefer to use a simpler model for estimation or prediction purposes. Consider the choice between model (1), with $X\beta = X_1\beta_1 + X_2\beta_2$ and normal ε, and the smaller linear model using X_1 alone as explanatory variables, where X_1 is $n \times k_1$ and X_2 is $n \times k_2$. The standard treatment using the methods of section 1 is to test the null hypothesis $\beta_2 = 0$, but a question remains as to what level of significance to use. An alternative viewpoint is to choose the model which is estimated to have smaller prediction errors. Specifically, let n future, out-of-sample, observations be:

$$\tilde{Y} = \tilde{X}\beta + \tilde{\varepsilon} \tag{20}$$

under the assumption that the larger model (1) is the true model. Let the model be selected which has a smaller expected sum of squared prediction errors.

Using the small model with X_1 alone and denoting the corresponding maximum-likelihood estimate of β by $\hat{\beta}_l$ [consisting of $(X_1'X_1)^{-1}X_1'Y$ and 0], one easily evaluates $E(\hat{\beta}_l - \beta)(\hat{\beta}_l - \beta)'$. Then using the estimated small model and the predictor $\tilde{X}\hat{\beta}_l$ for $\tilde{Y}$, one finds the expected sum of squared prediction errors to be:

$$E(\tilde{X}\hat{\beta}_l - \tilde{Y})'(\tilde{X}\hat{\beta}_l - \tilde{Y}) = E(\hat{\beta}_l - \beta)'\tilde{X}'\tilde{X}(\hat{\beta}_l - \beta) + E\tilde{\varepsilon}'\tilde{\varepsilon}$$
$$= k_1\sigma^2 + \beta_2'X_2'[I - X_1(X_1'X_1)^{-1}X_1']X_2\beta_2 + n\sigma^2. \tag{21}$$

Using the large model (1) and letting $\hat{\beta} = (X'X)^{-1}X'$, we have:

$$E(X\hat{\beta} - \tilde{Y})'(\tilde{X}\hat{\beta} - \tilde{Y}) = (k_1 + k_2)\sigma^2 + n\sigma^2. \tag{22}$$

Comparing (21) and (22), we find that the small model, though not being the true model, should be used if and only if:

$$\beta_2'X_2'[I - X_1(X_1'X_1)^{-1}X_1']X_2\beta_2 \equiv \beta_2'X_{2.1}'X_{2.1}\beta_2 < k_2\sigma^2, \tag{23}$$

where $X_{2.1}$ is the matrix of residuals of the regression of X_2 on X_1. To apply the criterion (23), one may replace $\beta_2'X_{2.1}'X_{2.1}\beta_2$ by its unbiased estimate $\hat{\beta}_2'X_{2.1}'X_{2.1}\hat{\beta}_2 - k_2\sigma^2$, and replace σ^2 in the resulting inequality by the unibased estimate s^2 to yield:

$$\hat{\beta}_2'X_{2.1}'X_{2.1}\hat{\beta}_2 < 2k_2s^2 \equiv 2k_2(Y - X\hat{\beta})'(Y - X\hat{\beta})/(n - k_1 - k_2) \tag{24}$$

as the condition for selecting the small model. This criterion amounts to setting the critical value of the F ratio $\hat{\beta}_2' X_{2.1}' \hat{\beta}_2 / k_2 s^2$ for testing the null hypothesis $\beta_2 = 0$ equal to 2. It is the C_p criterion of Mallows (1973) and is motivated by the desire for more accurate prediction. Comparing (21) and (22) we observe that omitting the variables X_2 might yield a better model for prediction even when (1) is the true model and $\beta_2 \neq 0$.

The information criterion of Akaike (1973, 1974) is also motivated by the desire for more accurate prediction. However, instead of using the expected squared prediction errors, one uses the following expected information:

$$E[\ln g(\tilde{y}, \theta_0) - \ln f(\tilde{y}, \theta)] \tag{25}$$

to measure how good the density function $f(\cdot)$ of the model used for predicting a future observation y is, as compared with the true model $g(\cdot)$. Akaike has implemented this criterion by estimating (25), suggesting the criterion for selecting a model if its maximum log likelihood minus the number of estimated parameters is the highest among the competing models. A model having more parameters will tend to have a higher value for its maximum log likelihood, but this value has to be reduced by the number of parameters estimated. Sawa (1978) has provided a better estimate of (25) for linear regression models while Chow (1981a, b) has provided better estimates of (25) for general statistical models and simultaneous-equation models.

5. THE POSTERIOR-PROBABILITY CRITERION. Another criterion for selecting models is the Jeffrey–Bayes posterior-probability criterion. Let $p(M_j)$ be the prior probability for model M_j to be correct and $p(\theta \mid M_j)$ be the prior density for the k_j-dimensional parameter vector θ_j conditioned on M_j being correct. Assume that a random sample of n observations $(y_1, y_2, \ldots, y_n) = Y$ is available. By Bayes's theorem the posterior probability of the jth model being correct is:

$$p(M_j \mid Y) = \frac{p(M_j) p(Y \mid M_j)}{p(Y)} = \frac{p(M_j) p(Y \mid M_j)}{\sum_j p(M_j) p(Y \mid M_j)} \tag{26}$$

where

$$p(Y \mid M_j) = \int L_j(Y, \theta) p(\theta \mid M_j) \, d\theta \tag{27}$$

with $L_j(Y, \theta_j)$ denoting the likelihood function for the jth model. Since $p(Y)$ is a common factor for all models, the model with the highest posterior probability of being correct is the one with the maximum value for:

$$p(M_j) p(Y \mid M_j) = p(M_j) \int L_j(Y, \theta) p(\theta \mid M_j) \, d\theta.$$

If the prior probabilities $p(M_j)$ are equal for the models, the one with the highest $p(Y \mid M_j)$ will be selected.

To evaluate $p(Y | M_j)$ for large samples we apply a theorem of Jeffreys (1961, pp. 193ff.) on the posterior density $p(\theta | Y, M_j)$ of θ_j given model M_j:

$$p(\theta | Y, M_j) = \frac{L_j(Y, \theta)p(\theta | M_j)}{p(Y | M_j)}$$

$$= (2\pi)^{-k_j/2} |S|^{1/2} \exp[-\tfrac{1}{2}(\theta - \hat{\theta}_j)' S(\theta - \hat{\theta}_j)][1 + 0(n^{-1/2})],$$

$$(28)$$

where $\hat{\theta}_j$ is the maximum-likelihood estimate of θ_j and the inverse covariance matrix is $S = -[(\partial^2 \ln L_j)/(\partial\theta \, \partial\theta')]_{\hat{\theta}} \equiv nR_j$. $0(n^{-1/2})$ is a function of order $n^{-1/2}$. Thus, for large samples, the posterior density of a parameter vector θ in model j is asymptotically normal with mean equal to the maximum-likelihood estimate $\hat{\theta}_j$ and covariance matrix which can be approximated by the inverse of S. Evaluating both sides of (28) at $\theta = \hat{\theta}_j$ and taking natural logarithms, we obtain, noting $|S| = |nR_j| = n^{k_j}|R_j|$,

$$\ln p(Y | M_j) = \ln L_j(Y, \hat{\theta}_j) - \frac{k_j}{2} \ln n - \tfrac{1}{2} \log |R_j|$$

$$+ \frac{k_j}{2} \ln 2\pi + \ln p(\hat{\theta}_j | M_j) + 0(n^{-1/2}). \qquad (29)$$

If we retain only the first two terms $\ln L_j(Y, \hat{\theta}_j)$ and $-k_j(\tfrac{1}{2} \ln n)$ in (29), we obtain the formula of Schwarz (1978) for approximating $\log p(Y | M_j)$.

In practice $\ln p(Y | M_j)$ may not be well approximated by using only the first two terms of (29), as it will depend on the prior density $p(\theta | M_j)$ of the parameter vector chosen for each model M_j. Bayesian statisticians, including Jeffreys (1961), Pratt (1975), and Leamer (1978), among others, have recognized the difficult problem of choosing a prior distribution $p(\theta | M_j)$ for the parameters of each model to be used to compute $p(Y | M_j)$. Unlike the estimation of parameters by Bayesian methods, even for large samples the choice of models by the posterior-probability criterion is very sensitive to the prior distribution $p(\theta | M_j)$ assumed for each model.

In this essay I have summarized some of the important ideas and methods employed in hypothesis testing and model selection in econometrics. The choice of an econometric model is a complicated subject. Many approaches have to be explored in practice for choosing and evaluating econometric models. Some of these approaches are discussed in Chow and Corsi (1982) and in Belsley and Kuh (1986).

BIBLIOGRAPHY

Akaike, H. 1973. Information theory and an extension of the maximum likelihood principle. In *Proceedings of the 2nd International Symposium for Information Theory*, ed. B. Petrov and F. Csáki, Budapest: Akademiai Kiadó.

Akaike, H. 1974. A new look at the statistical model identification, *IEEE Transactions on Automatic Control* AC-19, 716–23.

Belsley, D. and Kuh, E. 1986. *Model Reliability*. Cambridge, Mass.: MIT Press.

Belsley, D., Kuh, E. and Welsch, R. 1980. *Regression Diagnostics*. New York: Wiley.

Box, G. and Jenkins, G.M. 1970. *Time-Series Analysis: Forecasting and Control*. San Francisco: Holden-Day.

Chow, G. 1960. Tests of equality between sets of coefficients in two linear regressions. *Econometrica* 28, 591–605.

Chow, G. 1980. The selection of variates for use in prediction: a generalization of Hotelling's solution. In *Quantitative Econometrics and Development*, ed. L. Klein, M. Nerlove and S.C. Tsiang, New York: Academic Press.

Chow, G. 1981a. A comparison of the information and posterior probability criteria for model selection. *Journal of Econometrics* 16, 21–33.

Chow, G. 1981b. Evaluation of econometric models by decomposition and aggregation. In *Methodology of Macro-Economic Models*, ed. J. Kmenta and J. Ramsey, Amsterdam: North-Holland.

Chow, G. 1983. *Econometrics*. New York: McGraw-Hill.

Chow, G. and Corsi, P. (eds) 1982. *Evaluating the Reliability of Macro-Economic Models*. London: Wiley.

Cox, D. 1961. Tests of separate families of hypotheses. In *Proceedings of the 4th Berkeley Symposium on Mathematical Statistics and Probability*, Berkeley: University of California Press.

Cox, D. 1962. Further results on tests of separate families of hypotheses. *Journal of the Royal Statistical Society* Series B24, 406–24.

Hausman, J. 1978. Specification tests in econometrics. *Econometrica* 46, 1251–72.

Jeffreys, H. 1961. *Theory of Probability*. 3rd edn, Oxford: Clarendon Press.

Leamer, E. 1978. *Specification Searches*. New York: Wiley.

Mallows, C. 1973. Some comments on C_p. *Technometrics* 15, 661–75.

Newey, W. 1985. Maximum likelihood specification testing and conditional moment tests. *Econometrica* 53, 1047–70.

Neyman, J. and Pearson, E. 1928. On the use of interpretation of certain test criteria for the purpose of statistical inference. *Biometrika* 20A, Part I, 175–240; Part II, 263–294.

Pratt, J. 1975. Comments. In *Studies in Bayesian Econometrics and Statistics*, ed. S. Fienberg and A. Zellner, Amsterdam: North-Holland.

Quandt, R. 1974. A comparison of methods for testing nonnested hypotheses. *Review of Economics and Statistics* 56, 92–9.

Sawa, T. 1978. Information criteria for discriminating among alternative regression models. *Econometrica* 46, 1273–92.

Schwarz, G. 1978. Estimating the dimension of a model. *Annals of Statistics* 6, 461–4.

Silvey, S. 1959. The Lagrangian multiplier test. *Annals of Mathematical Statistics* 30, 389–407.

Wald, A. 1943. Tests of statistical hypotheses concerning several parameters when the number of observations is large. *Transactions of the American Mathematical Society* 54, 426–82.

White, H. 1982. Maximum likelihood estimation of misspecified models. *Econometrica* 50, 1–25.

Wu, D. 1973. Alternative tests of independence between stochastic regressors and disturbances. *Econometrica* 41, 733–50.

Least Squares

HALBERT WHITE

The method of least squares is a statistical technique used to determine the best linear or nonlinear regression line. The method, developed independently by Legendre (1805), Gauss (1806, 1809) and Adrain (1808), has a rich and lengthy history described in an excellent six-part article by Harter (1974–6). Least squares is the technique most widely used for fitting regression lines because of its computational simplicity and because of particular optimality properties described below. Primary among these are the facts that it gives the best linear unbiased estimator (BLUE) in the case of linear regression and that it gives the maximum likelihood estimator (MLE) in the case of regression with Gaussian (normal) errors.

A regression line is a model of the expectation of a random variable, denoted Y, given a specified set of conditioning variables, denoted X. Y is called the 'dependent' or 'explained' variable, and X is called the vector of 'independent' or 'explanatory' variables. We denote the conditional expectation of Y given X as $E(Y|X)$. A model of this conditional expectation is a function, say f, which depends on the explanatory variables X, and on a vector of parameters, say β, chosen in such a way that for some value of the parameters β^*, $f(X, \beta^*)$ provides the best fitting approximation to $E(Y|X)$.

There are numerous ways in which to measure the goodness of fit of any particular approximation. Perhaps the most important and commonly used criterion is that of mean squared error. The mean squared error of a random variable Z as an approximation to (or estimate of) a random variable Y is defined as

$$\mathrm{mse}(Z, Y) = E[(Y - Z)^2].$$

Here, $(Y - Z)^2$ is the squared error of Z as an approximation to (estimate of) Y. The smaller the mean squared error, the better, because the closer Z is to Y on average. This criterion penalizes an overestimate of Y by the same amount that it penalizes an underestimate of Y of equal magnitude. Of all the functions

118

of X which one might use as an approximation to Y, the best approximation in this sense is given by $E(Y|X)$. That is,

$$\text{mse}[E(Y|X), Y] \leqslant \text{mse}[g(X), Y]$$

for all functions g of X.

Typically, the conditional expectation $E(Y|X)$ is unknown, so one may approximate $E(Y|X)$ using the model $f(X, \beta)$, choosing β^* to satisfy

$$\text{mse}[f(X, \beta^*), E(Y|X)] \leqslant \text{mse}[f(X, \beta), E[Y|X]]$$

for all allowable values of β. It can be shown that this holds if and only if

$$\text{mse}[f(X, \beta^*), Y] \leqslant \text{mse}[f(X, \beta), Y],$$

for all allowable values of β. Thus, $f(X, \beta^*)$ is equivalently a best approximation to $E(Y|X)$ or a best approximation to Y in this sense.

Because the relevant expectations are usually unknown, it is not possible to find β^* directly by solving the problem

$$\min_{\beta} \text{mse}[f(X, \beta), Y].$$

Fortunately, the needed expectation can be estimated if one has sample information on Y and X. In economics, this may take the form of time-series, cross-section, or panel (time-series cross-section) observations. Given a sample of n observations on Y and X, denoted (Y_t, X_t), $t = 1, \ldots, n$, it follows generally from the law of large numbers that

$$n^{-1} \sum_{t=1}^{n} [f(X_t, \beta) - Y_t]^2 = E\{[f(X, \beta) - Y]^2\} + o_{as}(1),$$

where $o_{as}(1)$ denotes terms vanishing with probability one (i.e. almost surely) as n tends to infinity. A useful estimator for β^* can therefore be found by solving the problem

$$\min_{\beta} n^{-1} \sum_{t=1}^{n} [f(X_t, \beta) - Y_t]^2,$$

or the equivalent problem

$$\min_{\beta} \sum_{t=1}^{n} [Y_t - f(X_t, \beta)]^2.$$

This method of estimating β^* is the *method of least squares*, and the resulting estimator is the *least squares estimator*, denoted $\hat{\beta}_{LS}$. The quantity $r(Y_t, X_t, \beta) = Y_t - f(X_t, \beta)$ is the 'residual'. The summation above is the 'sum of squared residuals', and it is this sum to which the word 'squares' refers in the phrase 'least squares'. Substituting $\hat{\beta}_{LS}$ into r, gives the 'estimated residual', $\hat{r}_t = r(Y_t, X_t, \hat{\beta}_{LS})$; substituting $\hat{\beta}_{LS}$ into $f(X_t, \beta)$ yields the 'fitted value' $\hat{Y}_t = f(X_t, \hat{\beta}_{LS})$. Thus, $Y_t = \hat{Y}_t + \hat{r}_t$. The quantity $\sum_{t=1}^{n} Y_t^2$ is the 'total sum of squares', the quantity $\Sigma_{t=1}^{n} \hat{Y}_t^2$ is the 'explained sum of squares', and the quantity $\Sigma_{t=1}^{n} \hat{r}_t^2$ is the 'unexplained sum of squares'.

The properties of $\hat{\beta}_{LS}$ are of particular importance; these depend crucially on the properties of Y_t, X_t, and the function $f(X, \beta)$. White (1981) studies the properties of $\hat{\beta}_{LS}$ under the following assumptions:

(A1) $\{Y_t, X_t\}$ is a sequence of independent identically distributed (i.i.d.) random variables;

(A2) $f: \mathbb{R}^k \times B \to \mathbb{R}$ is a measurable function on $\mathbb{R}^k$, $k \in N = \{1, 2, \ldots\}$, for each β in B, a compact subset of $\mathbb{R}^p$, $p \in N$, and a continuous function on B for each x in $\mathbb{R}^k$;

(A3) $q(Y_t, X_t, \beta) = [Y_t - f(X_t, \beta)]^2$ is dominated by an integrable function, i.e., there exists $d: \mathbb{R}^{k+1} \to \mathbb{R}$ such that for all (y, x) in $\mathbb{R}^{k+1}$ and β in B, $q(y, x, \beta) \leq d(y, x)$ and $E[d(Y_t, X_t)] < \infty$;

(A4) $E([Y_t - f(X_t, \beta)]^2)$ has a unique minimum at β^* in B. With these conditions, White proves the following result.

THEOREM 1: Given A1–A4, $\hat{\beta}_{LS} = \beta^* + o_{as}(1)$.

Thus, the least squares estimator $\hat{\beta}_{LS}$ converges almost surely to β^*, the parameter value such that $f(X_t, \beta^*)$ provides the minimum mse approximation to Y_t and $E(Y_t | X_t)$.

An approximate sampling distribution for $\hat{\beta}_{LS}$ exists using the following conditions.

(A4') A4 holds, and β^* is interior to B;

(A5) $f(x, \cdot)$ is continuously differentiable of order two on B for each x in $\mathbb{R}^k$;

(A6) The elements of $\nabla q(Y_t, X_t, \beta)' \nabla q(Y_t, X_t, \beta)$ and $\nabla^2 q(Y_t, X_t, \beta)$ are dominated by integrable functions, where ∇ denotes the gradient operator with respect to β;

(A7) The matrices

$$A^* = E[\nabla^2 q(Y_t, X_t, \beta^*)] \quad \text{and} \quad B^* = E[\nabla q(Y_t, X_t, \beta^*)' \nabla q(Y_t, X_t, \beta^*)]$$

are positive definite. The result is

THEOREM 2: Given

A1–A4', A5–A7,

$$n^{1/2}(\hat{\beta}_{LS} - \beta^*) \xrightarrow{d} N(0, A^{*-1} B^* A^{*-1}).$$

Further,

$$\hat{A}^{-1} \hat{B} \hat{A}^{-1} = A^{*-1} B^* A^{*-1} + o_{as}(1),$$

where

$$\hat{A} = n^{-1} \sum_{t=1}^{n} \nabla^2 q(Y_t, X_t, \hat{\beta}_{LS}),$$

$$\hat{B} = n^{-1} \sum_{t=1}^{n} \nabla q(Y_t, X_t, \hat{\beta}_{LS})' \nabla q(Y_t, X_t, \hat{\beta}_{LS}).$$

This implies that to test $H_0: s(\beta^*) = 0$ vs. $H_a: s(\beta^*) \neq 0$, where s is a $v \times 1$ vector function, one can form the Wald statistic

$$W = ns(\hat{\beta}_{LS})' [\nabla s(\hat{\beta}_{LS}) \hat{A}^{-1} \hat{B} \hat{A}^{-1} \nabla s(\hat{\beta}_{LS})']^{-1} s(\hat{\beta}_{LS})$$

which has the χ_v^2 distribution approximately in large samples under H_0.

An important special case arises when

$$f(X_t, \beta) = \beta_1 + X_t \beta_2,$$

where $\beta' = (\beta_1, \beta_2')$, with β_1 a scalar and β_2 a $k \times 1$ vector. This is the '(standard) linear model'. In this case,

$$\hat{\beta}_{LS} = (X'X)^{-1} X'Y,$$

where X is the $n \times k + 1$ matrix with rows $(1, X_t)$, and Y is the $n \times 1$ vector with elements Y_t. This form for $\hat{\beta}_{LS}$ is called the 'ordinary least squares estimator'.

Results for the linear model similar to Theorems 1 and 2 above follow by retaining (A1) and imposing

(A2') $f(x, \beta) = \beta_1 + x\beta_2$, for $x \in \mathbb{R}^k$, $\beta' = (\beta_1, \beta_2') \in \mathbb{R}^{k+1}$;

(A3') $E(Y_t^2) < \infty$, $E(X_t X_t') < \infty$;

(A4'') det $E(X_t' X_t) > 0$.

White (1980a) proves the following result.

THEOREM 3: Given A1, A2', A3', and A4'',

$\hat{\beta}_{LS} = \beta^* + o_{as}(1)$, where $\beta^* = [E(X_t' X_t)]^{-1} E(X_t' Y_t) < \infty$.

An asymptotic normality result holds, using the conditions

(A3'') $E(Y_t^4) < \infty$, and $E[(X_t X_t')^2] < \infty$;

(A5') det $E(X_t' r_t^* r_t^{*'} X_t) > 0$, where $r_t^* = r(Y_t, X_t, \beta^*)$.

The result is

THEOREM 4: Given A1, A2', A3'', A4'', and A5',

$$n^{1/2}(\hat{\beta}_{LS} - \beta^*) \xrightarrow{d} N(0, A^{*-1} B^* A^{*-1}),$$

where

$$A^* = E(X_t' X_t)$$

and

$$B^* = E(X_t' r_t^* r_t^{*'} X_t).$$

121

Further,

$$\hat{A}^{-1}\hat{B}\hat{A}^{-1} = A^{*-1}B^*A^{*-1} + o_{as}(1),$$

with

$$\hat{A} = X'X/n, \quad \text{and} \quad \hat{B} = X'\hat{\Omega}X/n,$$

where $\hat{\Omega}$ is the $n \times n$ diagonal matrix with diagonal elements $\hat{r}_t^2$.

To test the linear hypothesis H_0: $R\beta^* = r$ vs H_a: $R\beta^* \neq r$, where R is a given $v \times k + 1$ matrix and r is a given $v \times 1$ vector, one can compute

$$W = n(R\hat{\beta}_{LS} - r)'[R(X'X/n)^{-1}X'\hat{\Omega}X/n(X'X/n)^{-1}R']^{-1}(R\hat{\beta}_{LS} - r).$$

Under H_0, this has the χ_v^2 distribution approximately in large samples.

Similar results hold in situations more general than the case of i.i.d. observations. See e.g. Domowitz and White (1982) and Gallant and White (1987).

In applications, it is often assumed (with or without justification) that the model $f(X, \beta)$ is correctly specified; that is, there exists β^0 in B such that

$$E(Y|X) = f(X, \beta^0) \quad \text{a.s.}$$

For discussion of nonlinear least squares estimation in this context, the reader is referred to Jennrich (1969), Hannan (1971), Klimko and Nelson (1978), White (1980b) and White and Domowitz (1984).

Because of the popularity of the linear model, we discuss the properties of $\hat{\beta}_{LS}$ for the correctly specified case in more detail. We adopt the following assumptions.

(B1) $\{Y_t, X_t\}$ is a sequence of independently distributed random variables such that

(a) $E(Y_t) < \infty$, and there exists $\beta^0 \in \mathbb{R}^{k+1}$, $\beta^{0'} = (\beta_1^0, \beta_2^{0'})$ such that

$$E(Y_t|X_t) = \beta_1^0 + X_t\beta_2^0, \quad t = 1, 2, \ldots;$$

(b) For all $t = 1, 2, \ldots$, $E(Y_t^4) < \infty$, $E[(X_tX_2')^2] < \infty$, and

$$\text{var}(Y_t|X_t) = \sigma_0^2 \neq 0.$$

(B2) $f(x, \beta) = \beta_1 + x\beta_2$, for $x \in \mathbb{R}^k$, $\beta' = (\beta_1, \beta_2') \in \mathbb{R}^{k+1}$;
(B3) There exist

$$\delta > 0 \quad \text{and} \quad \Delta < \infty$$

such that

$$E|Y_t^2|^{1+\delta} < \Delta \quad \text{and} \quad E|X_tX_t'|^{1+\delta} < \Delta, t = 1, 2, \ldots;$$

(B4) There exists $\delta > 0$ such that for all n sufficiently large $\det E(X'X/n) > \delta$.

With these conditions we have

THEOREM 5: Given B1a, and B2–B4,

$$\hat{\beta}_{LS} = \beta^0 + o_{as}(1)$$

If (B1(b)) also holds, then

$$n^{1/2}(\hat{\beta}_{LS} - \beta^0) \xrightarrow{d} N(0, \sigma_0^2 [E(X'X/n)]^{-1}).$$

Further, $\hat{\sigma}^2 (X'X/n)^{-1} = \sigma_0^2 [E(X'X/n)]^{-1} + o_{as}(1)$

To test $H_0: R\beta^0 = r$ versus $H_a: R\beta^0 \neq r$, compute

$$W = n(R\hat{\beta}_{LS} - r)'[R(X'X/n)^{-1}R']^{-1}(R\hat{\beta}_{LS} - r)/\hat{\sigma}^2.$$

Under H_0, this has the χ_v^2 distribution approximately in large samples.

When (B1(b)) is not available, asymptotic normality results for $\hat{\beta}_{LS}$ may still hold. We impose

(B3′) There exist $\delta > 0$ and $\Delta < \infty$ such that $E|Y_t^4|^{1+\delta} < \Delta$ and $E|(X_t X_t')^2|^{1+\delta} < \Delta$, for all $t = 1, 2, \ldots$;
(B5) There exists $\delta > 0$ such that for all n sufficiently large,

$$\det n^{-1} \sum_{t=1}^{n} E(X_t' \varepsilon_t \varepsilon_t' X_t) > \delta,$$

where

$$\varepsilon_t = Y_t - E(Y_t | X_t).$$

White (1980c) proves the following result.

THEOREM 6: Given B1a, B2, B3′, B4, and B5,

$$n^{1/2}(\hat{\beta}_{LS} - \beta^0) \xrightarrow{d} N(0, A^{0-1}B^0 A^{0-1}),$$

with

$$A^0 = E(X'X/n) \quad \text{and} \quad B^0 = E(X'\Omega X/n)$$

where Ω is the $n \times n$ diagonal matrix with diagonal elements ε_t^2. Further,

$$\hat{A}^{-1}\hat{B}\hat{A}^{-1} = A^{0-1}B^0 A^{0-1} + o_{as}(1)$$

with

$$\hat{A} = X'X/n, \quad \text{and} \quad \hat{B} = X'\hat{\Omega}X/n,$$

where $\hat{\Omega}$ is as previously defined.

This result allows hypothesis testing even when the 'errors' ε_t exhibit heteroskedasticity of unknown form. To test H_0: $R\beta^0 = r$ versus H_a: $R\beta^0 \neq r$, compute

$$W = n(R\hat{\beta}_{\text{LS}} - r)'[R(X'X/n(X'X/n)^{-1}R']^{-1}(R\hat{\beta}_{\text{LS}} - r).$$

Under H_0, this has the χ_v^2 distribution approximately in large samples.

Under slightly different assumptions, the properties of $\hat{\beta}_{\text{LS}}$ can be specified for samples of any size. Retaining (B1) and (B2), we replace (B3) and (B4).

(B3″) For all $t = 1, 2, \ldots$, $E(Y_t^2) < \infty$ and $E(X_t X_t') < \infty$;
(B4′) For any $n \geq k + 1$, $P[\det X'X > 0] = 1$.

Now we have

THEOREM 7: Given B1(a), B2, B3″, and B4′, for any $n \geq k + 1$,

$$E(\hat{\beta}_{\text{LS}} | X) = \beta^0 \quad \text{a.s.}$$

so that $E(\hat{\beta}_{\text{LS}}) = \beta^0$.

That is, $\hat{\beta}_{\text{LS}}$ is unbiased, conditionally and unconditionally.

Modifying B1, we obtain the sampling distribution for $\hat{\beta}_{\text{LS}}$ in samples of any size.

(B1′) $\{Y_t, X_t\}$ is a sequence of independent random variables such that $E(Y_t^2) < \infty$, and for some $\beta^{0\prime} = (\beta_1^0, \beta_2^{0\prime})$ in $\mathbb{R}^{k+1}$,

$$Y_t | X_t \sim N(\beta_1^0 + X_t \beta_2^0, \sigma_0^2), \quad 0 < \sigma_0^2 < \infty, t = 1, 2, \ldots .$$

We have the following version of the 'classical' sampling distribution theorem for the least squares estimator.

THEOREM 8: Given B1′, B2, B3″, and B4′, for any $n \geq k + 1$,

$$\hat{\beta}_{\text{LS}} | X \sim N(\beta^0, \sigma_0^2(X'X)^{-1})$$

and

$$(n - k - 1)\hat{\sigma}_{\text{LS}}^2/\sigma_0^2 | X \sim \chi_{n-k-1}^2,$$

where $\hat{\sigma}_{\text{LS}}^2 = (Y'Y - Y'X(X'X)^{-1}X'Y)/(n - k - 1)$ is independent of $\hat{\beta}_{\text{LS}}$ conditional on X.

To test the linear hypothesis H_0: $R\beta^0 = r$ vs H_a: $R\beta^0 \neq r$ one can use Fisher's F-statistic

$$F = \frac{(R\hat{\beta}_{\text{LS}} - r)'[R(X'X)^{-1}R']^{-1}(R\hat{\beta}_{\text{LS}} - r)/v}{\hat{\sigma}_{\text{LS}}^2/(n - k - 1)}.$$

Under H_0, this has Fisher's F-distribution with $v, n - k - 1$ degrees of freedom. When $v = 1$, another statistic is available. Given a $1 \times k + 1$ weighting vector w, and a scalar w_0, one can test H_0: $w\beta^0 = w_0$ vs H_a: $w\beta^0 \neq w_0$, using Student's t-statistic

$$t = (w\hat{\beta}_{\text{LS}} - w_0)/[\hat{\sigma}_{\text{LS}}^2 w'(X'X)^{-1}w]^{1/2}.$$

Under H_0, this has Student's t-distribution with $n - k - 1$ degrees of freedom.

Finally, the least squares estimator for the correctly specified linear model has desirable efficiency properties. The Gauss–Markov Theorem states that the ordinary least squares estimator is the best linear unbiased estimator (BLUE) in the sense that any other estimator constructed as a linear combination of Y – say $W'Y$, where W is a $k + 1 \times n$ matrix depending only on X – which is unbiased (i.e. $E(W'Y) = \beta^0$), has a variance-covariance matrix which differs from that of $\hat{\beta}_{LS}$ by a positive semi-definite matrix. This holds whether or not Y_t has a normal distribution conditional on X_t. When Y_t does have the normal distribution conditional on X_t, $\hat{\beta}_{LS}$ is the maximum likelihood estimator (MLE) and is therefore the best unbiased estimator, as the MLE attains the Cramer–Rao bound, conditional on X. For a more detailed discussion of the least squares estimator in this context, see Theil (1971), Johnston (1984) and White (1984).

BIBLIOGRAPHY

Adrain, R. 1808. Research concerning the probabilities of errors which happen in making observations. *Analyst* 1, 93–109.

Domowitz, I. and White, H. 1982. Misspecified models with dependent observations. *Journal of Econometrics* 20, 35–58.

Gallant, A.R. and White, H. 1987. *A Unified Theory of Estimation and Inference for Nonlinear Dynamic Models*. Oxford: Basil Blackwell.

Gauss, C.F. 1806. II Comet vom Jahr 1805. *Monatliche Correspondenz zur Beförderung der Erd- und Himmelskunde* 14, 181–6.

Gauss, C.F. 1809. *Theoria Motus Corporum Coelestium in Sectionbus Conicis Solem Ambientium*. Hamburg: F. Perthes and I.H. Besser.

Hannan, E.J. 1971. Nonlinear time-series regression. *Journal of Applied Probability* 8, 767–80.

Harter, H.L. 1974–6. The method of least squares and some alternatives, Parts I–VI. *International Statistical Review* 42, 147–74, 235–64, 282; 43, 1–44, 125–90, 269–78; 44, 113–59.

Jennrich, R. 1969. Asymptotic properties of nonlinear least squares estimators. *Annals of Mathematical Statistics* 40, 633–43.

Johnston, J. 1984. *Econometric Methods*. New York: McGraw-Hill.

Klimko, L. and Nelson, P. 1978. On conditional least squares estimation for stochastic processes. *Annals of Statistics* 6, 629–42.

Legendre, A.M. 1805. *Nouvelles méthodes pour la determination des orbites des comètes*. Paris: Courcier.

Theil, H. 1971. *Principles of Econometrics*. New York: Wiley & Sons.

White, H. 1980a. Using least squares to approximate unknown regression functions. *International Economic Review* 21, 149–70.

White, H. 1980b. Nonlinear regression on cross-section data. *Econometrica* 48, 721–46.

White, H. 1980c. A heteroskedasticity-consistent covariance matrix estimator and a direct test for heteroskedasticity. *Econometrica* 48, 817–38.

White, H. 1981. Consequences and detection of misspecified nonlinear regression models. *Journal of the American Statistical Association* 76, 419–33.

White, H. 1984. *Asymptotic Theory for Econometricians*. Orlando: Academic Press.

White, H. and Domowitz, I. 1984. Nonlinear regression with dependent observations. *Econometrica* 52, 143–62.

Likelihood

A.W.F. EDWARDS

A statistical model for phenomena in the sciences or social sciences is a mathematical construct which associates a *probability* with each of the possible outcomes. When two different models are to be compared as explanations for the same observed outcome, or perhaps two variants of the same model differing only in the value of some adjustable parameter, the probability of obtaining this particular outcome can be calculated for each, and is then known as the *likelihood* for the hypothesis (or parameter value) given the particular outcome or 'data'.

Likelihoods and probabilities are easily (and frequently) confused, and it is for this reason that in 1921 R.A. Fisher introduced the separate word 'likelihood' to draw attention to the different properties and uses of the two concepts.

The first of these is that the variable quantity in a likelihood statement is the hypothesis, the outcome being that actually observed, in contrast to the usual form of a probability statement which refers to a variety of outcomes, the hypothesis being assumed, or fixed. Thus a manufacturer of aircraft components using a well-tried process giving a known proportion of defective items will be able to calculate the *probabilities* with which 1, 2, 3, ... defective components will appear in a batch, and will be able to plan his inspection procedures accordingly; but when he later changes to an improved manufacturing process with an as-yet unknown proportion of defectives he will be able to calculate the *likelihoods* of various proportions given the numbers of defective items actually observed in a particular batch. As we shall see, such likelihoods provide information about the true, but unknown, proportion.

The second different property arises directly from the first. If all the outcomes of a statistical model are considered, their total probability will be 1 since one of them must occur and they are mutually exclusive; but since, in general, hypotheses are not exhaustive – one can usually think of another one – it is not to be expected that the sum of two or more likelihoods has any particular meaning, and indeed there is no addition law for likelihoods corresponding to the addition law for probabilities. It follows that it is only *relative* likelihoods that are informative; absolute values are not relevant.

The most important application of likelihood is in parametric statistical models. To take Fisher's original example (1921), the distribution of the sample correlation coefficient r depends, in the case of the bivariate normal model, only on the value of the correlation parameter ρ of the model. Thus for any assumed value of ρ, the distribution of r for samples of a given size may be computed. But 'What we can find from a sample is the *likelihood* of any particular value of ρ, if we define the likelihood as a quantity proportional to the probability that, from a population having that particular value of ρ, a sample having the observed value r should be obtained. So defined, probability and likelihood are quantities of an entirely different nature.'

By way of notation, let $P(R|\rho)$ be the probability density function of the random variable R given the population parameter ρ. Then we write

$$L(\rho\|r) \propto P(r|\rho)$$

for the likelihood of ρ given a particular value r, the double vertical line $\|$ being used to indicate that the likelihood of ρ is not *conditional on r* in the technical probability sense. In the example of the correlation coefficient $L(\rho\|r)$ is a continuous function of $\rho(-1 \leqslant \rho \leqslant +1)$, known as the *likelihood function*.

The value of ρ which maximizes $L(\rho\|r)$ for an observed r is known as the *maximum-likelihood estimate* of ρ and is denoted by $\hat{\rho}$; expressed in general form as a function of r it is known as the *maximum-likelihood estimator*. Since the pioneering work of Fisher in the early 20th century it has been known that maximum-likelihood estimators possess certain desirable properties under repeated-sampling (consistency and asymptotic efficiency), and for this reason they have come to occupy a central position in repeated-sampling theories of statistical inference.

However, partly as a reaction to some unsatisfactory features which repeated-sampling theories display, and partly as a defence against a full-blown Bayesian theory of statistical inference, likelihood has been increasingly seen as a fundamental concept enabling hypotheses and parameter values to be compared directly.

The basic notion, introduced by Fisher in 1912 whilst still an undergraduate at Cambridge, is that the likelihood ratio between two hypotheses or parameter values is to be interpreted as the degree to which the data support the one hypothesis against the other. Thus a likelihood ratio of 1 corresponds to indifference between the hypotheses, whereas the maximum-likelihood value of a parameter is the value best-supported by the data, other values being ranked by their lesser likelihoods accordingly.

Such an approach, unsupported by any appeals to repeated-sampling criteria, is ultimately dependent on the primitive notion that, other things being equal, the best hypothesis or parameter-value is the one which would explain what has in fact happened with the highest probability. The strong intuitive appeal of this can be captured by recognizing that it is the value which would lead, on repeated sampling, to a precise repeat of the observed data with the least expected delay. In this sense it offers the best statistical explanation of the data.

In addition to specifying that relative likelihoods measure degrees of support, the likelihood approach requires us to accept that the likelihood contains all the information we can extract from the data about the hypotheses in question on the assumption of the specified statistical model – the so-called *Likelihood Principle*. These two ideas are conveniently expressed together as:

The Likelihood Axiom: Within the framework of a statistical model, *all* the information which the data provide concerning the relative merits of two hypotheses is contained in the likelihood ratio of those hypotheses on the data, and the likelihood ratio is to be interpreted as the degree to which the data support the one hypothesis against the other (Edwards, 1972).

The likelihood approach has many advantages apart from its intuitive appeal. It is easy to apply because the likelihood function is usually simple to obtain analytically or easy to compute numerically. It leads directly to the important statistical concept of sufficiency, and illuminates many of the controversies surrounding repeated-sampling theories of inference, especially those concerned with ancillarity and conditioning. Likelihoods are multiplicative over independent data sets, facilitating the combination of information (for this reason *log-likelihoods*, or *supports*, are often preferred because information is then combined by addition). Most importantly it is compatible with Bayesian statistical inference in that the posterior Bayes distribution for a parameter is, by Bayes' Theorem, found by multiplying the prior distribution by the likelihood function. Thus, where a parameter *distribution* can be countenanced (and this is the Achilles' heel of Bayesian inference) all the information the data contain about the parameter is transmitted via the likelihood function, in accordance with the Likelihood Principle. It is indeed difficult to see why the medium through which such information is conveyed should depend on the purely external question of whether the parameter may be considered to have a probability distribution, and this is another powerful argument in favour of the Likelihood Principle.

There are disadvantages to the likelihood approach, however, though some of these may be attributed to its relatively undeveloped state. It is not always clear how to extract information about a parameter of interest in the presence of other unknown parameters (so-called 'nuisance parameters'), and the comparison of likelihoods for hypotheses with differing degrees of freedom is problematical. This last difficulty is probably associated with the lack of any notion of 'goodness-of-fit' in the likelihood approach, and future work may well remedy this by admitting the need for the incorporation of some repeated-sampling ideas of goodness-of-fit.

In practical terms the adoption of the Likelihood Axiom as the basis of statistical inference often means little more than a re-interpretation of existing practices, since maximum-likelihood estimates are already so widely used, but in terms of theory it brings a great clarification to large areas of statistics, sweeping away many problems associated with, for example, the interpretation of confidence intervals.

Widely-used already in the biological sciences, especially genetics, likelihood is a powerful notion wherever statistical *inference* is required; however, it is not relevant to decision theory and may therefore be expected to have a lesser impact in fields where action, rather than pure inference, is the goal.

In spite of having been widely discussed by statisticians interested in the logic of inference throughout most of the 20th century, the only book devoted exclusively to it is *Likelihood* (Edwards, 1972), which contains comprehensive references to earlier work, especially that of R.A. Fisher; of conventional statistical textbooks only that by Cox and Hinkley (1974) contains relevant material. The history of likelihood is given by Edwards (1974).

BIBLIOGRAPHY

Cox, D.R. and Hinkley, D.V. 1974. *Theoretical Statistics.* London: Chapman & Hall. Distributed in USA by Halsted Press.

Edwards, A.W.F. 1972. *Likelihood.* Cambridge and New York: Cambridge University Press. Paperback edn, 1984.

Edwards, A.W.F. 1974. The history of likelihood. *International Statistical Review* 42, 9–15.

Fisher, R.A. 1912. On an absolute criterion for fitting frequency curves. *Messenger of Mathematics* 41, 155–60.

Fisher, R.A. 1921. On the 'Probable Error' of a coefficient of correlation deduced from a small sample. *Metron* 1(4), 3–32.

129

Martingales

ALAN F. KARR

A martingale is a mathematical model of a fair game, or of some other process that is incrementally random noise. The term, which also denotes part of a horse's harness or a ship's rigging, refers in addition to a gambling system in which every losing bet is doubled; it was introduced into probability theory by J. L. Doob. Among stochastic processes, martingales have particular constancy properties with respect to conditioning. The time parameter may be either discrete or continuous, but since the latter is more important in economic applications, we concentrate on it.

Suppose that on a basic probability space there is defined a *history* $\mathcal{H} = (\mathcal{H}_t)_{t \geqslant 0}$ representing observable events as a function of time. For each t, $\mathcal{H}_t$ is the σ-algebra comprising events determined by observations over the interval $[0, t]$, so that $\mathcal{H}_s \subseteq \mathcal{H}_t$ when $s \leqslant t$. Then a stochastic process $M = (M_t)_{t \geqslant 0}$ is a *martingale* with respect to this history if

(a) For each t, M_t is $\mathcal{H}_t$-measurable (i.e., the state of the process at t is observable over $[0, t]$);

(b) $E[|M_t|] < \infty$ for each t;

(c) The 'martingale property' holds; whenever $s \leqslant t$,

$$E[M_t | \mathcal{H}_s] = M_s. \tag{1}$$

When no history is specified, it is usually understood that $\mathcal{H}_t = \sigma(M_s; s \leqslant t)$.

One specific consequence is that $E[M_t] = E[M_0]$ for each t, so that a martingale is constant in the mean.

Written as

$$E[M_t - M_s | \mathcal{H}_s] = 0, \qquad s \leqslant t,$$

the martingale property implies that the optimal (in the sense of minimum mean squared error, or MMSE) predictor of a future increment of a martingale is zero. Thus, a martingale is indeed a mathematical idealization of a fair game. In some ways this property is clearest in differential form: assuming that the differential

dM_t, which always extends *forward* in time from t, can be defined, then M is a martingale provided that

$$E[dM_t | \mathscr{H}_t] = 0 \qquad (2)$$

for each t. Thus, a martingale can be interpreted as a 'noise' process, in which the MMSE prediction of the differential dM_t is simply zero; in many applications this interpretation becomes quite literal. Martingales are also analogous to the residuals in a regression problem, where what remains unexplained by the model should reduce, ideally, to chance variation.

One can also define *supermartingales*, for which (1) becomes

$$E[M_t | \mathscr{H}_s] \leqslant M_s, \qquad (3)$$

and *submartingales*, in which the sense of the inequality in (3) is reversed. A supermartingale represents a less-than-fair game.

All martingales are in some sense convex combinations of (generalizations of) two key examples, namely the Wiener and Poisson processes. If (W_t) is a Wiener process (Brownian motion), then the processes W_t and $W_t^2 - t$ are both martingales; in fact, these properties characterize the Wiener process. In discrete time, martingales generalize sums of independent, mean zero random variables; the Wiener process, which has independent and stationary increments, is a continuous time counterpart of these partial sum processes.

If (N_t) is a point process (or counting process), with N_t the number of events occurring in $[0, t]$, then under quite general assumptions there exists a nonnegative, predictable (a technical term, which in practice means left-continuous) random process (λ_t), the stochastic intensity of N, such that the process $M_t = N_t = \int_0^t \lambda_s ds$ is a martingale. Since $\lambda_t dt = E[dN_t | \mathscr{H}_t]$, M represents the new information realized as a function of time, and because of this and applications in statistics and state estimation, is known as the innovation martingale. For a Poisson process, which like the Wiener process has independent and stationary increments, the stochastic intensity is deterministic and equal to the rate of the process.

Square integrable martingles are especially important. A martingale M is *square integrable* if $\sup_t E[M_t^2] < \infty$, and in this case there exists a predictable process $\langle M \rangle$, the *predictable variation* of M, such that $M_t^2 - \langle M \rangle_t$ is a martingale. That the predictable variation is incrementally a conditional variance is confirmed by the differential relationship

$$d\langle M \rangle_t = E[(dM_t - E[dM_t | \mathscr{H}_t])^2 | \mathscr{H}_t] = E[(dM_t)^2 | \mathscr{H}_t].$$

Here the second equality holds because M is a martingale.

For the Wiener process $\langle W \rangle_t \equiv t$ in particular, the predictable variation is deterministic, a property characteristic of processes with independent increments. For a point process N with stochastic intensity λ, the predictable variation of the innovation martingale $dM_t = dN_t - \lambda_t dt$ is given by $d\langle M \rangle_t = \lambda_t dt$, which implies that a point process is locally and conditionally Poisson, in the sense that the incremental conditional mean and variance coincide.

Existence of the predictable variation is proved via the Doob-Meyer decomposition theorem, a cornerstone of the theory. The principal theoretical results pertaining to martingales fall into three classes: inequalities, convergence theorems and optimal sampling theorems.

So-called maximal inequalities, which provide upper bounds for probabilities of the form $P\{\sup_{s \leqslant t} |M_s| > c\}$, are not only of inherent interest, but also the key tools for proving convergence theorems. Moreover, these inequalities form the basis of a profound connection between martingales and classical mathematical analysis.

Under various assumptions, given a martingale M there exists a random variable M_∞ such that $M_t \to M_\infty$ almost surely as $t \to \infty$. Convergence obtains both almost surely and in L^1 if M is uniformly integrable, and in this case $M_t = E[M_\infty | \mathscr{H}_t]$ for each t. Not all martingales converge, however; those that fail to converge include, for example, the Wiener process and most innovation martingales.

Optional sampling theorems require the further concept of a stopping time. A random time T (a random variable with values in $[0, \infty]$, interpreted at the time at which some event occurs – with $T = \infty$ corresponding to its not occurring) is a *stopping time* of the history $\mathscr{H}$ if $\{T \leqslant t\} \in \mathscr{H}_t$ for each t. Intuitively, whether a stopping time has occurred by t can be determined from observations over $[0, t]$, and does not require prescient knowledge of the future. The rule by which a gambler quits a game must be a stopping time. Associated with a stopping time T is a σ-algebra $\mathscr{H}_T$ representing events determined by observations over the random time interval $[0, T]$ in the same way that for deterministic t, $\mathscr{H}_t$ corresponds to the interval $[0, t]$.

Martingale property extends from deterministic times to stopping times, and imply in particular that an unfair game cannot be made fair by means of a stopping time. More precisely, if M is a martingale and S and T are stopping times with $S \leqslant T$, then under broad – albeit not universal – conditions,

$$E[M_T | \mathscr{H}_s] = M_s. \tag{4}$$

With $S = 0$ in (4), taking expectations yields $E[M_T] = E[M_0]$. The corresponding result for supermartingales,

$$E[M_T | \mathscr{H}_s] \leqslant M_s, \tag{5}$$

demonstrates that an unfair game cannot be made fair via a stopping time, and dooms gambling systems without infinite resources to eventual failure.

Significant applications of martingales include mathematical statistics (likelihood ratio processes are martingales), queueing theory, filtering and prediction (for example, in signal processing) and economics.

A common feature of these applications is that they involve a random system 'driven' by a martingale in precisely the same manner that a dynamical system is driven by a forcing function. Given a (square integrable) martingale M and a predictable process C fulfilling integrability restrictions, the stochastic integral process

$$(C * M)_t = \int_0^t C_s dM_s$$

is itself a martingale, for which M acts as driving term. (Since M may change state discontinuously, whether endpoints are included in the interval of integration must be specified; in this case, the integral is over the closed interval $[0,t]$.) Construction of stochastic integrals is a difficult, subtle problem: none of the conventional definitions can be applied pathwise (typically the sample paths of M are not of bounded variation), and instead one must employ sophisticated probability theory. The predictable variations satisfy

$$d\langle C*M\rangle_t = C_t^2 d\langle M\rangle_t.$$

Economic applications include, e.g., models of securities prices.

In applications, the inclusion of a 'dt'-integral is often desirable or necessary, leading to *semimartingales*, which are random processes Z of the form

$$Z_t = \int_0^t A_s ds + \int_0^t C_s dM_s, \tag{6}$$

where M is a martingale, C is a predictable process and A fulfils a technical property known as progressive measurability. (Integrability conditions must be satisfied as well.) The differential version of (6) is

$$dZ_t = A_t dt + C_t dM_t. \tag{7}$$

If the processes A and C, rather than specified exogenously, are functionals of Z, then (7) becomes a stochastic differential equation

$$dZ_t = \mu(Z_t)dt + \sigma(Z_t)dM_t, \tag{8}$$

or, more generally,

$$dZ_t = \mu(Z_s; s \leqslant t)dt + \sigma(Z_s; s \leqslant t)dM_t. \tag{9}$$

These equations can be solved–however, not using pathwise methods–under a variety of assumptions, but essentially only when the driving term is a martingale. For example, if the martingale is the Wiener process, solutions to (8) and (9) are known as diffusions and Itô processes, respectively, and the resultant theory as the Itô calculus, after its principal inventor, K. Itô. Alternatively, if M is the innovation martingale associated with a point process N then, *inter alia*, solutions to (8) can be used to construct recursive methods for filtering to extract signals from noise.

BIBLIOGRAPHY

Brémaud, P. 1981. *Point Processes and Queues: Martingale Dynamics*. Berlin: Springer-Verlag.

Hall, P. and Heyde, C.C. 1980. *Martingale Limit Theory and its Applications*. New York: Academic Press.

Kallianpur, G. 1980. *Stochastic Filtering Theory*. New York: Springer-Verlag.

Karr, A.F. 1986. *Point Processes and their Statistical Inference*. New York: Marcel Dekker.

Lipster, R.S. and Shiryayev, A.N. 1978. *Statistics of Random Processes*, I and II. Berlin: Springer-Verlag.

Metivier, M. and Pellaumail, J. 1980. *Stochastic Integration*. New York: Academic Press.

Shiryayev, A.N. 1981. Martingales: recent developments, results and applications. *International Statistical Review* 49, 199–233.

Maximum Likelihood

R.L. BASMANN

Maximum likelihood is primarily a strategy for measuring the relative empirical 'support' that an observed sample X of data affords rival statistical hypotheses and parameter estimates. A statistical model is described by a completely specified form of probability function or probability density function, $f(x; \theta)$, along with ranges for the observable random variable, x, and the parameter vector, θ. (See the example (1d–e) below.) θ may contain more than one parameter element; for instance, if the parent density is the familiar normal density function, then $\theta = (\mu, \sigma^2)$.

For every parameter vector θ, the density $f(x; \theta)$ expresses a distinct *simple* statistical hypothesis. These compose the set H of all admissible simple hypotheses for the inference problem at hand. (H and its proper subsets are called *composite* statistical hypotheses.) In some inference problems one or more parameters in θ are assigned definite numerical values. The method of maximum likelihood *estimation* assigns a definite statistic as estimator of each parameter in θ whose value is not thus preassigned by the problem. In other words maximum likelihood estimation selects a unique *simple* hypothesis from the admissible set (cf. Fisher, 1925, p. 701).

The method of maximum likelihood provides the keystone for a coherent general theory and heuristic of statistical estimation. Other estimation methods exist for selecting a unique simple hypothesis from an admissible set. When other parameter estimates are preferred it is usually because they are believed to be 'closer' in some sense to parent population parameters. However, observed data afford less empirical support to such estimates than to their maximum likelihood counterparts. One merit of the maximum likelihood approach to parameter estimation is that it weighs the 'cost' of getting greater 'closeness' of parameter estimates in terms of the initial support and likelihood of the hypothesis.

Preservation of the empirical information in observations with economy of its organization has been the prime goal of the maximum likelihood approach since its first use by Daniel Bernoulli (1777, pp. 3–23; 1961, pp. 1–18). Bernoulli was concerned by the information loss that besets the casting away of 'outliers' in estimating the mean of several discrepant observations. Modern maximum likelihood theory dates from R.A. Fisher's introduction of the concept of *sufficient statistic* (1920, pp. 768–9). The definite form and paramaters of the parent density create *statistical information* in the observed sample X. In many cases it is possible to compress *all* of this statistical information about $f(x; \theta)$ into a set of *sample statistics* no more numerous than the components of the parameter vector, θ. (Sample statistics are functions of observations in X. See the statistic $x_{[T]}$ below.) Their forms may depend on the form of $f(x; \theta)$, but their values are independent of θ. In such cases, this minimal set of sample statistics, called a minimal sufficient statistic, can always be found by the method of maximum likelihood.

Problems of support for hypotheses are logically prior to estimation. Maximum likelihood shapes the concepts of prior and initial 'support' for statistical hypotheses. Statisticians use concepts of *prior* (to observation) and *posterior support* for statistical hypotheses. 'Prior support' often means the support accumulated through observations taken previously to the present sample X. *Initial support* is the objective support for a statistical hypothesis previous to knowledge of any observations (Edwards, 1972, pp. 35–6). *Posterior support* (after taking the first observations) is the product of the *initial support* and the *likelihood* of the hypothesis on the observations. The dependence of posterior support on initial support and likelihood is expressed formally by *Bayes's formula*.

The crucial step in evaluating posterior support is to interpret the nature of *initial support* and to choose an algebraic form to express it. There are several competing interpretations of the nature of initial support for statistical hypotheses; the likelihood concept of observational support has fashioned all of them to some degree or other. In applications the specific mathematical form of the likelihood function profoundly influences the choice of mathematical form for the initial support.

The classic example is the Rev. Thomas Bayes's billiard table experiment, described in the famous memoir of 1763. The account by Todhunter (1865, Arts 547–9) is followed here. In Bayes's inference problem, the statistician knows the length, a, of the table. The unknown distance, x_0, travelled by the first ball rolled on the table, is the object of inference. Without changing the physical set-up of Bayes' experiment, we let the object of inference be the length, a, of the billiard table. In the present illustration the length, a, of the table, as well as x_0 is unknown to the statistician. The change permits using a single example in several other contexts.

The physical set-up is a table with ends AB and CD. Length of the table is denoted by a. A ball is rolled from AB towards CD, stopping on the table a distance x from AB. Bayes assumed that the chance of the ball stopping no further from AB than x is – expressed in modern notation –

$$\Pr\{X \leqslant x\} = 0, \qquad x < 0,$$

$$= \frac{x}{a}, \qquad 0 \leqslant x < a,$$

$$= 1, \qquad x \geqslant a. \qquad \text{(1a–c)}$$

The probability density function for (1a–c) is

$$f(x; a) = \frac{1}{a}, \qquad 0 < x < 1,$$

$$= 0, \qquad \text{otherwise.} \qquad (1d\text{–}e)$$

Repeated trials yield a series of $T + 1$ observed distances, $x_0, x_1, \ldots, x_T$. The statistician is given the following data: (a) the *hypothesis* (1a–c) and (b) the observations $X = \{x_1, \ldots, x_T\}$. The statistician is not given the observed x_0. Making the additional assumption (also made by Bayes) that outcomes of trials are independent, the statistician constructs the *likelihood function* of a, namely,

$$L(a; X) = a^{-T}, \qquad (2a\text{–}d)$$

where $a \geqslant x_{[T]}$, and

$$x_{[T]} = \max\{x_1, \ldots, x_T\};$$

$$L(a; X) = 0, \qquad \text{otherwise.}$$

The likelihood function is maximum for $a = x_{[T]}$. The value of this statistic is independent of the unknown parameter, a. Maximizing (2a–d) compresses all of the information in the T observations into a single statistic, namely, $x_{[T]}$, which is *minimal sufficient* for a in (1a–e).

The simple hypothesis that is most strongly supported by the observations is that the length of the table is $x_{[T]}$. Let the simple hypothesis, H_0: $a = a_0$ be considered in relation to the most supported alternative hypothesis, H_1: $a = x_{[T]}$. The empirical support by the sample X for H_0 relative to H_1 is, as we have seen above, the ratio of their respective likelihoods, called the *likelihood ratio*. In this example, the likelihood ratio is

$$L_R(a_0, a_1; X) = \left[\frac{a_0}{x_{[T]}} \right]^{-T} \quad \text{for } a_0 \geqslant x_{[T]},$$

$$= 0, \qquad \text{otherwise.} \qquad (3a\text{–}b)$$

On the *likelihood principle* (J. Berger and R. Wolpert, 1984) the likelihood ratio contains *all* of the information that can be extracted from X concerning the relative support an observed X accords any two alternative hypotheses in question. In the present case, the likelihood ratio (3a–b) measures the degree to which the realized observations X support the one hypothesis against the other.

Two important tasks of maximum likelihood are to be discerned in this example: (1) Specific possible future samples of observations tend to become *irrelevant* (I. Hacking, 1965, pp. 148–9), given $x_{[T]}$ in the realized sample X. (2) The *prior support* for a definite set of hypotheses has been diminished by observing the sample X. Once realized, the empirical datum $x_{[T]}$ makes all smaller observations irrelevant to the inference problem. Moreover the realized $x_{[T]}$ makes zero the compound initial and empirical support for any or all hypotheses H_0 for which $a_0 < x_{[T]}$.

In the case of Bayes' billiard table data, most statisticians would agree that, after the observed sample X, the posterior support for any relevant hypothesis about a is given by the posterior density function,

$$g(a; x_{[T]}) = \frac{T(x_{[T]})^T}{a^{T+1}}, \qquad a > x_{[T]},$$

$$= 0, \qquad \text{otherwise.} \qquad (4a-c)$$

This is R.A. Fisher's *fiducial probability* density of the unknown parameter a given the parent distribution function (1a–c); (Fisher, 1956, p. 70). There would not be a consensus in respect of the appropriate rationale for (4a–c) even in this case. However, what is important here is that all approaches make the form of the parent density function $f(x; \theta)$, which determines that of the likelihood function, $L(X; \theta)$, shape the initial support, or prior density, function that is to be used in *Bayes' formula*.

Suppose that, before any observation is reported, a statistician reasons in this fashion:

'The best prediction of x I can make in advance of observation is one of those values of x, (say) x^*, for which the maximum of $f(x; \theta)$ would be reached. So, in advance of observation, let the *initial* support be directly proportional to $f(x^*; \theta)$.'

If the parent density has the normal form with $\theta = \{\mu, \sigma^2\}$, then the initial support would be proportional to $(1/\sigma)$, $\sigma > 0$. In the present case, the same rationale also leads to initial support being made proportional to the parent density (1d), for $a > 0$. Used with the likelihood function (2a–c) in the continuous *Bayes' formula*, it would produce the posterior density (4a–c). Jeffreys (1983, pp. 117–25) proferred a reasoned set of rules for selection of prior density functions that leads to the same choice of initial support function.

The need for brevity in the illustration above precludes description of the more complex problems of interpreting and assigning prior support for interesting econometric hypotheses. However, the reader may usefully consult Zellner (1984, pp. 306–21).

In many statistical investigations the sample statistics that maximize a likelihood function $L(\theta; X)$ converge in probability to the parameters of the parent density function $f(x; \theta)$ for every admissible parameter vector θ. In such cases – important exceptions occur in economic simultaneous equations structures – the maximum likelihood statistic affords a useful starting point in the search for 'best' *estimators* of the parameters in vector θ. This is especially true of minimal sufficient statistics.

Maximum likelihood estimates are often replaced by alternative estimators which in some sense tend to be 'closer' to the parameter to be estimated. One desideratum of 'closeness' is *unbiasedness*, the equality of an estimator's expected value and the 'true' value of the parameter. The best known example is the degrees of freedom adjustment of the maximum likelihood estimator of the variance of *normal* density functions that was initiated by Gauss (1823), Art. 38, p. 47). The maximum likelihood estimate from a sample of T observations is multiplied by the factor $T/(T-1)$. However this achievement of unbiasedness in the estimator is purchased at a cost in terms of likelihood. The relative likelihood of the adjusted estimate of the components of θ is 97 per cent for sample size 10 and slightly less than 99 per cent for sample size 20. Another cost is the greater *mean squared error* of the unbiased variance estimator. F.Y. Edgeworth (1908, pp. 393–394) and R.A. Fisher (1912), p. 159) were critical of this practice.

Achieving unbiasedness at the expense of increased mean squared error is not always viewed as an acceptable improvement of maximum likelihood estimates. The maximum likelihood statistic $x_{[T]}$ for (1a–e), multiplied by $(T+1)/T$, is the *uniformly minimum variance unbiased* estimator of a. This may be regarded as a 'better' estimator than the maximum likelihood estimator $x_{[T]}$. Its mean squared error relative to that of the maximum likelihood estimator decreases from 1 to $1/2$ as the sample size T increases towards infinity. However, the improvement is purchased at a cost of support. Relative support, the likelihood ratio, declines from 50 per cent to slightly less than 37 per cent with increasing sample size. Another useful alternative is the Pitman scale estimator of a, which is obtained by multiplying $x_{[T]}$ by $(T+2)/(T+1)$. A slight bias is accepted, and the mean squared deviation is slightly smaller than the variance of the minimum variance unbiased estimator. The mean squared error of the scale estimator relative to that of the maximum likelihood estimator decreases from $3/4$ to $1/2$ as T increases indefinitely. However, the likelihood support for the Pitman estimator relative to the maximum likelihood estimator declines from 66.7 per cent to slightly less than 37 per cent with increasing sample size.

Many advantages attend statistical inference based on maximum likelihood and the coherent estimation theory it makes possible. However, fragmentary specification of parent density functions, commonly resorted to in many estimation problems, precludes the use of maximum likelihood methods. In such circumstances the various desiderata, unbiasedness, minimum variance (in restricted classes of estimators), and 'large-sample' efficiency call for ad hoc justification in the subject matter sciences themselves.

BIBLIOGRAPHY

Berger, J. and Wolpert, R. 1984. *The Likelihood Principle*. Institute of Mathematical Statistics Monograph Series, Haywood, Cal.

Bernoulli, D. 1777. Diiudicatio maxime probabilis plurium obferuationum difcrepantium atque verificillima inductio inde formanda. In *Acta Academiae Scientiarum Imperialis Petropolitanae*, Petropoli: Typis Academiae Scientiarum, 3–33. Reprinted 1961, with foreword by M.G. Kendall and observations by L. Euler in *Biometrika* 48, 1–18.

Edgeworth, F. 1908. On the probable errors of frequency constants. *Journal of the Royal Statistical Society* 71, June, 381–97.

Edwards, A.W.F. 1972. *Likelihood*. Cambridge and New York: Cambridge University Press.

Fisher, R.A. 1912. On an absolute criterion for fitting frequency curves. *Messenger of Mathematics* 41, 155–60.

Fisher, R.A. 1920. A mathematical examination of the methods of determining the accuracy of an observation by the mean error, and by the mean square error. *Monthly Notices of the Royal Astronomical Society* 80, 758–70.

Fisher, R.A. 1925. Theory of statistical estimation. *Proceedings of the Cambridge Philosophical Society* 22, 700–25.

Fisher, R.A. 1956. *Statistical Methods and Scientific Inference*. Edinburgh and London: Oliver & Boyd; New York: Hafner Publishing Company.

Gauss, C.F. 1823. *Theoria Combinationis Observationum Erroribus Minimis Obnoxiae*. Gottingen: Apud Henricum Dieterich.

Hacking, I. 1965. *Logic of Statistical Inference*. Cambridge: Cambridge University Press.

Jeffreys, H. 1983. *Theory of Probability*. 3rd edn, Oxford: Clarendon Press.

Todhunter, I. 1865. *A History of the Mathematical Theory of Probability*. Cambridge and London: Macmillan.

Zellner, A. 1984. *Basic Issues in Econometrics*. Chicago: University of Chicago Press.

Meaningfulness and Invariance

LOUIS NARENS AND R. DUNCAN LUCE

Few disavow the principle that scientific propositions should be meaningful in the sense of asserting something that is verifiable or falsifiable about the qualitative, empirical situation under discussion. What makes this principle tricky to apply in practice is that much of what is said is formulated not as simple assertions about empirical events – such as a certain object sinks when placed in water – but as laws formulated in rather abstract, often mathematical, terms. It is not always apparent exactly what class of qualitative observations corresponds to such (often numerical) laws. Theories of meaningfulness are methods for investigating such matters, and invariance concepts are their primary tools.

The problem of meaningfulness, which has been around since the inception of mathematical science in ancient times, has proved to be difficult and subtle; even today it has not been satisfactorily resolved. This article surveys some of the current ideas about it and illustrates, through examples, some of its uses. The presentation requires some elementary technical concepts of measurement theory (such as representation, scale type, etc.), which are below explained in MEASUREMENT.

INTUITIVE FORMULATION AND EXAMPLES

The following example, taken from Suppes and Zinnes (1963), nicely illustrates part of the problem in a very elementary way. Which of the following four sentences are meaningful?

(1) Stendhal weighed 150 on 2 September 1839.

(2) The ratio of Stendahl's weight of Jane Austen's on 3 July 1814 ˌas 1.42.

(3) The ratio of the maximum temperature today to the maximum temperature yesterday is 1.10.

(4) The ratio of the difference between today's and yesterday's maximum temperature to the difference between today's and tomorrow's maximum temperature will be 0.95. Suppose that weight is measured in terms of the ratio

140

scale $\mathscr{W}$ (which includes among its representations the pound and kilogram representations and all those obtained by just a change of unit) and that temperature is measured by the interval scale $\mathscr{T}$ (which includes the Fahrenheit and Celsius representations). Then Statement (2) is meaningful, since with respect to each representation in $\mathscr{W}$ it says the same thing, i.e., its truth value is the same no matter which representation in $\mathscr{W}$ is used to measure weight. That is not true for Statement (1), because (1) is true for exactly one representation in $\mathscr{W}$ and false for all of the rest. Thus we say that (1) is 'meaningless'. Similarly, (4) is meaningful with respect to $\mathscr{T}$, but (3) is not.

The somewhat intuitive concept of meaningfulness suggested by these examples is usually stated as follows: Suppose a qualitative or empirical attibute is measured by a scale $\mathscr{S}$. Then a numerical statement involving values of the representation is said to be *meaningful* if and only if its truth (or falsity) is constant no matter which representation in $\mathscr{S}$ is used to assign numbers to the attribute. There are obvious formal difficulties with this definition, for example the concept of 'numerical statement' is not a precise one. More seriously, it is unclear under what conditions this is the 'right definition' of meaningfulness, for it does not always lead to correct results in some well-understood and non-controversial situations. Nevertheless, it is the concept most frequently employed in the literature, and invoking it often provides insight into the correct way of handling a quantitative situation – as the following still elementary but somewhat less obvious example shows.

Consider a situation where M persons rate N objects (e.g. M judges judging N contestants in a sporting event). For simplicity, assume person i rates objects according to the ratio scale $\mathscr{R}_i$. The problem is to find an ordering on the N objects that aggregates in a reasonable way the persons' judgements. It will be assumed that their judgements cannot be coordinated in such a way that, for $\mathscr{R}_i$ in $\mathscr{R}_i$ and R_j in $\mathscr{R}_j$, meaning can be given to the assertion $R_i = R_j$. (The difficulties underlying such a coordination are essentially those that arise in attempting to compare individual utility functions. The latter problem – 'the interpersonal comparison of utilities' – has been much discussed in the literature, as for example in Narens and Luce (1983) and Sen (1979). It is generally conceived that there are great, if not insurmountable, difficulties in carrying out such comparisons.) Any rule that does not involve coordination can be formulated as follows: First, it is a function F that assigns to an object the value $F(r_1, \ldots r_M)$ whenever person i assigns the number r_i to the object. Second, object a is ranked just as high as b if and only if the value assigned by F to a is at least as great as that assigned by F to b. In practice F is often taken to be the arithmetic mean of the ratings $r_1, \ldots r_M$ (e.g. Pickering et al., 1973). Observe, however, that this choice of F, in general, produces a non-meaningful ranking of objects, as is shown in the following spacial case: Suppose $M = 2$ and, for $i = 1, 2$, R_i is person's i representation that is being used for generating ratings, and $R_1(a) = 2$, $R_1(b) = 3$, $R_2(a) = 3$, and $R_2(b) = 1$. Then the arithmetical mean of the ratings of a, 2.5, is greater than that for b, 2, and thus a is ranked above b. However, meaningfulness requires the same order if any other representations of persons 1 and 2 rating scales are used, for example, $10R_1$ and $2R_2$. But for this choice of representations, the arithmetic mean of a, 13, is less than that of b, 16, and thus b is ranked higher than a. It is easy to check that the geometrical mean,

$$F(r_1, \ldots, r_M) = (r_1, \ldots, r_M)^{1/M},$$

gives rise to a meaningful rule for ranking objects. It can be shown under plausible conditions that all other meaningful rules give rise to the same ranking as given by the geometric mean.

More subtle applications of the above concept of meaningfulness have been given, and the interested reader should consult Batchelder (1985) and Roberts (1985) for a wide range of social science examples.

In some contexts, this concept of meaningfulness presents certain technical difficulties that require some modification in the definition of meaningfulness (e.g., see Roberts and Franke, 1976, and Falmagne and Narens, 1983).

THEORIES OF MEANINGFULNESS BASED ON INVARIANCE

The above approach to meaningfulness lacks a serious account as to why it is a good concept of meaningfulness; that is, it lacks a sound theory as to why it should yield correct results. Formulating a serious account is difficult. One tack (Krantz et al., 1971; Luce, 1978; Narens, 1981) is to observe that if meaningfulness expresses valid qualitative relationships, then it must correspond to something purely qualitative, and therefore it should have a purely qualitative description. A long tradition in mathematics for formulating intrinsic qualitative relationships, one going back at least to 19th-century geometry and the famous Erlanger Programme of Felix Klein, is to do so in terms of transformations that leave the situation invariant. Formally, let $\mathscr{X}$ be the given qualitative situation (e.g. a relational structure), and K be a set of isomorphisms of $\mathscr{X}$ into itself. A qualitative relation $R(x_1, \ldots, x_n)$ is said to be K-*invariant* if and only if for each $x_1, \ldots, x_n$ in the domain of $\mathscr{X}$ and each f in K,

$$R(x_1, \ldots, x_n) \quad \text{iff} \quad R[f(x_1), \ldots, f(x_n)].$$

In mathematics, 'intrinsic' has usually been associated with a special type of K-invariance, namely when K is the group (under function composition) of all isomorphisms of $\mathscr{X}$ *onto* itself. These isomorphisms are called *automorphisms*, and this type of invariance is called *automorphism invariance*. The automorphism group has many desirable mathematical properties, including, of course, that the primitive relations that define the qualitative situation are all automorphism invariant. For measurement, it often seems appropriate to use the larger set of all isomorphisms of $\mathscr{X}$ *into* itself, the $1-1$ *endomorphisms*. The resulting invariance is called *endomorphism invariance*. One theory of meaningfulness identifies qualitative meaningfulness with autmorphism invariance, and another identifies it with endomorphism invariance. Both are based on structure preserving concepts and so relate readily to measurement concerns, since measurement, at least theoretically, is based upon related structure preserving concepts. Although little philosophical justification exists for either of these concepts, they, and especially automorphism meaningfulness, appear to lead to many correct results. For example, automorphism meaningfulness provides a basis of dimensional analysis (as described below). Under these theories, quantitative forms of meaningfulness result from forming images of qualitative meaningful relations by proper means of measurement.

DIMENSIONAL ANALYSIS

In at least four areas of science invariance ideas of meaningfulness have played a fundamental and major role: dimensional analysis in classical physics, the question of meaningful statistical assertions, relativistic physics, and mathematics (especially geometry). Since some applications of the first two have been to economics and other social sciences (de Jong, 1967; Roberts 1985), a brief summary of their main ideas is provided.

Dimensional analysis involves two major concepts: a structure of physical variables – those quantities for which units can be specified – represented as a finite dimensional, multiplicative vector space, and the assumption that any physical law that can be formulated as a relation among variables and constants represented in this space must satisfy an invariance property, called 'dimensional invariance', which is described below. When fully articulated, these two propositions imply Buckingham's (1914) theorem: any such law can be expressed as a function of one or more dimensionless quantities (i.e. real numbers), each of which is a product of powers of some of the variables involved.

Typical applications. Accepting for the moment the correctness of these two major premises of dimensional analysis, consider how they may be used. Without question, the simplest and most widespread use is to check an equation for dimensional consistency. Only quantities with the same dimensions can be added or set equal to one another. An equation failing this property simply cannot describe anything of empirical significance if dimensional invariance is a valid property of physical laws. For a discussion with some economic examples, see Osborne (1978). Most scientists have employed such checks whether or not they are aware of dimensional analysis.

There is, in addition, a much more powerful application of the method. Suppose a process or system is sufficiently well understood so that all of the relevant variables are known. This is a very strong assumption, one we are often unsure of, especially in incompletely developed areas of science. It is, however, met in physical situations when we have a full understanding of the laws at work but are, none the less, unable to solve the resulting equations. In such cases, by using elementary methods of linear algebra, it is possible systematically to develop a set of independent dimensionless combinations of the relevant variables. In that case, Buckingham's theorem tells us that the law is some unspecified function of these dimensionless quantities. If one of the variables of the system is viewed as the dependent one and if it appears in just one of the dimensionless combinations, then it can be solved for. This results in an expression for the dependent variable that is a product of powers of the other variables in that dimensionless combination times an unspecified function of all the other dimensionless quantities. For example, as has been shown in a number of books on the subject, it is easy to derive from dimensional considerations that the lift and drag of an idealized airfoil must be proportional to the square of the velocity, to the density of the air, to the area of the airfoil, to an explicit function of the angle of attack, and to an unknown function of a dimensionless quantity called the 'Reynolds' number'. Many other examples of the effective use of these techniques are routinely found in texts on engineering and applied physics (e.g. Sedov, 1959).

Constructing the dimensional structure. In order to understand the method well enough to see how applicable it may be beyond physics, two issues need to be addressed: where does the vector space representation come from, and why should we postulate that laws are dimensionally invariant? The latter question has attracted more attention than the former, although the concept of dimensional invariance becomes rather transparent once the qualitative underpinnings of the structure of quantities are worked out.

The basic tying together of the dimensions of classical physics are measurement structures involving triples of interrelated attributes. These consist of a conjoint structure, say $\langle A \times P, \gtrsim \rangle$, that has at least one operation on either A, P, or $A \times P$ such that it together with the ordering induced on that component by $\gtrsim$ forms a positive concatenation structure with a ratio scale representation. Further, the operation and conjoint structure are interconnected by a qualitative distribution law. For example, if the operation $\circ$ is on A, then it is said to be *distributive* if, for a, b, c, d in A and p, q in P, whenever $(a, p) \sim (c, q)$ and $(b, p) \sim (d, p)$, then $(a \circ b, p) \sim (c \circ d, q)$. (This definition was given independently by Narens and Luce (1976) and Ramsay (1976).) For example, if A represents a set of masses and P a set of velocities and the ordering is by the amount of kinetic energy, then the usual concatenation operation for masses is distributive in this triple. Under plausible solvability and Archimedean conditions, it can be shown (Narens and Luce, 1976; Luce and Narens, 1985; Narens, 1985) that the conjoint ordering has a representation in terms of products of powers of the ratio scale representations of the operations. This fact is reflected in the ordinary pattern of units as products of powers of others, for example the unit of energy is gm^2/t^2. The laws captured by these distributive triples are the most elementary ones that relate several dimensions.

If there are sufficiently many of these distributive triples and if they are sufficiently redundant so that there is a finite basis to the structure, then they can be simultaneously represented numerically as a finite dimensional, multiplicative vector space (Krantz et al., 1971; Luce, 1978; Roberts, 1980). Three major things are used to accomplish this development: a theory of ratio scale representations of concatenation structures, a theory of representations of conjoint structures, and the qualitative concept of an operation being distributive in the conjoint structure. Most traditional accounts attempt to make do only with the first of

144

these elements, usually for the special case of extensive structures, and as a result it is obscure where the rest of the structure comes from.

Relation to meaningfulness. It is plausible that laws formulated within this structure should be meaningful in the sense of invariance under automorphisms of the structure. By a well-known theorem of mathematical logic, it can be shown that this is true of any law that can be defined through (first-order) predicate logic in terms of the primitive relations of the structure. Luce (1978; see also Roberts, 1980) showed that automorphism invariance is equivalent to the following numerical requirement known as dimensional invariance: suppose the numerical law admits a particular combination of values of the relevant variables as a possible configuration of the system in question – that is, these values satisfy the law governing the system. Suppose, further, that an admissible transformation is carried out on these values in the sense that separate admissible transformations are made on each basis variable of the multiplicative vector space and all other variables are transformed as prescribed by that space. Then, according to dimensional invariance, when the combination of values satisfying the law is subject to an admissible dimensional transformation of the sort described, the transformed values also satisfy the law. (Ramsay (1976), in essence, defined 'dimensional invariance' as automorphism invariance, and he showed that distribution of a bisymmetric operation is sufficient to ensure automorphism invariance. He did not, however, show that his conditions imply a multiplicative vector space of units or the product of powers representation. That means that he did not show that his conditions imply the usual concept of dimensional invariance that was described above.)

There seems to be a wide consensus within the physical community that physical laws should be dimensionally invariant, although that community is not very clear – indeed, there is disagreement – as to why this is the case. Attempts have been made to argue for this property on a priori grounds and as a consequence of a concept of physical similarity (Buckingham, 1914; Bridgman, 1931; Causey, 1969; Luce, 1971; Osborne, 1978), but none of these seem as satisfactory as arguing for it in terms of automorphism invariance, which appears to be a more fundamental concept, one that is stated in purely qualitative terms. Thus, it seems to the authors that equivalence to automorphism invariance provides a more rigorous and better foundation for dimensional analysis than do the ones customarily given by physicists and engineers.

Extension beyond classical physics. The current theories for dimensional analysis fail to account adequately for measurements of either relativistic or quantum quantities. For example, at the representational level, relativistic velocity seems to work perfectly well since it continues to be distance divided by time, but because it is a bounded structure and its 'addition' operation is not distributive in the conjoint structure relating distance, velocity, and duration, the existing theorems do not account for why it can be included in the overall dimensional structure. The variables of quantum theory are far more perplexing, and little has been done to incorporate them in such a structure.

A question of natural interest to economists is whether dimensional methods are applicable to their sort of problems. An attempt to show that they are is given in de Jong (1967) and Osborne (1978) (also, see Roberts, 1985). Certainly there are some uses, such as the verification of dimensional consistency of equations. What seems to be lacking in the economic situation, however, is a sufficiently rich set of elementary laws of the type captured as distributive triples in order to set up a full vector space of dimensions like the one found in physics. A similar observation holds for other areas such as psychophysics, which is perhaps as close as any other to creating such a structure. It appears that additional basic work on these measurement questions is needed before it will be possible to bring to bear the full power of these highly useful methods to economics.

Input–output functions. A part of the theory, however, has proved to be promising for both economic and other social science concerns. This involves laws that describe input–output relations among variables of known scale types. In these cases, dimensional invariance simply says that the function relating them must have the following homogeneity property: The effect of admissible scale transformations on the input (independent) variables results in an admissible transformation on the output (dependent) variable. Such a homogeneity condition imposes severe restrictions on the form of the function when all of the input variables are dimensionally independent and even when they are all constrained to have the same dimension (Falmagne and Narens, 1983; Luce, 1959). For example, if there is just one ratio scale input, a ratio scale output, and a strictly increasing output function, then the function must be proportional to a power of the independent variable; if the output is an interval scale, then logarithmic functions can also arise. Such limitations have proved effective in some psychological applications (Luce, 1959; Osborne, 1970, 1976; Iverson and Pavel, 1981; Falmagne, 1985; Roberts, 1985), and they constitute a substantial part of de Jong's (1967) book.

It must be recognized, however, that they really are a presumed application of dimensional analysis in areas that do not have enough structure to justify its use, that is, dimensional invariance is assumed for these special cases without having a theory as to why this should be so. Moreover, one of two very strong assumptions is involved, namely that either all of the independent variables are dimensionally independent or they all have the same dimension.

MEANINGFULNESS AND STATISTICS

Another area of importance to social scientists in which invariance notions are believed to be relevant is the application of statistics to numerical data. The role of measurement considerations in statistics and of invariance under admissible scale transformations was first emphasized by Stevens (1946, 1951); this view quickly became popularized in numerous textbooks, and it resulted in extensive debates in the literature. Continued disagreement exists, mainly created by confusion arising from the following simple facts: measurement scales are characterized by groups of admissible transformations of the real numbers.

Statistical distributions exhibit certain invariances under appropriate transformation groups, often the same groups (especially the affine transformations) that arise from measurement considerations. Because of this, some have concluded that the suitability of a statistical test is determined in part by whether or not the measurement and distribution groups are the same. Thus, it is said that one may be able to apply a test, such as a *t*-test, that rests on the Gaussian distribution to ratio or interval scale data, but surely not to ordinal data, because the Gaussian is invariant under the group of affine transformations – which arises in both the ratio and interval case but not in the ordinal one. Neither half of the assertion is correct: first, a significance test should be applied only when its distributional assumptions are met, and they may very well hold for some particular representation of ordinal data. And, second, a specific distributional assumption may well not be met by data arising from ratio scale measurement. For example, reaction times, being times, are measured on a ratio scale, but they are rarely well approximated by a Gaussian distribution.

What is true, however, is that any proposition (hypothesis) that one plans to put to statistical test or to use in estimation had better be meaningful with respect to the scale used for the measurements. In general, it is not meaningful to assert that two means are equal when the quantities are measured by an ordinal scale, because equality of means is not invariant under strictly increasing transformations. Thus, no matter what distribution holds and no matter what test is performed, the result may not be meaningful because the hypothesis is not. In particular, if an hypothesis is about the measurement structure itself, for example that the representation is additive over a concatenation operation, then it is essential that the hypothesis be automorphism invariant and that, moreover, the hypotheses of the statistical test be met without going outside the transformations of the measurement representation.

BIBLIOGRAPHY

Batchelder, W.H. 1985. Inferring meaningful global network properties from individual actors' measurement scales. In *Research Methods in Social Networks*, ed. L. Freeman, D. White and A.K. Romney, Chicago: Nelson Hall.

Bridgman, P. 1931. *Dimensional Analysis*. New Haven: Yale University Press.

Buckingham, E. 1914. On physically similar systems: illustrations of the use of dimensional equations. *Physical Review* 4(4), 345–76.

Causey, R.L. 1969. Derived measurement, dimensions, and dimensional analysis. *Philosophy of Science* 36, 252–70.

de Jong, F.J. 1967. *Dimensional Analysis for Economists*. Amsterdam: North-Holland.

Falmagne, J.-C. 1985. *Elements of Psychophysical Theory*. New York: Cambridge University Press.

Falmagne, J-C. and Narens, L. 1983. Sales and meaningfulness of quantitative laws. *Synthese* 55, 287–325.

Iverson, G.J. and Pavel, M. 1981. Invariant properties of masking phenomena in psycho-acoustics and their theoretical consequences. In *Symposium in Applied Mathematics of AMS-SIAM*, ed. S. Grossberg, Providence, RI: American Mathematical Society, Vol. 13, 17–24.

Krantz, D.H., Luce, R.D., Suppes, P. and Tversky, A. 1971. *Foundations of Measurement*. Vol. 1, New York: Academic Press.

Luce, R.D. 1959. On the possible psychophysical laws. *Psychological Review* 66(2), 81–95.

Luce, R.D. 1964. A generalization of a theorem of dimensional analysis. *Journal of Mathematical Psychology* 1(2), 278–84.

Luce, R.D. 1971. Similar systems and dimensionally invariant laws. *Philosophy of Science* 38(2), 157–69.

Luce, R.D. 1978. Dimensionally invariant numerical laws correspond to meaningful qualitative relations. *Philosophy of Science* 45(1), 1–16.

Luce, R.D. and Narens, L. 1985. Classification of concatenation measurement structures according to scale type. *Journal of Mathematical Psychology* 29(1), 1–72.

Narens, L. 1981. A general theory of ratio scalability with remarks about the measurement-theoretic concept of meaningfulness. *Theory and Decision* 13(1), 1–70.

Narens, L. 1985. *Abstract Measurement Theory*. Cambridge, Mass.: MIT Press.

Narens, L. and Luce, R.D. 1976. The algebra of measurement. *Journal of Pure and Applied Algebra* 8, 197–233.

Narens, L. and Luce, R.D. 1983. How we may have been misled into believing in the interpersonal comparability of utility. *Theory and Decision* 15, 247–60.

Osborne, D.K. 1970. Further extensions of a theorem of dimensional analysis. *Journal of Mathematical Psychology* 7(2), 236–42.

Osborne, D.K. 1976. Unified theory of derived measurement. *Synthese* 33, 455–81.

Osborne, D.K. 1978. On dimensional invariance. *Quality and Quantity* 12(1), 75–89.

Pfanzagl, J. 1968. *Theory of Measurement*. New York: Wiley. 2nd edn, Vienna: Physica, 1971.

Pickering, J.F., Harrison, J.A. and Cohen, C.D. 1973. Identification and measurement of consumer confidence: methodology and some preliminary results. *Journal of the Royal Statistical Society*, Series A 136(1), 43–63.

Ramsay, J.O. 1976. Algebraic representation in the physical and behavioral sciences. *Synthese* 33(2–4), 419–53.

Roberts, F.S. 1980. On Luce's theory of meaningfulness. *Philosophy of Science* 47(3), 424–33.

Roberts, F.S. 1985. Applications of the theory of meaningfulness to psychology. *Journal of Mathematical Psychology* 229(3), 311–32.

Roberts, F.S. and Franke, C.H. 1976. On the theory of uniqueness in measurement. *Journal of Mathematical Psychology* 14(3), 211–18.

Sedov, L.I. 1959. *Similarity and Dimensional Methods in Mechanics*. New York: Academic Press. English translation by M. Holt and M. Friedman of the 1956 Russian edn.

Sen, A. 1979. Interpersonal comparisons of welfare. In *Economics and Human Welfare*, ed. M. Boskin, New York: Academic Press.

Stevens, S.S. 1946. On the theory of scales of measurement. *Science* 103, 677–80.

Stevens, S.S. 1951. Mathematics, measurement and psychophysics. In *Handbook of Experimental Psychology*, ed. S.S. Stevens, New York: Wiley.

Suppes, P. and Zinnes, J.L. 1963. Basic measurement theory. In *Handbook of Mathematical Psychology*, Vol. 1, ed. R.D. Luce, R.R. Bush and E. Galanter, New York: Wiley.

Mean Value

SOO HONG CHEW

What is mean value? Conventional wisdom tells us that it represents, typifies or in some way measures the central tendency of a distribution. Familiar examples of mean value include the median, mode, arithmetic mean, geometric mean, harmonic mean and root-mean-square or more generally the rth root of the rth moment of a positive random variable.

A mean value arises when the following question is asked. In examining the 'effect' due to a given distribution of some quantity of interest, what value if *equally distributed* would result in the same overall effect? The *mean moon*, for example, is a fictitious moon which moves around the earth with a uniform speed and in the same time as the real moon. Typically, the effect of interest is measured by an index corresponding to the context of application. The most common measure – the sum of the quantities concerned – gives rise to the arithmetic mean.

CERTAINTY EQUIVALENCE AND REPRESENTATIVE INCOME. The arithmetic mean was long considered a good rule-of-thumb for ordering risky prospects. In what has come to be known as the St Petersburg paradox, individuals are offered a lottery that pays 2^n dollars if in a sequence of independent coin tosses, the first head appears on the nth trial. While its expected payoff is infinite, few would find it to be worth much more than a few dollars. To account for this discrepancy, Bernoulli proposed in 1738 the expectation of a 'moral worth' function as an alternative to the arithmetic mean. In particular, he adopted a logarithmic model of moral worth which yields a finite geometric mean as the *certainty equivalence* – the sure outcome which is as attractive as a given monetary lottery – of the St Petersburg lottery.

In the literature on income inequality, the concept of an *equally-distributed-equivalent* or *representative* income was proposed by Kolm (1969), Atkinson (1970) and Sen (1973). The representative income is defined to be the level of income which if distributed equally would result in the same overall level of social welfare as the existing income distribution. Given a representative income

m as a mean value, there is a corresponding *relative (absolute) index of income inequality* I_R (I_A) given by:

$$I_R(F) = 1 - \frac{m(F)}{\mu(F)}, \tag{1}$$

and

$$I_A(F) = \mu(F) - m(F), \tag{2}$$

where $\mu(F)$ refers to the arithmetic mean of the given income distribution F. Most measures of income inequality can be written in terms of expression (1) or (2).

EXAMPLES OF QUASILINEAR MEANS. For a vector $x = (x_1, \ldots, x_N)$, a natural class of effect indices is given by the sum $\Sigma_{i=1}^N v(x_i)$ of a continuous and strictly monotone function v of the x_i's. The resulting mean value m_v called the *quasilinear mean* is given by:

$$v[m_v(x)] = \frac{1}{N} \sum_{i=1}^N v(x_i). \tag{3}$$

Examples of mean values which are special cases of (3) include the earlier mentioned arithmetic mean ($v \equiv x$), geometric mean ($v \equiv \log x$), harmonic mean ($v \equiv 1/x$), root-mean-square ($v \equiv x^2$) and the rth moment mean ($v \equiv x^r$).

For a probability distribution function F, the quasilinear mean $m_v(F)$ is given by:

$$m_v(F) = v^{-1}\left[\int v(x) \, dF(x)\right]. \tag{4}$$

The first axiomatic characterization of (3) was proved in 1930 by Nagumo and Kolmogorov independently. De Finetti extended their result in the following year to (4) for simple (finite) probability distributions on a compact interval. Characteristic properties of the quasilinear mean will be discussed under the next heading.

As a model of certainty equivalence, the quasilinear mean corresponds to the *expected utility hypothesis* with v as the von Neumann–Morgenstern utility function. In this sense, Ramsey (1926) and von Neumann and Morgenstern (1947) provided other independent axiomatizations of the quasilinear mean.

It was suggested in a pioneering paper of Dalton (1920) that any measure of income inequality has an underlying social welfare function, which he further assumed to be additively separable (i.e. utilitarian) and symmetric. Dalton's approach was made precise in Atkinson (1970) which is equivalent to adopting the quasilinear mean as a model of the representative income. Atkinson considered specifically the one-parameter class of relative measures based on the rth moment mean m_r as the representative income.

PROPERTIES OF THE QUASILINEAR MEAN. We represent the given distribution of the quantity of interest by a probability distribution function of an interval J of the real line $\mathbb{R}$. The *support* of a probability distribution function F denoted by supp(F) consists of each point x such that every open set around x has positive mass. The smallest closed interval containing supp(F) is denoted by conv supp(F). The degenerate probability distribution function whose support consists of a single point x is denoted by δ_x. A vector $(x_1, \ldots, x_N) \in J^n$ can be represented as a simple probability distribution $\Sigma_{i=1}^N (1/N)\delta_{x_i}$ with equal probability $1/N$ assigned to each outcome x_i. We denote by $x_\uparrow = (x_{[1]}, \ldots, x_{[N]})$, the *increasing rearrangement* of $x = (x_1, \ldots, x_N)$.

A *mean value* is defined to be any functional on D_J satisfying the following fundamental property.

Property I (Intermediate Value Property):

$\forall F \in D_J, m(F) \in$ conv supp(F).

Property I tells us that the mean value of a probability distribution function lies between its lowest realizable outcome and its highest realizable outcome. Consequently, it implies the following:

Property SC (Consistency with Sure Outcomes):

$\forall x \in J, m(\delta_x) = x$.

We will present additional properties of the quasilinear mean below. One such property is consistency with the *first-degree stochastic dominance* partial order denoted by $\leqslant^1$.

Property FSD (First-Degree Stochastic Dominance):

$\forall F, G \in D_J, F \leqslant^1 G$ implies that $m(F) \leqslant m(G)$.

Property I is implied by Property FSD which is often taken to be a universal property of mean values. While it is appealing in the certainty equivalence context, there are other mean values that do not necessarily satisfy this property.

The following is a characteristic property of the quasilinear mean.

Property Q (Quasilinearity or Substitution): $\forall F, G, H \in D_J$, and $\forall \beta \in (0, 1)$, $m(F) = m(G) \Rightarrow$

$m(\beta F + [1 - \beta]H) = m(\beta G + [1 - \beta]H)$.

A sequence of probability distributions $\{F_n\} \subset D_J$ is said to *converge in distribution* (or *weakly converge*) to a probability distribution $F \in D_J$ denoted by

$$F_n \xrightarrow{\mathcal{D}} F$$

if $F_n(x) \to F(x) \forall x$ such that F is continuous at x. It is known that

$$F_n \xrightarrow{\mathcal{D}} F \quad \text{if and only if} \quad \int_J f \, dF_n \to \int_J f \, dF$$

for every bounded and continuous function f on J. The following is a definition of continuity often used in utility theory and in statistics.

Property CD (Continuity in Distribution):

$$\text{If } F_n \xrightarrow{\mathcal{D}} F, \quad \text{then} \quad m(F_n) \to m(F).$$

Note that the quasilinear mean is continuous in the above sense if and only if v is bounded on J. This rules out the arithmetic mean among others as being continuous. The quasilinear mean, however, always satisfies the following weaker notions of continuity.

Property CC (Compact Continuity): If

$$\{F_n\}_{n=0}^{\infty} \subset D_J \xrightarrow{\mathcal{D}} F \in D_J$$

and $\text{supp}(F_n) \subset K$ for some compact $K \subset J$, then

$$m(F) = \text{Lim}_{n \to \infty} m(F_n).$$

The truncation of a probability distribution $F \in D_J$ by an interval $K \subset J$ is denoted by F_K.

Property E (Extension): $\forall F \in D_J$, $m(F) = \text{Lim}_{n \to \infty} m(F_{K_n})$ for any increasing family of compact sets $\{K_n\}$ whose limit is J.

Property CC and Property E and implied by Property CD. Property CC essentially requires Property CD to hold on D_K for any compact interval $K \subset J$. Property E defines the mean value of a distribution F without compact support by the limit of the sequence of mean values of the truncated distributions F_{K_n} if the limit does not depend on the particular choice of the K_n. In this sense, the arithmetic mean of the Cauchy distribution which has unbounded support does not exist.

In the income inequality literature, a distribution is more unequal than another if the more equal distribution is obtained as a result of a sequence of transfers from a higher income individual to a lower income individual. This idea was captured by Hardy, Littlewood and Polya's (1934) definition of the majorization partial order and the corresponding definition of Schur-concavity. In utility theory, Rothschild and Stiglitz (1970) extended the above to the notion of *mean-preserving-increase* in risk on $D_{[A, B]}$. More generally, we say that a distribution G *dominates* another distribution F in the *second degree*, denoted by $G \geqslant^2 F$, if $\forall x \in J$,

$$\int_{-\infty}^{x} [G(z) - F(z)] \, dz \leqslant 0,$$

with equality as x approaches ∞. In this sense, the dominated distribution is more risky (less equal) than G. Consider:

Property SSD (Second-Degree Stochastic Dominance): $\forall F, G \in D_J$, $F \geqslant^2 G$ implies that $m(F) \geqslant m(G)$.

It is known that m_v satisfies the above if and only if v is concave. In the sequel, we will examine other mean values that possess some of the properties discussed here. The mode specifically does not satisfy any of the properties except Property I.

152

WEIGHTED QUASILINEAR MEANS. In addition to the continuous and strictly monotone v function in m_v, we introduce a non-vanishing *weighting* function w. For each x_i in a vector $x \in J^N$, we assign a weight of $w(x_i)$. The resulting mean value m_{vw} called the *weighted quasilinear mean* is given by:

$$v[m_{vw}(x)] \sum_{i=1}^{N} w(x_i) = \sum_{i=1}^{N} v(x_i) w(x_i). \tag{5}$$

For $F \in D_J$, m_{vw} can be expressed as:

$$\int_J \{v(x) - v[m_{vw}(F)]\} w(x) \, dF(x) = 0. \tag{6}$$

An example of m_{vw} in mechanics is the following. For a simple pendulum of length L, the period of vibration T is given by $(2\pi/g^{1/2})L^{1/2}$, where g is the acceleration due to gravity. In general, the period of vibration of a pendulum with radial mass distribution F is given by the same formula except that L is now the ratio of the second moment (moment of inertia) to the first moment, i.e., $L = \int x^2 \, dF(x)/\int xF(x)$. The length L – the length of an *equivalent* simple pendulum which yields the same period of vibration – is an example of the m_{vw} mean with $v \equiv w \equiv x$.

In general, we may define the *ratio moment mean* $m_{s,t}$ by restricting m_{vw} to those with $v \equiv x^s$ and $w \equiv x^t$. It is easy to show $\forall F \in D_J$ that $m_{s,t}$ increases in s and in t. In addition to the equivalent length L, the popularly used coefficient of variation provides another context in which $m_{1,1}$ arises:

$$\text{Coefficient of Variation} = [m_{1,1} - \mu]^{1/2}. \tag{7}$$

Note that expression (7) yields an absolute measure of income inequality with an inequality-preferring (risk-preferring)$m_{1,1}$ as the model of the representative income.

Other uses of the $m_{s,t}$ moment mean include:

$m_{1,2}$ = standard deviation · coefficient of skewness, and
$m_{2,2}$ = standard deviation · (coefficient of kurtosis + 3).$^{1/2}$

The following property is shared by m_{vw} and m_v.

Property B (Betweenness): $\forall F, G \in D_J$, and $\beta \in [0, 1]$,

$$m(F) \leqslant m(G) \Rightarrow m(\beta F + [1 - \beta]G) \in [m(F), m(G)].$$

While betweenness appears to be a natural property for mean values, we will consider shortly mean values that do not satisfy it. The following is a characteristic property of m_{vw}.

Property SI (Substitution-Independence): Suppose $\exists F, G, H \in D_J$, and β, $\gamma \in (0, 1)$ such that

$$m(F) = m(G) \neq m(H)$$

and

$$m(\beta F + [1 - \beta]H) = m(\gamma G + [1 - \gamma]H),$$

then $\forall H' \in D_J$,

$$m(\beta F + [1-\beta]H') = m(\gamma G + [1-\gamma]H').$$

Clearly, if w is continuous on J, then m_{vw} is compact continuous (Property CC). It can be shown that m_{vw} will be continuous in distribution if w and $v \cdot w$ are both bounded on J. Chew (1983) proved that m_{vw} is the only mean value satisfying Properties SC, B, SI, CC and E. To be consistent with Property FSD (Property SSD), we further require v and w to satisfy: $\forall s \in J$,

$$w(\cdot)[v(\cdot) - v(s)] \text{ is increasing (concave).} \tag{8}$$

RANK-DEPENDENT QUASILINEAR MEAN. Symmetry of a social welfare function was thought to be necessary for an inequality measure to be *impartial* in the sense of being invariant with respect to permutations of incomes among individuals within the population. We consider here mean values that are not inherently symmetric. Impartiality is attained by restricting our evaluations to rank-ordered income vectors.

The median provides an immediate example of a rank-dependent mean value. The Gini arithmetic mean m_{Gini} (Sen, 1973) derived from:

$$\text{Gini index} = 1 - \frac{m_{\text{Gini}}}{\mu} \tag{9}$$

provides another example. For an income vector $x_\uparrow \in J^N$, the Gini mean is given by:

$$m_{\text{Gini}}(x_\uparrow) = \sum_{i=1}^{N} \frac{[2(N-i)+1]}{N^2} x_{[i]}. \tag{10}$$

For a distribution $F \in D_J$, we have that:

$$m_{\text{Gini}}(F) \equiv \int_J z \, d\{1 - [1 - F(z)]^2\}. \tag{11}$$

The above is a special case of the *rank-dependent quasilinear mean* m_v^g. For a probability distribution $F \in D_J$, we have:

$$m_v^g(F) = v^{-1}\left[\int_J [v(x) \, dg[F(x)]\right], \tag{12}$$

where $g: [0, 1] \rightarrow [0, 1]$ is nondecreasing and v is continuous and strictly monotone. The quasilinear mean results when g is the identity map. In statistics, the rank-dependent mean corresponds to the class of L-estimators. We tabulate in Table 1 a number of well known m_v^g means with $v = x$, which we denote by m^g.

Table 1

m^g	Probability transformation function g	
Median	Step function at $p = 1/2$	
α-Winsorized mean	$g(p) = \begin{cases} 0 \\ p \\ 1 \end{cases}$	$\begin{aligned} &p \in [0, \alpha] \\ &p \in (\alpha, 1 - \alpha) \\ &p \in [1 - \alpha, 1] \end{aligned}$
α-trimmed mean	$g(p) = \begin{cases} 0 \\ p/(1 - 2\alpha) \\ 1 \end{cases}$	$\begin{aligned} &p \in [0, \alpha] \\ &p \in (\alpha, 1 - \alpha) \\ &p \in [1 - \alpha, 1] \end{aligned}$
Gini mean	$g(p) = 1 - (1 - p)^2$	
s-Gini mean (Donaldson and Weymark, 1980)	$g(p) = 1 - (1 - p)^s$	

It is clear that m_v^g satisfies Properties I, FSD, CC and E. If v is bounded, then it will be continuous in distribution. In addition, it satisfies Property SSD if and only if v and g are both concave (Chew, Karni and Safra, 1986).

We state a characteristic property of m_v^g in the following. We say that x and y are *rank preserving* if, for each i,

$$x_{[i]} \in [y_{[i-1]}, y_{[i+1]}] \quad \text{and} \quad y_{[i]} \in [x_{[i-1]}, x_{[i+1]}].$$

The pair (w, z) is said to be a *rank-preserving rearrangement* of (x, y) if w and z are rank-preserving and, for each i,

$$\{w_{[i]}, z_{[i]}\} = \{x_{[i]}, y_{[i]}\}.$$

Property CI (Commutative Independence): $\exists \alpha \in (0, 1)$ such that $\forall p \in \Delta^{N-1}$, x, $y \in J^N$ with x and y being rank-preserving and $x_\uparrow \leqslant y_\uparrow$,

$$m\left\{ \sum_{i=1}^{N} p_i \delta_{m[\alpha\delta_{x_{[i]}} + [1-\alpha)\delta_{y_{[i]}}]} \right\} = m\left\{ \alpha\delta_m\left(\alpha \sum_{i=1}^{N} p_i \delta_{w_{[i]}} \right) + (1-\alpha)\delta_m\left(\sum_{i=1}^{N} p_i \delta_{z_{[i]}} \right) \right\} \quad (13)$$

for any rank-preserving arrangement (w, z) of (x, y).

Recently, Quiggin (1982) provided a generalization of expected utility for simple probability distributions which corresponds to the m_v^g model with $g(1/2) = 1/2$. Yaari (1987) independently axiomatized a theory of preference corresponding to m_v^g with $v \equiv x$. Chew (1985b) axiomatized the m_v^g mean in terms of Properties SC, FSD, CI, CC and E.

IMPLICIT-WEIGHTED QUASILINEAR MEAN. The mean values introduced thus far are defined explicitly in terms of operations relative to the given probability distribution. We present here a general class of implicitly defined mean values which are closely related to the M-estimator in robust statistics proposed by Huber (1964). The *implicit-weighted quasilinear mean* $m_{v(\cdot)w(\cdot,\cdot)}$ is defined to be the solution of:

$$\int_J [v(x) - v(s)]w(x, s)\,dF(x) = 0, \qquad (14)$$

where $w(x, s)$ is nonvanishing and $[v(\cdot) - v(s)]w(\cdot, s)$ is strictly monotone for each s. We have the weighted quasilinear mean when $w(x, s) \equiv w(x)$ and the quasilinear mean when $w \equiv$ constant.

Huber (1964) proposed a class of robust location estimators as the solution of

$$\int \phi(x - s)\,dF(x) = 0. \qquad (15)$$

The Huber estimators are special cases of M_{vw} with $v \equiv x$ and $w(x, s)[x - s] \equiv \phi(x - s)$. Fishburn (1986) axiomatized the case of (14) with w symmetric, i.e., $w(x, s) = w(s, x)$ and for each $s \in J$, $w(x, s)[v(x) - v(s)]$ strictly monotone in x.

An alternative way to write (14) is given by the following. First we define the *weighted transformed probability distribution* $F^{w(\cdot, s)}$ by:

$$dF^{w[\cdot, s)}(x) = w(\cdot, s)\,dF(x) \Big/ \int_J w(y, s)\,dF(y). \qquad (16)$$

Then implicit-weighted quasilinear mean is the solution of

$$s = v^{-1}\left[\int_J v(x)\,dF^{w(\cdot, s)}(x)\right]. \qquad (17)$$

In the case of the weighted quasilinear mean where w does not depend on s, (17) has the simpler form:

$$m_{vw}(F) = v^{-1}\left(\int_J v\,dF^w\right). \qquad (18)$$

It can be shown based on Chew (1985a) that the implicit m_{vw} mean is the most general class of mean values having the betweenness property in addition to Properties SC, CC and E. To satisfy FSD (SSD), we further require $w(\cdot, s)[v(\cdot) - v(s)]$ to be increasing (concave) for each $s \in J$.

A GENERAL FORM OF MEAN VALUE. There is a pattern in the preceding exposition. The mean value in each case is defined to be the solution of an equation of the following form:

$$v(s) = \int_J v\,d\phi_s(F), \qquad (19)$$

where for each $s \in J$, $\phi_s: D_J \to D_j$ is *support-attenuating*; $\forall F \in D_J$, conv supp$[\phi_s(F)]$ $\subset$ conv supp(F). If $\forall F \in D_J$, supp$(\phi_s(F)) = $ supp(F), then we say that ϕ_s is *support-*

preserving. Most of the mean values are defined relative to a support-preserving ϕ_s. The exceptions include the median, the α-trimmed mean and the α-Winsorized mean. The 'weighted' mean values would lose their support-preserving property when the weight function is allowed to vanish within the interior of J.

A mean value is an *explicit* one if ϕ_s does not depend on s. Otherwise, we have an *implicit* mean value. It is clear that any functional defined by (19) satisfies the intermediate value property. Conversely, any mean value functional $m(F)$ can be written in terms of (19) via the degenerate support-attenuating map $F \to \delta_{m(F)}$. If we require compact continuity, then ϕ_s needs to be *continuous* in the sense that $\phi_s(F_n)$ converges in distribution whenever F_n does.

Table 2 tabulates the known mean values and some new ones. All of these mean values satisfy Properties SC, I, CC and E (with w continuous and nonvanishing on J and g continuous and strictly increasing). These together with the stated characteristic properties yield the corresponding axiomatic characterizations of the respective mean values. Note that the unaxiomatized mean values in Table 2 are obtained by performing sequentially a 'weighting transformation' and a 'rank-dependent transformation' on the given distribution F. This is illustrated below:

$$F \to F^{w(\cdot, s)} \to g[F^{w(\cdot, s)}(\cdot)],$$

versus

$$F \to g[F(\cdot)] \to \{g[F(\cdot)]\}^{w(\cdot, s)}.$$

Table 2

Mean value	Probability transformation	Characteristic properties
Quasilinear mean	identity	Q, B or FSD
Weighted quasilinear mean	$F \to F^w$	SI, B
Rank-dependent quasilinear mean	$F \to g[F(\cdot)]$	CI, FSD
Rank-dependent weighted quasilinear mean	$F \to g[F^w(\cdot)]$	
Weighted rank-dependent quasilinear mean	$F \to \{g[F(\cdot)]\}^w$	
Implicit-weighted quasilinear mean	$F \to F^{w(\cdot, s)}$	B
Rank-dependent implicit-weighted quasilinear mean	$F \to g[F^{w(\cdot, s)}(\cdot)]$	
Implicit weighted-rank-dependent quasilinear mean	$F \to \{g[F(\cdot), s]\}^{w(\cdot, s)}$	
Mean value	$F \to \phi_s(F)$	

157

In general, we can compose a support-preserving map $_s$ by performing a sequence of such weighting and rank-dependent transformations with a number of w and g functions.

BIBLIOGRAPHY

Atkinson, A.B. 1970. On the measurement of inequality. *Journal of Economic Theory* 2, 244–63.

Bernoulli, D. 1738. Specimen theoriae novae de mensura sortis. *Commentarii Academiae Scientiarum Imperialas Petropolitanae* 5, 175–92; translated as 'Exposition of a new theory on the measurement of risk', *Econometrica* 22 (1954), 23–6.

Chew, S.H. 1983. A generalization of the quasilinear mean with applications to the measurement of income inequality and decision theory resolving the Allais paradox. *Econometrica* 51, 1065–92.

Chew, S.H. 1985a. Implicit weighted and semi-weighted utility theories, M-estimators, and non-demand revelation of second price auctions for uncertain auctioned objects. Working Paper No. 155, Department of Political Economy, Johns Hopkins University.

Chew, S.H. 1985b. An axiomatization of the rank-dependent quasilinear mean generalizing the Gini mean and the quasilinear mean. Working Paper No. 156, Department of Political Economy, Johns Hopkins University; revised 1986.

Chew, S.H., Karni, E. and Safra, Z. 1986. Risk aversion in the theory of expected utility with rank-dependent probabilities. *Journal of Economic Theory.*

Dalton, H. 1920. The measurement of inequality of incomes. *Economic Journal* 20, 348–61.

Donaldson, D. and Weymark, J.A. 1980. A single-parameter generalization of the Gini indices of inequality. *Journal of Economic Theory* 22, 67–86.

de Finetti, B. 1931. Sul concetto di media. *Giornale dell' Intituto Italiano degli Attuari* 2, 369–96.

Fishburn, P.C. 1986. Implicit mean value and certainty equivalence. *Econometrica* 54, 1197–1205.

Hardy, G.H., Littlewood, J.E. and Polya, G. 1934. *Inequalities.* Cambridge: Cambridge University Press.

Huber, P.J. 1964. Robust estimation of a location parameter. *Annals of Mathematical Statistics* 35, 73–101.

Kolm, S.-Ch. 1969. The optimal production of social justice. In *Public Economics*, ed. J. Margolis and H. Guitton, London/New York: Macmillan.

Kolmogorov, A. 1930. Sur la notion de la moyenne. *Rendiconti Academia dee Lincei* 6(12), 388–91.

Nagumo, M. 1930. Uber eine Klasse der Mittelwerte. *Japan Journal of Mathematics* 7, 71–9.

von Neumann, J. and Morgenstern, O. 1947. *Theory of Games and Economic Behavior.* 2nd edn, Princeton: Princeton University Press.

Quiggin, J. 1982. Anticipated utility theory. *Journal of Economic Behavior and Organization* 3, 323–43.

Ramsey, F.P. 1926. Truth and probability. In F.P. Ramsey, *The Foundations of Mathematics*, ed. R.B. Braithwaite, London: Routledge & Kegan Paul, 1931; New York: Humanities Press, 1950.

Rothschild, M. and Stiglitz, J.E. 1970. Increasing risk: I. A definition. *Journal of Economic Theory* 2, 225–43.

Sen, A. 1973. *On Economic Inequality.* Oxford: Oxford University Press.

Yaari, M.E. 1987. The dual theory of choice under risk: risk aversion without diminishing marginal utility. *Econometrica* 55, 95–115.

Measurement

R. DUNCAN LUCE AND LOUIS NARENS

Most mathematical sciences use quantitative methods, and the theory of measurement is devoted to making explicit the qualitative assumptions that give rise to them. This is accomplished by first stating the qualitative assumptions – empirical laws of the most elementary sort – in axiomatic form and then showing that there are structure preserving mappings, often but not always isomorphisms, from the qualitative structure into the quantitative one. The set of such mappings forms what is called a *scale* of measurement.

A theory of the possible numerical scales plays an important role throughout measurement – and therefore throughout science – since, just as the qualitative assumptions of a class of structures narrowly determine the nature of the possible scales, so also the nature of the underlying scales greatly limits the possible qualitative structures that give rise to such scales. Our two major themes, which reflect relatively new research results, are, first, that the possible scales that are useful in science are necessarily very limited and, second that once a type of scale is selected (or assumed to exist) for a qualitative structure, then a great deal is known about that structure and its quantitative models.

There are several general references to the axiomatic theory. Perhaps the most elementary and the one with the most examples is Roberts (1979). Pfanzagl (1968) and Krantz et al. (1971) are on a par, with the latter more comprehensive. Narens (1985) is the mathematically most sophisticated, and covers much of the material mentioned here. We cite only references not included in one of these surveys.

1. AXIOMATIZABILITY

The Qualitative Setup. The qualitative situation is usually conceptualized as a *relational structure* $\mathscr{X} = \langle X, S_0, S_1, \ldots \rangle$, where the $S_0, S_1, \ldots$ are relations of finite order on X. The set of relations can be either finite or infinite. X is called the *domain* of the structure and the S_i its *primitive relations*. In most applications, S_0 will be some type of ordering relation, and when this is the case it will be written as $\gtrsim$. The following are some examples of qualitative structures used in measurement situations. The first, which goes back to Helmholtz, has for its domain a set X of objects with the property of having mass. There are two primitive relations. The first, $\gtrsim$, is a binary ordering according to mass (which may be determined, for example, by using an equal-arm pan balance so that $x \gtrsim y$ means that the pans either remain level or the one containing x drops). The second relation, $\circ$, is a ternary one that can be interpreted as a binary operation. Empirically, it is defined as follows: if x and y are placed in the same pan and are exactly balanced by z, then we write $x \circ y \sim z$, where $\sim$ means equivalence in the attribute. The structure $\langle X, \gtrsim, \circ \rangle$ was used by Helmholtz in developing an axiomatic treatment of the measurement of mass.

A second example is from economics. Suppose $C_1, \ldots C_n$ are sets each consisting of different amounts of a commodity, and $\gtrsim$ is a preference ordering exhibited by a person or an institution over the set of possible commodity bundles $C = X_i C_i$. The resulting structure $\mathscr{E} = \langle C, \gtrsim \rangle$, known as a *conjoint* one, can among other things be used to induce ordering of an individual's preferences for the commodities associated with each component.

The third example, due to B. de Finetti, has as its domain an algebra $\mathscr{E}$ of subsets, called 'events', of some non-empty set Ω. The primitives of the structure consist of an ordering relation $\gtrsim$ of 'at least as likely as', the events Ω and $\varnothing$, and the set theoretical operations of union $\cup$, intersection $\cap$, and complementation $\sim$. The relational structure

$$\mathscr{P} = \langle \mathscr{E}, \gtrsim, \Omega, \varnothing, \cup, \cap, \sim \rangle$$

is intended to characterize qualitatively probability-like situations. The primitive $\gtrsim$ can arise from many different processes, depending upon the situation. In one, which is of considerable importance to Bayesians, $\gtrsim$ represents a person's ordering of events according to how likely they seem using whatever basis he or she wishes in making the judgements. In such a case, $\mathscr{P}$, is thought of as a subjective or personal probability structure. In another $\gtrsim$ is based on some probability model for the situation (possibly one coupled with estimated relative frequencies), as in much of classical probability theory.

Representation and Scales. A key notion in the theory of measurement is that of a *representation*, which is defined to be a structure preserving map ϕ of the qualitative relational structure $\mathscr{X}$ into a quantitative one, $\mathscr{R}$, in which the domain is a subset of the real numbers. Representations are either isomorphisms or in cases where equivalences play an important role (e.g. conjoint structures where trade-off between components is the essence of the matter) as homomorphisms, in which case equivalence classes of equivalent elements are assigned the same number. We say 'ϕ is a $\mathscr{R}$-representation for $\mathscr{X}$'.

For the past three decades, measurement theorists have been exploring certain types of qualitative structures for which numerical representations exist. The questions faced are, first, to establish that the set of $\mathscr{R}$-representations is non-empty for some choice of $\mathscr{R}$, and second to characterize how two such

$\mathscr{R}$-representations are related or, equivalently, to state how to generate all of them once one is specified. The first is called the existence problem and the second, the 'uniqueness' problem. Several examples will be cited.

For the qualitative mass structure $\mathscr{X} = \langle X, \succsim, \circ \rangle$ described above, the qualitative representing structure is taken to be $\mathscr{R} = \langle \text{Re}^+, \geqslant, + \rangle$, where Re^+ is the positive real numbers, and $\geqslant$ and $+$ have their usual meanings in the real number system. The set of $\mathscr{R}$-representations of $\mathscr{X}$ consist of all functions ϕ from X into Re^+ such that for each x and y in X, (i) $x \succsim y$ iff $\phi(x) \geqslant \phi(y)$, and (ii) $\phi(x \circ y) = \phi(x) + \phi(y)$. Such a function is called a *homomorphism*, and the set of all of them is called a *scale*. In addition to Helmholtz, others including O. Hölder, P. Suppes, Luce and A. A. A. Marley and J.-C. Falmagne have stated axioms about the primitives of $\mathscr{X}$ that are sufficient to show the existence of such homomorphisms and to show that any two homomorphisms ϕ and ψ are related by multiplication, that is, there is some real $r > 0$ such that $\psi = r\phi$. In the language introduced later by S. S. Stevens (1946), such a form of measurement is said to be a 'ratio scale'. For the case where $\circ$ is an operation (defined for all pairs), F. S. Roberts (1979) and Luce and Narens (1985) have given necessary and sufficient conditions for such a representation. A complete characterization, such as this one, is rather unusual in measurement; sufficient conditions are far more the rule.

Representations of the structure $\mathscr{C} = \langle X_i C_i, \succsim \rangle$ of commodity bundles are usually taken in economics to be n-tuples $\langle \phi_1, \ldots, \phi_n \rangle$ of functions, where ϕ_i maps C_i into Re, such that for each x_i, y_i in C_i, $i = 1, \ldots, n$,

$$(x_1, \ldots, x_n) \succsim (y_1, \ldots, y_n) \quad \text{iff} \quad \sum_i \phi(x_i) \geqslant \sum_i \phi(y_i).$$

In the measurement literature such a representation is called 'additive'. G. Debreu, Luce and J. W. Tukey, D. Scott, A Tversky and others, have given axioms on $\mathscr{C}$ for which existence of an additive representation can be shown, and that any two representations $(\phi_1, \ldots, \phi_n)$ and $(\psi_1, \ldots, \psi_n)$ are related by affine transformations of the form $\psi_i = r\phi_i + s_i$, $i = 1, \ldots, n$, $r > 0$. In Stevens's nomenclature, the set of such representations are said to form an 'interval scale'.

In the example of the subjective probability structure $\mathscr{P} = \langle \mathscr{E}, \succsim, \Omega, \varnothing, \cup, \cap, \sim \rangle$, the usual sort of representation is a probability function P from $\mathscr{E}$ into $[0, 1]$, that is, for all A, B in $\mathscr{E}$, (i) $P(\Omega) = 1$, $P(\varnothing) = 0$, (ii) $A \succsim B$ iff $P(A) \geqslant P(B)$, (iii) if $A \cap B = \varnothing$, then $P(A \cup B) = P(A) + P(B)$.

A number of authors have given sufficient conditions in terms of the primitives for P to exist. Fine (1973) gives a good summary of a variety of approaches to probability. In the probability case, unlike the previous two, if P and Q are two representations for $\mathscr{P}$, then $P = Q$; that is, the representation is uniquely determined. Such scales were called 'absolute' by Stevens.

Empirical Usefulness of Axiomatic Treatments. One advantage of a measurement approach to some scientific questions is that it offers an alternative way of testing quantitative models other than simple goodness of fit. Since the axiomatic approach isolates a series of properties that are in some sense thought to be basic, it leads to the validation or invalidation of specific axioms rather than the entire model. In particular, this approach often makes clear where the source of the problem is and thus gives insight into how the model must be altered. An example of this, familiar to economists, has arisen in the theory of subjective expected utility. In its simplest form the domain is gambles of the form $x \circ_A y$ in which x is the outcome if event A occurs and y if A fails to occur, where x and y may themselves be gambles, and the theory postulates a preference ordering $\succsim$ over the outcomes and gambles. The classical axiomatization (for a summary, see Fishburn, 1970) establishes conditions on preferences over gambles so that there exists a probability measure P on the algebra of events, as in a probability structure, and a 'utility function' U over the gambles such that U preserves $\succsim$ and

$$U(x \circ_A y) = P(A)U(x) + [1 - P(A)]U(y). \tag{1}$$

A series of empirical studies (for summaries see Allais and Hagen, 1979, and Kahneman and Tversky, 1979) have made clear that this representation, which can be readily defended on grounds of rationality, is inadequate to describe human behaviour. Among its axioms, the one that appears to be the major source of difficulty is the 'extended sure-thing principle'. It may be stated as follows: suppose A, B and C are events, with C disjoint from A and B, then

$$x \circ_A y \succsim x \circ_B y \quad \text{iff} \quad x \circ_{A \cup C} y \succsim x \circ_{B \cup C} y. \tag{2}$$

It is easy to verify that this is a necessary condition if equation (1) holds, and it seems to be one that people are unwilling to abide by. Any modification of the theory that is to be descriptive of human behaviour must abandon it.

A related example of the interplay of axioms and data, also of interest to economists, is the measurement of risk (references can be found in Weber, 1984; Luce and Weber, 1986).

It must be acknowledged that the isolation of properties in the axiomatic approach has an apparently happenstance quality. The choice of axioms for an empirical structure is by no means uniquely determined; there is an infinity of equivalent axiom systems for any infinite structure, and it is by no means clear why we tend to select the ones we do. It is entirely possible for the failure of the model to be described easily in terms of one axiomatization, and to be totally obscure in another. Furthermore, not everyone values the overall axiomatic approach to scientific (in contrast to mathematical) questions; in particular, it has been sharply attacked by Anderson (1981), pp. 347–56.

Another use of axiomatic methods and of the notion of scale (see *Representations and Scales* above) is in the study of meaningfulness, which is treated under MEANINGFULNESS AND INVARIANCE.

2. ORDERED STRUCTURES

Two types of 'quantitative' representations have played a major role in science: systems of coordinate geometry and the real number system (the latter being the one-dimensional specialization of the former). The latter is our focus. The absolutely simplest case, included in all of the above examples, is the representation of $\langle X, \succsim \rangle$ into $\langle \text{Re}, \geqslant \rangle$, that is, the case where there is a mapping ϕ from X into Re such that $x \succsim y$ iff $\phi(x) \succsim \phi(y)$. It follows readily that in such situations $\succsim$ must be transitive, connected, and reflexive. Such relations are given many different names including *weak order*. When a weak order is antisymmetric, it is called a *total* or *simple order*. Cantor showed that necessary and sufficient conditions for $\langle X, \succsim \rangle$ to be represented in $\langle \text{Re}, \geqslant \rangle$ are that $\succsim$ be a weak order and there be a finite or countable dense subset Y of X that is *order dense* in X (i.e. for each $x \succ z$, there exists a y in Y such that $x \succ y \succ z$). For many purposes, this subset plays the same role as do the rational numbers within the system of real numbers.

In order for the representation to be onto either $\langle \text{Re}, \geqslant \rangle$ or $\langle \text{Re}^+, \geqslant \rangle$, which is often the case in physical measurement, two additional conditions are necessary and sufficient: *Dedekind completeness* (each non-empty bounded subset of X has a least upper bound in X) and *unboundedness* (there is neither a least nor a greatest element).

In measurement axiomatizations, one usually does not postulate a countable, order-dense subset, but derives it from axioms that are intuitively more natural. For example, when there is a binary operation of combining objects, it follows from a number of properties including an Archimedean axiom which states that no object is infinitely larger than or infinitesimally close to another object. When the structure is Dedekind complete and the operation is monotonic, it is also Archimedean. Dedekind completeness and Archimedeaness are what logicians call 'second order axioms', and in principle they are incapable of direct empirical verification.

The most fruitful and intensively examined measurement structures are those with an associative, positive binary operation. This has been the basis of most physical measurement. It has been apparent for some time that few important phenomena of the behavioural and social sciences can be modelled, directly or indirectly, in this way. The development of a general non-associative and non-positive theory began in 1976, and it is moderately well understood in certain symmetric situations. This, and its specialization to associative structures, is the focus of the rest of this article.

3. SCALE TYPES

Classification. As was noted in the examples, scale type has to do with mappings of one numerical representation of a structure into other equally good ones. For some fixed numerical structure $\mathscr{R}$, a *scale* of the structure $\mathscr{X}$ is the collection of all $\mathscr{R}$-representations of $\mathscr{X}$. Much the simplest case, the one to which we confine most of our attention, occurs when $\mathscr{X}$ is totally ordered, the domain of $\mathscr{R}$ is either Re or Re$^+$, and the $\mathscr{R}$-presentations are all *onto* the domain and so are isomorphisms. Such scales are then usually described in terms of the group of real transformations that take one representation into another. As Stevens noted, four distinct groups of transformations have appeared in physical measurement: any strictly increasing function, any linear function $rx + s$, $r > 0$, any *similarity* transformation rx, $r > 0$, and the identity map. The corresponding scales are called *ordinal, interval, ratio*, and *absolute*. (Throughout this article, ratio scales are assumed to be onto Re^+ thereby ruling out cases where an object is assigned the number 0.)

The first three scale types exhibit a property called *homogeneity*, namely, that for each element x in the qualitative structure and each real number r in the domain of $\mathscr{R}$, there is a representation that maps x into r. Homogeneity is typical of physical measurement and it plays an important role in the formulation of many physical laws. We may ask two general types of questions about it: what are the possible groups associated with homogeneous scales, and what are the general classes of structures that can yield homogeneous scales?

It is easiest to formulate answers to these questions in terms of automorphisms of the qualitative structures, that is, in terms of isomorphisms of the structure onto itself. The elements of the scale and the automorphisms of the structure are in one-to-one correspondence, since if ϕ and ψ are two representations and juxtaposition denotes function composition, then $\psi^{-1}\phi$ is an automorphism, and if ϕ is a representation and α is an automorphism, then, $\psi = \phi\alpha$ is a representation.

It is not difficult to see that homogeneity of a scale simply corresponds to there being an automorphism that takes any element of the domain of the structure into any other element. This can be made more specific. Let M be a positive integer, then $\mathscr{X}$ is said to be *M-point homogeneous* iff each strictly ordered set of M points can be mapped by an automorphism into any other strictly ordered set of M points. A structure that is not homogeneous for any positive M is said to be 0-*point homogeneous*; one that is homogeneous for every finite M is said to be ∞-*point homogeneous*.

Another important feature of a scale is its degree of redundancy, which we may formulate as follows: a scale is said to be *N-point unique*, where N is a non-negative integer, iff for every two representations ϕ and ψ in the scale, if ϕ and ψ agree at N distinct points, then $\psi - \phi$. By this definition, ratio scales are 1-point unique, interval scales are 2-point unique, and absolute scales 0-point unique. Scales, like ordinal ones, that take infinitely many points to determine a representation are said to be ∞-*point unique*. Equally, we speak of the structure being *N-point unique* iff every two automorphisms that agree at N distinct points are identical, and it is ∞-*point unique* iff it is not N-point unique for any non-negative N.

The abstract concept of scale type can be given in terms of these concepts. The *scale type* of $\mathscr{X}$ is the pair (M, N) such that M is the maximum degree of homogeneity and N is the minimum degree of uniqueness of $\mathscr{X}$. For the cases under consideration, it can be shown that $M \leqslant N$. Ratio scales are of type $(1, 1)$ and interval scales of type $(2, 2)$. Narens (1981a,b) showed that the converses of both statements are true. And Alper (1987) showed that if $M > 0$ and $N < \infty$, then $N = 1$ or 2. The group in the $(1, 2)$ case consists of transformations of the form $rx + s$, where s is any real number and r is any element of a non-trivial, proper subgroup of the group $\langle \text{Re}^+, \cdot \rangle$. One example is $r = k^n$, where $k > 0$ is fixed and n ranges over the integers. So a structure is homogeneous iff it is of type $(1, 1)$, $(1, 2)$, $(2, 2)$, or (M, ∞). In the latter case, it is not known which values of M, aside from ∞, can occur. The ordinal case is (∞, ∞). We focus on the first three cases.

Unit Representation of Homogeneous Concatenation Structures. Given that we know the possible homogeneous scale types, the next question is: Which structures have scales of those types? The answer is not known completely, but for ordered structures with binary operations it is completely understood. This is useful since, as was noted, they play a central role in much physical measurement and, as we shall see below, they arise naturally in two distinct ways of interest to social scientists.

Consider real concatenation structures of the form $\mathscr{R} = \langle \text{Re}^+, \geqslant, *' \rangle$, where $\geqslant$ has its usual meaning and we have replaced $+$ by a general binary, numerical operation, denoted $*'$, that is strictly increasing in each variable. The major result is that if $\mathscr{X}$ satisfies $M > 0$ and $N < \infty$ – a sufficient condition for the latter is that $*'$ be continuous (Luce and Narens, 1985) – then the structure can be mapped canonically into an isomorphic one that is of the form $\langle \text{Re}^+, \geqslant, * \rangle$, where there is a function f from Re^+ onto Re^+ such that (i) f is strictly increasing, (ii) $f(x)/x$ is strictly decreasing, and (iii) for all x, y in Re^+, $x * y = yf(x/y)$ (Cohen and Narens, 1979). This type of canonical representation is called a *unit representation.* Observe that it is invariant under the similarities of a ratio scale:

$$rx * ry = ryf(rx/ry) = r[yf(x/y)] = r(x*y).$$

The two most familiar examples of unit representations are ordinary additivity, for which $f(z) = 1 + z$ and so $x * y = x + y$, and bisymmetry, for which $f(z) = z^c$ and so $x * y = x^c y^{1-c}$. Situations where such representations arise are discussed later.

The three different scale types can be distinguished by means of a simple property of the function f (Luce and Narens, 1985). Consider the values of $\rho > 0$ for which $f(x^\rho) = f(x)^\rho$ for all $x > 0$. The structure is of scale type $(1,1)$ iff $\rho = 1$; of type $(1,2)$ iff for some fixed $k > 0$ and all integers n, $\rho = k^n$; and of type $(2,2)$ iff $\rho > 0$. The $(2,2)$ condition imposes a very tight constraint on f, namely, that there be constants c, d in $(0, 1)$ such that

$$f(z) = \begin{cases} z^c, & \text{if } z > 1 \\ 1, & \text{if } z = 1 \\ z^d, & \text{if } z < 1. \end{cases}$$

If, as is the usual practice in the social sciences but not in physics, we construct the structure on Re by taking logarithms, the case of the $(2,2)$ operation becomes

$$x * y = \begin{cases} cx + (1-c)y, & \text{if } x > y \\ x, & \text{if } x = y \\ dx + (1-d)y, & \text{if } x < y. \end{cases}$$

Structures leading to this *dual bilinear* representation are called *dual bisymmetric* (when $c = d$, the 'dual' is dropped). They lead to an interesting generalization of the theory of subjective expected utility for gambles (section 6).

4. AXIOMATIZATION OF CONCATENATION STRUCTURES

Given this understanding of the possible representations of homogeneous, finitely unique concatenation structures, it is natural to return to the classical question of axiomatizing the qualitative properties that lead to such representations. Until a few years ago, the only two cases that were understood axiomatically were those leading to additivity and averaging (see below). We know more now, although our knowledge remains incomplete.

Additive Representations. The key mathematical result underlying extensive measurement, due to O. Hölder, states that when a group operation and an ordering interlock so that the operation is monotonic and is Archimedean in the sense that sufficient copies of any positive element will exceed any fixed element, then the group is isomorphic to an ordered subgroup of the additive real numbers. Basically, the theory of extensive measurement restricts itself to the positive subsemigroup of such a structure. Extensive structures can be shown to be of scale type (1, 1). Various generalizations involving partial operations (defined for only some pairs of objects) have been developed. (For a summary, see Krantz et al., 1971, chs 2, 3, and 5.) Not only are these structures more realistic, they are essential to an understanding of the partial additivity that arises in probability structures. These structures can be shown to be of scale type (0, 1).

The representation theory for extensive structures not only asserts the existence of a numerical representation, but provides a systematic procedure (involving the Archimedean property) for constructing one to any preassigned degree of accuracy. This construction, directly or indirectly, underlies the extensive scales used in practice.

The second classical case, due to J. Pfanzagl, leads to weighted average representations. The conditions are monotonicity of the operation, a form of solvability, an Archimedean condition, and bisymmetry $[(x \circ y) \circ (u \circ v) \sim (x \circ u) \circ (y \circ v)]$ which replaces associativity. One method of developing these representations involves two steps: first the bisymmetric operation is recorded as a conjoint one (see section 5) as follows: $(u, v) \succsim' (x, y)$ iff $u \circ v \succsim x \circ y$; and second, the conjoint structure is recoded as an extensive operation on one of its components. This reduces the proof of the representation theorem to that of extensive measurement, that is to Hölder's theorem, and so it too is constructive.

NON-ADDITIVE REPRESENTATIONS

The most completely understood generalization of extensive structures, called *positive concatenation structures* or PCSs for short, simply drops the assumption of associativity. Narens and Luce (see Narens, 1985) showed that this was

166

sufficient to get a numerical representation and that, under a slight restriction which has since been removed, the structure is 1-point unique, but not necessarily 1-point homogeneous. Indeed, Cohen and Narens (1979) showed that the automorphism group is an Archimedean ordered group and so is isomorphic to a subgroup of the additive real numbers; it is homogeneous only when the isomorphism is to the full group. As in the extensive case, one can use the Archimedean axiom to construct representations, but the general case is a good deal more complex than the extensive one and almost certainly will require computer assistance to make it practical.

For Dedekind complete PCSs that map onto Re^+ there exists a nice criterion for 1-point homogeneity, namely, that for each positive integer and every x and y, $n(x \circ y) = nx \circ ny$, where by definition $1x = x$ and $nx = (n-1)x \circ x$. The form of the representations of all such homogeneous representations was described earlier.

The remaining broad type of concatenation structures consists of those that are indempotent, i.e. for all x, $x \circ x = x$. The following conditions have been shown to be sufficient for indempotent structures to have a numerical representation (Luce and Narens, 1985): $\circ$ is an operation that is monotonic and satisfies an Archimedean condition (for differences) and a solvability condition that says for each x and y, there exist u and v such that $u \circ x = y = x \circ v$. If, in addition, such a structure is Dedekind complete, it can be shown that it is N-point unique with $N \leqslant 2$.

5. AXIOMATIZATION OF CONJOINT STRUCTURES

A second major class of measurement structures, widely familiar from both physics and the social sciences, are those, based on two or more independent variables effecting a tradeoff in the to-be-measured dependent variable. The familiar physical relations among three basic attributes, such as kinetic energy $= mv^2/2$, where m is the mass and v the velocity of a moving body, illustrates both their commonness and importance in physics. Such conjoint structures are equally common in the behavioural and social sciences: preference between commodity bundles or between gambles; loudness of pure tones as a function of signal intensity and frequency; tradeoff between delay and amount of a reward etc. Although there is some theory for more than two independent variables in the additive case, for present purposes we confine attention to the two variable case $\langle X \times Y, \succsim \rangle$.

As for concatenation structures, the simplest case to understand is the additive one in which the major non-structural properties are:

(i) Independence (monotonicity): if $(x, y) \succsim (x', y)$ holds for some y then it holds for all y in Y, and the parallel statement for the other component. Note that this property allows us to induce natural orderings, $\succsim_X$ and $\succsim_Y$, on X and Y.

(ii) Thomsen condition: if $(x, z) \sim (u, y')$ and $(u, y) \sim (x', z)$, then $(x, y) \sim (x', y')$.

(iii) An Archimedean condition which says, for each component, if $\{x_i\}$ is a bounded sequence and for some non-equivalent y and z it satisfies $(x_i, y) \sim (x_{i+1}, z)$, then the sequence is finite.

These, together with some solvability in the structure, are sufficient to prove the existence of an interval scale, additive representation (for a summary of various results, see Krantz et al., 1971, chs 6, 7 and 9). The result has been generalized to non-additive representations by dropping the Thomsen condition, which leads to the existence of a non-additive numerical representation. The basic strategy is to define on one component, say X, an operation $*_X$ that captures the information embodied in the tradeoff between components. The induced structure $\langle X, \succsim_X, *_X \rangle$ can be shown to consist of two PCSs pieced together at an element that acts like a natural zero of the concatenation structure. The results for PCSs are then used to construct the representation. As might be anticipated, $*_X$ is associative if and only if the conjoint structure satisfies the Thomsen condition.

The important case of a conjoint structure having an operation on one of its components that is coupled to the conjoint structure by means of a distribution law is taken up in section 4 of MEANINGFULNESS AND INVARIANCE.

6. GAMBLING STRUCTURES

Rationality Assumptions in the Traditional Theory. As was noted earlier, an extensive literature on preferences among gambles exists. The major theoretical development is the axiomatization of subjective expected utility (SEU), which is a representation satisfying equation (1). Although such axiomatizations are defensible theories in terms of principles of rationality, they fail as descriptions of human behaviour. The rationality axioms invoked are of three quite distinct types.

First, preference is assumed to be transitive. This assumption has been shown to fail in various empirical contexts (especially multifactor ones), with perhaps the most pervasive and still ill-understood example being the 'preference reversal phenomenon', discovered by P. Slovic and S. Lichtenstein and investigated extensively, by among others, Grether and Plott (1979) (see references there to the earlier work). Nevertheless, transitivity is the axiom that is least easily given up. Even subjects who violate it are not inclined to defend their 'errors'. A few attempts have been made to develop theories without it, but so far they are complex and have not received much empirical scrutiny (Bell, 1982; Fishburn, 1982, 1985).

The second type of rationality postulates 'accounting' principles in which two gambles are asserted to be equivalent in preference because when analysed into their component outcomes they are seen to be identical. For example, if $x \circ_A y$ is a gamble and $(x \circ_A y) \circ_B z$ means that the event B occurs first and then, independent of it, A occurs, then on accounting grounds $(x \circ_A y) \circ_B y \sim (x \circ_B y) \circ_A y$ is rational, since on both sides x is the outcome when A and B both occur (though in opposite orders) and y otherwise. One of the first 'paradoxes' of utility theory, that of M. Allais, is a violation of an accounting equation which assumes that certain probability calculations also take place.

The third type of rationality condition is the extended sure-thing principle, equation (2). Its failure, which occurs regularly in experiments, is substantially the 'paradox' earlier pointed out by D. Ellsberg. Subjects have insisted on the reasonableness of their violations of this principle (MacCrimmon, 1967).

Some Generalizations of SEU. Kahneman and Tversky (1979) proposed a modification of the expected utility representation designed to accommodate the last two types of violations. Luce and Narens (1985) developed a somewhat related and more comprehensive theory, based on the dual bilinear representation described above. The representation takes the form:

$$U(xo_A y) = \begin{cases} S^+(A)U(x) + [1 - S^+(A)]U(y), & \text{if } U(x) > U(y) \\ U(x), & \text{if } U(x) = U(y) \\ S^-(A)U(x) + [1 - S^-(A)]U(y), & \text{if } U(x) < U(y), \end{cases}$$

where the S^i are weights, not necessarily probabilities. In such a structure, the accounting equation $(x \circ_A y) \circ_B y \sim (x \circ_B y) \circ_A y$ mentioned above necessarily holds. Another simple and often postulated accounting equation is $x \circ_A y \sim y \circ\tilde{~}_A x$, which holds in the model iff $S^+(A) + S^-(\tilde{~}A) = 1$. They show that any further accounting equations not derived from the latter equation and the model force the bisymmetric case, i.e., $S^+ = S^-$. The extended sure-thing principle, which is not an accounting equation, is equivalent to: for events A, B, C with C disjoint from A and B and $i = +, -,$

$$S^i(A) \geqslant S^i(B) \quad \text{iff} \quad S^i(A \cup C) \geqslant S^i(B \cup C),$$

which of course is true when the S's are probability measures. It follows easily that if the accounting equation $x \circ_A y \sim y \circ\tilde{~}_A x$ holds and if the S^i, $i = +, -$, are probability functions, then $S^+ = S^-$, and so the SEU model holds.

No axiomatic justification has yet been given for this model, and it has yet to be subjected to searching empirical criticism. However, it does predict most of the empirical failures of the SEU model.

Another interesting line of development, involving a different weighting than in traditional SEU, can be found in Chew (1980, 1983).

BIBLIOGRAPHY

Allais, M. and Hagen, O. (eds) 1979. *Expected Utility Hypotheses and the Allais Paradox.* Dordrecht: Reidel.

Alper, T.M. 1987. A classification of all order-preserving homeomorphism groups that satisfy uniqueness. *Journal of Mathematical Psychology.*

Anderson, N.H. 1981. *Foundations of Information Integration Theory.* New York: Academic Press.

Bell, D. 1982. Regret in decision making under uncertainty. *Operations Research* 30, 961–81.

Chew, S.H. 1980. Two representation theorems and their application to decision theory. University of British Columbia, PhD dissertation.

Chew, S.H. 1983. A generalization of the quasilinear mean with applications to measurement of income inequality and decision theory resolving the Allais paradox. *Econometrica* 51, 1065–92.

Cohen, M. and Narens, L. 1979. Fundamental unit structures: a theory of ratio scalability. *Journal of Mathematical Psychology* 20, 193–232.

169

Fine, T. 1973. *Theories of Probability*. New York: Academic Press.

Fishburn, P.C. 1970. *Utility Theory for Decision Making*. New York: Wiley.

Fishburn, P.C. 1982. Nontransitive measurable utility. *Journal of Mathematical Psychology* 26, 31–67.

Fishburn, P.C. 1985. Nontransitive preference theory and the preference reversal phenomenon. *International Review of Economics and Business* 32, 39–50.

Grether, D.M. and Plott, C.R. 1979. Economic theory of choice and the preference reversal phenomenon. *American Economic Review* 69, 623–38.

Kahneman, D. and Tversky, A. 1979. Prospect theory: an analysis of decision under risk. *Econometrica* 47, 263–91.

Krantz, D.H., Luce, R.D., Suppes, P. and Tversky, A. 1971. *Foundations of Measurement*. Vol. 1, New York: Academic Press.

Luce, R.D. and Narens, L. 1985. Classification of concatenation measurement structures according to scale type. *Journal of Mathematical Psychology* 29, 1–72.

Luce, R.D. and Webber, E. 1986. An axiomatic theory of conjoint, expected risk. *Journal of Mathematical Psychology* 30, 188–205.

MacCrimmon, K.R. 1967. Descriptive and normative implications of the decision theory postulates. In *Risk and Uncertainty*, ed. K. Borch and J. Mossin, New York: Macmillan, 3–32.

Narens, L. 1981a. A general theory of ratio scalability with remarks about the measurement-theoretic concept of meaningfulness. *Theory and Decision* 13, 1–70.

Narens, L. 1981b. On the scales of measurement. *Journal of Mathematical Psychology* 24, 249–75.

Narens, L. 1985. *Abstract Measurement Theory*. Cambridge, Mass.: MIT Press.

Pfanzagl, J. 1968. *Theory of Measurement*. New York: Wiley. 2nd edn, Vienna: Physica, 1971.

Roberts, F.S. 1979. *Measurement Theory*. Reading, Mass.: Addison-Wesley.

Stevens, S.S. 1946. On the theory of scales of measurement. *Science* 103, 677–80.

Weber, E. 1984. Combine and conquer: a joint application of conjoint and functional approaches to the problem of risk measurement. *Journal of Experimental Psychology, Human Perception and Performance* 10, 179–94.

Monte Carlo Methods

JOHN G. CRAGG

The term 'Monte Carlo methods' is used to refer to two different, though closely related, techniques. The first meaning, currently the less common one among economists, is the evaluation of definite integrals by use of random variables. The idea is to evaluate $\int_a^b F(x) \, dx$ (where x may be a vector) by estimating $\int_a^b [F(x)/p(x)] p(x) \, dx$. Here $p(x)$ is the density function of a random variable defined over $[a, b]$. The original problem has been converted into one of estimating the mean of $F(x)/p(x)$. It can be solved by using a random sample drawn from $p(x)$ and calculating the average value of $F(x)/p(x)$.

Despite widespread occurrence of intractable integrals in economics, Monte Carlo methods in this sense have been little used (except to the extent that the second meaning can be encompassed within the first), possibly because explicit parameters for $F(x)$ are usually unknown and so only general analytical solutions are of interest. Promising opportunities for application may arise in Bayesian econometrics where fully parameterized (and often very intractable) definite integrals are the rule rather than the exception. A good example of use of Monte Carlo methods in this sense is provided in Kloek and van Dijk (1978).

The second meaning of 'Monte Carlo methods' refers to repeated simulation of a stochastic model to investigate the properties of statistical techniques applied to it. The techniques under investigation typically are derived from general principles such as maximum likelihood which provide no guarantee of reliability in finite samples. The Monte Carlo procedure is adopted when analytical derivation of finite sample properties of methods appears not to be feasible.

More explicitly, suppose that some observable economic variables of interest, y, are generated according to $y = g(\varepsilon; x, \theta)$ where ε are unobserved random variables of specified distribution, x are other observable variables on which the analysis of y can be conditioned and θ are unknown parameters. Monte Carlo methods investigate the properties of the statistical techniques which are used to infer properties of the process generating y. They do this by applying the techniques to artificially generated data coming from this model. Repeated samples of ε are obtained from the specified distribution and samples of y are

171

generated using chosen values of x and θ. The techniques being investigated are applied to these artificial sets of data on y to provide samples of inferences made by the techniques. Properties of the procedures may then be established by statistical inference. Since all aspects of the data generation are known, the extent to which the techniques are reliable can be assessed.

The Monte Carlo method involves substitution of computer resources for human resources of the sort needed to perform abstract mathematical derivations (as the title of the classic paper by Summers (1965) indicated). Despite the increase in technical expertise among economists, progress in computing technology continues to be so rapid that one may well expect application of the technique to become more rather than less common. The volume of work using Monte Carlo methods is already vast and is steadily growing. A good recent survey of some of this literature is Hendry (1984).

Monte Carlo methodology is highly dependent on the ability of computers to generate pseudo-random numbers that mimic the random processes hypothesized to generate economic data. None of the variety of techniques available for this purpose can produce truly independent sets of random numbers. (Kennedy and Gentle, 1980, provides a good discussion of random number generation.) As a result there may be a legitimate worry that the lack of independence interacts with the complicated processes in many econometric specifications to produce misleading results. In addition to careful examination of the random number generators used and their properties, one practical way to lessen this danger is to use within a Monte Carlo study different random number generators that employ substantially different methods. The results of the sub-experiments using the different generators can then be compared to establish that they are in agreement with each other. To date such validation seems rare. Indeed, explicit reference to the type of random-number generator being used is not common, despite the known weaknesses of some generators for which efficient computer code has been readily available.

The usual criticisms of the Monte Carlo technique concern the lack of precision of the findings and their dependence on a particular specification. The first is largely a problem of sample size and efficiency of experiment design. A variety of techniques, largely stemming from Hammersley and Handscombe (1964), is available to increase efficiency, of which the most common and generally useful is employment of control variate estimators whose distributions are known and which are likely to be closely related to the techniques of interest. These variance-reducing techniques make use of the fact that all parameters of the generating process are known by the investigator; this knowledge can therefore be exploited in discovering the properties of techniques used when such information is not available. Some authors indeed would restrict the term 'Monte Carlo' to studies that exploit these possibilities to obtain efficiency. However, with the ready availability of cheap computation facilities, high degrees of precision may often be achieved even without such techniques. In so far as more sophisticated experimental design requires more complicated computer programming, the gain in efficiency may be illusory.

172

The problem of results being dependent on specific parameters is apparently more serious, but can be overemphasized. Two approaches to reducing the problem can be adopted. First, the parameters can be varied and the effect of the variation can be studied. Although past studies have tended to use many replications at each of a very few points in the relevant parameter space, it may instead be sensible to allow the parameters, θ and/or x, to vary from replication to replication.

With this approach, the problem becomes one of fitting a 'response surface' to describe the ways in which the properties of the econometric techniques depend on the various parameters or conditions of the different replications of an experiment. In principle, it should be possible to discover the properties of the finite-sample distribution to any desired degree of accuracy using standard statistical approximation techniques. Though this might seem to indicate that Monte Carlo techniques can replace exact derivation of the sampling distribution of estimators, the lack of precision and completeness of any Monte Carlo study and the difficulty of finding a revealing and parsimonious response-surface representation in the absence of knowledge of what aspects of the experimental situation are critical should not be minimized. Furthermore, in the past Monte Carlo studies have run into serious problems from not appreciating features of the small sample distributions of techniques being studied, such as the lack of moments for some simultaneous equation estimators or the difficulties encountered on the unit circle in moving average models. However, exact results, even when available, may also be difficult to interpret or apply.

A second approach to the problem of the specificity of Monte Carlo results is to conduct experiments using parameters fitted to a sample of data that are believed to arise from the process of interest. Thus the values of θ estimated from actual data on y and the corresponding values of x are employed. These provide a presumption that the Monte Carlo experiment is investigating the relevant part of the parameter space. This approach largely overcomes the specificity problem in the sense that the Monte Carlo study can answer the question whether the inferences drawn about the processes generating the data would tend to be made if data had in fact been generated by the supposed process with the estimated parameters. While the results can not be generalized to other applications of the techniques readily, this may not be important if indeed the application is important and interesting and the Monte Carlo investigation is inexpensive.

A major weakness that standard Monte Carlo methodology shares with traditional exact sample results is the specification of particular distributions for ε. It is often doubtful that these describe adequately the process generating economic data. To some extent, 'bootstrap' techniques (cf. Efron, 1982), which involve using the empirical distribution of residuals in a study, overcome this, providing a more concrete incorporation of Monte Carlo techniques into the process of making statistical inferences about processes generating data.

A side benefit that Monte Carlo studies may provide is validation of computer software. They may also reveal computational problems of particular methods that are not immediately obvious. Because Monte Carlo studies involve repeated use of estimating or testing techniques, they may uncover programming bugs or computational difficulties which would not surface in only a few applications Furthermore, results vastly at difference with those expected, for example from asymptotic theory, may in particular instances indicate failures in computer programming rather than weakness of the econometric methods.

BIBLIOGRAPHY

Efron, B. 1982. *The Jackknife, the Bootstrap and Other Resampling Plans*. Philadelphia: SIAM.

Hammersley, J.M. and Handscombe, D.C. 1964. *Monte Carlo Methods*. London: Methuen; New York: Wiley.

Hendry, D.F. 1984. Monte Carlo experimentation in econometrics. In *Handbook of Econometrics*, Vol. II, ed. M. Intriligator, Amsterdam: North-Holland, 937–76.

Kennedy, W.J., Jr. and Gentle, J.E. 1980. *Statistical Computing*. New York: Marcel Dekker.

Kloek, T. and van Dijk, H.K. 1978. Bayesian estimates of equation system parameters: an application of integration by Monte Carlo. *Econometrica* 46, 1–19.

Summers, R.M. 1965. A capital-intensive approach to the small sample properties of various simultaneous equation estimators. *Econometrica* 33, 1–41.

Multivariate Time Series Models

CHRISTOPHER A. SIMS

The staple of econometrics textbooks, the simultaneous equations model, is a multivariate model; and when the data are time series it becomes a multivariate time series model. John Geweke (1978) laid out the connection of the notation and standard assumptions of simultaneous equations modelling to the corresponding concepts in the theory of vector stochastic processes. Multivariate time series modelling of economic data is none the less a topic distinct from simultaneous equations modelling. We go on to discuss why such a distinction exists, the nature of it, and the prospects for making it less sharp.

DEALING WITH OVER-PARAMETERIZATION

Both static multivariate models and univariate time series models can easily grow to involve too many unknown parameters. There is usually no obvious limit to how far back in time temporal dependencies might go or on how complex dynamic effects could be, so there is no obvious bound on the number of parameters in a univariate time series model. Every variable in a multivariate model might interact with every other one meaning there are in the order of n^2 channels of interaction to be parameterized in an n variable model. While this is a finite number, when n is large n^2 can be the same order of magnitude as sample size. When many time series models are modelled jointly, these two sources of parameter proliferation interact multiplicatively.

Classical simultaneous equations methodology takes no explicit account of overparameterization. It presumes there is a model, called the unrestricted reduced form model, for the conditional distribution of the endogenous variables given the exogenous or predetermined variables, and that this model can be estimated.

The focus of the econometric theory is then on how to translate the estimated unrestricted reduced form parameters into efficient estimates of parameters with a more direct economic interpretation, called structural parameters. The number of free parameters is important only in determining whether the model is identified,

175

in the sense that the vector of structural parameters maps into a unique vector of reduced form parameters.

In fact, in a large time series simultaneous equations model it is commonly the case that the unrestricted reduced form model has more parameters than there are data points. Even where this is not true, it is commonly the case that models with nearly as many free structural parameters as there are reduced form coefficients (models which are not strongly over-identified) have far too many parameters.

It is now well understood that classical statistical methods can founder when naively applied to models with too many unknown parameters. Often estimated models are used as certainty equivalents – as if the estimated values of their parameters were known exactly. In this case, applying a false simplifying restriction to a model will reduce expected losses in a decision theory problem if the restriction is not too false and is related to the loss function appropriately. In practice, therefore, econometricians tend to use heavily restricted, simple models, relaxing restrictions when there is enough information in the data to justify doing so.

It is possible to think of inference within approximate, small models whose specification depends on the data as part of a procedure for inference within an infinite dimensional parameter space (see Sims, 1972b). Thus in practice it is reasonable to adjust the size of the model in interaction with the data. The problem with the usual implementations of simultaneous equations methodology is not that they make parameterization of the model data dependent, but that they do so while documenting and reporting results according to a theory of inference which ignores the actual specification process.

The various methods grouped under the heading of multivariate time series modelling have in common that they confront the problem of over-parameterization directly. They include prescriptions for how to adjust the model form to obtain a reasonable relation between number of unknown parameters and data points, or in the case of some Bayesian methods a prescription for how to avoid the bad practical consequences of large numbers of parameters without actually reducing the number of them.

By explicitly declaring a strategy for allowing model complexity to depend on the amount and nature of available data, multivariate time series methods open the possibility of separating the application of complexity-controlling model simplifications from the imposition of controversial hypotheses about economic behaviour. Thus time series models may be able to play the role of an unrestricted reduced form where the classical unrestricted reduced form is unusable.

They differ from standard simultaneous equations theory also in that they introduce classes of restrictions on models motivated by hypotheses about the joint dynamic behaviour of the variables. The classical theory focuses attention on analysis of each model equation separately, as a distinct behavioural mechanism. Sometimes knowledge or hypotheses about behaviour do not take this form. Also, restrictions arrived at equation by equation may interact in unexpected ways to imply unreasonable joint behaviour.

176

MULTIVARIATE TIME SERIES MODELLING STRATEGIES

Static multivariate modelling procedures include principal components, factor analysis, ridge regression, canonical correlation and multiple-indicator-multiple-cause (MIMC) approaches, among others. Univariate time series procedures include ARIMA modelling (Box–Jenkins), autoregressive modelling and spectral analysis, among others. Multivariate time series modelling procedures for the most part combine aspects of some well known multivariate modelling strategy with some well known time series modelling strategy, so as to control the dimensionality of the parameter space on the two fronts at once – across variables and across time.

Index models. Sargent and Sims (1977) introduced a class of models they call index models. if $y(t)$ is a $k \times 1$ vector stochastic process, an index model for it takes the form

$$y(t) + a * z(t) + e(t), \tag{1}$$

where '$*$' stands for convolution, so that

$$a * z(t) = \sum_{s=-\infty}^{\infty} a(s)z(t-s). \tag{2}$$

The $q \times 1$ vector stochastic process z, the 'index', is taken to have dimension q much less than k, and in most applications interpretation is more natural if $a(s) = 0$ for $s < 0$ (so that only current and past z's influence current y – the z-to-y relation is 'causal' in the jargon of engineering). The model (1) does not determine the properties of the y process, even once a is specified, unless we restrict the joint behaviour of z and e.

One appealing specification is to require that the elements of the e vector be mutually uncorrelated and that the z process be uncorrelated with the e process. Since this implies in general that there is no way to construct current z from current and past x, even if a and the autocovariance function of e are known. Sargent and Sims call this the 'unobservable index' model. It turns out to have the computationally appealing property that, when translated into the frequency domain, it implies that the spectral density matrix at each frequency has the same structure as the covariance matrix of the data in a factor analysis model. Since estimates of the spectral density matrix at sufficiently separated frequencies are independent, the unobservable index model can be treated as a set of independent factor analysis models. There are complications (e.g., the spectral density matrix generally has complex numbers in off-diagonal entries), but the theory of inference for this model is well worked out by Geweke (1977). In this framework, intertemporal parameterization is controlled by the usual frequency domain technique of smoothing the spectral density, while cross-variable parameterization is controlled by keeping q relatively small – keeping down the number of indexes or dynamic factors.

177

An alternative way to complete the index model is to assert that

$$z(t) = b * y(t - 1), \tag{3}$$

with $b(s) = 0$ for $s < 0$, and that $e(t)$ is uncorrelated with $y(s)$ for all $s < t$. Here, of course, z can be constructed from current and past x, so the model is called an 'observable index' model. If we ignore the special nature of the right-hand-side variables, the model is a special case of the MIMC regression model. Also, when we rewrite it as

$$y(t) = (a * b) * y(t - 1) + e(t) \tag{4}$$

and recall that e is uncorrelated with lagged y, the model is recognizable as the autoregressive representation for y, linear in y but parameterized so that the coefficients of lagged y's are quadratic functions of a relatively small number of parameters. The model thus combines MIMC and autoregressive modelling as the unobservable index model combines factor analysis and spectral analysis.

State space models. In a flexible framework borrowed from engineering, y is modelled as generated by a stochastic 'state vector' z which evolves according to

$$z(t) = Az(t - 1) + v(t). \tag{5}$$

The equation for y is

$$y(t) = Hz(t) + e(t). \tag{6}$$

Equation (5) is the 'state equation' and (6) the 'observation equation' in engineering jargon. It is nearly always assumed that e and v are serially uncorrelated and uncorrelated with each other. Because the z vector can be expanded to include lagged values of itself and/or lagged y's, the possible dynamics are rich and the requirement that e and v be serially uncorrelated is not restrictive. H and A can be allowed to depend on time without affecting the model's tractability.

When v has a full rank covariance matrix, z is just a stochastic process uncorrelated with e. The model is therefore close to the unobservable index model. However, state space models are ordinarily estimated with different techniques. If A and H are known, the Kalman filter provides a convenient method for at the same time finding the likelihood function of the data and forming estimates of the z series. When A and H are unknown, the Kalman filter becomes part of an iterative procedure for choosing A and H to maximize likelihood. Because this iterative procedure is computationally expensive, state space models tend to keep z of small dimension and give A and H simple forms as functions of a small number of parameters. The unobservable index model in the frequency domain, on the other hand, retains its computational tractability only if it is not heavily restricted – otherwise the independence of inference across frequencies is lost.

State space time series modelling is discussed in more detail in Harvey (1981) and, from an engineering perspective, in Kumar and Varaiya (1986).

Bayesian vector autoregression. The problem of inference in regression models with large numbers of right-hand-side variables, which can be approached with MIMC models when there are several equations considered jointly, can also be approached with Bayesian techniques or the nearly equivalent 'ridge regression' techniques. Such methods have in fact been applied to univariate or bivariate time series models by Shiller (1973) and Leamer (1972), in a form specialized to take account of a prior belief that coefficients are smaller on more distantly lagged variables and/or similar on adjacent lags. Litterman (1982) suggested a tractable family of specifications for Bayesian prior beliefs about the coefficients in a multivariate autoregression. His specification makes the prior mean for the model a set of possibly correlated random walks, that is a model in which for each i the best predictor of $y_i(t+s)$ based on data up to time t is $y_i(t)$, for all $s > 0$. However, the mean is less important than the covariance matrix of coefficients. His simplest suggestion is to have all coefficients independent, with variances shrinking as the length of the lag increases. He suggests a number of other possibilities as well. Recently, e.g. in Doan, Litterman and Sims (1984), these methods have been extended to allow random time variation in the coefficients. Litterman has published forecasts using a simple model of this type since 1980; the results have been comparable with the performance of commercial forecasting services. They have been relatively better at longer-term forecasts, and they have been relatively good for real variables and relatively bad for prices. See McNees (1986) for more detailed discussion.

Block structure. A notion which arises in every approach to practical multivariate time series modelling is that of dividing the list y of series into groups corresponding to 'sectors' and limiting the nature of feedback among some sectors. This idea is not in itself a complete modelling strategy, but it is a method for limiting the dimensionality of the parameter space which applies to all time series modelling strategies.

Most commonly, it is assumed that y consists of two subvectors x and z, such that

$$x(t) = f[z(s), x(s-1), s \leq t; e(t)], \tag{7}$$

with $z(s)$ independent of $e(t)$, all s and t. In a usage which has been standard in econometrics for at least 25 years, this condition is called exogeneity of z in the equation (7). I showed (Sims, 1972a) that in the case where (7) is linear with $e(t)$ entering additively, exogeneity of z in (7) implies a restriction on the representation of y as a vector stochastic process which is testable with little in the way of other maintained hypotheses. Since exogeneity assumptions are an important building block in most dynamic simultaneous equations models, their testability is a valuable tool in checking model adequacy.

Economists usually decide which variables are plausibly treated as exogenous by invoking intuitive notions of causal priority. It is therefore useful to observe that the restriction on the joint stochastic process for x and z implied by exogeneity of z in (7) is a causal ordering on x and z, with z first in the ordering, using Granger's (1969) definition of causality.

Causality is a nebulous concept, and Granger's is not a uniquely appealing way to make it precise. None the less, it is formally similar to a number of other proposed precise definitions of causality (see Sims, 1977) and has some intuitive appeal.

The statement 'x does not Granger-cause y' is not the same as 'y is Granger-causally prior to x'. Thomas Doan, in an unpublished paper several years ago, observed that if we use Granger's definition of 'x_i causes x_j' in a given multivariate time series model, this relation ('x_icx_j' for short) is not transitive and therefore does not induce a causal ordering on the variables. The relation can be restricted, however, to become transitive. We can treat the relation 'c' as a set of ordered pairs of indexes, so that inclusion of the pair $\langle i, j \rangle$ implies that x_icx_j. We define a new relation 'C' as the largest subset of 'c' which is transitive, that is, satisfies the condition that x_iCx_j and x_jCx_k imply x_jCx_k. Then C is well-defined and 'c' can be read as 'Granger-causes' and 'C' as 'is Granger-causally prior to'.

Doan showed that x_iCx_j implies that the complete vector of series in the model, x, can be partitioned into two pieces, one containing x_i and the other containing x_j, such that no variable in the piece containing x_j Granger-causes any of the variables in the piece containing x_i. Thus when these results are specialized to linear time series models, a model with a Granger-causal ordering is one displaying a block triangular structure in its moving average and autoregressive representations. Putting the matter another way, x_iCx_j is equivalent to the assertion that there is some block of variables containing x_i and not x_j which are autonomous, in the sense that the best forecasts which can be made based on past values of variables in the block is as good as the best which can be made when past values of x_j are available as well. This is stronger than the assertion that x_j are available as well. This is stronger than the assertion that x_i does not Granger-cause x_j, which means that the best forecast of x_i itself based on past values of all variables in the x vector other than x_j is as good as the best forecast when past values of x_j are available as well. The assertion x_icx_j does not by itself connect to an assertion about exogeneity, while x_iCx_j implies that there is some set of equations in x in which x_j appears and x_i is exogenous.

Whatever one thinks of its independent appeal as a definition of causality, Granger causality forces into the open the implicit notion of causal priority underlying exogeneity assumptions in econometrics. Economists often assume exogeneity as a matter of convenience or dogmatism without subjecting these assumptions to critical examination. For example, it is common for models to 'treat as exogenous' policy variables, both because to do otherwise makes use of the models for policy analysis conceptually difficult and because in the policy maker's choice problem there is indeed a sense in which policy variables are 'causally prior'. But treating policy variables as exogenous for purposes of statistical inference amounts to asserting that they are causally prior in Granger's sense. Once we understand Granger's definition, it is easy to see that it is not the same notion of causal priority as that which makes policy variables causally prior in the policy maker's choice problem. Thus the causal priority of policy variables to policy makers does not justify treating those variables as statistically exogenous.

If (7) contains unknown parameters, and if there is another relation to determine z which contains a different set of unknown parameters, then exogeneity of z in (7) implies that estimation of (7)'s parameters in isolation is as efficient as estimating them jointly with the parameters of the relation determining z. Engle, Hendry and Richard (1983) (henceforth EHR) argue that this implication of exogeneity is in fact its essence, arriving thereby at a new definition of the word.

EHR's approach rests on the notion that an economic model is completely characterized by the function specifying the joint distribution of the data as a function of the parameters. In this framework, a single equation in a model is of separate interest only if it corresponds to a distinct group of parameters. Two sets of equations involving the same parameters and describing the same joint distribution of the data are equivalent. But economists have ordinarily regarded distinct equations or blocks of equations as corresponding to distinct behavioural mechanisms. If our model contains one block of equations determining economic behaviour of Thailand, and another determining economic behaviour of the US, we can ask whether US GNP is exogenous for the model of Thailand. With the standard approach, exogeneity of US GNP depends only on whether there are mechanisms (equations, in a complete model) by which disturbances to Thai economic behaviour influence determination of US economic behaviour. This is an assertion about the true stochastic structure of the world, not about what parameters of the Thai and US models are unknown. But in the EHR approach, if our model contained, say, a parameter representing the rate of technological change in the electronics industry, which was the same in both countries but unknown, no variable from either country would be exogenous in the other.

[A good Bayesian will be suspicious of the distinction I draw here between real randomness in behaviour and uncertainty about parameter values. In a single-agent decision problem this suspicion would be justified. In considering professional communication about scientific inference, the distinction between objective randomness in behaviour and uncertainty about parameters is useful, though (see Sims, 1982).]

Another way to see the drawbacks of the EHR approach is to note that in predictive applications of a model, even when the parameters are all known (or more often, when uncertainty in them is ignored), the block structure induced by exogeneity assumptions is a valuable concept. It allows us to characterize patterns of influence in conditional prediction. But the EHR approach leaves the notion of exogeneity undefined when there are no unknown parameters.

The EHR analysis is worth studying to understand how the usual presumption that analysis conditioning on an exogenous variable can in fact lead to inefficient estimators. This is a subtle point which they illustrate well. But it will remain useful to restrict models by asserting that disturbances in certain equations do not feed back in to the determination of certain variables. This kind of restriction is an assertion about exogeneity in its original sense, not about EHR exogeneity.

It seems to me worthwhile to reserve the original sense of 'exogeneity' and to think of EHR exogeneity as a different, related notion.

Granger causal ordering asserts that disturbances in one block of equations do not feed back into determination of variables in a certain block – ever. Sometimes it may not be reasonable to make such an assertion, yet it may be reasonable to assert that the feedback occurs only with a delay with some known lower bound. Block structure based on such feedback delay imposes restrictions on the time series model as does a Granger causal ordering, unless the feedback delay is exactly one time unit.

Feedback delay of one time unit between an equation block and a block of variables in the equations is the assumption of predeterminedness. Predeterminedness is a common assumption both in textbooks and applied work. For much of simultaneous equations theory predetermined variables can play the same role as exogenous variables. In standard set-ups, where each equation has its own set of parameters, predeterminedness coincides with EHR's notion of weak exogeneity.

Because of the arbitrariness of the time unit in economic data, an assertion that intuition or theory tells us there should be a feedback delay of one time unit, but no more, ought to be inherently suspicious. In a model which imposes many predeterminedness assumptions, it ought to be general practice to test for feedback delay of two or more periods. If feedback delays in the model are hardly ever more than one period, the specification ought to be regarded as implausible, even though, since the one-period delay imposes no restrictions in itself, it cannot be tested.

Comparing modelling approaches. Each of the modelling strategies discussed above helps to attack the problem of over-parameterization in multivariate time series models. They differ in their amenability to interpretation of various kinds and in their computational tractability.

In models where one has a great deal of a priori knowledge about the dynamic properties of a low dimensional driving process, the state space approach is attractive. It makes using the priori knowledge easy; and in this situation estimates of the historical path of the state process, which emerge naturally in the state space approach, will be important.

The observable index model has many of the same advantages. Its disadvantage is that it has seen little actual use, so that there will be less advice available when the anomalies which crop up so often in applying nonlinear models arise. Also, to the extent that the observable index is kept in a rather general form instead of being specialized in a more or less ad hoc way to a form involving very few unknown parameters (as stated space models usually are), it will be computationally less tractable than state space models.

The unobservable index model in the frequency domain is perhaps the most tractable of the approaches discussed here, so long as one limits oneself to testing the hypothesis that a low dimensional index model fits the data and to separating the spectral density into components due to the indexes and due to disturbance terms. It requires considerable additional computational work, however, to generate forecasts and estimates of the historical values of the unobserved indexes. Because it is naturally handled in the frequency domain, it is easy to interpret when the behavioural mechanisms being considered make separate predictions about high and low frequency or seasonal and non-seasonal frequency behaviour.

Bayesian vector autoregressions are computationally easy in some respects, being less dependent on iterative solution methods than the other approaches. However, they avoid the consequences of over-parameterization without actually reducing the dimension of the matrices involved in computation, so that for large models they may make large demands on computer memory. They also do not apply easily to situations where there is a priori reason to believe that much of the observed covariation of the data represents common responses to an underlying index or state of low dimension.

The multivariate approaches described above other than block structuring are in themselves symmetric in variables. Only the Bayesian VAR approach explicitly avoids the practice of treating model specifications arrived at by examining the data as if they were actually given a priori. However, index models and state space models do provide a framework for generation of reasonable probability models of multiple time series without invocation of the distinct, theory-based a priori knowledge about each equation in the system required with the standard simultaneous equations approach. They therefore share with the Bayesian VAR approach the promise of providing a basis for separating the purely instrumental parts of model specification, which are actually part of the estimation process, from the imposition of restrictions which are grounded in a priori knowledge or hypotheses about behaviour.

Imposition of block structure is ordinarily done by a process asymmetric in the variables, strongly influenced by a priori knowledge. We might look for exogeneity of US variables in the model for Thailand, but even if the data seemed compatible with it we would not be likely to impose exogeneity of Thai variables in a model of the US. The same is true of many of the simplifying assumptions routinely invoked in making state space models tractable. In both cases, though, the restrictions differ from the substantive restrictions commonly invoked in standard simultaneous equations modelling in that the connection of the restrictions to the behaviour of the joint probability model for the multiple time series is relatively transparent. In standard models the interaction of hundreds or thousands of restrictions imposed casually on individual equations tends to lead to unexpected anomalies in system behaviour.

CHECKING TIME SERIES MODELS FOR ACCURACY

Because there are different approaches to multivariate time series modelling, one commonly is in the position of comparing two or more models for the same data, neither of which is nested in the other. If two models are both nominally unstructured, one may want to know if they fit equally well and whether they are much different. If instead one model is the kind of mathematically intricate, behaviourally simplified model which emerges from modern stochastic dynamic equilibrium theories, while the other is an unstructured multivariate time series model, it is not likely that the equilibrium theory model fits as well as the other, but one may still wish to compare the models. The equilibrium model may provide interpretive insight into the unstructured model if the two are similar in important respects.

Though it might seem so on the surface, this problem of model comparison is not a version of the usual problem of comparing non-nested models. The literature on non-nested models takes the parameterization of each of the models as a firmly maintained hypothesis. In non-Bayesian time series modelling parameterizations are more or less explicitly data-dependent, with more elaborate dynamics emerging when more data are available. And of course the classical literature on non-nested model comparison can be no help at all in comparing a Bayesian to a non-Bayesian time series model.

In comparing model fits, there is a natural measure: recursively generated forecast errors. By these I mean the sequence of forecast errors when the entire modelling strategy is updated at each date t in the sampling period based on data through time t and forecasts made based on the resulting sequence of updated models. Non-Bayesian strategies, though, make the process of using the data to arrive at a model parameterization time-consuming and somewhat subjective, so that it is not practical to reproduce the whole process at each date in the sample. Furthermore, it would be impossible to assume that the researcher's subjective judgements about model form at early dates in the sample were not being influenced by what he knows about the data later in the sample. Bayesian strategies do provide a completely explicit procedure for updating the model based on new data. Even they, however, usually involve some search over a few 'hyperparameters', and this search is seldom reproduced in constructing recursive forecast errors.

There is, unfortunately, no easier alternative to recommend. It is important to remember that even measures of fit nominally based on recursively computed residuals are unreliable when they condition on a particular finite parameterization which has been arrived at after substantial exploration of the data. In fact, in a simple linear regression model it is well known that the sum of squared recursive residuals (weighted by their conditional variances) is the same as the sum of squared 'within-sample' residuals. In other models as well, going through the sample recursively to generate 'out of sample' errors with a model whose parametric form reflects experimentation with the entire sample provides no reliable information about actual out of sample performance.

Some econometricians, recognizing the dependence of the usual specification choice procedures on the data but not willing to abandon or modify those procedures, argue that one can only use actual out of sample performance as a measure of fit. This is a discouraging prescription, however, since historically it is clear that econometric models are revised every few years, so that the best currently available models never have a very extensive record of out of sample forecast performance. And for non-time-series models, there is often no realistic prospect of new data becoming available which would provide a predictive test of the model before decisions based on the results must be taken.

184

COMPARING TIME SERIES MODELS

It is not always reasonable to compare time series models by comparing how well they fit. For example one might have available both an uninterpreted Bayesian vector autoregression (VAR) and a fully interpreted behavioural equilibrium model, both applying to the same time series. The latter is likely to contain few parameters and be difficult to solve, but also to be easier to interpret and draw conclusions from. Even if it does not fit as well as the VAR model, we might for some purposes contemplate using it. We would then like to know whether it differs from the better-fitting VAR in substantively important respects.

If the application for the models is known and specific, there will be certain variables or parameters in the model whose conditional distributions given the data are important to the application. Ideally, one compares the models by checking whether they have different implications for these conditional distributions. Where the applications are diverse or ill defined, model comparison becomes correspondingly more difficult.

For models which are linear in variables, the impulse responses, plots of the conditional mean of all variables given unit disturbances to each equation's error term, provide a useful framework for model comparison. If the model is stationary, the impulse responses are also plots of the coefficients of the model's moving average representation and thus a complete summary of the model's second-order properties. They display typical modes of behaviour for variables in the system; they should look qualitatively like plots of the variables being modelled. And they have the units of the variables in the system, so that there is an intuitively reasonable scale for what constitute large differences in impulse responses across models.

For nonlinear models, there is no set of summary measures as appealing as the impulse responses. Where the nonlinearity is not too strong, one can simulate data from the nonlinear models and compare the impulse responses from linear models fitted to the simulated data. Where the focus is on conditional projections and forecasting of the future based on the most recent data, models can be compared by generating conditional distributions of future data with Monte Carlo methods.

LINES OF CONVERGENCE

It seems likely that the distinction between standard simultaneous equations methods and multivariate time series modelling methods will erode. Simultaneous equations methods, by taking a sophisticated view of dynamic structure and cross-equation serial correlation, can in principle begin to approach multiple time series modelling. Franz Palm (1983) has combined a variant of the Bayesian VAR framework with equation-by-equation simultaneous equations specification.

Keynesian macroeconomic theory connects handily to simultaneous equations econometric theory. It emphasizes separate analysis of consumption, investment, money demand, etc., followed by derivation of conclusions about dynamic behaviour generated by interaction of these distinct mechanisms. Macroeconomic theories based on models of individual optimization under uncertainty tend not to lead to the same clean distinctions among sectors or mechanisms. Empirical analysis of such theories leads restricted multiple time series models to be compared with unrestricted models. In this enterprise classical simultaneous equations theory offers little help. To the extent that this latter type of macroeconomic model becomes more common, emphasis on multiple time series modelling methodology in econometrics is likely to increase.

On the other hand, as multiple time series models are treated more seriously in economics, peole will want to use their results. One way or another this forces users of such models to confront the identification problem and thereby is likely to lead to use of formal methods for addressing this problem. A multiple time series model which treats identification formally will in some respects not look very different from a classical simultaneous equations model.

BIBLIOGRAPHY

Doan, T., Litterman, R. and Sims, C.A. 1984. Forecasting and conditional projection using realistic prior distributions. *Econometric Reviews* 3(1), 1–100; Reply, 131–44.

Engle, R., Hendry, D. and Richard, J.-F. 1983. Exogeneity. *Econometrica* 51, 277–304.

Geweke, J. 1977. The dynamic factor analysis of economic time series. In *Latent Variables in Socioeconomic Models*, ed. D.J. Aigner and A.S. Goldberger, Amsterdam: North-Holland.

Geweke, J. 1978. Testing the exogeneity specification in the complete dynamic simultaneous equations model. *Journal of Econometrics* 7, 163–85.

Granger, C.W.J. 1969. Investigating causal relations by econometric models and cross-spectral methods. *Econometrica* 37, 424–38.

Harvey, A. 1981. *Time Series*. New York: Halsted Press.

Kumar, P.R. and Varaiya, P. 1986. *Stochastic Systems: Identification, Estimation and Adaptive Control*. New Jersey: Prentice-Hall.

Leamer, E. 1972. A class of informative priors and distributed lag analysis. *Econometrica* 40, 1059–81.

Litterman, R. 1982. Specifying vector autoregressions for macroeconomic forecasting. In *Studies in Bayesian Economics and Statistics*, Vol 3 *In Honor of Bruno de Finetti*, ed. P. Good, Amsterdam: North-Holland.

McNees, S. 1986. Forecasting accuracy of alternative techniques: a comparison of US macroeconomic forecasts. *Journal of Business and Economic Statistics* 4, 4–23.

Palm, F. 1983. Structural econometric modeling and time series analysis: an integrated approach. In *Applied Time Series Analysis of Economic Data*, ed. A. Zellner, Washington, DC: US Census Bureau, 199–233.

Sargent, T.J. and Sims, C. 1977. Business cycle modeling without pretending to have too much a priori economic theory. In *New Methods in Business Cycle Research: Proceedings from a Conference*, ed. C.A. Sims, Minneapolis: Federal Reserve Bank of Minneapolis, 45–109.

Shiller, R. 1973. A distributed lag estimator derived from smoothness priors. *Econometrica* 41, 775–88.

Sims, C.A. 1972a. Money, income and causality. *American Economic Review* 62, 540–52.

Sims, C.A. 1972b. Distributed lag estimation when the parameter space is explicitly infinite dimensional. *Annals of Mathematical Statistics* 42, 1622–36.

Sims, C.A. 1977. Exogeneity and causal ordering in macroeconomic models. In *New Methods in Business Cycle Research: Proceedings from a Conference*, ed. C.A. Sims, Minneapolis: Federal Reserve Bank of Minneapolis.

Sims, C.A. 1982. Scientific standards in econometric modeling. In *Current Developments in the Interface: Economics, Econometrics, Mathematics*, Dordrecht, Boston and London: D. Reidel, 317–37.

Non-parametric Statistical Methods

JOSEPH L. GASTWIRTH

Basic statistics and econometrics courses stress methods based on assuming that the data or error term in regression models follow the normal distribution. Indeed, the efficiency of least squares estimates relies on the assumption of normality. In order to lessen the dependence of statistical inference on that assumption statisticians developed methods based on rank tests whose sampling distribution, under the null hypothesis, do not depend on the form of the underlying density function.

The simplest and oldest (Arbuthnott, 1710) non-parametric test is the sign test used to test whether the median of a population equals a specified value v_0. Let $x_1, \ldots, x_n$ be a sample of size n and let $s(x, v_0) = 1$ if $x > v_0$; $= 0$ otherwise. Then the statistic

$$S = \sum_{i=1}^{n} s(x_i, v_0) \tag{1}$$

has a binomial distribution with mean $n/2$ and variance $n/4$ if v_0 is the true median, as $P[s(x) = 1] = 1/2$ regardless of the form of the density function. This contrasts with the classical t-test whose exact sampling distribution depends on normality.

The sign test also yields an estimate and confidence interval for v the median when that parameter is unknown. The idea (see Hettmansperger, 1984 for details) is that we can vary v in the definition of $s(x)$ until we find that value or values for which S equals its expected value $(n/2)$, that is, the estimate $\hat{v}$ satisfies

$$\sum_{i=1}^{n} s(x_i, \hat{v}) = 0 \tag{2}$$

and is simply the sample median. In contrast with the test statistic, the estimator derived from the sign test is not distribution-free although distribution-free

187

confidence intervals are available. These are based on the binomial distribution of S and it can be demonstrated that the interval

$$[x_{(k+1)}, x_{(n-k)}], \tag{3}$$

where $x_{(i)}$ are the ordered observations, is a $100(1 - \alpha)$ per cent confidence interval for v when k satisfies $P[S \leqslant k] = \alpha/2$.

More interesting uses of non-parametric tests occur when samples from two populations are compared. Suppose we desire to see whether male and female college graduates earn similar wages after working for five years. We are testing whether the earning distribution of females, $G(x)$ equals that, $F(x)$, of males. One possible alternative is that $G(x) = F(x - \Delta)$, that is, the female distribution is shifted up by Δ. If the distributions are found to be significantly different we will then estimate Δ.

To resolve the issue, we take random samples $x_1, \ldots, x_m$ from $F(x)$ and $y_1, \ldots, y_n$ from $G(x)$. Consider the combined sample of $N = m + n$ observations. Under the null hypothesis that the two distributions are the same, that is, $F(x) = G(x)$, it can be shown that each of the original observations has probability $1/N$ of being the kth largest in the pooled sample. Thus the ranks in the combined sample that the ny's have can be considered as a random sample of n integers chosen from $1, \ldots, N$, irrespective of the form of the distribution function $F(x)$. Any test which is solely a function of the ranks that one group of observations has in the combined sample is called a rank test. If we let R_i be the rank y_i has in the ordered combined sample of N, then the Wilcoxon (1945) test is defined as $W = \Sigma R_i$, and its distribution is that of the sum of n randomly selected integers from $1, 2, \ldots, N$. Since the average of the first N integers is $(N + 1)/1$, under the null hypothesis the expected value of W is $n(N + 1)/2$. Furthermore, its variance is $nm(N + 1)/12$ and its standardized form

$$\frac{W - n(N+1)/2}{\sqrt{nm(N+1)/12}} \tag{4}$$

rapidly approaches the unit normal variate as n and m increase. If the observed value of W is much larger than expected, for example the standardized form exceeds $\pm z_{\alpha/2}$, where α is the pre-set significance level we reject the hypothesis that the x's and y's have the same distribution in favour of the alternative and conclude that the distribution of the y's is shifted to the right, i.e. $\Delta > 0$.

So far we have limited our attention to ensuring that the probability of rejecting the hypothesis that both populations are the same when it is indeed true, is small (5 per cent or less). The advantage of rank statistics is that this calculation is the same regardless of the form of the density function of the variable. On the other hand, we also desire to reject the null hypothesis when the two populations truly differ. If c is the critical point of a test of size α (often 0.05), that is, the probability, when the null hypothesis is true, of obtaining a value $> c$, is $\leqslant \alpha$, written $P_0[W > c] \leqslant \alpha$, then the power of the test is the probability of $[W > c]$ calculated under the alternative assumption (e.g. $\Delta = 1$). While the size (α) of the

Wilcoxon (or any rank test) does not depend on the form of the underlying density function, its power does. The remarkable fact about the Wilcoxon test is that it is about 95 per cent as powerful as the usual t-test for normal data. Hence, one pays a rather small price in terms of loss of power for guaranteeing that the Type I error (size) is not affected by the form of the density.

The Wilcoxon test also has an equivalent form, due to Mann and Whitney (1947), based on comparing each of the x's with each of the y's. Let

$$I_{ij} = \begin{cases} 1, & \text{if } y_i > x_j \\ 1/2, & \text{if } y_i = x_j \\ 0, & 0 \quad \text{otherwise.} \end{cases} \tag{5}$$

The statistic $W = \Sigma\Sigma I_{ij}$, counts the number of times a y observation exceeds an x observation. Notice that

$$\Sigma R_i = W + n(n+1)/2 \tag{6}$$

since, if the y's are the smallest n observations in the total of $m + n$, $W = 0$ and $\Sigma R_i = n(n+1)/2$. As we move the y's up to obtain our sample ranks every time a y exceeds an x both ΣR_i and W increase by 1. This form of the Wilcoxon test has two desirable features. First, W/mn estimates an interesting parameter, $P[X < Y]$, the probability that a randomly selected y (female earnings) exceeds a randomly selected x (male earnings) under the null hypothesis that $F = G$, $P[X < Y]$ should equal $1/2$. This measure can also indicate whether 'progress' towards equality is made over time. Secondly, the amount of shift, Δ, that needs to be added to the y's so that

$$\Sigma R_i(x_i, y_j + \Delta) - n(N+1)/2 = 0, \tag{7}$$

that is, the Wilcoxon test calculated on the old x's and the new $(y_i + \Delta)$'s equals its expected value under H_0, can be expressed as the *median* of the mn differences $(y_i - x_j) = D_{ij}$ (see Lehmann, 1975, p. 82) and is an alternative estimate of the difference between the location parameters of the two distributions.

So far we have only used the sum of the ranks of the observation of our sample (y's) as a test statistic. More generally one can use a statistic of the form $\Sigma a(R_i)$, where R_i is the rank of y_i and $a(R_i)$ is specified by $a[R_i/(N+1)]$, where $a(u)$ is a function on $(0, 1)$. The following basic result, due to Chernoff and Savage (1958), shows that there is a non-parametric test with the same large sample power as the best parametric test for the problem when the density function $f = F'$ is known:

Theorem 1. Let $x_1, \ldots, x_m; y_1, \ldots, y_n$ be two independent samples from the distributions $F(x)$ and $G(x) = F(x - \Delta)$, respectively, and assume that $f = F'$ has finite Fisher information, that is $I = \int (f'/f)^2 f \, \mathrm{d}x < \infty$. The asymptotically most powerful rank test of H_0: $\Delta = 0$ against $\Delta \neq 0$ is based on the function

$$a(u) = I^{-1/2} f'[F^{-1}(u)]/f[F^{-1}(u)], \qquad 0 < u < 1, \tag{8}$$

189

and is asymptotically as powerful as the best parametric (maximum likelihood) procedure. In particular, if $F(x) = \Phi(x)$, the standard normal distribution, $a(u) = \Phi^{-1}(u)$ and generates the normal scores test. The Wilcoxon test is the optimal test for data from the logistic law. For further examples see Hajek and Sidak (1967).

The next problem one faces is how to choose the rank test or score function $a(u)$ as almost any reasonable test is consistent. To guide this choice we use the Pitman efficiency $e(T_1, T_2)$ which compares the power of two tests of the $H_0: \Delta = 0$ against a sequence of alternatives $\Delta = \sigma/\sqrt{N}$ which approach the null hypothesis as the sample size increases. The Pitman efficiency $e(T_1, T_2)$ can be interpreted as the limiting ratio of the sample sizes required by the tests T_1 and T_2 to achieve the same limiting power π against the same sequence of alternatives. For example, if the Pitman efficiency of test T_1 relative to T_2 $e(T_1, T_2) = 1/2$, then the test T_2 requires approximately half as many observations as the test T_1 to achieve the same large sample power for critical regions of the same size α. Moreover, the relative efficiencies of the corresponding estimates is also given by $e(T_1, T_2)$. The Pitman efficiency can be easily computed. The efficiency of T_1 (based on $a_1(u)$) relative to the best test, T_2, on data from the density f_2 is given by

$$\langle a_1, a_2 \rangle = \int a_1(u) a_2(u) \, du, \tag{9}$$

where a_2 is obtained from (8). By the symmetry of the inner product T_2 has this same efficiency relative to the best test, T_1, for data from the density f_1. The fact that the functions $a(u)$ generating the most powerful rank tests for a wide family of densities are in $L^2(0, 1)$ yields insight into other problems as well. If one truly knew the form of the density, why use a rank test instead of the usual maximum likelihood test? Suppose one knew something about the density, for example that it was either f_1 or f_2 (normal or double exponential): Is there a reasonably powerful rank test for this problem? Considering the functions a_1, a_2 as vectors in $L^2(0, 1)$, it is clear that a test corresponding to the angle bisector will maximize the minimum efficiency when data come from either density. In fact, the robust test obtained in this manner is nearly 90 per cent as efficient as the best tests when they fit the model. On the other hand, if the normal scores test is used when the data are from a double-exponential, it has only 64 per cent efficiency. This general problem is discussed in Gastwirth (1966) and Birnbaum and Laska (1967).

The reason we reviewed the two-sample problem at length is that the relative efficiencies of the tests and derived parameter estimates (Hodges and Lehmann, 1963; Bauer, 1972) typically extend to their analogues in regression and linear models. Thus, once an appropriate nonparametric test is selected it can be used for the same family of possible error distributions in more complex general linear models.

Before discussing regression models we note that an alternative approach to account for the effect of covariates is to stratify the data into homogeneous

190

subgroups, compare the two samples in each subgroup using the same rank test and combine the *results* into our summary statistic. In the male–female earnings example one might stratify the data by occupation. The Wilcoxon procedure was generalized by van Elteren (1960) and developed further by others (see Oosterhoff, 1969) and yields a summary estimate of the parameter $P[X < Y]$. General rank tests were considered by Puri (1965).

The first analogues of rank tests for analysis of variance (Friedman, 1937; Brown and Mood, 1951; Kruskal and Wallis, 1952) and regression models (Theil, 1950) were based on extending the Wilcoxon and median tests and Kendall's measure, τ, of dependence of bivariate data (Sen, 1968). The generalizability of tests based on score functions, $a(u)$ to these more general situations was made possible by the results of Jureckova (1969, 1971). The analogues of the normal equations of least squares are a non-linear system of equations which can be 'linearized' by her techniques. We next introduce these ideas in the simple linear regression model

$$Y_i = \alpha + x_i\beta + e_i, \qquad (10)$$

where e_i are i.i.d. with mean 0 and the x_i's are fixed known numbers. To test whether the slope $\beta = 0$, ordinary least squares theory uses

$$\hat{\beta} = \frac{\sum (x_i - \bar{x})y_i}{\sum (x_i - \bar{x})^2} \qquad (11)$$

which has a variance $\sigma^2 / \Sigma(x_i - \bar{x})^2$ and mean 0 if $\beta = 0$. The extension of the Wilcoxon procedure replaces the y_i in the numerator of (11) by their ranks, R_i; that is, considers the statistic

$$T = \sum (x_i - \bar{x})R_i. \qquad (12)$$

If $H_0: \beta = 0$ holds, then the y_i's are i.i.d. variates with location parameter α and the ranks of the y_i's, just like their numerical values, should be uncorrelated with $(x_i - x)$, that is $E(T) = 0$. Moreover,

$$\text{var}(T) = \frac{nN(N+1)}{12} \sum (x_i - \bar{x})^2.$$

To estimate β we consider T as a function of a possible value of β, that is

$$T(\beta) = \sum (x_i - \bar{x})R(y_i - \alpha - \beta x_i), \qquad (13)$$

where $R(y_i - \alpha - \beta x_i)$ is the rank of the residual $y_i - \alpha - \beta x_i$. Because the ranks of the y's do not depend on α, that is if the intercept of the line were increased (or decreased), the ranks of the $y_i - \alpha - \beta x_i$ would remain the same, one can take $\alpha = 0$. If β^* is the true value of β then

$$E[T(\beta^*)] = 0 \qquad (14)$$

and we can estimate β by the value $\hat{\beta}$ which satisfies

$$T(\hat{\beta}) = \Sigma(x_i - \bar{x})R(y_i - \hat{\beta}x_i) = 0. \qquad (15)$$

Unfortunately, $\hat{\beta}$ typically must be obtained by numerical means although its distribution in large samples approaches a normal law. If an estimate of α is also desired, the median of the $\{y_i - \hat{\beta}x_i\}$ can be used.

Rank tests and estimates of β based on other score functions, $a(u)$ replace R_i by $a(R_i/N + 1)$ etc. The relative efficiency of these procedures is the same as their values in the two sample problem so that knowledge of nature of the error distribution should be used in selecting a non-parametric test. A large literature (Hettmansperger, 1984) has been devoted to obtaining nonparametric methodology for the multiple regression and linear models. The basic idea of estimation is to find the vector β minimizing

$$\sum a\left[\frac{R(Y_i - x_i'\beta)}{N+1}\right](Y_i - x_i'\beta), \tag{16}$$

in the model

$$y = [1\ X]\binom{\alpha}{\beta} + e,$$

where $Y = (Y_1, \ldots, Y_n)'$, 1 is an $n \times 1$ column of 1's, X is the $N \times p$ matrix of regression constants and β the regression parameters. Various conditions may be imposed on the score function, a, in (16) for example $a(u) = a(1 - u)$ and $a(u)$ is an increasing function, in order that the measure (16) is a proper measure of dispersion. The mathematical methods of finding the estimate β in (16) involve solving a set of non-linear equations satisfying

$$\sum_{i=1}^{N} (x_{ij} - \bar{x}_j)a[R(y_i - x_i'\beta)] \simeq 0, \qquad j = 1, \ldots, p \tag{17}$$

which play the role of the normal equations of OLS.

Although methods based on rank tests are less sensitive to the distributional assumptions of classical procedures, they lose their distribution-free character when the observations are dependent. For example, the distribution of the sampling distribution of the sign test or first order autoregressive processes with the same ρ depends on the form of the underlying distribution (Wolff et al., 1967). Thus, the usual diagnostic checks based on examining the residuals should be carried out even when the regression model is fitted by nonparametric or other robust methods (Huber, 1972; Bickel, 1973; Hogg, 1974). Of course, the dependence also affects the distribution of least squares estimates and Gastwirth and Rubin (1971) show that the level of the test using the sample mean is more sensitive to dependence than the sign or Wilcoxon procedures.

BIBLIOGRAPHY

Arbuthnott, J. 1710. An argument for divine providence taken from the constant regularity observed in the birth of both sexes. *Philosophical Transactions* 27, 186–90.

Bauer, D.F. 1972. Constructing confidence sets using rank statistics. *Journal of the American Statistical Association* 67, 687–90.

Bickel, P.J. 1973. On some analogs to linear combination of order statistics in the linear model. *Annals of Statistics* 1, 597–616.

Birnbaum, A. and Laska, E. 1967. Efficiency robust two-sample rank tests. *Journal of the American Statistical Association* 62, 1241–51.

Brown, G.W. and Mood, A.M. 1951. On median tests for linear hypotheses. *Proceedings of the 2nd Berkeley Symposium*, 159–66.

Chernoff, H. and Savage, I.R. 1958. Asymptotic normality and efficiency of certain nonparametric test statistics. *Annals of Mathematical Statistics* 29, 972–94.

van Elteren, P. 1960. On the combination of independent two sample tests of Wilcoxon. *Bulletin de l'Institut Internationale de Statistique* 37(3), 351–60.

Friedman, M. 1937. The use of ranks to avoid the assumption of normality implicit in the analysis of variance. *Journal of the American Statistical Association* 32, 675–701.

Gastwirth, J.L. 1966. On robust procedures. *Journal of the American Statistical Association* 61, 929–48.

Gastwirth, J.L. and Rubin, H. 1971. The behavior of the level of rank tests on dependent data. *Journal of the American Statistical Association* 66, 816–20.

Hajek, J. and Sidak, Z. 1967. *Theory of Rank Tests*. New York: Academic Press.

Hettmansperger, T.P. 1984. *Statistical Inference Based on Ranks*. New York: Wiley.

Hodges, J.L., Jr. and Lehmann, E.L. 1963. Estimates of location based on rank tests. *Annals of Mathematical Statistics* 34, 598–611.

Hogg, R.V. 1974. Adaptive robust procedures: a partial review and some suggestions for future research. *Journal of the American Statistical Association* 69, 909–27.

Hollander, M. and Wolfe, D.A. 1973. *Nonparametric Statistical Methods*. New York: Wiley.

Huber, P.J. 1972. Robust statistics: a review. *Annals of Mathematical Statistics* 43, 1041–67.

Jureckova, J. 1969. Asymptotic linearity of a rank statistic in regression parameter. *Annals of Mathematical Statistics* 40, 1889–950.

Jureckova, J. 1971. Nonparametric estimate of regression coefficients. *Annals of Mathematical Statistics* 42, 1328–38.

Kruskal, W.H. and Wallis, W.A. 1952. Use of ranks in one criterion variance analysis. *Journal of the American Statistical Association* 57, 583–621.

Lehmann, E.L. 1975. *Nonparametrics: Statistical Methods Based on Ranks*. San Francisco: Holden-Day.

Mann, H.B. and Whitney, D.R. 1947. On a test of whether one of two random variables is stochastically larger than the other. *Annals of Mathematical Statistics* 18, 50–60.

Oosterhoff, J. 1969. *Combination of One-Sided Statistical Tests*. Amsterdam: Mathematical Centre.

Puri, M.L. 1965. On the combination of independent two sample tests of a general class. *Review of the ISI* 33, 229–41.

Sen, P.K. 1968. Estimates of the regression coefficient based on Kendall's tau. *Journal of the American Statistical Association* 63, 1379–89.

Theil, H. 1950. A rank invariant method of linear and polynomial regression analysis. *Proceedings: Koninklijke Nederlandse Akademie van Wetenschappen*, Series A 53, 386–92.

Wilcoxon, F. 1945. Individual comparison by ranking methods. *Biometrics* 1, 80–83.

Wolff, S.S., Rubin, H. and Gastwirth, J.L. 1967. The effect of autoregression dependence on a nonparametric test. *Professional Group on Information Theory* IEEE, IT-13, 311–13.

Outliers

WILLIAM S. KRASKER

Nearly all empirical investigations in economics, particularly those involving linear structural models or regressions, are subject to the problem of anomalous data, commonly called outliers. Roughly speaking, there are three sources of outliers. First, the distribution of the model's random disturbances often has longer tails than the normal distribution, resulting in a greatly increased chance of larger disturbances. Second, the data set may contain erroneous numbers, or 'gross errors'. The data bases most prone to gross errors are large cross sections, particularly those compiled from surveys; gross errors can result from misinterpreted questions, incorrectly recorded answers, keypunch errors, etc. Third, the model itself, typically linear in (transformations of) the variables, is only an approximation to reality. It is apt to be a poor representation of the process generating the data for extreme values of the explanatory variables. This source of outliers applies even to, say, macroeconomic time series, where the likelihood of gross errors is minimal.

Outliers resulting from heavy-tailed but still symmetric disturbance distributions can greatly decrease the efficiency of least squares, while gross errors can in addition cause substantial biases. These potentially damaging effects of anomalous data have been recognized for many years; indeed, the first published work on least squares (Legendre, 1805) recommended that outliers be removed from the sample before estimation. The wisdom of this and other approaches that give the observations unequal weights was debated throughout the 19th century.

Despite considerable evidence that error distributions tend to be heavy tailed, many statisticians were reluctant to modify least squares, which was known to be optimal when the disturbances are normally distributed. There were notable exceptions, however, such as Simon Newcomb, an astronomer and mathematician as well as an economist. Newcomb (1886) introduced the idea of modelling the disturbance distribution as a mixture of normal distributions with differing variances; the implied marginal distribution then has heavier tails than the normal. Newcomb also proposed a 'weighted least squares' alternative that, it turns out, is similar to a 1964 proposal of Peter Huber, discussed below, which has numerous desirable robustness properties. (The contributions of Newcomb and other late-19th and early 20-century statisticians are discussed in more detail by Stigler, 1973.)

There was a rapid increase in interest in robustness in the mid 1900s, in part due to the work of John Tukey (see, e.g. Tukey, 1960). Robustness research benefited greatly in the 1960s from the formalization of certain desirable robustness properties of estimators. The first is 'efficiency robustness': one would like an estimator to maintain a high efficiency for all symmetric disturbance distributions that are 'close to' the normal distribution. Peter Huber (1964) found a one-parameter family of estimators, indexed by $c > 0$, that have a certain optimal minimax efficiency-robustness property. Suppose the regression model is $y_i = x_i\beta + u_i (i = 1, \ldots, n)$, where y_i is the ith observation on the dependent variable, x_i is the k-dimensional row vector containing the ith observation on the explanatory variables, u_i is the ith disturbance, and β is the k-vector of parameters to be estimated. Then the Huber estimate b is the vector that solves the equations

$$0 = \psi_c(y_i - x_i b)x_{ij} \qquad (j = 1, \ldots, k),$$

where $\psi_c(t) \equiv \max[-c, \min(t, c)]$ and where the choice of parameter c depends on the scale of the disturbance distribution and the desired tradeoff between robustness and efficiency. As $c \to \infty$, the Huber estimator reduces to ordinary least squares, whereas if c is never zero, the estimator is similar to the method of least absolute residuals, which had been studied as early as Laplace (1818) and which gained some popularity in the 1950s (see Taylor, 1974). The Huber estimator and over sixty others were compared for small samples in the 'location' problem (regression on just a constant term) in an extensive 1970–71 Monte Carlo study (Andrews et al., 1972). The results suggested that the asymptotic properties hold quite will in samples as small as twenty.

Though the Huber estimators, and others designed for efficiency robustness, maintain a high efficiency even for heavy-tailed disturbance distributions, they are not resistant to other sources of outliers, such as low-probability gross errors. A second desirable robustness property, introduced by Hampel (1968, 1971) and corresponding to the mathematical concept of uniform continuity, is that if gross errors are generated with small probability, then, irrespective of the distribution of those gross errors, the estimator's bias should be small. Estimators having this property are called 'qualitatively robust'. Hampel quantified this relationship by means of an estimator's 'sensitivity', which he defined as the right-hand derivative of the maximum possible bias, with respect to the probability of gross errors, evaluated at probability zero.

Modifications of the Huber estimator designed to make it qualitatively robust were proposed by several researchers in the 1970s (see Krasker and Welsch (1982) for further discussion). They have the general form

$$0 = v(x_i)\psi_c((y_i - x_i b)/(w(x_i))x_{ij} \qquad (j = 1, \ldots, k),$$

195

where w and v are non-negative weight functions that allow for the downweighting of observations with outlying values for the explanatory variables, called 'leverage points'. The proposals of Krasker (1980) and Krasker and Welsch (1982) also have a certain efficiency property among estimators with the same sensitivity to gross errors. The idea of finding an estimator that has maximum efficiency subject to a bound on the sensitivity was developed by Hampel (1968).

If an estimator is qualitatively robust, its asymptotic bias will be small provided the probability of gross errors is sufficiently small. However, this property does not tell us how the estimator will behave if the gross errors are, say, ten per cent of the data. One crude measure of this behaviour, introduced by Hampel (1968, 1971) and called the 'breakdown point', is the smallest probability of gross errors that can cause the asymptotic bias to be arbitrarily large. Equivalently, it is the largest fraction of gross errors in the data that the estimator can handle before it becomes totally unreliable. By the 1980s it was clear that the most common qualitatively robust regression estimators, such as those listed earlier, have low breakdown points when k, the number of parameters, is large. Several alternative estimators were proposed that have breakdown points equal to $\frac{1}{2}$, the largest possible value. Examples are the 'repeated medians' estimator of Siegel (1982), the projection-pursuit approach of Donoho and Huber (1983) and the estimator proposed by Rousseeuw (1984), which minimizes the median of the squared residuals (rather than their sum). However, all of these estimators are computationally burdensome unless k is small, and in fact, it appears that the computational difficulties are an inherent feature of high-breakdown multivariate procedures that transform naturally under linear changes in the coordinate system.

One of the most important uses for high-breakdown procedures is simply to facilitate the identification of outliers, which are often masked by non-robust estimators. For example, in a simple regression, a single outlier associated with an extreme value of the explanatory variable can have so much influence on the least-squares estimate that its own residual is very small. Thus, mere examination of the residuals from a non-robust fit can fail to reveal the anomalous observations. This problem becomes much more severe in higher dimensions, where even many qualitatively robust estimators can break down due to a small cluster of outlying observations. Belsley, Kuh and Welsch (1980) have proposed a variety of methods for identifying outliers in regression.

For statistical inference, as opposed to data analysis, identification of the outliers is only a small part of the problem. An important difficulty is that it is often impossible to determine solely from the data whether an outlying observation results from aberrant data, or whether the true regression function is slightly non-linear. Typically either of these possibilities will 'explain' the outlier, but for inference their implications may be very different. In these circumstances it seems essential to place a prior on the amount of curvature in the regression function, but this is difficult to do, particularly when there are several explanatory variables. One approach is outlined in Krasker, Kuh and Welsch (1983, section 5).

Finally, although the preceding remarks have dealt with regression, outliers occur and have similar consequences in many other statistical contexts, such as discrete or censored dependent variable models, stochastic parameter models, or linear structural models. The most reliable way to identify outliers in these contexts is to estimate robustly the model's underlying parameters, and check for observations that deviate greatly in an appropriate sense from the model's prediction. For example, Krasker and Welsch (1985) have presented a qualitatively robust weighted-instrumental-variables estimator for simultaneous-equations models, analogous to their proposal for regression. In general, however, methods for dealing with outliers in models of the kind just mentioned are far less developed than those for regression.

BIBLIOGRAPHY

Andrews, D.F., Bickel, P.J., Hampel, F.R., Huber, P.J., Rogers, W.H. and Tukey, J.W. 1972. *Robust Estimates of Location: Survey and Advances.* Princeton: Princeton University Press.

Belsley, D.A., Kuh, E. and Welsch, R.E. 1980. *Regression Diagnostics.* New York: John Wiley and Sons.

Donoho, D.L. and Huber, P.J. 1983. The notion of breakdown point. In *A Festschrift for Erich L. Lehmann,* ed. P. Bickel, K. Doksum and J.L. Hodges, Jr, Belmont, Cal.: Wadsworth International Group.

Hampel, F.R. 1968. Contributions to the theory of robust estimation. PhD thesis, Berkeley, University of California.

Hampel, F.R. 1971. A general qualitative definition of robustness. *Annals of Mathematical Statistics* 42, 1887–96.

Huber, P.J. 1964. Robust estimation of a location parameter. *Annals of Mathematical Statistics* 35(1), 73–101.

Krasker, W.S. 1980. Estimation in linear regression models with disparate data points. *Econometrica* 48, 1333–46.

Krasker, W.S., Kuh, E. and Welsch, R.E. 1983. Estimation for dirty data and flawed models. In *Handbook of Econometrics,* Vol 1, ed. Z. Griliches and M.D. Intriligator, Amsterdam: North-Holland.

Krasker, W.S. and Welsch, R.E. 1982. Efficient bounded-influence regression estimation. *Journal of the American Statistical Association* 77(379), September, 595–604.

Krasker, W.S. and Welsch, R.E. 1985. Resistant estimation for simultaneous-equations models using weighted instrumental variables. *Econometrica* 53(6), 1475–88.

Laplace, P.S. de. 1818. *Deuxième supplément à la théorie analytique des probabilités.* Paris: Courcier. Reprinted in *Oeuvres de Laplace,* Vol. 7, Paris: Imprimerie Royale, 1847, 569–623. Reprinted in *Oeuvres complètes de Laplace,* Vol. 7, Paris: Gauthier-Villars, 1886, 531–80.

Legendre, A.M. 1805. On the method of least squares. Trans. in *A Source Book in Mathematics,* ed. D.E. Smith, New York: Dover Publications, 1959.

Newcomb, D. 1886. A generalized theory of the combination of observations so as to obtain the best result. *American Journal of Mathematics* 8, 343–66.

Rousseeuw, P.J. 1984. Least median of squares regression. *Journal of the American Statistical Association* 79(388), December, 871–80.

Siegel, A.F. 1982. Robust regression using repeated medians. *Biometrika* 69, 242–4.

Stigler, S.M. 1973. Simon Newcomb, Percy Daniell, and the history of robust estimation, 1885–1920. *Journal of the American Statistical Association* 68(344), December, 872–9.

Taylor, L.D. 1974. Estimation by minimizing the sum of absolute errors. In *Frontiers of Econometrics,* ed. P. Zarembka, New York: Academic Press.

Tukey, J.W. 1960. A survey of sampling from contaminated distributions. In *Contributions to Probability and Statistics,* ed. I. Olkin, Stanford: Stanford University Press.

Prediction

P. WHITTLE

Any rational theory of prediction must be based upon a model. Enoch Powell expresses this view when he says, 'The prophets were not soothsayers; they were expounders.'

We shall formulate models in discrete time, so that the time variable t can be assumed to take integral values. The value of a variable x at time t will be denoted x_t. We shall frequently denote the observation taken at time t by y_t (usually vector-valued) and shall then denote the *observation history*

$$(y_t, y_{t-1}, \ldots)$$

available at time t by Y_t. The estimate of a quantity u based upon Y_t will be denoted $u^{(t)}$. Thus $x_{t+m}^{(t)}$ is, for positive m, the predictor of x_{t+m} formed at time t. The linear *linear least square* (LLS) criterion chooses $u^{(t)}$ as the linear function of Y_t that minimizes the mean square deviation $E[u - u^{(t)}]^2$ (or a matrix analogue if u is vector-valued). If all variables are jointly normally distributed (*Gaussian*, henceforth), then this $u^{(t)}$ can also be characterized as the conditional expectation $E[u \mid Y_t]$ or as the maximum likelihood (ML) estimate of u for given Y_t.

There are two techniques useful in the calculation of such estimates and predictors: *recursive methods* (associated with Markov models) and *generating function methods* (associated with cases in which structure is time-invariant and prediction errors are stationary).

If x and y are random vectors of zero mean then we shall use $\operatorname{cov}(x, y)$ to denote the cross-covariance matrix $E(xy')$, and shall write $\operatorname{cov}(x, x)$ simply as $\operatorname{cov}(x)$.

RECURSIVE METHODS: MARKOV MODELS AND THE KALMAN FILTER. Consider the dynamic equation, typical of many econometric models:

$$x_{t+1} = Ax_t + \varepsilon_{t+1}. \tag{1}$$

Here the process variable x is supposed to be a vector, and so A, a corresponding square matrix, and ε_t is assumed to be vector white noise of zero mean and with covariance matrix N. One special feature of this model is that it is linear; another is that it is Markov (at least if ε is Gaussian). This is, that x is a state variable which constitutes a complete description, in that all aspects of the future which can be predicted from

$$X_t = (x_t, x_{t-1}, \ldots)$$

can also be predicted from x_t.

Suppose indeed that just $(x_t, x_{t-1}, \ldots)$ is observable at time t, so that $Y_t = X_t$. From (1) we deduce the solution

$$x_{t+m} = A^m x_t + \sum_{s=0}^{m-1} A^s \varepsilon_{t+m-s} \tag{2}$$

for a future value x_{1+m} in terms of the current state x_t and future noise. Now, the white noise character of ε implies that $E[\varepsilon_{t+\tau} | X_t] = 0$ for $\tau > 0$. That is, a future noise value is unpredictable in that it has no better predictor than its unconditioned mean value: zero. We deduce then from (2) the simple expression for the predictor $x_{t+m}^{(t)} = E[x_{t+m} | X_t]$:

$$x_{t+m}^{(t)} = A^m x_t \qquad (m \geqslant 0). \tag{3}$$

This obeys the recursion in m:

$$x_{t+m+1}^{(t)} = A x_{t+m}^{(t)} \qquad (m \geqslant 0). \tag{4}$$

In other words, one predicts into the future just by solving the dynamic equation (1) with future noise set equal to its best prediction: zero. The predictor (3) would be *exact* for sequences $\{x_t\}$ generated from the noise-free version of (1):

$$x_{t+1} = A x_t. \tag{5}$$

In the case (1) of noisy dynamics we see from (2) and (3) that the m-step prediction error will have covariance matrix

$$\operatorname{cov}[x_{t+m}^{(t)} - x_{t+m}] = \sum_{s=0}^{m-1} A^s N (A')^s. \tag{6}$$

All these results remain true whatever the nature of A (and indeed have analogues if A is time-varying). If A has all its eigenvalues inside the unit circle, then system (1) is stable and will generate a stationary process. In other cases, $\{x_t\}$ will not be stationary, but conclusions (3), (4) and (6) still hold, and the prediction errors are stationary in time. For example, if A has a k-fold eigenvalue at unity, then the noise-free equation (5) will generate a polynomial trend in time of degree $k - 1$ (which (3) will predict exactly) and the actual dynamic equation (1) will generate a disturbed such tend. If A has other eigenvalues on the unit circle, then (1) will generate disturbed cyclicities (*undamped*, and possibly of polynomially increasing amplitude). Allowance of these possibilities provides the most 'structural' way of incorporating trends and seasonalities. If A has eigenvalues outside the unit circle, then (5) will have exponentially growing solutions (again predicted exactly by (3)) and (1) will have disturbed such solutions.

However, it will seldom be the case that the full state variable x will be observable. One must in general regard x as the state variable of an ideal Markov model, and indeed as a latent variable, which can be observed only partially. The usual and natural assumption is that, at time t, one can observe a vector y_t related to x by

$$y_{t+1} = Cx_t + \eta_{t+1}, \tag{7}$$

where $\{\varepsilon_t, \eta_t\}$ jointly constitute vector white noise with covariance matrix

$$\mathrm{cov}\begin{pmatrix} \varepsilon \\ \eta \end{pmatrix} = \begin{pmatrix} N & L \\ L' & M \end{pmatrix}. \tag{8}$$

Relations (1) and (7) together express process and observation structure.

Let us denote $x_t^{(t)}$ by $\hat{x}_t$, the estimate of current state based on current observations. From (1), (7) and the properties of LLS estimates one can deduce that $\hat{x}_t$ obeys the recursion

$$\hat{x}_{t+1} = A\hat{x}_t + H_t(y_{t+1} - C\hat{x}_t), \tag{9}$$

where the matrix H_t is determined in terms of

$$V_t = \mathrm{cov}(\hat{x}_t - x_t) \tag{10}$$

by the recursions

$$V_{t+1} = N + AV_tA' - (L + AV_tC')(M + CV_tC')^{-1}(L' + CV_tA') \tag{11}$$

$$H_t = (L + AV_tC')(M + CV_tC')^{-1}. \tag{12}$$

Relation (9) constitutes the celebrated *Kalman filter* (a 'filter' being an operation for generating one sequence from another; in this case $\{\hat{x}_t\}$ from $\{y_t\}$). The shortest of its many proofs is quite short (see, for example, Whittle, 1983, p. 147).

There are many points to be made about the Kalman filter. It is an updating relation, to be used in real time, to produce the new estimate of current state $\hat{x}_{t+1}$ from the old one $\hat{x}_t$ as a new observation y_{t+1} becomes available. It takes the form of the dynamic equation (1) of the model itself, but driven, not by noise, but by the *innovation* $(y_{t+1} - C\hat{x}_t)$. The innovation is to be interpreted as that part of the new observation y_{t+1} which is not predictable from previous observations Y_t.

Once one has the state estimate, then prediction is simple. Because both process noise ε and observation noise η are supposed white one has

$$x_{t+m}^{(t)} = A^m \hat{x}_t, \qquad (m \geqslant 0)$$

$$y_{t+m}^{(t)} = CA^{m-1}\hat{x}_t, \qquad (m > 0). \tag{13}$$

Recursion (9) and relations (13) explain between them virtually all recursions (in t or m) between predictors to be found in the literature.

If appropriate conditions are satisfied (referred to as *observability* or *detectability* conditions), then, in the absence of plant and observation noise, the error in state estimate $\hat{x}_t - x_t$ will tend to zero with increasing t. Under these same conditions the matrices V_t and H_t will tend to limit values V and H in the noisy case. Further, the matrix $\Omega = A - HC$ will be a stability matrix (so that Ω^s tends to zero exponentially fast with increasing s).

The Kalman filter (9) can then be written

$$\hat{x}_{t+1} = \Omega\hat{x}_t + Hy_{t+1} \tag{14}$$

with 'solution'

$$\hat{x}_t = \sum_{s=0}^{\infty} \Omega^s Hy_{t-s} \tag{15}$$

are of state and observation, and not of the parameters of the model itself, which are presumed known for present purposes.

$$g_{xy}(z) = \sum_{s=-\infty}^{\infty} z^s \operatorname{cov}(x_t, y_{t-s}),$$

a matrix function of the scalar marker variable z. Generating functions such as $g_{xy}(z)$ are closely related to Fourier ideas and the frequency concept; the power series becomes a Fourier series if we set $z = \exp(i\omega)$.

Suppose that $g_{xx}(z)$ has a *canonical factorization*

$$g_{xx}(z) = B(z)B(z^{-1})' \tag{16}$$

where both $B(z) = \sum_{s=0}^{\infty} b_s z^s$ and $B(z)^{-1}$ are analytic in $|z| \leq 1$. Then the stationary process $\{x_t\}$ has both a *moving average representation*

$$x_t = \sum_{s=0}^{\infty} b_s \varepsilon_{t-s}, \tag{17}$$

where $\{\varepsilon_t\}$ is white noise with $\operatorname{cov}(\varepsilon) = I$, and an *autoregressive representation*

$$\sum_{s=0}^{\infty} a_s x_{t-s} = \varepsilon_t, \tag{18}$$

where a_s is the coefficient of z^s in the expansion of $B(z)^{-1}$ in non-negative powers of z.

Suppose X_t is the observable at time t. Then, by the argument which led us from (2) to (3), the optimal predictor is:

$$x_{t+m}^{(t)} = \sum_{s=m}^{\infty} b_s \varepsilon_{t+m-s} \tag{19}$$

and this can be expressed explicitly in terms of X_t:

$$x_{t+m}^{(t)} = \sum_{s=0}^{\infty} \gamma_s x_{t-s} \tag{20}$$

by using (18) to express the ε variables of (19) in terms of the x variables. One can express this solution for the optimal prediction coefficients γ_s in generating function form

$$\sum_{s=0}^{\infty} \gamma_s z^s = [z^{-m} B(z)]_+ B(z)^{-1}, \tag{21}$$

where the operator $[\ ]_+$ has the effect that all terms in negative powers of z in the series enclosed by the brackets are discarded.

Suppose, as is more usual, that x_t is not completely observable, but that at time t one has observed the values $y_t, y_{t-1} \ldots$ of some associated variable y. Then the predictor will now have the form $x^{(t)}_{t+m} = \sum_{s=0}^{\infty} \gamma_s y_{t-s}$, and the generalization of solution (21) is:

$$\sum_{s=0}^{\infty} \gamma_s z^s = [z^{-m} g_{xy} (g_{yy}^-)^{-1}]_+ (g_{yy}^+)^{-1}. \tag{22}$$

Here we have omitted the z-arguments for simplicity, and have assumed that the matrix generating function $g_{yy}(z)$ has canonical factorization

$$g_{yy} = g_{yy}^+ g_{yy}^-. \tag{23}$$

$$x^{(t+1)}_{t+m} = x^{(t)}_{t+m} + H(y_{t+1} - y^{(t)}_{t+1}) \tag{24}$$

$$A(T) x_t = \varepsilon_t$$

$$y_t + C(T) x_t = \eta_t, \tag{25}$$

where $A(T) = \sum_{s=0}^{\infty} A_s T^s$, $C(T) = \sum_{s=0}^{\infty} C_s T^s$, and T is the backwards translation operator, with effect $Tx_t = x_{t-1}$. We make the same assumptions about the noise variables as before: that they are white with covariance matrix (8).

Then appeal to the fact that $x^{(t)}$ can be regarded as an ML estimator (in the Gaussian case) as well as an LLS estimator leads to the conclusion that it satisfies a recursion

$$\begin{bmatrix} N & L & A(T) \\ L' & M & C(T) \\ A(T^{-1})' & C(T^{-1})' & 0 \end{bmatrix} \begin{bmatrix} \lambda \\ \mu \\ x \end{bmatrix}_\tau^{(t)} = - \begin{bmatrix} 0 \\ y_\tau \\ 0 \end{bmatrix}, \quad (\tau \leqslant t) \tag{26}$$

(see Whittle, 1983, p. 155). Here λ and μ specify Lagrangian multiplier sequences whose significance will emerge shortly, and the lag operator T operates on the running argument τ, not on the fixed value t.

Note that relations (26) determine estimates of past and present state $x^{(t)}_\tau (\tau \leqslant t)$. However, once these have been derived, then predictors are easily calculated recursively from:

$$A(T) x^{(t)}_\tau = 0. \quad (\tau > t) \tag{27}$$

Equivalently, (26) can be regarded as holding for all τ, with λ, μ, set equal to zero for $\tau > t$.

Relations (26) constitute an equation system to be solved, semi-infinite if observation indeed extends back into the indefinite past. Write the system as:

$$\Phi(T)\xi_\tau = \zeta_\tau. \tag{28}$$

Then a reduction that provides as explicit a solution for $x_t^{(t)}$ as is possible in the general case in the following. Suppose that the Hermitian matrix generating function $\Phi(z)$ has canonical factorization

$$\Phi(z) = \Phi^+(z)\Phi^-(z). \tag{29}$$

Then under generalized observability conditions it is permissible to partially invert (26) to:

$$\Phi^{-1}(T)\xi_\tau = \Phi^+(T)^{-1}\zeta_\tau \qquad (\tau \leqslant t) \tag{30}$$

with the formal end condition $\xi_\tau = 0(\tau > t)$. Relation (30) for $\tau = t$ gives an explicit solution for $x_t^{(t)}$ in terms of Y_t; the relation for $\tau = t - 1$ then determines $x_{t-1}^{(t)}$ etc.

To see the wider significance of this approach one must consider the wider purpose of prediction. One will usually require predictions (or estimates of unobservables) to support actions. Suppose actions are chosen to minimize the expectations $E(Q)$ of some quadratic function Q of process and action variables. It follows then from the certainty equivalence theorem that LLS (or ML) predictors are the optimal ones to use. However, suppose that one instead minimizes a criterion $-\theta^{-1} \log E \exp(-\frac{1}{2}\theta Q)$. Here θ is a measure of risk-sensitivity, implying risk-seeking behaviour (optimism) for $\theta > 0$ and risk-aversion (pessimism) for $\theta < 0$. This risk-sensitivity modifies the estimators, which we shall now term *minimal stress* estimates, for reasons explained in Whittle and Kuhn (1986). Remarkably, the above analysis still goes through, with the simple change that Φ has the modified definition

$$\Phi(T) = \begin{bmatrix} N & L & A(T) \\ L' & M & C(T) \\ A(T^{-1})' & C(T^{-1})' & -\theta R \end{bmatrix}.$$

Here R is a matrix corresponding to a component $\Sigma_t(x'Rx)_t$ of Q which penalizes deviations of the process variable from a desired profile. Moreover, one can now establish the identity

$$\begin{bmatrix} N & L \\ L' & M \end{bmatrix} \begin{bmatrix} \lambda \\ \mu \end{bmatrix}_\tau^{(t)} = \begin{bmatrix} \varepsilon \\ \eta \end{bmatrix}_\tau^{(t)}$$

which relates λ and μ to the minimal stress estimates of noise.

BIBLIOGRAPHY

Durbin, J. 1984. Present position and potential developments: some personal views on time series analysis. *Journal of the Royal Statistical Society Series* 147, 161–73. This survey article contains a substantial reference list.

Whittle, P. 1983. *Prediction and Regulation.* 2nd edn. Oxford: Blackwell and University of Minnesota Press.

Whittle, P. and Kuhn, J. 1986. A Hamiltonian formulation of risk-sensitive linear/quadratic/Gaussian control. *International Journal of Control* 43, 1–12.

Principal Components

T. KLOEK

The principal components of a set of m variables are m artificially constructed variables with the following properties. The first component 'explains' as much as possible of the total variance of the original variables. The second has the same property under the additional condition that it is uncorrelated with the first, and so on. It often happens that a few principal components account for a large part of the total variance of the original variables. In such a case one may omit the remaining components. The effect is a substantial reduction of the dimension of the problem. The method is used to explore the relations present in a set of data or to combat the problems created by multicollinearity.

As in linear regression, several approaches are possible. One may view the principal components as the solution to a simple mathematical plane fitting problem, or one may assume a statistical model with an unknown covariance matrix, which is to be estimated. A normality assumption may (but need not) be added, with the consequence that the method of maximum likelihood is available.

If we have a statistical model with an m-vector of random variables ξ with covariance matrix, Σ, the kth principal component can be defined as $\pi_k = \xi' a_k$ where a_k is the eigenvector (characteristic vector) of Σ that corresponds to the kth eigenvalue (characteristic root, latent root), the eigenvalues λ_k being arranged in descending order

$$\lambda_1 \geqslant \lambda_2 \cdots \geqslant \lambda_m. \tag{1}$$

If Σ is estimated by S the same operations of taking eigenvectors and eigenvalues are carried out with respect to S. The mathematics of this approach is explained in almost every book on multivariate statistical analysis. A classic in this field is Anderson (1958). In the econometrics literature a detailed account is given in Dhrymes (1970).

A descriptive approach starts with an $n \times m$ matrix X consisting of n observations on each of m variables. Then the principal components are the columns of $P = XA$, where A is the matrix of eigenvectors of $X'X$. As in (1) the eigenvectors are always arranged according to the descending order of the eigenvalues. The first principal component p_1 may also be obtained as the result of minimizing the sum of the squares of the residuals E defined as

$$E = X - pa',$$ (2)

where p is an n-vector and a an m-vector. This approach to the subject is described in detail by Theil (1971, 1983).

Since both p and a are unknown we need an additional constraint in order to obtain unique results. Most authors choose $a'a = 1$, some $p'p = 1$. The choice is arbitrary and a matter of convenience. Here, it is henceforth assumed that $a'a = 1$, and more generally that $A'A = I$. Another consequence of the fact that both p and a are unknown is that our problem does not have the simple linear structure of least squares regression. Hence the resulting A and P depend (in a non-trivial way) on the origin and scale of the original variables. In the statistical approach the variables are usually measured from their means, in the descriptive approach this is not always the case. If all variables are measured in the same units, there is a natural solution to the problem of the units of measurement. If this is not the case one often chooses the solution to take correlations rather than covariances. (This holds for Σ and S in the statistical approach but it may also be applied to $X'X$ in the descriptive approach.)

Geometrically, the principal components transformation is equivalent to rotating the scatter (in the descriptive approach) or the density (in the statistical approach). Consider the case $m = 2$ and suppose that the scatter has the form of an ellipse. Then the principal components transformation is equivalent to rotating the ellipse in such a way that the principal axes of the ellipse coincide with the axes of the coordinate system. Equivalently, one might rotate the coordinate axes in such a way that they coincide with the principal axes of the ellipse. More details on the geometry of principal components are given by Fomby et al. (1984, pp. 287–93).

The main purpose of applying principal components is *reduction of the dimension* of a data set. The idea originated with Hotelling (1936) and in the present author's opinion it can be interpreted as a mathematician's reaction on Thurstone's (1931) paper on factor analysis. Indeed, Hotelling applies his approach to psychological test scores. It was precisely for this type of data the psychologists developed factor analysis.

The main difference between factor analysis and principal components can be given as follows. In factor analysis it is assumed that Σ can be decomposed as:

$$\Sigma = CC' + D,$$

where C is an $m \times h$ matrix and D a diagonal matrix of order $m \times m$. If

$$h < \tfrac{1}{2}[2m + 1 - \sqrt{(8m + 1)}]$$

this assumption implies restrictions on the elements of Σ, while the principal components approach does not impose any restrictions on Σ.

205

A well-known economic example of dimension reduction was given by Stone (1947), who took 17 time-series from the US national accounts in the period 1922–38. They describe several income and expenditure aggregates relating to consumers, producers and government. It appeared that in this period the first three principal components accounted for more than 97 per cent of the total variance of these 17 series (the first 80.8 per cent, the second 10.6 per cent, the third 6.1 per cent). The first principal component appears to be highly correlated with total income, the second with the annual change in income, the third with time. It should be emphasized that usually such simple interpretations are not available. More details are given by Stone (1947); also by Theil (1971).

Dimension reduction may also be desirable in the so-called *undersized sample* problem. Consider a (linear) simultaneous equation model. Suppose one wants to estimate the parameters of a simple structural equation by means of two-stage least-squares or a similar method. Then the first step requires the regressions of the current endogenous variables at the right-hand side of the equation on the total set of predetermined variables. This is impossible if $n < m$ (the number of predetermined variables), but it may also have undesirable properties if $n < 2.5\,m$, say. In large models, but even in models of medium size, these rules may be violated. Kloek and Mennes (1960) proposed to tackle this problem by replacing the m predetermined variables by a limited number of principal components. For a further discussion and modifications, see Amemiya (1966). The limitations of this approach were discussed by Fisher (1965).

Dimension reduction may also be desirable in more general regressions with *multicollinear* explanatory variables. The principal components of these variables can play a very useful role in clarifying the consequences of multicollinearity for the estimates of the regression parameters and their estimated covariance matrix. The case where one eigenvalue (λ_m) is relatively very small is particularly simple. Consider the linear regression model

$$y = X\beta + \varepsilon,$$

where y is an n-vector containing the observations on the variable to be explained, X and $n \times m$ matrix, as before, containing n observations on each of m explanatory variables, β a vector of unknown parameters to be estimated and ε a vector of disturbances, with zero means and covariance matrix $\sigma^2 I$. Let A denote the matrix of eigenvectors of $X'X$ and Λ the diagonal matrix containing the corresponding eigenvalues, then we have $X'X = A\Lambda A'$ with $A'A = I$. Then the inverse satisfies $(X'X)^{-1} = A\Lambda^{-1}A'$ and v_{ii}, the ith diagonal element of the covariance matrix $V = \sigma^2(X'X)^{-1}$, can be written as

$$v_{ii} = \sigma^2 \sum_j a_{ij}^2(1/\lambda_j),$$

where a_{ij} is the typical element of A. So v_{ii} is small if the a_{ij}^2 that correspond to small values of λ_j are small and large in the opposite case. This knowledge is helpful in understanding the problem of multicollinearity. Fomby et al. (1984) give a more extensive treatment and more references.

The next question is whether the relationship between principal components and multicollinearity can be exploited in order to solve the problems created by multicollinearity. It has been suggested that one might delete a number of principal components. Since the possibility exists that some of the principal components with small variances have a strong influence on the variable to be explained, it cannot be guaranteed that deleting these is a good choice. This may be decided by means of a preliminary test.

When applying the principal components method we transform a set of variables into linear combinations that are uncorrelated. Theil (1976) extends this approach in the context of the Rotterdam model of consumer demand. He constructs linear combinations of commodities that are *preference independent* and, hence, have a diagonal matrix of price coefficients in his demand system. In an example (p. 287) he transforms beef, pork and chicken into artificial preference independent commodities called inexpensive meat, beef/pork contrast and antichicken. He also gives an example containing clothing, footwear and other goods. His discussion on pages 311 and 312 is illustrative for the interpretation problems that may arise.

In general, one may say that principal components have elegant mathematical properties, but that their interpretation in applications is often far from simple.

BIBLIOGRAPHY

Amemiya, T. 1966. On the use of principal components of independent variables in two-stage least-squares estimation. *International Economic Review* 7, September, 283–303.

Anderson, T.W. 1958. *An Introduction to Multivariate Statistical Analysis*. New York: Wiley.

Dhrymes, P.J. 1970. *Econometrics*. New York: Harper & Row.

Fisher, F.M. 1965. The choice of instrumental variables in the estimation of economy-wide econometric models. *International Economic Review* 6, September, 245–74.

Fomby, T.B., Hill, R.C. and Johnson, S.R. 1984. *Advanced Econometric Methods*. New York: Springer.

Hotelling, H. 1936. Analysis of a complex of statistical variables into principal components. *Journal of Educational Psychology* 24, July, 417–41, 498–520.

Kloek, T. and Mennes, L.B.M. 1960. Simultaneous equations estimation based on principal components of predetermined variables. *Econometrica* 28, January, 45–61.

Stone, J.R.N. 1947. On the interdependence of blocks of transactions. *Journal of the Royal Statistical Society*, Series B 9, Supplement, 1–45.

Theil, H. 1971. *Principles of Econometrics*. Amsterdam: North-Holland; New York: Wiley.

Theil, H. 1976. *Theory and Measurement of Consumer Demand*. Vol. 2, Amsterdam: North-Holland.

Theil, H. 1983. Mathematical and statistical methods in econometrics. In *Handbook of Econometrics*, Vol. 1, ed. Z. Griliches and M.D. Intriligator, Amsterdam: North-Holland.

Thurstone, L.L. 1931. Multiple factor analysis. *Psychological Review* 38, 406–27.

Randomization

JAMES O. BERGER

Randomization refers to the selection of an element a, from a set A, according to some probability distribution P on A.

EXAMPLE 1. In the 1970 United States draft lottery it was necessary to order eligible males randomly for possible later induction into the armed services. In an attempt to do this fairly, capsules representing each day of the year were mixed in a large drum and selected by drawing. Those individuals with birthdays on the day corresponding to the first capsule drawn would be drafted first; those with birthdays corresponding to the second capsule drawn would be drafted second, and so on. The set A was thus the set of all sequences of capsules corresponding to days 1 through 366 of the year (1970 was a leap year). The sequence of capsules that was actually drawn began $a = (258, 115, 365, 45, 292, 250, \ldots)$.

The goal of the randomization was to be 'fair', so that any such sequence had the same chance of occurring. Choosing a according to the uniform probability distribution on A would have achieved this fairness, the uniform distribution being that which assigns equal probability to each a in A. Interestingly, the mixing process used with the capsules was not very good, and the capsules with large numbers ended up being drawn sooner than capsules with small numbers (on the average). Thus the actual randomization used was not the uniform distribution, and resulted in bias against individuals with late birthdays (see Rosenblatt and Filliben, 1971).

Randomization is very commonly used to select winners (or losers) as in example 1. Lotteries are the most common examples. There are also technical roles for randomization in such fields as statistics and game theory, and it is to these roles we now turn.

The use of randomization in statistics is very widespread, particularly in experimental design.

208

EXAMPLE 2. Two medical treatments A and B are to be tested, and 20 patients are available for the experiment. From the 20 patients, 10 are randomly selected using *simple random sampling* (i.e., the selection is done in such a way that any 10 people would have the same chance of being chosen). These 10 are given treatment A, with the remaining 10 being given treatment B.

The major reason for use of randomization in example 2 is to help prevent possible (unintentional) experimental bias. For instance, the doctors administering the treatments might well have feelings as to which treatment is better for a patient with given characteristics, and could (perhaps subconsciously) allow these feelings to affect the assignment of patients to treatment, if given that responsibility. Historical examples of (unintentional) experimenter-induced bias abound, to the extent that randomization of treatment assignment is now standard practice in most statistical experimentation. The statistician most responsible for the widespread adoption of randomization was R.A. Fisher (see Fisher, 1966).

Modes of randomization, considerably more complicated than that in example, 2 are used in sophisticated experimental designs. The major reason for such sophistication is that, while random assignment of treatments can help prevent experimenter-induced bias, it can result in 'unlucky bias'. In example 2, for instance, the sickest people could (by bad luck) all end up in the group chosen to receive treatment A. To help prevent such an eventuality, and to reduce variance, randomization is often combined with use of *control* in experimental design. (See Cox, 1958; Fisher, 1966; and Anderson and McLean, 1974, for general discussions. Moore, 1979, gives an excellent nontechnical introduction to the subject.)

Another use of randomization in statistics, and also in game theory, is to choose an action or statistical answer randomly. The motivation in game theory is easiest to perceive.

EXAMPLE 3. Each of two players in a game is to choose 'odd' or 'even'. If their choices match, player I wins; otherwise player II wins. This game is to be played repeatedly.

It is clear that if either player falls into a recognizable pattern of choosing 'odd' or 'even', the other player can adapt his strategy to this pattern and win repeatedly. Thus it might be wise for the players to adopt *random* strategies, whereby their choice of 'odd' or 'even' is determined by a chance mechanism. For instance, a simple random strategy is to flip a fair coin, choosing 'odd' if a head occurs and 'even' if a tail occurs (and, of course, keeping the coin flip secret). This would correspond to choosing 'odd' and 'even' with probability 0.5 each.

In a general game having a set A of available strategies, a *randomized strategy* is simply a choice from A according to a probability distribution, P, on A. Each P corresponds to a different randomized strategy. (Some of these strategies can, of course, be quite bad.) Randomized strategies play a crucial role in game theory (cf. Thomas, 1984; and Berger, 1985).

Some proponents of the frequentist approach to statistics advocate use of randomized statistical strategies. The reason is that one could be in a situation where it is impossible, say, to find a statistical test having type I error probability of 0.05, unless one is willing, for certain data, to allow the possibility of deciding at random whether to accept or reject the hypothesis. This can put the statistician in the rather untenable position of having to flip a coin at the end of the analysis, with heads leading to 'rejection at the 0.05 level' and tails leading to acceptance. The careful experimenter, seeing the statistician draw conclusions from his data in his fashion, will not be thrilled. Use of randomized statistical strategies has thus never been very widespread.

Implementing a desired randomization is not as easy as one might expect; witness the fiasco described in example 1. The most common method used today is based on random number tables or random number generators in computers.

EXAMPLE 1 (CONT.). The most direct method of generating a uniform random sequence would be to label the days as 001, 002, 003, ..., 366, and use a random number table or generator to obtain a sequence of three-digit random numbers. Simply list the three-digit random numbers in the order they occur (ignoring any three-digit numbers, other than those above, which happen to be generated). Note that it is necessary to label day 1 as 001, day 15 at 015, and so on; if the labels of the days were allowed to have different numbers of digits, they would have different probabilities of being generated. (Any one-digit number has three times the chance of being generated, by a uniform random number generator, as does a three-digit number.) See Moore (1979) for further discussion at an introductory level. Note that computers also have available software for generating probability randomizations other than the uniform.

BIBLIOGRAPHY

Anderson, V.L. and McLean, R.A. 1974. *Design of Experiments.* New York: Marcel Dekker.
Berger, J. 1985. *Statistical Decision Theory and Bayesian Analysis.* New York: Springer-Verlag.
Cox, D.R. 1958. *Planning of Experiments.* New York: Wiley.
Fisher, R.A. 1966. *The Design of Experiments.* 8th edn, New York: Hafner.
Moore, D.S. 1979. *Statistics, Concepts and Controversies.* San Francisco: Freeman.
Rosenblatt, J.R. and Filliben, J.J. 1971. Randomization and the draft lottery. *Science* 171, 306-8.
Thomas, L.C. 1984. *Games, Theory and Applications.* New York: Wiley.

Random Variables

I. RICHARD SAVAGE

Scientific statements often have a probabilistic element, for example, 'In population Ω the distribution of individual income, I, can be approximated by a log-normal distribution'. The formal interpretation of this statement requires a moderate amount of structure, such as,

> The population Ω has n members, $\omega_1, \ldots, \omega_n$. Associated with each ω is an income, $I(\omega)$. Each ω has the same probability $P(\omega_i)$ of being observed so that $P(\omega_i) = 1/n$ for $i = 1, \ldots, n$. Finally, $P(I \leq t) \doteq F(t, \alpha, \beta, \gamma)$ for $-\infty < t < \infty$ where F is the 3-parameter log-normal distribution function.

For this formal description, the following terms are often used. The set of all *elementary events*, ω, that is Ω, is the *sample space*. A function, such as $I(\omega)$ defined on Ω, is called a *random variable*. The *distribution function* of $I(\omega)$ is given by the probabilities of the events that if ω_i is selected, then $I(\omega_i) \leq t$ as a function of t. In this example, $F(t, \alpha, \beta, \gamma)$ is a *model* for the distribution of I. The model contains unspecified *parameters*, α, β, γ, which could depend on units of measurement, the population, time, etc. The sign $\doteq$ indicates the approximation.

BASIC PROPERTIES OF RANDOM VARIABLES

In studying a random variable, $X(\omega)$, attention is focused on finding probabilities of events described in terms of $X(\omega)$, such as, $a \leq X(\omega) \leq b$, or in terms of concepts derived from those probabilities, such as, the average or *expected value* of $X(\omega)$, see (16). Other approaches could have been taken: the development could use expected value instead of probability as the basic concept, or the sample space concept could be omitted, proceeding directly to distribution functions. The approach taken here is in the mainstream. The theory requires a σ-field of sets, $\mathscr{F}$, whose members are subsets of Ω; that is, if $A \in \mathscr{F}$ then the complement of A is in $\mathscr{F}$, $\Omega \in \mathscr{F}$, and if $A_i \in \mathscr{F}$ for $i = 1, 2, \ldots$, then $\cup A_i \in \mathscr{F}$. The basic theory permits us to compute probabilities of events, B, only when $B \in \mathscr{F}$; these sets are called *measurable*. For the real line we select the smallest σ-field which includes all intervals of the form $(-\infty, t]$. Random variables must be *measurable*; that is, events defined in terms of a random variable must belong to $\mathscr{F}$. Thus, if X is a random variable, then for each t it is required that $\{\omega: X(\omega) \leqslant t\} \in \mathscr{F}$.

All probabilities of events determined in terms of $X(\omega)$ can be obtained from the *distribution function* of X, denoted by $F(t)$, where $F(t) = P(X \leqslant t)$ for $-\infty < t < \infty$.

The necessary and sufficient conditions for $F(t)$ to be a distribution function are:

(a) $F(s) \leqslant F(t)$ for $-\infty < s < t < \infty$.

(b) $\underset{t \to -\infty}{\text{limit}} F(t) = 0$.

(c) $\underset{t \to \infty}{\text{limit}} F(t) = 1$.

(d) $\underset{x \to t'}{\text{limit}} F(x) = F(t)$. $\qquad\qquad$ (1)

Notice, F can be used to compute probabilities for events not of the form $X \leqslant t$, for examples,

$$P(X = t) = F(t) - \underset{x \to t^-}{\text{limit}} F(x),$$

and

$$P(a \leqslant X \leqslant b) = F(b) - \underset{x \to a^-}{\text{limit}} F(x).$$

Every distribution function has a unique decomposition of the form,

$$F = w_{\text{ac}} F_{\text{ac}} + w_s F_s + w_d F_d, \qquad\qquad (2)$$

where $w_{\text{ac}} + w_s + w_d = 1$, $0 \leqslant w_{\text{ac}}$, w_s, w_d. Here F_{ac} is an *absolutely continuous* distribution function, that is, there exists a function f_{ac} such that

$$F_{\text{ac}}(t) = \int_{-\infty}^{t} f_{\text{ac}}(x) \, dx \qquad -\infty < t < \infty. \qquad\qquad (3)$$

The function f_{ac} is a *density*. Notice

$$f_{\text{ac}} \geqslant 0 \quad \text{and} \quad \int f_{\text{ac}} = 1.$$

The distribution function F_s is *singular* in that although it is not identically zero, its derivative exists and is zero almost everywhere. The distribution function F_d

is *discrete*, that is, it is a right continuous step function with at most countably many jumps at $\{t_i\}$. The *probability function* f_d for F_d is zero everywhere except on $\{t_i\}$ where

$$f(t_i) = F(t_i) - \lim_{x \to t_i^-} F(x).$$

The most common situations are the *discrete distributions* ($w_d = 1$) and the (*absolutely*) *continuous distributions* ($w_{ac} = 1$). In the discrete case the most common situation is the non-negative integer lattice, that is $\{t_i\} = \{i\}$ where the range of i is a set of non-negative integers, see Table 1.

In Table 1, x is used to designate a value of the random variable. All values that have a positive probability of occurrence are called the *support*. Also found in the 'support' column are specific restrictions on the constants or parameters of the probability function. In Table 1

$$A! = \Gamma(A+1) = \int_0^\infty x^A e^{-x} \, dx, \qquad A \geqslant -1, \tag{4}$$

and when A is a non-negative integer,

$$\binom{B}{A} = \frac{B(B-1)\cdots(B-A+1)}{A!}. \tag{5}$$

The name of a random variable or of a distribution, for example $B(p)$, is used also to represent the random variable. The symbol $\sim$ between two random variables means that they have the same distribution function, and in the case of discrete random variables, that they have the same probability function. Notice

$$B(1) \sim U(1) \sim \text{Degenerate}(1) \sim \text{Geometric}(1),$$

$$B(p) \sim B(1, p),$$

$$B(n, 0) \sim P(0) \sim \text{Degenerate}(0),$$

$$B(n, p) \sim n - B(n, 1-p).$$

In Table 2

$$\mathscr{B}(a, b) = \frac{\Gamma(a)\Gamma(b)}{\Gamma(a+b)}. \tag{6}$$

For the continuous distributions (Table 2), there are many interesting variations which arise from transformations (12). For example, $\sigma N(0, 1) + \mu$ with $\sigma \geqslant 0$ defines a normal random variable with expectation μ and variance σ^2, that is, $N(\mu, \sigma^2) \sim \sigma N(0, 1) + \mu$. The 3-parameter log-normal is obtained from Table 2(10) with the transformation $x = [(y - \alpha)/\beta]^\gamma$, $y > \alpha$, $\beta > 0$, $\gamma > 0$ and the real root is used. Two useful connections between discrete and continuous random variables are

$$P[B(n, p) \geqslant k] = P[\beta(k, n-k+1) \leqslant p] \quad \text{for} \quad k = 0, \ldots, n, \, 0 \leqslant p \leqslant 1, \tag{7}$$

213

Table 1. Discrete distributions

Name	Probability function	Support	Characteristic function	Mean	Variance
(1) Degenerate (x_0)	1	$x \in \{x_0\}$	e^{itx_0}	x_0	0
(2) Bernoulli (p) $B(p)$	$f(0)=1-p$ $f(1)=p$	$x\in\{0,1\}$ $0\leqslant p\leqslant 1$	$1-p+pe^{it}$	p	$p(1-p)$
(3) Binomial (n,p) $B(n,p)$	$\binom{n}{x}p^x(1-p)^{n-x}$	$x\in\{0,1,\ldots,n\}$ n is a positive integer $0\leqslant p\leqslant 1$	$(1-p+pe^{it})^n$	np	$np(1-p)$
(4) Poisson (λ) $P(\lambda)$	$e^{-\lambda}\lambda^x/x!$	$x\in\{0,1,\ldots\}$ $0\leqslant\lambda$	$e^{-\lambda(1-e^{it})}$	λ	λ
(5) Geometric (p)	$(1-p)^{x-1}p$	$x\in\{1,2,\ldots\}$ $0<p\leqslant 1$	$\dfrac{pe^{it}}{1-(1-p)e^{it}}$	$\dfrac{1}{p}$	$\dfrac{1-p}{p^2}$
(6) Uniform (a) $U(a)$	$1/a$	$x\in\{1,2,\ldots,n\}$ a is a positive integer	$\dfrac{e^{it}(1-e^{ita})}{a(1-e^{it})}$	$\dfrac{1+a}{2}$	$\dfrac{a^2-1}{12}$
(7) Hypergeometric	$\dfrac{\binom{n}{x}\binom{m}{r-x}}{\binom{m+n}{r}}$	$x\in\{0,1,\ldots,\min(m,n)\}$ n,m,r non-negative integers with $r\leqslant m+n$		$\dfrac{rn}{m+n}$	$\left(\dfrac{m+n-r}{m+n-1}\right)r\,\dfrac{mn}{(m+n)^2}$
(8) Multinomial	$n!\sum_{j=1}^{J}(p_j^{x_j}/x_j!)$	$x_j=0,1,\ldots$ $\sum x_j=n$ $p_j\geqslant 0, j=1,\ldots,J$ $\sum p_j=1$	$\left(\sum p_j e^{it_j}\right)^n$	$EX_j=np_j,$ $j=1,\ldots,J$	$\sigma_j^2=np_j(1-p_j)$ $\sigma_{jk}=-np_jp_k$ $j\neq k$

Table 2. Continuous distributions

Name	Density	Support	Characteristic function	Mean	Variance
(1) Exponential	e^{-x}	$x \in (0, \infty)$	$1/(1-it)$	1	1
(2) Logistic	$\dfrac{e^{-x}}{(1+e^{-x})^2}$	$x \in (-\infty, \infty)$	$\pi t \operatorname{cosech} \pi t$	0	$\pi^2/3$
(3) Normal $(0, 1)$ $N(0, 1)$	$\dfrac{1}{(2\pi)^{1/2}} e^{-x^2/2}$	$-\infty < x < \infty$	$e^{-t^2/2}$	0	1
(4) Uniform $(0, 1)$ $U(0, 1)$	1	$x \in (0, 1)$	$(e^{it}-1)/it$	$1/2$	$1/12$
(5) Chi-Square (n) $\chi^2(n)$	$\dfrac{1}{2^{n/2}\Gamma(n/2)} e^{-x/2} x^{(n/2)-1}$	$x \in (0, \infty)$ $n \in (0, \infty)$	$(1-2it)^{-n/2}$	n	$2n$
(6) Cauchy	$[\pi(1+x^2)]^{-1}$	$x \in (-\infty, \infty)$	$e^{-|t|}$	See (16)	See (16)
(7) Student's $t(n)$ $t(n)$	$\dfrac{1}{n^{1/2}\mathscr{B}\left(\frac{1}{2}, \frac{n}{2}\right)} \left(1+\dfrac{x^2}{n}\right)^{-[(n+1)/2]}$	$x \in (-\infty, \infty)$ $n \in (0, \infty)$		0 if $n > 1$	$n/(n-2)$ if $n > 2$
(8) Fisher's $F(m, n)$ $F(m, n)$	$C \dfrac{x^{(m-2)/2}}{(n+mx)^{(n+m)/2}}$ with $C = \dfrac{m^{m/2}n^{n/2}}{\mathscr{B}(m/2, n/2)}$	$x \in (0, \infty)$ $m \in (0, \infty)$ $n \in (0, \infty)$		$\dfrac{n}{n-2}$ if $n > 2$	$\dfrac{2n^2(n+m-2)}{m(n-2)^2(n-4)}$ if $n > 4$

215

216

Table 2. *continued*

Name	Density	Support	Characteristic function	Mean	Variance
(9) Beta (a, b) $\beta(a, b)$	$\dfrac{x^{a-1}(1-x)^{b-1}}{\mathscr{B}(a, b)}$	$x \in (0, 1)$ $a, b \in (0, \infty)$		$\dfrac{a}{a+b}$	$\dfrac{ab}{(a+b)^2(a+b+1)}$
(10) Lognormal	$(2\pi x^2)^{-1/2} \exp[-(\ln x)^2/2]$	$x \in (0, \infty)$		$e^{1/2}$	$e^2 - e$
(11) Extreme value	$e^{-x-e^{-x}}$	$x \in (-\infty, \infty)$	$\Gamma(1-it)$	0.577	$\pi^2/6$
(12) Weibull	$cx^{c-1}e^{-x^c}$	$x \in (0, \infty)$ $c \in (0, \infty)$		$\Gamma(c^{-1}+1)$	$\Gamma(2c^{-1}+1)$ $-[\Gamma(c^{-1}+1)]^2$
(13) Bivariate normal	See (61)				

and

$$P[P(\lambda) < a] = P[\chi^2(2a) \geqslant 2\lambda] \quad \text{for} \quad a = 1, 2, \ldots \quad \text{and} \quad \lambda > 0. \tag{8}$$

ELEMENTARY MANIPULATIONS OF RANDOM VARIABLES

An absolutely continuous distribution does not have a unique density; the value of an integral is not changed if the integrand is changed on a countable number of points or a set of Lebesgue measure 0.

For $0 < \alpha < 1$, the α-*percentile* of a random variable X, denoted by x_α, is defined by

$$x_\alpha = \inf\{x: F(x) \geqslant \alpha\}. \tag{9}$$

Deciles, quartiles and medians (50-percentiles) are special cases.

If $X = X(\omega)$ is a random variable, then for any (measurable) function $g(\cdot)$ one obtains the random variable

$$Y = Y(\omega) = g[X(\omega)] = g(X)$$

with

$$F_Y(y) = P(Y \leqslant y) = P[g(X) \leqslant y] = \int_{\{x:\, g(x) \leqslant y\}} dF_X(x). \tag{10}$$

where F_X is the distribution function of X. In the discrete case, the $\int$ is a summation and $dF(x)$ is the probability function. In the absolutely continuous case, $dF(x)$ becomes $f(x)\,dx$ where f is a density function.

If $g(\cdot)$ is a strictly increasing function,

$$F_Y(y) = F_X[g^{-1}(y)], \tag{11}$$

and further, in the absolutely continuous case when g', the derivative of g, is assumed to exist, then

$$f_Y(y) = f_X[g^{-1}(y)][dg^{-1}(y)/dy]. \tag{12}$$

If $g(x) = \mu + \sigma x$, and $\sigma > 0$, then

$$f_Y(y) = \sigma^{-1} f_X[(y - \mu)/\sigma]. \tag{13}$$

In this monotone increasing case

$$y_\alpha = g^{-1}(x_\alpha). \tag{14}$$

Notice, if g is strictly decreasing, then in (12) replace $(g^{-1})'$ by $|(g^{-1})'|$ and (14) becomes

$$y_\alpha = g^{-1}(x_{1-\alpha}). \tag{15}$$

The *expected value* of X, denoted by EX, is defined by

$$EX = \int_{-\infty}^{\infty} x\,dF(x) \quad \text{provided} \quad \int_{-\infty}^{\infty} |x|\,dF(x) < \infty; \tag{16}$$

217

this last condition is sometimes relaxed to either

$$-\int_{-\infty}^{0} x \, dF(x) < \infty \quad \text{or} \quad \int_{0}^{\infty} x \, dF(x) < \infty.$$

In the discrete case,

$$EX = \sum xf(x), \tag{17}$$

and in the absolutely continuous case,

$$EX = \int_{-\infty}^{\infty} xf(x) \, dx. \tag{18}$$

If $Y = g(X)$, then

$$EY = \int_{-\infty}^{\infty} g(x) \, dF_X(x). \tag{19}$$

So we write $Eg(X)$ and it is not necessary to compute $F_Y(y)$.

Assume $g(x)$ is *convex* on an interval I which includes the support of X; that is, for x_1 and $x_2 \in I$ and $\alpha \in [0, 1]$,

$$g[\alpha x_1 + (1 - \alpha)x_2] \leqslant \alpha g(x_1) + (1 - \alpha)g(x_2). \tag{20}$$

(If $g''(x) \geqslant 0$ for $x \in I$, then g is convex.) Then *Jensen's inequality* is:

$$Eg(X) \geqslant g(EX), \tag{21}$$

provided both expected values exist. In particular,

$$EX^2 \geqslant (EX)^2, \tag{22}$$

so the *variance*, denoted by σ^2 and defined by

$$\sigma^2 = EX^2 - (EX)^2, \tag{23}$$

satisfies $\sigma^2 \geqslant 0$. An equivalent definition is

$$\sigma^2 = E(X - EX)^2. \tag{24}$$

A continuous distribution is *unimodal* with mode x_0 if $F(x)$ is convex for $x \in (-\infty, x_0)$, and $1 - F(x)$ is convex for $x_0 \in (x, \infty)$. The discrete X is *unimodal* if there is a unique x which maximizes its probability function. The discrete examples (except for the uniform) for most choices of the parameters are unimodal, and when the probability function has several maximizing values, they are contiguous.

218

Following are results and definitions for often-used expectations, if they exist (16):

$$\text{Mean of } X = \mu = EX. \tag{25}$$

$$k\text{th moment of } X = \alpha_k = EX^k, \quad \text{so} \quad \mu = \alpha_1. \tag{26}$$

$$k\text{th absolute moment of } X = E\,|\,X\,|^k. \tag{27}$$

$$k\text{th central moment of } X = \mu_k = E(X - \mu)^k, \text{ so that } \sigma^2 = \mu_2, \text{ see (24).} \tag{28}$$

$$E\{N(0,\,1)\}^{2k+1} = 0,$$

and

$$E\{N(0,\,1)\}^{2k} = (2k)!\,/k!\,2^k \text{ for } k, \text{ a non-negative integer.} \tag{29}$$

Characteristic function of X, $\phi_X(t)$ or $\phi(t)$ is defined by

$$\phi(t) = E\,e^{itX}. \tag{30}$$

Always $\phi(0) = 1$, $|\phi(t)| \leqslant 1$, ϕ is uniformly continuous in t, and there is a one-to-one correspondence between distribution functions and characteristic functions. This correspondence is made explicit by

The *inversion formula*: If ϕ is the characteristic function of X, then

$$F(x + \Delta) - F(x - \Delta) = \lim_{T \to \infty} \int_{-T}^{T} \frac{1}{\pi} \frac{\sin t\Delta}{t} e^{-itx} \phi(t)\,dt \tag{31}$$

provided $x - \Delta$ and $x + \Delta$ are continuity points of F.

$\phi(t)$ is a characteristic function if and only if ϕ is continuous, $\phi(0) = 1$ and ϕ is non-negative definite; that is, for all $n(\geqslant 1)$, $t_1, \ldots, t_n$, and $h_1, \ldots, h_n$

$$\sum_{j=1}^{n} \sum_{k=1}^{n} h_j \phi(t_j - t_k) \bar{h}_k \geqslant 0, \tag{32}$$

where $\bar{h}$ is the complex conjugate of h.

The characteristic function of X is real if and only if

$$X \sim -X; \tag{33}$$

that is, X has a symmetric (about 0) distribution.

If $Y = aX + b$, then

$$\phi_Y(t) = e^{ibt} \phi_X(at). \tag{34}$$

If X and Y are independent (50), then

$$\phi_{X+Y}(t) = \phi_X(t)\phi_Y(t). \tag{35}$$

The *moment generating function of X is* $m(t) = Ee^{tX}$ and

$$\ln m(t) \text{ is the } \textit{cumulant generating function.} \tag{36}$$

If X has support on the non-negative integers, then the *probability generating function of X* is

$$\theta(t) = Et^X, \qquad \text{for } 0 \leqslant t \leqslant 1,$$

and

$$P(X = k) = \frac{1}{k!} \frac{d^k \theta(t)}{dt^k}\bigg|_{t=0}, \qquad \text{for } k = 1, 2, \ldots \tag{37}$$

If the kth moment of X exists, then

$$EX^k = d^k m(t)/dt^k |_{t=0} = i^{-k} d^k \phi(t)/dt^k |_{t=0}, \quad \text{for } k = 1, 2, \ldots. \tag{38}$$

The *kth cumulant* is the kth derivative of the cumulant generating function evaluated at 0. For $P(\lambda)$ the cumulant generating function is $\lambda(e^t - 1)$ so all the $P(\lambda)$ cumulants are λ. In general, the cumulants can be expressed in terms of the central moments and vice versa.

Many inequalities can be obtained from the *Markov inequality*:

If $P[g(X) \geqslant 0] = 1$ and $A > 0$, then $P[g(X) \geqslant A] \leqslant Eg(X)/A$. (39)

The *Chebychev inequality* is one consequence of

$$P(|X - \mu| \geqslant \lambda) \leqslant \frac{E|X - \mu|^p}{\lambda^p}, \quad \lambda > 0 \quad \text{and} \quad p > 0, \tag{40}$$

and another is the *Bernstein inequality*: If $x \geqslant 0$, then

$$P(X \geqslant x) \leqslant \text{ind}_{t \geqslant 0} [e^{-xt} m(t)]. \tag{41}$$

SEVERAL RANDOM VARIABLES

To this point we have mentioned the possibility of several random variables being defined on the same Ω. Now the discussion will focus on two random variables, say $X_1 = X_1(\omega)$ and $X_2 = X_2(\omega)$, for example, X_1 could be Income and X_2 could be Savings. So if ω_0 is an individual, then $[X_1(\omega_0), X_2(\omega_0)]$ is the income and savings of ω_0.

The *distribution function* is defined by

$$F(x_1, x_2) = F_{X_1, X_2}(x_1, x_2) = P(X_1 \leqslant x_1 \text{ and } X_2 \leqslant x_2). \tag{42}$$

Notice,

$$\lim_{x_1 \to -\infty} F(x_1, x_2) = \lim_{x_2 \to -\infty} F(x_1, x_2) = 0, \tag{43}$$

$$F_{X_1}(x_1) = \lim_{x_2 \to \infty} F(x_1, x_2),$$

$$F_{X_2}(x_2) = \lim_{x_1 \to \infty} F(x_1, x_2), \tag{44}$$

$$F(x_1 + \Delta, x_2 + \varepsilon) - F(x_1, x_2 + \varepsilon) - F(x_1 + \Delta, x_2) + F(x_1, x_2)$$
$$= P(x_1 < X_1 \leqslant x_1 + \Delta \text{ and } x_2 < X_2 \leqslant x_2 + \varepsilon) \geqslant 0, \qquad (45)$$

when $\Delta \geqslant 0$ and $\varepsilon \geqslant 0$, and

$$F \text{ is right continuous in each of its arguments.} \qquad (46)$$

Conditions (43)–(46) are necessary and sufficient for F to be a distribution function; (45) is the analogue of $F(x)$ being an increasing function in the univariate case (1). The discrete bivariate distributions offer no surprises when compared to the univariate case, but there are many special cases of mixed continuous and discrete situations. And there are simple continuous examples where nothing like a density could exist, such as

$$F(x, y) = \begin{cases} 0, & \text{for } x + y \leqslant 1 \\ \min(x, 1) + \min(y, 1) - 1, & \text{for } x + y \geqslant 1 \end{cases}. \qquad (47)$$

The random variables X and Y, are said to have the *joint density*, $f(x, y)$, provided

$$F(x, y) = P(X \leqslant x, Y \leqslant y) = \int_{-\infty}^{x} \int_{-\infty}^{y} f(s, t)\, \mathrm{d}s\, \mathrm{d}t,$$
$$\text{for } -\infty < x < \infty \quad \text{and} \quad -\infty < y < \infty. \qquad (48)$$

When continuous random variables are discussed, the usual meaning will be this absolutely continuous situation with a (joint) density.

The random variables X and Y are *independent* if and only if

$$P(X \in A, Y \in B) = P(X \in A)P(Y \in B), \qquad (49)$$

for all measurable sets A and B. A necessary and sufficient condition for the independence of X and Y, is

$$F(x, y) = F_X(x)F_Y(y) \quad \text{for } -\infty < x < \infty \quad \text{and} \quad -\infty < y < \infty; \qquad (50)$$

when there is a density or probability function, (50) is equivalent to

$$f(x, y) = f_X(x)f_Y(y) \quad \text{for } -\infty < x < \infty \quad \text{and} \quad -\infty < y < \infty. \qquad (51)$$

The expected value of a function of several random variables, say $Z = g(X, Y)$, can be found from

$$EZ = Eg(X, Y) = \iint g(x, y)\, \mathrm{d}F(x, y). \qquad (52)$$

Always,

$$E(aX + bY) = aEX + bEY, \qquad (53)$$

and if X and Y are independent,

$$EXY = (EX)[EY], \qquad (54)$$

221

provided both EX and EY exist. In these formulas one can replace X by $r(X)$ and Y by $s(Y)$ to obtain results, such as, (35) and (24). The *covariance* is defined by

$$\sigma_{X,Y} = E(X - \mu_X)(Y - \mu_Y) = EXY - \mu_X\mu_Y, \tag{55}$$

and the Pearson product moment *correlation* is defined by,

$$\rho_{X,Y} = \sigma_{X,Y}/\sigma_X\sigma_Y. \tag{56}$$

The Cauchy–Schwartz inequality is equivalent to $-1 \leqslant \rho \leqslant 1$. If X and Y are independent, then $\rho = 0$, but not conversely.

Assume the equations

$$u = u(x, y) \quad \text{and} \quad v = v(x, y) \tag{57}$$

have a unique inverse; that is,

$$x = x(u, v) \quad \text{and} \quad y = y(u, v) \tag{58}$$

and the *Jacobian* determinant,

$$J(x, y; u, v) = \det\begin{pmatrix} \dfrac{\partial x}{\partial u} & \dfrac{\partial y}{\partial u} \\[2mm] \dfrac{\partial x}{\partial v} & \dfrac{\partial y}{\partial v} \end{pmatrix}, \tag{59}$$

exists, is continuous and is never equal to 0. Then

$$f_{U,V}(u, v) = |J(x, y; u, v)| f_{X,Y}[x(u, v), y(u, v)]. \tag{60}$$

The above conditions are sufficient and in applications, even if they fail, a little analysis might show that (60) still holds. The linear transformation

$$Y_1 = \mu_1 + \sigma_1 X_1 \quad \text{and} \quad Y_2 = \mu_2 + \sigma_2[\rho X_1 + (1 - \rho^2)^{1/2} X_2]$$

of X_1 and X_2, two independent $N(0, 1)$ variables, yields

$$
\begin{aligned}
f_{Y_1,Y_2}(y_1, y_2) = \frac{1}{2\pi} \frac{1}{\sigma_1\sigma_2(1-\rho^2)^{1/2}} \exp\Bigg\{ & \frac{-1}{2(1-\rho^2)\sigma_1^2\sigma_2^2} \\
& \times [\sigma_2^2(y_1 - \mu_1)^2 - 2\rho\sigma_1\sigma_2(y_1 - \mu_1)(y_2 - \mu_2) \\
& + \sigma_1^2(y_2 - \mu_2)^2]\Bigg\},
\end{aligned} \tag{61}
$$

or

$$(Y_1, Y_2) \sim N(\mu, \Sigma). \tag{62}$$

In (62) $N(\mu, \Sigma)$ is a *bivariate normal* random variable with mean vector μ and variance–covariance matrix Σ where

$$\mu = \begin{pmatrix} \mu_1 \\ \mu_2 \end{pmatrix} \quad \text{and} \quad \Sigma = \begin{pmatrix} \sigma_1^2 & \rho\sigma_1\sigma_2 \\ \rho\sigma_1\sigma_2 & \sigma_2^2 \end{pmatrix}.$$

From the general bivariate normal density (61), one can show $Y_1 \sim N(\mu_1, \sigma_1^2)$ and $Y_2 \sim N(\mu_2, \sigma_2^2)$. The random variables Y_1 and Y_2 are independent if and only if $\rho = 0$.

To finish this introduction to bivariate distributions, we introduce the conditional probability of A given B,

$$P(A \mid B) = \frac{P(A \text{ and } B)}{P(B)}, \tag{63}$$

provided $P(B) > 0$. When X and Y are discrete random variables (defined on the same sample space), the conditional probability function of X given Y, is defined accordingly

$$f_{X \mid Y}(x \mid y) = \frac{f_{X,Y}(x, y)}{f_Y(y)}, \tag{64}$$

provided $f_Y(y) > 0$. For each y-value, $f_{X \mid Y}$ will be a probability function, and conditional expectations are defined by

$$E(X \mid Y = y) = \sum x f_{X \mid Y}(x, y). \tag{65}$$

The function in (65) has y as its argument. If $y = Y(\omega)$, then the conditional expectation becomes a random variable denoted by $EX \mid Y$. The conditional density may be defined as in (64) for the continuous case as well. For the bivariate normal (61), the conditional distribution of Y_1 given $Y_2 = y_2$ is

$$N\left[\mu_1 + \rho \frac{\sigma_1}{\sigma_2}(y_2 - \mu_2), (1 - \rho^2)\sigma_1^2\right]. \tag{66}$$

Conditioning on Y_2 reduces the variance of Y_1 and makes the expected value of Y_1 depend linearly on the specified value of Y_2 when $\rho \neq 0$.

ASYMPTOTIC THEOREMS FOR SUMS OF INDEPENDENT RANDOM VARIABLES

A random variable X with expectation μ is often observed near μ. And if there are several random variables, $X_1, \ldots, X_n$ each with expectation μ, then their average, $\bar{X}_n = \sum X_i / n$, should even be closer to μ. Now consider a sequence of random variables $X_1, \ldots, X_n, \ldots$, which are independent each with the same distribution and $EX_i = \mu$.

Weak Law of Large Numbers:

$$\lim_{n \to \infty} P(|\bar{X}_n - \mu| < \varepsilon) = 1, \quad \text{for every } \varepsilon > 0. \tag{67}$$

Strong Law of Large Numbers:

$$P\left(\lim_{n \to \infty} \bar{X}_n = \mu\right) = 1. \tag{68}$$

223

The mode of convergence in (67) is *in probability* or *weak*, and the mode of convergence in (68) is *with probability one* or *strong*. The difference between weak and strong statements is shown in the following example, $\bar{A}$ is the complement of A, and $\text{mod}_1 a = r$ where $a = a' + r$ with a' an integer and $0 \leqslant r < 1$. Let:

$$Z_n(\omega) = \begin{cases} 0, & \text{if } \omega \in \bar{A}_n \\ 1, & \text{if } \omega \in A_n \end{cases}, \tag{69}$$

where $\Omega = (0, 1)$, $A_n = (\text{mod}_1 \Sigma_1^n 1/i, \text{mod}_1 \Sigma_1^{n+1} 1/i)$ and the probability of a set in Ω is the length of the set. Then $P(A_n) \to 0$ so that Z_n converges in probability to 0. Also, every ω is in an infinite number of A_n so that Z_n does *not* converge with probability one.

Strong convergence implies weak convergence; when the Strong Law of Large Numbers applies, so will the Weak Law of Large Numbers. A sequence of random variables Z_n is said to converge in *mean square* to μ if and only if

$$E(Z_n - \mu)^2 \to 0. \tag{70}$$

Mean square convergence implies weak convergence. A consequence of the Chebychev inequality is:

Assume for each i and j that $EX_i = \mu$, $\sigma_{X_i, X_j} = \sigma_{ij}$

and $\displaystyle\sum_{i=1}^{n} \sum_{j=1}^{n} \sigma_{ij}/n^2 \to 0$; then $\bar{X}_n \to \mu$ in probability. $\qquad(71)$

Another type of convergence is *in distribution*. The sequence of random variables $X_1, X_2, \ldots, X_n, \ldots$ converge in distribution to X if and only if

$$F_X(x) = \lim_{n \to \infty} F_{X_n}(x)$$

at all continuity points of F_X. It is expressed as $X_n \leadsto X$. Note X and X_n can be defined on different sample spaces Ω and Ω_n so $P(X \in A, X_n \in B)$ would not be defined. The symbol $X - X_n$ requires X and X_n to be defined on the same space. Thus the conclusion of (67) is $\bar{X}_n \leadsto$ degenerate (μ). Note $B(n, \lambda/n) \leadsto P(\lambda)$ for fixed λ.

Also, $X_n a \leadsto Y$ means there are sequences $\{a_n\}$ and $\{b_n\}$ such that $a_n X_n + b_n \leadsto Y$. The assumptions of (72) imply $\bar{X}_n a \leadsto N(0, 1)$, $\bar{X}_n a \leadsto \mu$, $\bar{X}_n a \leadsto 0$. Read $X_n \leadsto Y$ as 'the limiting distribution of $\{X_n\}$ is the distribution of Y' or 'X_n converges to Y in distribution'. And read $X_n a \leadsto Y$ as 'the *asymptotic* distribution of $\{X_n\}$ is the distribution of Y'.

Central Limit Theorem. If each X_i is independent and has the same distribution with finite mean μ and finite variance σ^2, then

$$n^{1/2}(\bar{X}_n - \mu)/\sigma \leadsto N(0, 1). \tag{72}$$

The Weak Law of Large Numbers probabilistically says that $(\bar{X}_n - \mu)$ is small, but the Central Limit Theorem gives a much stronger statement since it implies that $n^{1/2}(X_n - \mu)$ is not large in a probabilistic sense.

Berry–Essen Theorem. Assume and define:

(a) $X_1, \ldots, X_n$ are independent, and $EX_i = 0$.

(b) For each i write $\sigma^2_{X_i} = \sigma^2_i$.

(c) $s^2_n = \sum\limits_{i=1}^{n} \sigma^2_i > 0$.

(d) For each i, $\gamma_i = E|X_i|^\Delta < \infty$, for some $2 < \Delta \leqslant 3$.

(e) $\Gamma_n^\Delta = \sum\limits_{i=1}^{n} \gamma_i$.   (73)

Then there exists constants $C_\Delta(C_3 \leqslant 7.5)$ such that

$$\max_{-\infty < x < \infty} \left| P[n\bar{X}_n/s_n < x] - \int_{-\infty}^{x} \frac{1}{(2\pi)^{1/2}} e^{-t^2/2} \, dt \right| \leqslant C_\Delta(\Gamma_n/s_n)^\Delta.$$

When the random variables are identically distributed, $C_\Delta(\Gamma_n/s_n)^\Delta$ is proportional to $n^{[(2-\Delta)/2]}$ which might be small enough to give useful bounds.

Some tools useful in proving limit theorems are: (31) and (35).

Consider a sequence of distribution functions $\{F_i\}$ and the corresponding sequence of characteristic functions $\{\phi_i\}$. Assume there exists a function $\phi(t)$ which is continuous at 0 and

$$\phi(t) = \lim_{i \to \infty} \phi_i(t) \text{ for every } t.$$

Then,

(a) $\phi(t)$ is a characteristic function, and if $F(x)$ is the associated distribution function,

(b) $F(x) = \lim\limits_{i \to \infty} F_i(x)$ at every x

which is a continuity point of F.   (74)

$(X_{n1}, X_{n2}) \leadsto (Y_1, Y_2)$ if and only if

$$t_1 X_{n1} + t_2 X_{n2} \leadsto t_1 Y_1 + t_2 Y_2$$ (75)

for each pair of real numbers (t_1, t_2).

Slutsky's Theorem. If for each n, the random variables X_n, Y_n, Z_n are defined on the same sample space, and

(a) $X_n \rightsquigarrow X$,

(b) $Y_n \rightsquigarrow a$,

(c) $Z_n \rightsquigarrow b$; then $\quad X_n Y_n + Z_n \rightsquigarrow aX + b$. $\qquad (76)$

Propagation of Error. Assume $[n^{1/2}(X_n - \mu_x), n^{1/2}(Y_n - \mu_y)]$ has a bivariate normal limiting distribution with mean vector $(0, 0)$ and variance–covariance matrix

$$\begin{pmatrix} \sigma_{XX} & \sigma_{XY} \\ \sigma_{XY} & \sigma_{YY} \end{pmatrix},$$

and $H(x, y)$ has continuous first derivatives,

$$\left[H_x(x, y) = \frac{\partial H(x, y)}{\partial x}, \ H_y(x, y) = \frac{\partial H(x, y)}{\partial y} \right]$$

in the neighbourhood of (μ_X, μ_Y); then

$$n^{1/2}[H(X_n, Y_n) - H(\mu_X, \mu_Y)] \rightsquigarrow N[0, H_x^2(\mu_X, \mu_Y)\sigma_X^2$$
$$+ 2H_x(\mu_X, \mu_Y)H_y(\mu_X, \mu_Y)\sigma_{XY} + H_y^2(\mu_X, \mu_Y)\sigma_Y^2], \qquad (77)$$

provided this variance is >0.

Although the limiting distribution of $n^{1/2}[H(X_n, Y_n) - H(\mu_X, \mu_Y)]$ exists and has finite moments, the moments of $H(X_n, Y_n)$ may not exist; for example, let $H(x) = 1/x$ and X_n be the average of n independent $P(\lambda)$ variables. Then $H(EX_n) = 1/\lambda$, and $EH(X_n) = \infty$ for every n.

Example: if

$$X_n \sim B(n, p) \quad \text{then} \quad n^{1/2}(X_n/n - p) \rightsquigarrow N[0, p(1 - p)];$$

from (72) where $X_n = \Sigma_{i=1}^n Y_i$, with the Y_i independent Bernoulli (p) random variables. Now consider $H(x) = \arcsin(x)^{1/2}$ so that $H_x(x) = 1/\{2[x(1 - x)]^{1/2}\}$, and thus,

$$n^{1/2}[\arcsin(X_n/n)^{1/2} - \arcsin(p)] \rightsquigarrow N(0, 1/4). \qquad (78)$$

The transformation is *variance stabilizing*.

There are many other classes of limit theorems, such as,

Law of the Iterated Logarithm: Assume

(a) $X_1, \ldots, X_n, \ldots$ are mutually independent with the same distribution.

(b) $EX_1 = 0$.

(c) $EX_1^2 = 1$. $\qquad (79)$

Then

$$P\left\{\lim_{n\to\infty}\frac{\sum\limits_{i=1}^{n}X_i}{[n\ln(\ln n)]^{1/2}}=(2)^{1/2}\right\}=1.$$

DISTRIBUTIONS RELATED TO THE NORMAL

Assume X, X_1, X_2, ..., X_i, ... are independent $N(0, 1)$; then the following definitions, examples and theorems apply:

$$\bar{X}_n=\sum_1^n X_i/n \quad\text{and}\quad S_n^2=\sum_1^n (X_i-\bar{X}_n)^2/(n-1)$$

are independent, and

$$\bar{X}_n\sim N(0, 1/n), \ S_n^2\sim (n-1)^{-1}\chi^2(n-1). \tag{80}$$

A more general result is: $\bar{X}_n$ and $D_n(X_1, ..., X_n)$ are independent provided D_n is translation invariant; that is, $D_n(X_1, ..., X_n)=D_n(X_1+a, ..., X_n+a)$ for every a.

$$\sum_{i=1}^{r} X_i^2\sim\chi^2(r) \text{ with } r \text{ a positive integer.} \tag{81}$$

If $\chi^2(r)$ and $\chi(s)^2$ are independent, then

$$\chi^2(r)+\chi^2(s)\sim\chi^2(r+s). \tag{82}$$

If X and $\chi^2(r)$ are independent, then

$$t = X/[\chi^2(r)/r]^{1/2} \tag{83}$$

has a t-distribution with r degrees of freedom, $t(r)$.

Student's Theorem: If $Y_1, ..., Y_n$ are independent $N(\mu, \sigma^2)$, then

$$\frac{n^{1/2}(\bar{Y}_n-\mu)^{1/2}}{\left[\dfrac{\Sigma (Y_i-\bar{Y}_n)^2}{n-1}\right]}\sim t(n-1). \tag{84}$$

$$\frac{\chi^2(n)-n}{(2n)^{1/2}}\rightsquigarrow N(0, 1). \tag{85}$$

$$t(n)\rightsquigarrow N(0, 1). \tag{86}$$

If $\chi^2(r)$ and $\chi^2(s)$ are independent, then

(a) $\beta=\dfrac{\chi^2(r)}{\chi^2(r)+\chi^2(s)}$ has a $\beta(r, s)$ distribution, and

(b) $F=\dfrac{[\chi^2(r)/r]}{[\chi^2(s)/s]}$ has an F-distribution with r and s degrees of freedom, $F(r, s)$.

$$\tag{87}$$

$$t^2(n) \sim F(1, n). \tag{88}$$

$$[F(r, s)]^{-1} \sim F(s, r). \tag{89}$$

$$rF(r, s) \underset{s \to \infty}{\rightsquigarrow} \chi^2(r). \tag{90}$$

Under the conditions of (84), if $n = n_1 + n_2$, then

$$S_1^2/S_2^2 \sim F(n_1 - 1, n_2 - 1),$$

where

$$S_1^2 = \sum_1^{n_1} \left[Y_i - \left(\sum_1^{n_1} Y_i/n_1 \right) \right]^2 \bigg/ (n_1 - 1),$$

and

$$S_2^2 = \sum_{n_1+1}^{n} \left[Y_i - \left(\sum_{n_1+1}^{n} Y_i/n_2 \right) \right]^2 \bigg/ (n_2 - 1). \tag{91}$$

ORDER STATISTICS

In this section assume $X, X_1, X_1, \ldots, X_n$ are independent real-valued random variables; each X has density f and distribution function F. Further, let $\{X_i\}$, when arranged in order from smallest to largest, be denoted by $X_{(1)}, \ldots, X_{(n)}$.

For $1 \leqslant r \leqslant n$, the density of $X(r)$ is

$$f_{X_{(r)}}(x) = \frac{n!}{(r-1)!(n-r)!} F^{r-1}(x)[1 - F(x)]^{n-r} f(x). \tag{92}$$

$$F_{X_{(n)}}(x) = F^n(x). \tag{93}$$

$$F_{X_{(1)}}(x) = 1 - [1 - F(x)]^n. \tag{94}$$

If $1 \leqslant r < s \leqslant n$, then

$$f_{X_{(r)}, X_{(s)}}(x, y) = \frac{n!}{(r-1)!(r-s-1)!(n-s)!} F^{r-1}(x)$$

$$\times [F(y) - F(x)]^{s-r-1}[1 - F(y)]^{n-s} f(x) f(y), \qquad -\infty < x < y < \infty. \tag{95}$$

$$f_{X_{(1)}, X_{(2)}, \ldots, X_{(n)}}(y_1, y_2, \ldots, y_n) = n! \prod_1^n f(y_i), \quad -\infty < y_1 < y_2 \cdots < y_n < \infty. \tag{96}$$

Theorem: If

(a) f is continuous where $f = F'$.

(b) For specified α and β satisfying $0 < \alpha < \beta < 1$, define x_α and x_β as the unique solution of $F(x) = \alpha$ and $F(x) = \beta$, respectively.

(c) $0 < f(x_\alpha) < \infty$ and $0 < f(x_\beta) < \infty$.

(d) $[m]$ is the largest integer not exceeding m.

Then,

$$n^{1/2}(X_{[\alpha n]} - x_\alpha, X_{[\beta n]} - x_\beta) \rightsquigarrow N\left\{ \begin{pmatrix} 0 \\ 0 \end{pmatrix}, \begin{bmatrix} \dfrac{\alpha(1-\alpha)}{f^2(x_\alpha)} & \dfrac{\alpha(1-\beta)}{f(x_\alpha)f(x_\beta)} \\[2mm] \dfrac{\alpha(1-\beta)}{f(x_\alpha)f(x_\beta)} & \dfrac{\beta(1-\beta)}{f^2(x_\beta)} \end{bmatrix} \right\}. \qquad (97)$$

Not all limit theorems involve sums of random variables (100). Theorem (97) appears to be an example, but consider the following:

$$P[X_{(k)} < x] = P\left\{ \sum_1^n B_i[F(x)] \geq k \right\}, \qquad (98)$$

where $B_1, \ldots, B_n$ are independent, Bernoulli $[F(x)]$ and $k = 1, 2, \ldots, n$.

Renyi Representation. If f is exponential [Table 2(1)], then

$$X_{(i)} = \sum_{j=1}^i Y_j/(n - j + 1), \qquad (99)$$

where the $\{Y_j\}$ satisfy the same conditions as the $\{X_i\}$.

Extreme Value Theorem. If $a_n X_{(n)} + b_n a \rightsquigarrow Z$, then Z is one of three types, the principal ones being the Extreme Value [Table 2(11)] and Weibull [Table 2(12)]. In particular, if F is normal, then there exist sequences of constants $\{A_n\}$ and $\{B_n\}$ such that

$$A_n X_{(n)} + B_{(n)} \rightsquigarrow \text{extreme value [Table 2(11)]}. \qquad (100)$$

FAILURE RATE (HAZARD RATE, FORCE OR MORTALITY, INTENSITY RATE)

Starting with Karl Pearson, families of distributions have been introduced to unify theory or applications. The exponential family (107) plays a central role in theoretical statistics, and the characterization of failure rates is central to the description of lifetimes of organizations, animals, equipment, etc.

Assume F satisfies:

(a) $F(0) = 0$;   (b) $f(x) = F'(x)$ exists for all $x \geq 0$.

Then define the *failure rate*, $r(t)$, by

$$r(t) = \frac{f(t)}{q - F(t)} \text{ for all } t \text{ such that } 1 - F(t) > 0. \tag{101}$$

The following classes of distributions are non-empty since the exponential [Table 2(1)] belongs to each of them. The names of the classes are suggestive of their applied interest.

IFR (DFR) – Increasing (Decreasing) Failure Rate:

$$r(t) \text{ increases (decreases) for } t \geqslant 0. \tag{102}$$

IFRA (DFRA) – Increasing (Decreasing) Failure Rate Average:

$$\frac{1}{t} \int_0^t r(u)\, du \text{ increases (decreases) for all } t > 0. \tag{103}$$

NBU (NWU) – New Better (Worse) than Used:

$$[1 - F(x + y)] \leqslant (\geqslant)[1 - F(x)][1 - F(y)] \text{ for all } x \geqslant 0,\, y \geqslant 0. \tag{104}$$

NBUE (NWUE) – New Better (Worse) than Used Expectation:

$$\text{(a) } \mu = \int_0^\infty xf(x)\, dx = \int_0^\infty [1 - F(x)]\, dx < \infty\, (\leqslant \infty),$$

$$\text{(b) } \int_t^\infty [1 - F(x)]\, dx \leqslant (\geqslant)\mu[1 - F(t)] \quad \text{for} \quad t \geqslant 0. \tag{105}$$

The classes obey the following inclusion relations:

$$\text{IFR} \subset \text{IFRA} \subset \text{NBU} \subset \text{NBUE},$$

and

$$\text{DFR} \subset \text{DFRA} \subset \text{NWUC} \subset \text{NWUE}. \tag{106}$$

A Weibull random variable [Table 2(12)] is IFR if $c \geqslant 1$, and is DFR if $c \leqslant 1$. There are many analytic results associated with these classes, for example, if X and Y are independent and NBUE, then $Z \sim X + Y$ is NBUE; however, the analogous implication fails for NWU.

Exponential Family. (107)

Many of the examples of densities (or probability functions) are of the form:

$$\exp[a(x)b(\theta) + c(x) + d(\theta)], \tag{108}$$

where x is a possible value of the random variable, and θ is a parameter.

230

Statistical Sufficiency. If $X_1, \ldots, X_n$ are independent each with the same density of form (108), and $T = \Sigma\, a(X_i)$, then

$$f_{X_1, \ldots, X_n \mid T}(x_1, \ldots, x_n \mid T, \theta) \tag{109}$$

does not depend on θ; that is, for purposes of making inferences about θ, all of the information in the sample, $\{X_i\}$, is in the sufficient statistic, $\Sigma\, a(X_i)$.

Theorem: If X has density (108), $b(\cdot)$ is one to one, $b(\theta)$ is an interior point of $\{b(\theta): d(\theta)$ is finite$\}$ and the derivatives denoted by $'$ and $''$ below exist. Then

(a) $Ea(X) = -d'(\theta)/b'(\theta)$.

(b) The Fisher information, I_θ, for a family of densities, $f(\cdot, \theta)$, is defined by

$$I_\theta = E\left[\frac{\partial \ln f(X_1, \theta)}{\partial \theta}\right]^2.$$

When X has a density in the form of (108),

$$I_\theta = -d''(\theta) + d'(\theta)[b''(\theta)/b'(\theta)].$$

When, as often happens, $b(\theta) = \theta$, the result becomes

$$I_\theta = -d''(\theta) = V[a(X)]. \tag{110}$$

Infinitely Divisible and Stable Random Variables. $\qquad\qquad\qquad$ (111)

A random variable, X, is *infinitely divisible* if and only if for every positive integer, n, there exists independent and identically distributed random variables, $\{X_{ni}\}$, such that $X \sim X_{n1} + X_{n2} + \cdots + X_{nn}$. Normal, Poisson, Cauchy and exponential random variables are infinitely divisible. A random variable, X, is *stable* if and only if for each choice of $a_1 \geq 0$ and $a_2 \geq 0$, there exists $a > 0$ and b such that $aX + b \sim a_1 X_1 + a_2 X_2$, where X_1 and X_2 are independent and $X \sim X_1 \sim X_2$. Stable random variables are unimodal, absolutely continuous and infinitely divisible. Normal random variables are the only stable random variables with finite variance; Cauchy random variables are stable.

The function, $\phi(t)$, is the characteristic function of an infinitely divisible random variable if and only if it has the form

$$\log \phi(t) = itA - \frac{\sigma^2}{2}t^2 + \int_{-\infty}^{0-}\left(e^{itu} - 1 - \frac{itu}{1+u^2}\right)dM(u)$$

$$+ \int_{0+}^{\infty}\left(e^{itu} - 1 - \frac{itu}{1+u^2}\right)dN(u), \tag{112}$$

231

where $M(u)$, $N(u)$ and σ^2 satisfy:

(a) $M(u)$ and $N(u)$ are non-decreasing on $(-\infty, 0)$ and $(0, \infty)$.

(b) $M(-\infty) = N(\infty) = 0$.

(c) $\displaystyle\int_{-\varepsilon}^{0} u^2 \, dM(u)$ and $\displaystyle\int_{0}^{\varepsilon} u^2 \, dN(u)$ are finite for every $\varepsilon > 0$.

(d) $\sigma^2 \geqslant 0$.

The representation is unique. [Define $\log \phi(t)$ so that $\log \phi(0) = 0$.]
  For stable random variables (112) must have either

(a) $\sigma^2 > 0$, $M(u) \equiv 0$, and $N(u) \equiv 0$, or

(b) $\sigma^2 = 0$, $M(u) = C_1 |u|^{-\alpha}$ for $u < 0$,

$$N(u) = -C_2 u^{-\alpha} \text{ for } u > 0 \text{ where } 0 < \alpha < 2, \ C_1 \geqslant 0, \ C_2 \geqslant 0 \text{ and } C_1 + C_2 > 0. \tag{113}$$

Conversely, functions satisfying these conditions are characteristic functions of stable random variables.

MIXTURES AND EXCHANGEABILITY

Assume the distribution of X depends on the random parameter θ. When $\theta = \theta_0$, let the conditional density of X be $f(x \mid \theta_0)$. Now assume θ is a random variable with density $f(\theta)$, and the marginal density of X is

$$f_X(x) = \int f(x \mid \theta) \, dF(\theta). \tag{114}$$

Since $f_X(x)$ is a weighted combination of the conditional densities of X, it is called a *mixture*.

Example: Assume X is Poisson (λ) and $\lambda \sim$ exponential, then

$$f_X(x) = \int_{0}^{\infty} \frac{e^{-\lambda} \lambda^x}{x!} e^{-\lambda} = 2^{-x}, \quad x = 0, 1, \ldots. \tag{115}$$

An interpretation of this example is that the λ associated with an individual reflects his accident-proneness, while X is the number of accidents.

Example: Let I be income and θ be sex. Then it is plausible that I given θ has a log-normal distribution with parameters dependent on θ. The marginal distribution of income would be of interest. The $P(\theta = \text{female})$ would have a simple sampling interpretation. The components of these examples appear in Bayesian models. $\qquad$ (116)

A condition, not as restrictive as independence and identical distribution of random variables, is

$$f_{X_1, \ldots, X_n}(x_1, \ldots, x_n) \equiv f_{X_1, \ldots, X_n}[x_{\pi(1)}, \ldots, x_{\pi(n)}], \tag{117}$$

where the identity holds for all $n \geqslant 1$ and all $n!$ permutations $[\pi(1), \ldots, \pi(n)]$ of $(1, \ldots, n)$. Random variables for which condition (117) holds are called *exchangeable random variables*. Note (117) is equivalent to the following generalization of (114):

$$f_{X_1, \ldots, X_n}(x_1, \ldots, x_n) = \int \prod_{i=1}^{n} f(x_i \mid \theta) \, dF(\theta). \tag{118}$$

Now consider sequences of random variables, $\{X_i\}$, where in contrast to exchangeability the labels on the random variables, $\{i\}$, are important. Much of applied statistics is concerned with

$$X_a \sim \sum_{m=1}^{M} t_{am} \beta_m + \varepsilon_a, \quad a = 1, \ldots, N, \tag{119}$$

where the $\{\varepsilon_a\}$ are independent and identically distributed. This is the regression model with M independent variables, $\{t_{am}\}$, and parameters $\{\beta_m\}$. Further complications involve structure on the errors.

(*Strictly*) *Stationary:* For every choice of k distinct integers $\{a_i\}$ and every integer t: (120)

$$(X_{a_1}, X_{a_2}, \ldots, X_{a_k}) \sim (X_{a_1 + t}, X_{a_2 + t}, \ldots, X_{a_k + t}) \tag{121}$$

This implies, for every a, $X_a \sim X_0$, so the random variables are identically distributed but not necessarily independent.

Weakly Stationary:

(a) $EX_a = \mu$, and

(b) EX_a^2 is finite

(c) $\sigma_{a,b} = C(|a - b|)$. (122)

where, specifically, the function C will be of the form

$$C(k) = \sigma^2 \int_{-\pi}^{\pi} \cos k\omega \, dG(\omega), \quad k = 1, 2, \ldots \tag{123}$$

In (123) G is a distribution function with support in $(-\pi, \pi)$, and $G(\omega) + G(-\omega) = 1$ at continuity points of G. If a sequence is weakly stationary, then there is a random variable X such that

$$\lim_{n \to \infty} P(|\bar{X}_n - X| > \varepsilon) = 0,$$

where $\varepsilon > 0$ and $\bar{X}_n = (X_1 + \cdots + X_n)/n$.

BROWNIAN MOTION OR WIENER PROCESSES

Now consider a random variable for each $t \in [0, \infty)$, that is, an uncountably infinite number of random variables. The notation will be $X(t, \omega)$ or $X(t)$. In the above discussion of n random variables, each ω gives an n-dimensional vector $[X_1(\omega), \ldots, X_n(\omega)]$. In the current situation, each ω gives a curve $X(t, \omega), 0 \leqslant t$.

233

We will not consider continuous time stochastic processes, $X(t)$ for $0 \leqslant t$, in general, but we will report results for *Brownian motion* or *Wiener processes*.

Definition of (standard) Brownian motion:

(a) $X(0) = 0$.

(b) The sample paths, $X(s, \omega)$ for $s \in [0, \infty)$, are continuous except for a set $A \in \Omega$ with $P(A) = 0$.

(c) If $0 \leqslant t_1 < t_2 < \cdots < t_k$, then the random variables $X(t_i) - X(t_{i-1})$ are independent, and

$$X(t_i) - X(t_{i-1}) \sim N(0, t_i - t_{i-1}) \text{ for } i = 2, \ldots, k. \tag{124}$$

Some properties of Brownian motion are:

$$\text{If } 0 \leqslant s < t, \quad \text{then} \quad [X(s), X(t)] \sim N\left[\begin{pmatrix} 0 \\ 0 \end{pmatrix}, \begin{pmatrix} s & s \\ t & t \end{pmatrix}\right]. \tag{125}$$

The sample paths are differentiable on a set of Lebesgue measure 0 with probability one. $\tag{126}$

If T replaces n and

$$X(T) \text{ replaces } \sum_{i=1}^{n} X_i, \text{ then (79) holds.} \tag{127}$$

For $a > 0$ define T_a as the least t with $X(t) \geqslant a$. Then

$$P(T_a \leqslant t) = 2P[X(t) \geqslant a] = P[t^{1/2} | N(0, 1)| \geqslant a]. \tag{128}$$

Assume $\mu < 0$ and define $W = \max_{0 \leqslant t}[X(t) + \mu t]$. Then,

$$P(W \geqslant w) = e^{2\mu w}, \quad w \geqslant 0. \tag{129}$$

Let T^* be the largest s such that $X(s) = 0$ for $0 \leqslant s \leqslant t^*$. Then,

$$P(T^* \leqslant t_0) = (2/\pi)\arcsin(t_0/t^*)^{1/2} \text{ for } 0 \leqslant t_0 \leqslant t^*. \tag{130}$$

Assume $X_1, \ldots, X_n$ are independent, and each X_i has the same distribution, F. Define the empirical distribution, F_n, by

$$F_n(x) = (\text{number of } X_i \leqslant x)/n \text{ for } -\infty < x < \infty. \tag{131}$$

The Glivenko–Cantelli Lemma asserts that

$$P\left[\lim_{\substack{n \to \infty}} \max_{-\infty < x < \infty} | F_n(x) - F(x)| = 0\right] = 1. \tag{132}$$

Further, if F is continuous, then for large values of n,

$$B_n(t) = n^{1/2}\{F_n[F^{-1}(t)] - t\} \quad \text{for} \quad 0 \leqslant t \leqslant 1 \tag{133}$$

behaves asymptotically like a *Brownian bridge*,

$$B(t) = X(t) - tX(1), \quad 0 \leqslant t \leqslant 1, \tag{134}$$

where X is Brownian motion.

A consequence is

$$\lim_{n \to \infty} P\left[\max_{-\infty < x < \infty} (n)^{1/2} | F_n(x) - F(x) | \geqslant t \right]$$

$$= 2 \sum_{m=1}^{\infty} (-1)^{m+1} \exp[-2m^2 t^2]. \qquad (135)$$

The Glivenko–Cantelli Lemma (132) is a generalization of the strong law (68), and (133, 134) is a generalization of the central limit theorem (72).

Brownian motion also provides limit theorems for *random walks*. Let $X_1, \ldots,$ $X_n, \ldots$ be independently and identically distributed random variables with mean μ and variance σ^2. Then

$$S_{tn} = \sum_{i=1}^{[tn]} X_i + (nt - [nt]) X_{[nt]+1}, \quad n \geqslant 1, \quad 0 < t,$$

particularly when X is a lattice random variable, is called a *random walk*. Its large sample properties, n large, can be found by treating

$$\frac{S_{tn} - \mu t n}{(n\sigma^2)^{1/2}} \qquad (136)$$

as a sequence of stochastic processes that behaves asymptotically as a Brownian motion, $X(t)$. Some properties of $X(t)$ that are of interest in this regard are:

$$\text{With probability 1, } X(t) = 0 \text{ infinitely often.} \qquad (137)$$

Assume T is a *stopping time*; that is, the event $T \leqslant t$ depends on the values of $X(s)$ only for $s \leqslant t$, and assume $ET < \infty$. Then

$$EX(T) = 0. \qquad (138)$$

Notice this implies the stopping time in (128) does not have finite expectation.

The nonlimiting case yields Wald's equation,

$$ES_N = \mu EN, \qquad (139)$$

where $\{N \leqslant n\}$ depends on $\{X_i\}$ for $i = 1, \ldots, n$.

Assume $a < 0 < b$ and T is the least t such that $X(T) \leqslant a$ or $X(T) \geqslant b$. Then

$$P[X(T) = b] = \frac{|a|}{|a| + b} \quad \text{and} \quad ET = |a| b. \qquad (140)$$

BIBLIOGRAPHY

Note. Some of the criteria used in selecting the references were clarity, availability and completeness. The Johnson and Kotz volumes are a storehouse of information about specific random variables, and Greenwood and Hartley gives extensive detail on available printed tables. The best entry to the current literature on random variables or other statistical-probabilistic topics is the *Current Index to Statistics* (published by the American Statistical Association and the Institute of Mathematical Statistics, 1984, volume 10, also available electronically as *MathScience* produced by the American Mathematics Society) which is a key-word, permuted-title index. Barlow and Proschan, David, Lukacs and Pollard are monographs on specialized topics. Comprehensive views of broad areas are given by Anderson, Chow and Teicher, Rao and Serfling. Ash gives a detailed mathematical setting for probability theory, and Lamperti quickly shows the power of the theory.

Anderson, T.W. 1984. *An Introduction to Multivariate Statistical Analysis.* 2nd edn, John Wiley, 1972.

Ash, R.B. 1972. *Real Analysis and Probability.* New York: Academic Press.

Barlow, R.E. and Proschan, F. 1975. *Statistical Theory of Reliability and Life Testing Probability Models.* New York: Holt, Rinehart and Winston.

Chow, Y.S. and Teicher, H. 1978. *Probability Theory: Independence Interchangeability, Martingales.* New York: Springer-Verlag.

David, H.A. 1981. *Order Statistics.* 2nd edn. New York: John Wiley.

Greenwood, J.A. and Hartley, H.O. 1962. *Guide to Tables in Mathematical Statistics.* Princeton: Princeton University Press.

Johnson, N.L. 1969. *Distributions in Statistics: Discrete Distributions.* Boston: Houghton Mifflin, chs 1–11.

Johnson, N.L. 1970a. *Continuous Distributions,* Vol. 1. Boston: Houghton Mifflin, chs 12–24.

Johnson, N.L. 1970b. *Continuous Distributions,* Vol. 2. Boston: Houghton Mifflin, chs 22–33.

Johnson, N.L. 1972. *Continuous Multivariate Distributions.* New York: John Wiley, chs 34–42.

Karlin, S. and Taylor, H.M. 1975. *A First Course in Stochastic Processes.* 2nd edn, New York: Academic Press.

Lamperti, J. 1966. *Probability: A Survey of Mathematical Theory.* New York: W.A. Benjamin.

Lukacs, E. 1970. *Characteristic Functions.* 2nd edn. New York: Hafner Publishing.

Pollard, D. 1984. *Convergence of Stochastic Processes.* New York: Springer-Verlag.

Rao, C. 1973. *Linear Statistical Inference and Its Applications.* 2nd edn, New York: John Wiley.

Serfling, R.J. 1980. *Approximation Theorems of Mathematical Statistics.* New York: John Wiley.

Regression and Correlation Analysis

D.V. LINDLEY

Correlation is a tool for understanding the relationship between two quantities. Regression considers how one quantity is influenced by another. In correlation analysis the two quantities are considered symmetrically: in regression analysis one is supposed dependent on the other, in an unsymmetric way. Extensions to sets of quantities are important.

Suppose that for each value of a quantity x, another quantity y has a probability distribution $p(y|x)$, the probability of y, given x. The mean value of this distribution, alternatively called the expectation of y, given x, and written $E(y|x)$, is a function of x and is called the regression of y on x. The quantity x is often called the independent variable, though a better term is regressor variable: y is the dependent variable. The regression tells us something about how y depends on x. The simplest case is linear regression, where $E(y|x) = \alpha + \beta x$ for parameters α and β: the latter is called the regression coefficient (of y on x). Other features of the conditional distribution $p(y|x)$ are usually considered in addition to the mean. The variance (or standard deviation) measures the spread of the y-values, for fixed x. A common case is where this is constant over x: the regression is then said to be homoskedastic. A further common assumption is that $p(y|x)$ is normal, or Gaussian. Then y is normally distributed about $\alpha + \beta x$ with constant variance σ^2.

The regression concept of y on x does not involve a probability distribution for the regressor x. If it does have one, $p(x)$, then x and y have a joint distribution given by $p(x, y) = p(y|x)p(x)$. This joint distribution yields variances, σ_{xx} and σ_{yy}, for x and y, and a covariance σ_{xy}. The correlation between x and y is then defined as $\rho_{xy} = \sigma_{xy}/(\sigma_{xx}\sigma_{yy})^{1/2}$. It is the ratio of the covariance to the product of the standard deviations and is clearly unaffected by a change of scale in either x or y (and since the variances and covariance are unaffected, by a change in origin). It is easy to show that $-1 \leqslant \rho_{xy} \leqslant 1$, and if x and y are independent, ρ_{xy}

237

is zero. When $\rho_{xy} = 0$, x and y are said to be uncorrelated. The correlation measures the association between x and y. If x and y have a joint distribution, then not only is there a regression of y on x, considered above, but also of x on y.

The linear, homoskedastic case is easily the most common one used in practice and has several important properties. We may write $y = \alpha + \beta x + \varepsilon$, where ε has zero mean and variance σ^2. If x has a distribution, then the factorization $p(x, y) = p(y|x)p(x)$ shows ε is independent of x and therefore ε and x are uncorrelated. Averaging we have $\mu_y = \alpha + \beta\mu_x$, relating the means, μ_x and μ_y, of x and y. A change of origin enables both of these to be put equal to zero, when $\alpha = 0$ and $E(y|x) = \beta x$, or $y = \beta x + \varepsilon$. Multiplying this last result by x and taking expectations, $\sigma_{xy} = \beta\sigma_{xx}$, as ε and x are uncorrelated. Consequently the regression coefficient of y on x equals σ_{xy}/σ_{xx}. Similarly the regression coefficient of x on y (if that regression is also linear homoskedastic) is σ_{xy}/σ_{yy} and the square of the correlation coefficient equals the product of the regression coefficients.

Returning to the relation $y = \beta x + \varepsilon$ and considering the variances of both sides, we obtain $\sigma_{yy} = \beta^2\sigma_{xx} + \sigma^2$ (again using the lack of correlation between x and ε). Hence $\sigma^2 = \sigma_{yy} - \sigma_{xy}^2/\sigma_{xx}$, on using $\beta = \sigma_{xy}/\sigma_{xx}$, and we have the important relationship that $\sigma^2 = \sigma_{yy}(1 - \rho_{xy}^2)$, showing that the variance σ^2, of y about the regression, is a proportion $(1 - \rho_{xy}^2)$ of the total variance of y, σ_{yy}. In the form $\sigma_{yy} = \beta^2\sigma_{xx} + \sigma^2$, we have the result that the total variance of y is made up of two additive components, that due to x, $\beta^2\sigma_{xx}$, and that about the regression line. The former is called the component of variance ascribable to x: the latter is the residual variance and, as we have just seen, is a proportion $(1 - \rho_{xy}^2)$ of the total. That ascribable to x is a proportion ρ_{xy}^2. This decomposition of variance is at the heart of analysis of variance techniques.

The ideas of regression and correlation are due to Galton and Pearson. The classic example has x the height of a father and y that of his son. Both regressions are linear, homoskedastic and normal, having positive regression coefficients which are less than one. Galton noticed that tall (short) fathers have sons who are, on average, shorter (taller) than themselves. This follows since, centring the values at the mean, or average height, $E(y|x) = \beta x < x$ if $x > 0$ corresponding to tall fathers, $\beta x > x$ if $x < 0$ for short ones. This is the phenomenon of regression (of heights) towards the mean and is necessary if the variability in heights is not to increase from one generation to the next. An illustration from economics might have x as the price of an item and y the number sold. There β will be negative reflecting the average decrease in numbers sold as the price increases. Here x might not have a probability distribution but be at the control of the seller.

The modern tendency is to make increasing use of regression and less of correlation. Part of the explanation for this is the importance of dependency relations, instead of associations, between quantities. Another reason is that in so many examples (as item price) the regressor variable is not random, so that σ_{xx} and σ_{xy} are meaningless and correlation ideas are unavailable. A third consideration is that correlation can be misleading. As an illustration of this let x be a quantity, symmetrically and randomly distributed about zero. Let $y = x^2$. Then $\sigma_{xy} = E(xy) = E(x^3) = 0$ by the symmetry about zero. Hence the correlation is zero whilst y and x are highly associated, one being the square of the other. Correlation ideas work well when all variables are normally distributed but less well otherwise. (If $y = x^2$, y cannot be normal.)

The ideas and definitions extend to the case where there are several regressor variables $x_1, x_2, \ldots, x_m$. Write $\mathbf{x} = (x_1, x_2, \ldots, x_m)$. Then $E(y \mid \mathbf{x})$ is the (multiple) regression of y on $\mathbf{x}$. In the linear case with means at zero, $E(y \mid \mathbf{x}) = \Sigma \beta_i x_i$ and β_i is the partial regression coefficient of y on x_i. The notation and nomenclature here are too brief and can be misleading, for β_i only measures the dependence of y on x_i in the presence of the other quantities in $\mathbf{x}$. Were, say x_m, to be omitted β_i, $i < m$, would typically change: indeed, the regression might not be linear. The cumbersome notation exemplified by $\beta_{2.134}$ ($i = 2, m = 4$) is sometimes used. In words, the coefficient of y on x_2, allowing for x_1, x_3 and x_4. The variance about the regression remains and the homoskedastic case, where this is constant, is the one usually considered.

In the linear case $E(y \mid \mathbf{x}) = \Sigma \beta_i x_i$ the x's can be functionally related. A common case is where $x_i = x^i$, the powers of a single quantity x. This is referred to as polynomial regression. It is usually more convenient to work with polynomials $P_i(x)$ of degree i in x which are orthogonal with respect to some measure. Then $E(y \mid \mathbf{x}) = \Sigma \beta_i P_i(x)$. Another possibility is where the x_i are periodic, say $\cos it$. Notice that the linearity is in the terms $P_i(x)$ – or the coefficients β_i – not in x.

If the regressor variables have a joint distribution then the covariances σ_{yi}, between y and x_i, and σ_{ij} between x_i and x_j are available. With more than one regressor variable additional concepts can be introduced. For example, if all the x's are held fixed except for x_i there is a conditional joint distribution of y and x_i given all the x's except x_i. This has a correlation, defined as above as the ratio of the conditional covariance to the product of the conditional standard deviations, and is called the partial correlation between y and x_i. The notation is exemplified by $\rho_{y2.134}$. This will, in general, depend on the fixed values of the regressor variables but is normally only used when it is constant. This happens if the joint distribution of y and $\mathbf{x}$ is multivariate normal.

In the case of a single regressor variable we saw that $1 - \rho_{xy}^2 = \sigma^2 / \sigma_{yy}$, where σ^2 is the residual variance of y, conditional on x. In the multiple case, continue to define σ^2 in this way conditional on all the quantities in $\mathbf{x}$. Then define R^2 by $(1 - R^2) = \sigma^2 / \sigma_{yy}$, in analogy with the single variable case. The positive square root R is called the multiple correlation coefficient (of y on $\mathbf{x}$). As before, we may write $\sigma_{yy} = \sigma^2 + R^2 \sigma_{yy}$, expressing the total variance of y additively in terms of the residual variance σ^2 and that due to the regression on $\mathbf{x}$. It is more common nowadays to work in terms of the variance components than R^2.

The mathematical theory of regression and correlation is now well understood. Centring at the means, all the concepts depend on the matrix of variances and covariances of y, the dependent variable, and $\mathbf{x}$, the set of regressor variables: σ_{yi} and σ_{ij}. The calculations are merely ways of rearranging these elements in convenient forms: correlations and components of variance in regression are just two possibilities. The real difficulty, and the real interest in regression lies in the interpretation of the results.

As an illustration consider the simple case of linear, homoskedastic regression of y on a single regressor variable x, written $y = \beta x + \varepsilon$, with β as the regression coefficient and ε as the residual variation, with zero mean and variance σ^2. All this says is that for any fixed x, y has mean βx and variance σ^2: and it is only this aspect of the dependence of y on x that is described. Suppose a large amount of data consisting of pairs (x_i, y_i) is collected and the fit $y = 2x + \varepsilon$ with $\sigma^2 = 2$ is established. (We discuss how this might be done below.) This shows a fairly close association between y and x. In order therefore to increase y it might be thought reasonable to set x to a high value. Suppose this is done, will this cause y necessarily to increase? Surprisingly, not so. Suppose there is another quantity z and the real relationships are that $y = -x + z + \varepsilon_1$, and $x\frac{1}{3}z + \varepsilon_2$ so that z is the basic quantity determining the situation. This clearly yields $y = 2x + \varepsilon$, with $\varepsilon = \varepsilon_1 - 3\varepsilon_2$, the observed relation. If now x is controlled at a large value without affecting z which is, under natural conditions, the main determinant of x, the effect will be to decrease y through $y = -x + z + \varepsilon_1$. Consequently a strong positive relationship between y and x need not imply an increase in y when x is increased. There can be an enormous difference between the association of y with x, when x is uncontrolled and allowed to vary freely, and the association when x is controlled. And the reason is the presence of another quantity z whose influence on x in the free system is disturbed by the control.

Whenever the regression of y on a set of quantities $\mathbf{x}$ is discussed, one has to beware of the possible presence of other, unobserved quantities $\mathbf{z}$ that could affect the relationship. A laboratory scientist, or even a social scientist doing a planned survey, can often guard against such hidden quantities by careful design or by appropriate randomization; but an economist, or anyone who has to rely on data from unplanned studies, has always to be on his guard against their effects. Another way of describing the difficulty is to distinguish carefully between association and causation. All regression and correlation analyses can do is study association: the underlying causal mechanism is not necessarily revealed. It is remarkable how little attention has been paid by statisticians to the meaning of causation, and to how it can be revealed by statistical analysis. Economists have had to rely on statistical analyses of randomly obtained data and some of the causal inferences they have drawn are totally unjustified by that data and the analyses.

We now consider the nature of these statistical analyses, confining ourselves predominantly to the case of homoskedastic, linear regression $y = \Sigma \beta_i x_i + \varepsilon$, ε having mean zero and variance σ^2. There the means have been supposed zero. There is usually no difficulty over this as the mean of each variable can ordinarily be estimated by the sample means, y and x_i. The quantities being discussed here are, in terms of the original data, the deviations, $y - y$ and $x_i - x_i$, from the sample means. The standard method of estimating the β's and σ^2 is least squares. This has been in use for two centuries and is still adopted by almost all data analysts. If that data is $(y_j, x_{ji}: i = 1, 2, \ldots, m; j = 1, 2, \ldots, n)$ consisting of n independent observations of y and the m regressor variables, then the least-squares estimates of β_i are provided by minimizing the sum of squares of residuals

$y - \Sigma \beta_i x_i$ for each of the n observations: that is $\Sigma_j (y_j - \Sigma_i \beta_i x_{ji})^2$. Matrix notation is most convenient. Write $\mathbf{y} = (y_1, y_2, \ldots, y_n)^T$, $\boldsymbol{\beta} = (\beta_1, \beta_2, \ldots, \beta_m)^T$ and X as the matrix with elements x_{ji}, observation j on variable x_j. Then $\mathbf{y} = X\boldsymbol{\beta}$ + residual and the sum of squares to be minimized over $\boldsymbol{\beta}$ is $(\mathbf{y} - X\boldsymbol{\beta})^T(\mathbf{y} - X\boldsymbol{\beta})$ with minimum given by $\hat{\boldsymbol{\beta}} = (X^T X)^{-1} X^T \mathbf{y}$. The variance σ^2 is estimated by the sum of squares at $\hat{\boldsymbol{\beta}}$ divided by $(n - m)$. The $\hat{\beta}$ are called the least-squares estimates of β_i.

The method is deservedly popular because it is relatively easy to use and interpret, and many convenient computer programs are available. Its long and successful history testifies to its merits. Unfortunately it has been discovered that there can be very real difficulties when m, the number of variables is large. With the availability of fast computers capable of handling a lot of data, it is not uncommon to have 40 or more variables. The difficulties then become noticeable. Before the arrival of such computing power, least squares was only used with few variables and the difficulties are scarcely noticeable. It is easy to appreciate what could go wrong: it is not so easy to correct it. Consider the case where the sum of squares is $\Sigma_j (y_j - \beta_j)^2$. This apparently special and degenerate case is, in fact, a canonical form for least squares and any multiple regression situation can be transformed to it by linear transformations. (In so doing, the meanings of the y's and β's will change.) The minimization is trivial with estimate $\hat{\beta}_j = y_j$, and the minimum value is zero. But we know that y_j differs from its expectation, here β_j, but in general $\Sigma_i \beta_i x_{ji}$, by an amount which has variance σ^2, so the average of $\Sigma_j (y_j - \hat{\beta}_j)^2$ ought to be about σ^2, and indeed this is the usual estimate of σ^2 as mentioned above. But here this estimate is zero, which is absurd. This first, rigorous demonstration that least squares is unsatisfactory was given by Charles Stein. He showed that whenever the number of variables exceeds two, there is an estimate which is, for every value of the regression coefficients, better than least squares. Better here means having smaller mean-square error, though the statement remains true under many other meanings. The efficiency varies with the true values of the β's. The result just quoted says that it is always less than one. It can be as low as $2/m$: with $m = 40$ this gives only 5% efficiency, a rather serious loss.

It is surprising how little attention Stein's result has received outside a small group, largely of theoreticians, yet its practical value could be enormous. Stein, and others, have produced estimates which improve on least squares but none has had much acceptance. Fairly early in the use of computers for regression analysis, it was appreciated that difficulties could arise when the matrix $X^T X$, which has to be inverted to obtain the least-squares estimates, is ill-conditioned, with determinant near zero. This is the matrix of sample variances and covariances of the regressor variables, a typical element being $\Sigma_r x_{ri} x_{rj}$ where the x's are deviations from their means, x_i. It will be ill-conditioned if, in the data, there is a near linear relationship between the regressor variables. One suggestion was to put the matrix into correlation form, dividing each row and each column by the sample standard deviation of the variable corresponding to that row or column, so making all diagonal elements one and each off-diagonal element equal to a sample correlation coefficient between x_i and x_j, and then subtracting a constant λ from each unit diagonal element. This leads to ridge regression estimates and ways of choosing λ have been proposed. If often works well but can fail.

These ideas all lie within a frequentist school of inference. In principle, a solution is available with the Bayesian paradigm for inference. Here, in addition to the distribution of y, given $\mathbf{x}$, is included a probability distribution for the regression parameter $\boldsymbol{\beta} = (\beta_1, \beta_2, \ldots, \beta_m)$. Inference is then made by calculating the revised probability distribution of $\boldsymbol{\beta}$ given the data. This procedure always avoids Stein's criticism provided the original distribution of $\boldsymbol{\beta}$ has total integral unity. (Least squares results from this procedure only if all the values of $\boldsymbol{\beta}$ are equally probable, a form which is not finitely integrable.) The practical difficulty is the choice of a distribution for $\boldsymbol{\beta}$. The ridge method can be produced for certain types of exchangeable distributions for $\boldsymbol{\beta}$. In the case of polynomial regression, a reasonable possibility is to suppose that the coefficients of the higher degree polynomials are likely to be smaller than those of lower degree. When the regressor variables refer to different quantities, a possibility is to suppose that few of them have an appreciable coefficient, and therefore influence y, but it is not known which are the determining ones.

This idea that only a few regressors matter has led to a lot of work on the choice of which to include in the regression. There are two broad ways to proceed. One can fit all the quantities available and then discard them one by one as long as the discarding has little effect. Or one can proceed in the reverse direction, introducing them one at a time only if they have an appreciable effect. In both of these methods it has to be decided how the effect is to be measured. The usual criterion is the change in the variance of y ascribable to $\mathbf{x}$; the quantity denoted above by $R^2 \sigma_{yy}$. Alternatively expressed, this is the change in the multiple correlation coefficient. For example, in the method where the variables are discarded, R^2 will decrease when a variable is omitted from the regression. Only if this decrease is small will the omission be granted. There are two difficulties here. First, it is possible for two quantities, separately to have little effect, but jointly to be of considerable importance, so that tests of them one at a time may be misleading. (The possibility of computing all 2^m regressions is too extravagant.) Second, it is not clear what is meant by saying the change in R^2 is 'small': how small? One possibility is to use an ordinary significance test, here a t-test. If significant the regressor causing the change can be included: if not, it is omitted. This is for some suitably chosen significance level. This has been thought to be unsatisfactory by some and other criteria have been proposed. It is here that the Bayesian and frequentist views part company. The usual Bayesian criterion for 'small' depends on the assumed distribution for the regression coefficients, but, in general, it seems to need more evidence to introduce a regressor when using the Bayesian approach than when employing a significance test. The former has been accused of favouring the hypothesis that the variable is not worth including. The Bayesian reply is that some 'significant' effects are spurious. Multiple regression techniques are so widely used today that one wonders how many effects of x_i on y reported in the literature are meaningful.

Regression concerns a relation, to take the linear, one variable form, $y = \beta x + \varepsilon$ between y and x. This treats y and x asymmetrically and does not lead to $x = \beta^{-1}y + \varepsilon'$ with ε' unrelated to y. There is, however, a symmetric form that is sometimes useful. Suppose two quantities, ξ and η, are exactly linearly related, $\eta = \beta\xi$, or equally $\xi = \beta^{-1}\eta$. Suppose that each is measured with error giving $y = \eta + \varepsilon, x = \xi + \varepsilon'$. Then the pair (x, y) may have linear regressions but the real interest lies in β, the coefficient of the exact relationship. This is often referred to as the case where both variables, independent and regressor, are subject to error. Ordinary least-squares techniques, even with a single regressor variable, require modification.

Linear multiple regression is part of the general theory of linear models in which, to use the notation above, $E(y \mid X) = X\beta$, the linearity being in the parameter β. Least squares and its Stein-type modifications are the standard techniques for analysis, together with the analysis of variance.

BIBLIOGRAPHY

Efron, B. and Morris, C. 1975. Data analysis using Stein's estimator and its generalizations. *Journal of the American Statistical Association* 70, 311–19.

Hoerl, A.E. and Kennard, R.W. 1970. Ridge regression: biased estimation of non-orthogonal problems. *Technometrics* 12, 55–67.

Seber, G.A.F. 1977. *Linear Regression Analysis.* New York: Wiley.

Vinod, H.D. and Ullah, A. 1981. *Recent Advances in Regression Methods.* New York: Dekker.

Zellner, A. 1971. *An Introduction to Bayesian Inference in Econometrics.* New York: Wiley.

Residuals

F.J. ANSCOMBE

Most commonly used statistical procedures, for analysis and interpretation of statistical data, rest on assumptions about the behaviour of the data. Quite often these assumptions can be adequately justified, and the procedures accepted as fair and reasonable. But that is not always so, and it behoves the analyst to check consistency of the data with the assumptions. Failure to do this may lead to a grossly misleading analysis and the drawing of wrong conclusions. Just how consistency can be checked depends on the complexity of the data. Often a step is calculation of *residuals*, which are measures of deviation between the observed values of a variable and the fitted (or estimated or predicted) values for that variable, calculated in accordance with the assumptions. The residuals, when found, are sometimes combined into a summary measure of goodness of fit, or sometimes they are displayed graphically, in various possible ways.

A very simple example of this kind of concern is afforded by the common practice of summarizing a single set of readings of a quantitative variable by the average of the readings and their standard deviation. Those two quantities would certainly form a good and convenient summary of the data, useful for a variety of purposes, if we knew that the readings were independent observations of a random variable following a normal (Gauss–Laplace) distribution, or something not very different from that. Usually in practice we do not have such knowledge. We can, however, check to see whether the distribution of the readings, shown perhaps by a histogram, is reasonably consistent with a normal distribution; and if the readings came to us arranged in some meaningful order we could look for evidence of serial dependence. If the readings contained one extreme outlier (a reading very far from all the others), the average and standard deviation calculated from all the readings could be quite different from those calculated from all the readings *except* that one outlier, and for most purposes the average and standard deviation of all the readings would be misleading.

The possibly devastating effect of outliers has suggested to some authorities that 'robust' measures of the centre and spread of a set of readings would be preferable to the traditional average and standard deviation – measures that rest on much weaker assumptions than a nearly normal distribution, measures that would be little affected by inclusion or exclusion of a few outliers if such occurred in the data. Instead of the average one could choose the median of the data, and instead of the standard deviation one could choose the median absolute deviation of readings from their median, or the interquartile range. Such robust measures cannot be said to rest on no assumptions at all – independence is assumed, for example – but they are safer to use if procedures must be used uncritically. A price is paid for the safety. The traditional assumptions permit a considerable body of simple inferential methods, that must be foregone or much modified when only the weaker assumptions for robust procedures are made. Thus in much statistical practice today, analytical procedures based on specific non-robust probabilistic assumptions are still often used, but checking conformity of the data with the assumptions is regarded as essential.

In the above discussion of summarizing a single set of readings of one variable, the word 'residual' has not been mentioned. Residuals could be defined as the differences between each of the readings and their average (or median or whatever central measure is adopted). The central measure is the 'fitted value', the same for all readings. An outlier is a reading whose residual is much larger in magnitude than nearly all the other residuals. In any graphical presentation of the data, the differences between individual readings and the common central value are easily seen, whether or not the residuals have been calculated; and therefore in this context it is hardly necessary to refer to residuals, even though it is just those differences that are of most interest.

The most widely used technique in the analysis of statistical data is linear regression, by which the association of a quantitative 'dependent' variable with one or more explanatory variables may be studied. Some of the considerations that arise concerning consistency of the data with the assumptions underlying linear regression can be seen in their simplest form if we consider linear regression of one dependent variable on just one explanatory variable.

For such simple linear regression, the standard least-squares calculation is based on the following theoretical description or 'model': the given number pairs (x_i, y_i) are related by

$$y_i = \beta_0 + \beta_1 x_i + \varepsilon_i \qquad (i = 1, 2, \ldots, n). \tag{1}$$

where β_0 and β_1 are constants and the 'errors' $\{\varepsilon_i\}$ are drawn independently from a normal probability distribution having zero mean and constant variance. The regression calculation leads to estimates b_0 and b_1 for β_0 and β_1, to the fitted values

$$\hat{y}_i = b_0 + b_1 x_i = \bar{y} + b_1(x_i - \bar{x}),$$

and to the residuals

$$e_i = y_i - \hat{y}_i.$$

TABLE 1. Four artificial data sets, each consisting of eleven (x, y) pairs

Data set		1–3	1	2	3	4	4
Variable		x	y	y	y	x	y
Obs. no.	1:	10.0	8.04	9.14	7.46:	8.0	6.58
	2:	8.0	6.95	8.14	6.77:	8.0	5.76
	3:	13.0	7.58	8.74	12.74:	8.0	7.71
	4:	9.0	8.81	8.77	7.11:	8.0	8.84
	5:	11.0	8.33	9.26	7.81:	8.0	8.47
	6:	14.0	9.96	8.10	8.84:	8.0	7.04
	7:	6.0	7.24	6.13	6.08:	8.0	5.25
	8:	4.0	4.26	3.10	5.39:	19.0	12.50
	9:	12.0	10.84	9.13	8.15:	8.0	5.56
	10:	7.0	4.82	7.26	6.42:	8.0	7.91
	11:	5.0	5.68	4.74	5.73:	8.0	6.89

The sum of squares of the latter, generally called the 'residual sum of squares', leads to an estimate of the variance of the distribution of errors. If the theoretical description were exactly correct (and all calculations were exact, without round-off error), these calculations would be entirely satisfactory, in the sense that b_0, b_1 and the residual sum of squares, together with the number of readings n and the first two moments of the x-values, would constitute sufficient statistics for the original data for all purposes with no loss of information. In practice, we do not know that the theoretical description is correct, we should generally suspect that it is not, and we cannot therefore heave a sigh of relief when the regression calculation has been made, knowing that statistical justice has been done.

Some of the possibilities for appropriateness or inappropriateness of the standard regression calculation are illustrated by the four artificial data sets given in Table 1. Each data set consists of eleven (x, y) pairs. For the first three data sets the x-values are the same, and they are listed only once. The four data sets have been constructed so as to yield the same standard output from a typical regression programme, as shown in Table 2. Thus if equation (1) is a correct theoretical description of the data, all four data sets are equivalent – they mean the same thing.

Regression programmes often list the residuals, in the order in which the data were entered. Since in the present case the data have been entered in a random order, probably little would be seen if the eye were run down such a listing, especially if it were in abominable floating-point notation. Only if the residuals are presented graphically, or perhaps combined into one or more overall measures of goodness of fit, is the viewer likely to realize how very different in character these four data sets are, and therefore how inadequate the information in Table 2 is. The simplest kind of graphical presentation of the data sets is just a scatterplot of the given (x, y) pairs, together with the fitted regression line, as in Figures 1–4.

TABLE 2. The same standard output of a
regression analysis of each of the data sets in
Table 1

Number of observations $(n) = 11$
Mean of the x's $(\bar{x}) = 9.0$
Mean of the y's $(\bar{y}) = 7.5$
Regression coefficient (b_1) of y on $x = 0.5$
Equation of regression line: $y = 3 + 0.5x$
Sum of squares of $x - \bar{x} = 110.0$
Regression sum of squares $= 27.50$ (1 d.f.)
Residual sum of squares of $y = 13.75$ (9 d.f.)
Estimated standard error of $b_1 = 0.118$
Multiple $R^2 = 0.667$

Figure 1, corresponding to data set 1, is the kind of thing most people would see in their mind's eye, if they were presented with the summary in Table 2. The theoretical description (1) seems to be perfectly appropriate here, and the summary fair and adequate. Figure 2 suggests forcefully that data set 2 does not conform with the theoretical description (1), but rather y has a smooth curved relation with x, possibly quadratic, and there is little residual variability. Figure 3 similarly suggests that (1) is not a good description for data set 3: all but one of the observations lie close to a straight line (not the one yielded by the standard regression calculation), namely

$$y = 4 + 0.346x;$$

and one observation is far from this line. Those are the essential facts that need to be understood and reported.

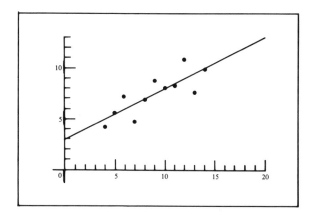

Figure 1

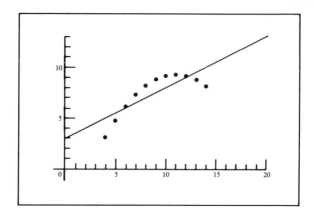

Figure 2

Figure 4, like Figure 1, shows data apparently conforming well with the theoretical description (1). If all observations are considered genuine and reliable, data set 4 is just as informative about the regression relation as data set 1; there is no reason to prefer either to the other. Yet in most circumstances we should feel that there was something unsatisfactory about data set 4. All the information about the slope of the regression line resides in one observation – if that observation were deleted the slope could not be estimated. Usually we are not quite sure that every observation is reliable. If any one observation were discredited and therefore deleted from data set 1, the remainder would tell much the same story. That is not so for data set 4. Thus the standard regression calculation ought to be accompanied by a warning that one observation has played a critical role. Of course, just one informative observation is much better than none. But we are usually happier about asserting a regression relation if the relation seems to permeate many of the observations and does not inhere mostly in one or two.

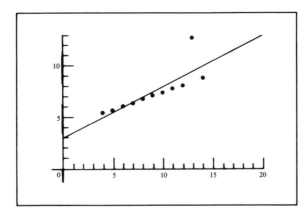

Figure 3

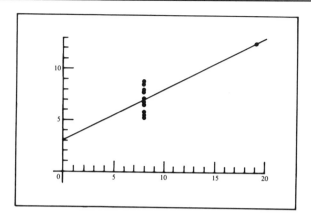

Figure 4

Each of the data sets 2, 3, 4 illustrates a peculiar effect in an extreme form. In less extreme forms such effects are often encountered in statistical analysis. There are other kinds of effect that can appear, such as residual variability changing progressively with *x*. But it is arguable that data sets 2, 3, 4 exemplify the three situations most important to recognize of they should occur, namely that the true regression relationship between the variables is not the linear one fitted, that there are one or more extreme outliers among the residuals, and that there are one or more highly influential *x*-values.

When regression is done on more than one explanatory variable, similar considerations arise. A simple two-dimensional scatterplot cannot now represent directly the whole of the data, in the style of Figures 1–4 above. It is found that plots of residuals against the fitted values, and also of residuals against the values of each explanatory variable in turn, are often effective in suggesting ways to improve the analysis; and other kinds of plots depending on residuals are sometimes made. The more variables there are, the greater are the possible complexities in the data, and the less sure we can be that all important effects will be perceived. That is the more reason for examining residuals carefully. Various specific test statistics can be formed from residuals and used to detect specific kinds of discrepancy between the data and the assumed theoretical description.

Examination of residuals has been most thoroughly developed for regression. But in many other cases when data are considered in light of a theoretical description, measures of difference between observed values and fitted values can be defined that behave like regression residuals and are similarly useful. Such residuals are, however, often not just simple differences between observed values and fitted values.

[Examination of residuals is discussed by Draper and Smith (1981), Cook and Weisberg (1982), Anscombe (1981), McCullagh and Nelder (1983), Cox and Snell (1968). The tables and figures given above are taken from Anscombe (1973). For robust methods see Tukey (1977) and Huber (1981).]

BIBLIOGRAPHY

Anscombe, F.J. 1973. *American Statistician* 27, 17–21.

Anscombe, F.J. 1981. *Computing in Statistical Science through APL.* New York: Springer-Verlag. (Especially Appendix 2.)

Cook, R.D. and Weisberg, S. 1982. *Residuals and Influence in Regression.* London: Chapman & Hall. (Especially Chapter 2.)

Cox, D.R. and Snell, E.J. 1968. *Journal of the Royal Statistical Society*, Series B 30, 248–75.

Draper, N.R. and Smith, H. 1981. *Applied Regression Analysis.* 2nd edn, New York: Wiley.

Huber, P.J. 1981. *Robust Statistics.* New York: Wiley.

McCullagh, P. and Nelder, J.A. 1983. *Generalized Linear Models.* London: Chapman & Hall.

Tukey, J.W. 1977. *Exploratory Data Analysis.* Reading, Mass.: Addison-Wesley.

Semiparametric Estimation

STEPHEN R. COSSLETT

A structural econometric model typically has the form $y = f(x, u, \theta)$, where y is a set of observed dependent variables; x a set of observed explanatory variables; u represents some unobserved variables, often called 'error' terms or stochastic terms; and θ is a parameter vector which is to be estimated. The main focus of econometric modelling is on specification of the function f. But estimation and inference also require assumptions about the statistical properties of u. Very little may be known about those variables, so one should be cautious of estimators that rely on a specific distribution function for them.

This applies particularly to a large class of non-linear econometric models that are commonly estimated by maximum likelihood (ML) under the assumption of normally distributed error terms. Examples are discrete choice models, censored and truncated regression models, and some disequilibrium models (see Maddala, 1983). In particular, let $y^* = v(x, \theta) + u$ be an unobserved (latent) variable and let y be the observed dependent variable: then $y = 1[y^* > 0]$ defines the binary choice model; $y = y^* \cdot 1[y^* > 0]$ defines the simplest version of the censored regression model; and in the truncated regression model neither y^* nor x is observed unless y^* is positive. (The indicator function $1[\cdot]$ equals one if its argument is true, and equals zero otherwise.) The sample (x_i, y_i), $i = 1, \ldots, n$, is assumed to be a cross-section with independent errors u_i.

The model can generally be rewritten in regression form as $y = g(x, \theta; F) + \varepsilon$ with $E[\varepsilon] = 0$, where F is the distribution function of u. A special case is the *single-index* model where $g(x, \theta; F) = h(v(x, \theta); F)$ for some given index function v — for example, the models given above with partially observed y^*.

Semiparametric (also called *distribution-free*) methods estimate θ consistently when F is unknown but f (or g) is specified. Some of the methods described below can handle more general kinds of unknown functional dependence, and border on the separate topic of non-parametric regression. If, on the other hand, g does not depend on F, one has the *nonlinear regression* model: while least squares and method of moments estimators are, strictly speaking, semiparametric estimators, that is also a separate topic (see, for example, Amemiya, 1983). For an account of adaptive estimation of nonliner regression models (i.e., semiparametric estimation with the same large-sample efficiency as if F were known), see Manski (1984).

The following headings cover some of the main directions of semiparametric estimation in econometrics.

LEAST ABSOLUTE DEVIATIONS AND RELATED METHODS

One can rewrite the model as $y = \mu(x, \theta; F) + \varepsilon$ where now median $[\varepsilon] = 0$ (instead of $E[\varepsilon] = 0$). If μ does not depend on F, and suitable regularity conditions hold, then θ is consistently estimated by minimizing the sum of absolute deviations $\Sigma_i |y_i - \mu_i|$ with respect to θ, where $\mu_i = \text{median}[f(x_i, u_i, \theta)]$. This applies to the censored regression model (Powell, 1984), and to the binary choice model, where the method reduces to the maximum score estimator (Manski, 1974 and 1985). An important feature of this approach is that the errors u_i need not be identically distributed.

Unlike many semiparametric estimators, Powell's least absolute deviations (LAD) estimator has a known asymptotic distribution: under the assumption of independent identically distributed (i.i.d.) errors, $\hat{\theta}$ converges at the rate $n^{-1/2}$ to a normal distribution with an explicit expression for the asymptotic variance (Powell, 1984). The asymptotic distribution of the maximum score estimator is not yet known; preliminary investigations indicate an $n^{-1/3}$ rate of convergence.

Manski's maximum score method is more than a special case of LAD, because it can be applied to the random utility model with any number of discrete choices, although only under the following condition. Let $u_{i,j}$ be the stochastic component of the utility function for case i and choice j; then the $u_{i,j}$ must be i.i.d. across choices for each case. This is quite restrictive. The only other practicable semiparametric method for polychotomous choice models is Gallant's semi-nonparametric approach (see below).

If the error distribution is known to be *symmetric*, then Powell's LAD method can be applied also to the truncated regression model by 'symmetric trimming': in effect, large positive residuals are trimmed to compensate for observations with large negative residuals having been dropped from the sample. Symmetry may be thought a rather artificial assumption. But if it holds, then symmetric trimming can be applied also to least squares estimation of both the censored and the truncated regression models (Powell, 1986), with considerable savings in computation when compared with LAD estimation.

NONPARAMETRIC MAXIMUM LIKELIHOOD ESTIMATION OF F

If θ were known, the error terms ε would be observable and would allow nonparametric maximum likelihood (NPML) estimation of F, say $\hat{F}(\cdot | \theta)$. Tractable NPML estimators are available for several cases, the best known being the Kaplan–Meier estimator for a censored distribution (Kaplan and Meier,

1958); there is a similar estimator in the truncated case (Lynden-Bell, 1971). In fact θ must also be estimated, for which two approaches have been developed.

Semiparametric maximum likelihood. Semiparametric maximum likelihood (SPML) estimation is possible if the likelihood function can be maximized over both θ and F. This is a theoretically attractive approach but is practical in only a few cases. The following examples are special in that the ML estimator exists without any prior smoothness assumptions on F.

A method for implementing the SPML estimator of the binary choice model is given by Cosslett (1983). Here F is the distribution function of the error term in the underlying regression model for y^*: a normal distribution would give the probit model, a logistic distribution the logit model. Both θ and F are consistently estimated, but the asymptotic distribution is not known.

Heckman and Singer (1984) give an algorithm for the SPML estimator of a mixture model of duration data (specifically, unemployment duration). The distribution function of durations for an individual, $G(t \mid u, x, \theta)$, depends on an unobserved characteristic u, so the distribution of observed durations is $\int G(t \mid u, x, \theta) \, dF(u)$. Heckman and Singer investigate the case where F is unknown but G is a given parametric function (the Weibull model). The classical parametric ML estimator is sensitive to misspecification of F. The SPML estimator of θ and F is shown to be consistent, but also in this case the asymptotic distribution is unknown.

Bias-corrected regression. Consider again a limited dependent variable model with the underlying regression equation $y^* = x(x, \theta) + u$ and the observed dependent variable y. Let $\eta(y, v(x, \theta); F)$ be an exogenous correction term such that $E[\eta] = E[y - y^*]$. Then, if F were known, θ could be consistently estimated from the regression $y = v(x, \theta) + \eta(y, v(x, \theta); F) + \varepsilon$. When F is normal, this is the basis of Heckman's two-stage estimator (see Maddala, 1983, ch. 8).

In fact F is unknown, but one can replace it by its NPML estimator (suitably trimmed if necessary to avoid instability at large values of residuals) and estimate

$$y = v(x, \theta) + \eta[y, v(x, \theta); \hat{F}(\cdot \mid \theta)] + \varepsilon$$

by least squares or method of moments. This is computationally awkward because the dependence of $\hat{F}$ on θ is not explicit: the most practical approach seems to be the EM algorithm, an iterative scheme where one alternately estimates F and θ.

Several authors have taken this approach, and we mention in particular the truncated regression estimator of Buckley and James (1979) (see also Miller and Halpern, 1982). Despite much research effort, a definitive proof of consistency of $\hat{\theta}$ has not yet been published.

SEMI-NONPARAMETRIC ESTIMATION

A straightforward response to misspecification of a distribution is to make it a member of a larger parametric family. If the number of parameters is allowed to grow with sample size, it may be possible to find an estimate $\hat{F}$ that converges to the true distribution. This has been formalized by Gallant, who coined the term 'semi-nonparametric' and established conditions under which the resulting least squares or maximum likelihood estimators of θ and F are strongly consistent (see Gallant and Nychka, 1987). The Phillips ERA (Phillips, 1983) can be used as a parametric representation of an unknown distribution function. A convenient special case of this is the Hermite expansion used by Gallant and Nychka, who investigate the nonlinear regression model with sample selection. (The method also works for more general classes of unknown functions.)

The dimensionality $k(n)$ of the parametric family containing $\hat{F}$ may be fixed *a priori* or may be data based. Once $k(n)$ is determined, existing parametric estimation methods can be used. The question of an operational data-based rule for $k(n)$ remains, and it is not known under exactly what circumstances the 'traditional' method is valid (add parameters as long as they are statistically significant). It also remains to be seen whether conventional statistical tests, which treat $k(n)$ as fixed, are asymptotically valid for any data-based selection rule.

INSTRUMENTAL VARIABLES

If the semiparametric model has the single-index form with a linear index function, i.e., $y = h(x \cdot \theta; F) + \varepsilon$, then integration by parts gives

$$\theta_j E[\partial h/\partial v] = -E[y\partial \ln p(x)/\partial x_j],$$

where $p(x)$ is the density of x. This of course assumes the existence of $\partial p(x)/\partial x_j$, so it does not hold for the coefficients of discrete explanatory variables or for the constant term. The term $E[\partial h/\partial v]$ depends on F and so is unknown, but the right-hand side can be consistently estimated by the covariance between y and the instrumental variable $\partial \ln p/\partial x_j$. Thus the coefficients θ_j of the continuous components of x can be estimated up to an overall scale factor (Stoker, 1986).

The problem of the unknown distribution of u has been replaced by that of the unknown distribution of x. Logically this is a simpler problem, because x is an observed variable and estimation of $\partial \ln p/\partial x$ does not involve the econometric model at all. The higher the dimensionality of x, the more difficult it will be to get adequate estimates of $\partial \ln p/\partial x$ from data sets of realistic size. Several standard methods available for nonparametric density estimation can also be used to estimate $\partial \ln p/\partial x$, including the semi-nonparametric approach of Gallant.

BIBLIOGRAPHY

Amemiya, T. 1983. Nonlinear regression models. In *Handbook of Econometrics*, Vol. 1, ed. Z. Griliches and M.D. Intriligator, Amsterdam: North-Holland.

Buckley, J. and James, I. 1979. Linear regression with censored data. *Biometrika* 66, 429–36.

Cosslett, S.R. 1983. Distribution-free maximum likelihood estimator of the binary choice model. *Econometrica* 51, 765–82.

Gallant, A.R. and Nychka, D.W. 1987. Semi-nonparametric maximum likelihood estimation. *Econometrica* 55.

Heckman, J. and Singer, B. 1984. A method for minimizing the impact of distributional assumptions in econometric models for duration data. *Econometrica* 52, 271–320.

Kaplan, E.L. and Meier, P. 1958. Nonparametric estimation from incomplete observations. *Journal of the American Statistical Association* 53, 457–81.

Lynden-Bell, D. 1971. A method of allowing for known observational selection in small samples aplied to 3CR quasars. *Monthly Notices of the Royal Astronomical Society* 155, 95–118.

Maddala, G.S. 1983. *Limited Dependent and Qualitative Variables in Econometrics.* Cambridge: Cambridge University Press.

Manski, C.F. 1974. Maximum score estimation of the stochastic utility model of choice. *Journal of Econometrics* 3, 205–28.

Manski, C.F. 1984. Adaptive estimation of non-linear regression models. *Econometric Reviews* 3, 145–94.

Manski, C.F. 1985. Semiparametric analysis of discrete response: asymptotic properties of the maximum score estimator. *Journal of Econometrics* 27, 303–33.

Miller, R. and Halpern, J. 1982. Regression with censored data. *Biometrika* 69, 521–31.

Phillips, P.C.B. 1983. ERA's: a new approach to small sample theory. *Econometrica* 51, 1505–25.

Powell, J.L. 1984. Least absolute deviations estimation for the censored regression model. *Journal of Econometrics* 25, 303–25.

Powell, J.L. 1986. Symmetrically trimmed least squares estimation for tobit models. *Econometrica* 54, 1435–60.

Stoker, T.M. 1986. Consistent estimation of scaled coefficients. *Econometrica* 54, 1461–81.

Sequential Analysis

JAMES O. BERGER

Statistical experiments are of either fixed sample or sequential design. A *fixed sample size* experiment is one in which the sample size taken for experimentation is predetermined, while a *sequential* experiment involves monitoring incoming data to help determine an appropriate time to stop experimentation.

To formalize these notions, suppose the data can be observed one-at-a-time; let $X_1, X_2, \ldots$ denote this possible stream of data. Examples include a series of products coming off an assembly line, a series of missiles being tested for accuracy, and a series of patients participating in a clinical trial.

A key concept is that of a *stopping rule*, R, which is a description of the manner in which the data stream will be used to determine cessation of the experiment.

Example 1. Consider the stopping rule R_1: stop experimentation after n observations have been taken. This stopping rule effectively defines what we earlier called a fixed sample size experiment, since we will take precisely n observations.

Example 2. Consider the stopping rules (where $\bar{X}_j = \Sigma_{i=1}^{j} X_i/j$) R_2: stop experimentation if $\bar{X}_{50} > 0.62$, or (failing that) when $n = 100$; R_3: after each new observation, X_j, check whether or not $\bar{X}_j \geqslant 0.5 + 0.823/\sqrt{j}$; if so, stop experimentation and otherwise take the next observation. Note that R_2 allows experimentation to stop only after 50 or 100 observations have been taken, while R_3 gives rise to the possibility of stopping after any observation.

To see why stopping rules such as R_2 and R_3 can be desirable, consider a clinical trial investigating a new treatment in which, for the jth participating patient, the observation is a Bernoulli (θ) random variable, X_i, which can assume the values 1 (denoting treatment success) or 0 (denoting treatment failure). Thus θ is the probability of the treatment being successful. Suppose that the standard (old) treatment is known to have a success probability of $\frac{1}{2}$, so it is desired to test the hypothesis (H_0) that $\theta \leqslant \frac{1}{2}$ (the old treatment is better) versus the hypothesis (H_a) that $\theta > \frac{1}{2}$ (the new treatment is better).

A typical fixed sample size test of these hypotheses would proceed by choosing a sample size, say $n = 100$, observing $X_1, \ldots, X_{100}$ from $n = 100$ independent patients, and then rejecting H_0 if $\bar{X}_{100} \geq 0.582$. This is an $\alpha = 0.05$ level test. (We make no judgement here concerning the appropriateness of formulating this problem as a statistical hypothesis test.)

Suppose now that the experimenters happen to look at the data after 50 patients have participated in the trial, and observe that, for all 50, the treatment proved successful. This would appear to be overwhelming evidence that the new treatment is better, and would lead reasonable people to stop the clinical trial and recommend adoption of the new treatment. It is a rather surprising fact that this conclusion would be *forbidden* by classical statistics, because the original design called for a sample of size 100. (Classical analyses do not allow deviation from original experimental protocol.) It would have been possible, however, to plan for such a possible eventuality by adopting a sequential design, whereby after every observation (or every few observations) the possibility of stopping is allowed. Indeed, R_2 and R_3 are two such stopping rules, and had either been employed, the above-mentioned clinical trial would certainly have stopped by the time the overwhelming evidence had accumulated.

As indicated in the above example, the advantage of a sequential experimental design is that it allows one to stop the experiment precisely when sufficient evidence has accumulated. The disadvantages of a sequential design are that it can be more expensive (often it is cheaper per observation if the data is collected at all at once or in large batches), and that it is harder to analyse from the classical perspective. This last point has to do with the fact that the stopping rule can significantly affect classical statistical measures.

Example 2 (*continued*). Suppose the stopping rule R_2 had been employed in the clinical trial (i.e., an *interim analysis* at the halfway point in the trial had been performed). Also, suppose that, if one did stop after 50 observations (i.e., if $\bar{X}_{50} > 0.62$), then H_0 would be rejected, and that, if the trial lasted for all 100 observations (i.e., if $\bar{X}_{50} \leq 0.62$ so that the experiment did not stop at the halfway point), then H_0 would be rejected when $\bar{C}_{100} > 0.582$. It can be shown that, for a *fixed* sample of 50 observations, rejecting H_0 when $\bar{X}_{50} > 0.62$ is an $\alpha = 0.05$ level test, as is rejecting H_0 if $\bar{X}_{100} > 0.582$ for a *fixed* sample size experiment with $n = 100$. For the experiment using R_2, however, it can be shown that the level is $\alpha = 0.083$. (One obtains an error probability larger than each of the separate $\alpha = 0.05$, because use of R_2 gives 'two chances' to reject H_0.) Thus, if R_1 had been used and $\bar{X}_{100} = 0.582$ had been observed, one could claim significant evidence against H_0 at the $\alpha = 0.05$ level, while if R_2 had been used, one could not claim significance at the $\alpha = 0.05$ level.

It should be mentioned that there is considerable controversy over the issue of whether use of stopping rules should affect statistical conclusions. When classical measures are used, there is no denying a substantial effect. But, interestingly, for certain other statistical measures, such as Bayesian measures, the stopping rule has *no* effect. Thus, employment of the Bayesian approach to statistics allows one to collect data without having to prespecify a rigid initial stopping rule, greatly increasing the flexibility of experimentation. For discussion of this issue, and support for the Bayesian viewpoint, see Berger and Wolpert (1984) and Berger (1985).

The founder of sequential analysis is generally acknowledged to be Abraham Wald, with Milton Friedman and W. Allen Wallis providing substantial motivational and collaborative support. Early history of sequential analysis is given in Wald (1947), which developed the basic formulation of the problem in terms of stopping rules and analysed a number of basic situations, such as the Sequential Probability Ratio Test (for testing between two simple hypotheses). Most of the subsequent work in sequential analysis has focused on either (i) evaluating classical measures, such as error probabilities, for special stopping rules (see Siegmund, 1985); or (ii) determining optimal stopping rules. This last problem is very difficult, and can be rephrased as the problem of deciding if enough information is already available to reach a decision, or if another (or several) observations should be taken. The mathematics of this problem is essentially that of Dynamic Programming. For general reviews of sequential analysis, see DeGroot (1970), Ghosh (1970), Govindarajulu (1981), Berger (1985), and Siegmund (1985).

BIBLIOGRAPHY
Berger, J. 1985. *Statistical Decision Theory and Bayesian Analysis.* New York: Springer-Verlag.
Berger, J. and Wolpert, R. 1984. *The Likelihood Principle.* Institute of Mathematical Statistics Monograph Series, Hayward, California.
DeGroot, M.H. 1970. *Optimal Statistical Decisions.* New York: McGraw-Hill.
Ghosh, B.K. 1970. *Sequential Tests of Statistical Hypotheses.* Reading, Mass.: Addison-Wesley.
Govindarajulu, Z. 1981. *The Sequential Statistical Analysis of Hypothesis Testing, Point and Interval Estimation, and Decision Theory.* Columbus: American Science Press.
Siegmund, D. 1985. *Sequential Analysis: Tests and Confidence Intervals.* New York: Springer-Verlag.
Wald, A. 1947. *Sequential Analysis.* New York: Wiley.

Eugen Slutsky

GIANCARLO GANDOLFO

Born in the Yaroslav province of Russia, Slutsky had troubled years as a student: he enrolled in the department of physics and mathematics at Kiev University, was expelled for taking part in student revolts, went abroad to the Munich Institute of Technology to study engineering and finally graduated in the department of law in 1911 back at Kiev University. He became a member of the faculty at Kiev Institute of Commerce in 1913 and full professor there in 1920. In 1926 he moved to Moscow as a staff member of the Conjuncture Institute; in 1934 he became a staff member of the Mathematical Institute of the University of Moscow and in 1936 a member of the Mathematical Institute of the Academy of Sciences, Moscow, a post which he held until his death.

Slutsky was a mathematician, statistician and economist. His fame as an economist rests mainly on one single contribution (1915), which went unnoticed until the 1930s, when it was discovered independently by Dominedò (1933, p. 790), Schultz (1935, pp. 439ff), and Allen (1936), and subsequently influenced the further development of consumer theory. Hicks – who, together with Allen (Hicks and Allen, 1934), had independently arrived at Slutsky's results – writes: 'The theory to be set out in this chapter and the two following is essentially Slutsky's ... The present volume is the first systematic exploration of the territory which Slutsky opened up' (Hicks, 1939, p. 19). Building on earlier work by Pareto (who had already derived the formulae which express the change in the consumer's demand when any one of its arguments changes, but without seeing their implications), Slutsky showed that the effect of a price change on the quantity demanded can be divided into two effects. One is the effect of a *compensated variation* of price; if a price increases and the consumer is given an income increase so as to make possible the purchase of the same quantities of all the goods previously purchased, the individual – though being in the position to purchase the preceding bundle of goods – will no longer consider it preferable to any other, and there will take place some kind of *residual variation* of demand. This is called the *residual variability* by Slutsky (the substitution effect in Hicks's

259

terminology). It should be noted that the compensated variation of price can also be defined in terms of the income change which leaves the consumer's *real* income unchanged, that is which causes the consumer to remain on the *same* indifference curve (this is the concept used by Hicks, 1939, in the text, while in the mathematical appendix he gives the same definition as Slutsky). Although the two definitions are equivalent for infinitesimal changes (as was first shown by Mosak, 1942), Slutsky's is preferable from the operational point of view since it does not require knowledge of the consumer's indifference map. The other effect is the *income effect*, which gives the change in the consumer's purchases when his money income changes at unchanged prices. The two effects turn out to be independent and additive and their algebraic sum gives the *price effect*: this is, in Hicks' terminology, the 'Fundamental Equation of Value Theory', also called the Slutsky Equation.

Slutsky proved the complete properties of the various effects and of the demand curves. The income effect may be either normal (demand increases as income increases: 'relatively indispensable goods' in Slutsky's terminology) or abnormal ('relatively dispensable' goods). The 'own' substitution effect is always negative ('The residual variability of a good in the case of a compensated variation of its price, is always negative', [1915] 1953, p. 42) and the cross substitution effect is symmetric ('The residual variability of the j-th good in the case of a compensated variation of the price p_i is equal to the residual variability of the i-th good in the case of a compensated variation of the price p_j', [1915] 1953, p. 43). The 'own' price effect, therefore, is necessarily normal in the case of relatively indispensable goods. Slutsky also proved the relation which implies that the individual demand functions are homogeneous of degree zero. He gave a definition of complementary and competing goods, and made an important methodological point which is usually overlooked in his contribution: he stressed the need for *experiment* in order to obtain all the values of the relevant magnitudes (which cannot be obtained by observation of existing budgets) which enter into the definition. This emphasis on the need for experimental verification of economic laws, which concludes his contribution, is worthy of note and obviously arises from his statistical background.

Slutsky did no other noticeable work in economics but made important contributions to mathematical statistics and probability theory.

In (1914) he suggested the use of a χ^2 variate to test the goodness of fit of a regression line ('line' is taken in the broad sense, i.e. including both straight lines and curves); as a logical consequence, he introduced the concept of *minimum chi-square estimator* ('the most probable values of the coefficients will be those which bring our χ^2 to a minimum', 1914, p. 83) as a general method of fitting regressions. This paper was written several years before R.A. Fisher's work on the subject.

Slutsky was one of the originators of the theory of stochastic processes and time-series analysis. In his renowned (1927) paper he proved several important theorems. One is that the summation of random causes may be the source of cyclic or undulatory processes, and that these waves will show an approximate regularity in the sense that they can be approximated quite well by a relatively small number of terms (sine curves) of the Fourier series. Another is the sinusoidal limit theorem, which states that under certain conditions the summation of random causes will tend to give rise to a specific sine wave. For example, if one takes a moving average (of two terms) of a random series n times and then takes the mth difference of the result, and lets $n \to \infty$ so that m/n tends to a constant c between zero and one, it follows that the series will tend to a sine wave with wavelength are $\cos(1-c)/(1+c)$. A corollary of these theorems is the famous Slutsky-Yule Effect (so named because it was also independently discovered by Yule): if a moving average of a random series is taken (for example to determine trend), this may *generate* an oscillatory movement in the series where none existed in the original data.

Slutsky also worked in the theory of probability, where he studied the concept of asymptotic convergence in probability (e.g. 1925, 1928, 1929). He spent the last years of his life in preparing tables for the computation of the incomplete gamma-function and the chi-square probability distribution (1950).

SELECTED WORKS

A bibliography (1912 46) is contained in the memorial article (in Russian) by A.N. Kolmogorov, in *Uspekhi Matematicheskikh Nauk*, Vol. 3, No. 4, 1948. This bibliography is reproduced in Allen (1950). A collection of selected papers was published posthumously in Russian (1960). On Slutsky's life and works see also the memorial article (in Russian) by N. Smirnov, in *Izvestiia Akademiia Nauk SSSR*, Mathematical Series, Vol. 12, 1948, and Allen (1950).

1914. On the criterion of goodness of fit of the regression lines and on the best method of fitting them to the data. *Journal of the Royal Statistical Society* 77, Pt I, December, 78 84.

1915. Sulla teoria del bilancio del consumatore. *Giornale degli Economisti e Rivista di Statistica* 51, July, 1 26. Trans. as 'On the theory of the budget of the consumer' in *Readings in Price Theory*, ed. K.E. Boulding and G.J. Stigler, London: Allen & Unwin, 1953, 26 56.

1925. Über stochastische Asymptoten und Grenzwerte. *Metron* 5, December, 3 89.

1927. The summation of random causes as the source of cyclic processes. (In Russian.) *Problems of Economic Conditions*, The Conjuncture Institute, Moscow, Vol. 3, No. 1. Revised English version in *Econometrica* 5, April 1937, 105 46.

1928. Sur un critérium de la convergence stochastique des ensembles de valeurs éventuelles. *Comptes rendu des séances de l' Académie des Sciences* 187, Paris, 17 July to 13 August.

1929. Quelques propositions sur les limites stochastiques éventuelles. *Compte rendu des séances de l' Académie des Sciences* 189, Paris, 2 September.

1950. *Tables for the computation of the incomplete Gamma-function and the Chi-square probability distribution.* (In Russian.) Ed. A.N. Kolmogorov, Moscow: Akademiia Nauk SSSR (posthumous).

1960. *Selected Works.* (In Russian.) Moscow: Akademiia Nauk SSSR (posthumous).

BIBLIOGRAPHY

Allen, R.G.D. 1936. Professor Slutsky's theory of consumers' choice. *Review of Economic Studies* 3, February, 120 29.

Allen, R.G.D. 1950. The work on Eugen Slutsky. *Econometrica* 18, July, 209–16.

Dominedò, V. 1933. Considerazioni intorno alla teoria della domanda, II-Le principali premesse e caratteristiche delle curve statiche. *Giornale degli Economisti e Rivista di Statistica* 48, November, 765–807.

Hicks, J.R. and Allen, R.G.D. 1934. A reconsideration of the theory of value. *Economica* 1, Pt I, February, 52–76; Pt II, May, 196–219.

Hicks, J.R. 1939. *Value and Capital.* Oxford: Clarendon Press. 2nd edn, 1946.

Mosak, J. 1942. On the interpretation of the fundamental equation of value theory. In *Studies in Mathematical Economics and Econometrics in Memory of Henry Schultz*, ed. O. Lange, F. McIntyre and T.O. Yntema, Chicago: University of Chicago Press, 69–74.

Samuelson, P.A. 1947. *Foundations of Economic Analysis.* Cambridge, Mass.: Harvard University Press. Enlarged edn, 1983.

Schultz, H. 1935. Interrelations of demand, price, and income. *Journal of Political Economy* 43, August, 433–81.

Spectral Analysis

C.W.J. GRANGER

A univariate discrete time-series x_t is said to be second-order stationary if its mean, variance and autocovariances $\mu_r = \text{cov}(x_t, x_{t-r})$ are all time invariant. If x_t has no strictly cyclical or deterministic components and is stationary, there are two mathematical relationships with important interpretations, the Cramer representation

$$x_t = \int_{-\pi}^{\pi} e^{it\omega}\, dz(\omega), \tag{1}$$

where

$$\left. \begin{aligned} E[dz(\omega)\, \overline{dz(\lambda)}] &= 0, & \omega \neq \lambda \\ &= f(\omega)\, dw, & \omega = \lambda \end{aligned} \right\} \tag{2}$$

and the spectral representation of the autocovariances

$$\mu_r = \int_{-\pi}^{\pi} e^{it\omega} f(\omega)\, dw. \tag{3}$$

Each relationship is a Fourier representation of the sequence on the left-hand side. The interpretation of (1) is that a stationary series can be thought of as a (non-countably infinite) sum of uncorrelated components. As x_t is a random sequence, so the components are random and each is associated with a particular frequency in the range from zero to π. As a frequency is proportional to the inverse of period, a component with frequency near π corresponds to the quickly changing oscillations in the data, that is the 'short-run', and those with low frequency in the range from zero to π. As frequency is proportional to the 'long-run'. These components will be uncorrelated fo different pairs of frequencies and the component with frequency ω will have a variance proportional to the value of the function $f(\omega)$ at ω, as shown in (2). These components, denoted by $dz(\omega)$ in (1), are complex for technical reasons. Because the components are

263

uncorrelated, the variance of x_t, denoted by μ_0, will be the sum (actually the integral) of the variances of the components, as seen in (3) by putting $r = 0$. Thus, the relative importance of components can be measured in terms of their contribution to the variance of x_t, which is seen directly from the plot of $f(\omega)$ against ω. $f(\omega)$, known as the spectral density function, has the property that it is non-negative and is symmetric about $\omega = 0$, so that $f(-\omega) = f(\omega)$. Once $f(\omega)$ is known, all the autocovariances are uniquely determined from it by (3). There is also a reverse relationship, so that if the sequence μ_r is known, then $f(\omega)$ is determined. There is thus a one-to-one relationship between the sequence μ_r and the spectral function $f(\omega)$.

There are basically two forms of analysis of a single stationary series. The so-called time-domain analysis involves estimation and interpretation of the autocovariances μ_r and then building a model that generates data giving this particular sequence μ_r. The frequency-domain or spectral analysis concentrates on the function $f(\omega)$. Because of the one-to-one relationship, each analysis provides exactly the same information about the series, at least in theory. In practice, certain types of analysis are easier in one domain than the other, and so familiarity with both is convenient.

If x_t is a stationary series with spectrum $f_z(\omega)$ and z_t is a series derived from it by a filter, such as

$$z_t = \sum c_j x_{t-j},$$

then z_t has spectrum $f_z(\omega)$ given by

$$f_z(\omega) = |c(z)|^2 f_z(\omega),$$

where $c(z) = \sum c_j z^j$ and $z = e^{iw}$.

The spectrum of an uncorrelated, or 'white noise', series ε_t is flat, taking the form

$$f(\omega) = \frac{\operatorname{var}(\varepsilon)}{2\pi}, \quad -\pi \leqslant \omega \leqslant \pi.$$

It follows that the spectrum of any stationary autoregressive or moving average model can be derived immediately, as these are filtered versions of white noise. Any series that has a spectrum highest at low frequencies will be smooth, but if the higher frequencies dominate the spectral shape, the series will be very unsmooth.

The theory can be extended to the case when the series contains a cycle, or near cycle, as then the spectrum will have a strong peak at the frequency of the cycle. For example, if a monthly series contains a seasonal, it will have spectral peaks at frequencies $2\pi k/12$, $k = 1, \ldots, 6$.

When analysing a single series, the estimated spectral shape is useful for detecting cycles in the data and for determining the relative importance of different frequency components, such as the long-run versus short-run components. If a theory suggests a particular temporal structure, such as white noise for changes of prices from an efficient market, this can be tested from the shape of the estimated spectrum. Experience shows that many macroeconomic series have a typical spectral shape, with a peak at zero frequency, often seasonal peaks and a smooth, generally declining background shape. This typical shape, which is by no means inevitable, does not necessarily coincide with a finite-variance, stationary model; but rather with a series known as integrated of order one. A series is so called if it needs to be differenced once to produce a series with spectrum which is everywhere positive but without a distinct peak or zero frequency. Using the filter result above, the spectrum of an integrated of order one series takes the form $f_x(\omega) = (1 - \cos \omega)^{-2} f_{\Delta x}(\omega)$ where $f_{\Delta x}(\omega)$ is the spectrum of the differenced series and does not have the typical shape. Other generalizations of the stationarity condition have been considered by Priestley (1981) for time-varying spectra and by Hatanaka and Suzuki (1967) for a variety of trending series.

Care has to be taken in estimating the spectrum as it seems that it is impossible to have an unbiased and consistent estimate. A variety of methods of estimation is available and several are discussed in the Proceedings of the IEEE, September 1982, *Special Issue on Spectral Estimation*, and in Koopmans (1974).

The usefulness of spectral techniques is increased when several series are considered. If x_t, y_t are both stationary, zero-mean series with no cycles, and they are also second-order jointly stationary so that the cross-covariances $\mu_r^{xy} = E[x_t, y_{t-r}]$ are not functions of time, then expanding the notation of (1) in an obvious way, the bivariate version of (2) is

$$E[dz_x(\omega) \overline{dz_y(\lambda)}] = 0, \qquad \omega \neq \lambda$$
$$= \mathrm{cr}(\omega)\,dw, \qquad \omega = \lambda$$

where $\mathrm{cr}(\omega)$ is the cross-spectrum. Equation (3) becomes

$$\mu_r^{xy} = \int e^{ir\omega}\,\mathrm{cr}(\omega)\,dw.$$

As $\mu_r^{xy} \neq \mu_{-r}^{xy}$ in general, $\mathrm{cr}(\omega)$ will not be a real function of frequency. A more convenient pair of functions is the coherence, defined by

$$C(\omega) = \frac{|\mathrm{cr}(\omega)|^2}{f_z(\omega) f_y(\omega)}$$

and the phase defined by

$$\Phi(\omega) = \tan^{-1}\left[\frac{\text{Imaginary part of } \mathrm{cr}(\omega)}{\text{Real part of } \mathrm{cr}(\omega)}\right].$$

If x_t, y_t are jointly stationary, they can be considered as sums of uncorrelated components where their components at different frequencies are also uncorrelated across series. Thus, the series are related only through corresponding frequency components, and the coherence measures the squared correlations of these components, so that essentially

$$C(\omega) = [\mathrm{corr}(dz_x(\omega), dz_y(\omega))]^2.$$

265

It is thus possible to find that a pair of series are highly related at low frequency (the long run) but little related at other frequencies. The phase diagram is generally less useful, but in a few simple cases can help determine a time-lag between the series. If $x_t = ay_{t-k} + z_t$, where y_t, z_t are independent stationary series, then $\Phi(\omega) = k\omega$ and so the lag k can be detected as the slope of a trend in $\Phi(\omega)$ plotted against ω. In this analysis k need not be an integer. However, for more complicated lagged relationships between x_t and y_t the phase diagram becomes very difficult to interpret.

For more than two series, spectra can be defined from partial autocorrelations, but a more and useful approach is that of band-pass regression discussed and applied by Engle (1974, 1980). Suppose that $x_i(\omega)$ represents the component of x_t consisting of frequencies around ω. Theoretically, such a series might be obtained by application of special filters. Similarly, if there are a number of explanatory series, y_{jt}, $j =$, ..., N, each will have corresponding components $y_{jt}(\omega)$. If the series are jointly stationary, then $x_t(\omega)$ should be explained just by the $y_j(\omega)$, as only similar frequency components are potentially correlated. This suggests a regression of the form

$$x_t(\omega) = \sum_j \beta_j(\omega) y_{jt}(\omega) + \text{residual}.$$

Economists might expect the β's to change with frequency, as long-run components may be explained in a different way than are seasonal or short-run components. The $\beta_j(\omega)$ can be estimated directly from the spectra and cross-spectra and although they can be complex, they are generally easy to interpret. In an application, Engle considered the consumption function to determine whether the marginal propensity to consume an additional dollar of income appeared to be different for high and low frequencies. Interpreting high frequencies as the transitory component and low frequencies as the permanent component of income, the permanent income hypothesis would suggest a substantial difference, but none was observed. These methods can also be used as a test for correct specification of a model.

In another multivariate situation, spectral techniques have been used to identify and interpret common factors in a group of series. Considering a group of interest rates, Singleton (1980) investigated how many independent noise sources there were acting as common factors, and found evidence for just two.

Although time domain modelling techniques are certainly more useful for forecasting and possibly for some policy selection situations, the frequency domain methods are helpful as complementary methods of analysis and for testing various types of economic theories. An early reference is Granger and Hatanaka (1964) which emphasizes interpretation, the more recent book by Koopmans (1974) being more comprehensive. A history of the use of spectral techniques in economics has been given by Granger and Engle (1984).

BIBLIOGRAPHY

Engle, R.F. 1974. Band spectrum regression. *International Economic Review* 15, 1–11.

Engle, R.F. 1980. Exact maximum likelihood methods for dynamic regressions and band spectrum regressions. *International Economic Review* 21, 391–407.

Granger, C.W.J. and Engle, R.F. 1984. Applications of spectral analysis in econometrics. Ch. 5 in *The Handbook of Statistics*, Vol. 3: *Time Series in the Frequency Domain*, ed. D.R. Brillinger and P.R. Krishnaiah, Amsterdam: North-Holland.

Granger, C.W.J. and Hatanaka, M. 1964. *Spectral Analysis of Economic Time Series*. Princeton: Princeton University Press.

Hatanaka, M. and Suzuki, M. 1967. The theory of the pseudospectrum and its application to non-stationary dynamic econometric models. Ch. 23 in *Essays in Mathematical Economics, in Honor of Oskar Morgenstern*, ed. M. Shubik, Princeton: Princeton University Press.

IEEE. *Proceedings*, September 1982.

Koopmans, L.H. 1974. *The Spectral Analysis of Time Series*. New York: Academic Press.

Priestley, M. 1981. *Spectral Analysis and Time Series*. New York: Academic Press.

Singleton, K.J. 1980. A latent time-series model of the cyclical behavior of interest rates. *International Economic Review* 21, 559–76.

Spline Functions

DALE J. POIRIER

In the everyday use of the word, a *spline* is a flexible strip of material used by draftsmen in the same manner as French curves to draw a smooth curve between specified points. The mathematical *spline function* is similar to the draftsman's spline in that its graph resembles the curve drawn by a mechanical spline. More formally, a spline function is a piecewise continuous function with a specified degree of continuity imposed on its derivatives. Usually the pieces are polynomials. The abscissa values which define the segments are referred to as *knots* or *joint points*, and the set of knots is referred to as the *mesh*. Examples of spline functions in economics are discussed below.

Although spline functions are a fairly simple mathematical concept, the development of spline functions is relatively new. The terminology and impetus for most contemporary work can be traced to the seminal work of I.J. Schoenberg (1946), although the basic idea can be found in the writings of E.T. Whittaker (1923), and in Schoenberg's (1946, p. 68) own modest opinion, in the earlier work of Laplace. Today the literature on spline functions comprises an integral part of modern approximation theory; see Schumaker (1981) for an accessible introduction and historical review. Furthermore, the many important contributions of Grace Wahba in the 1970s and 1980s (see Wegman and Wright, 1983, for references) have served to unite the approximation theory and statistics literatures.

The importance of spline functions in approximation theory can in large part be explained by the following best approximation property. Consider the data points (x_i, y_i) $(i = 1, 2, \ldots, n)$ and suppose without loss of generality that $0 < x_1 < x_2 < \cdots < x_n < 1$. Let $\lambda > 0$ and consider the optimization problem

$$\min_{f(\cdot)} \sum_{i=1}^{n} [y_i - f(x_i)]^2 + \lambda \int_0^1 [D^m f(x)]^2 \, dx, \tag{1}$$

where D^m denotes the differentiation operator of degree m and $f(\cdot)$ is a function defined on $[0, 1]$ such that $D^j f, j \leqslant m - 1$, is absolutely continuous and $D^m f$ is in the set of measurable square integrable functions on $[0, 1]$. The first term in (1) comprises the familiar least squares measure of fit and the second term comprises a measure of the smoothness in $f(\cdot)$. The parameter λ measures the tradeoff between fit and smoothness. The solution to (1) is a polynomial spline of degree $2m - 1$ with possible knots at all the data points. As $\lambda \to 0$, the solution is referred to as an *interpolating spline* and it fits the data exactly. The choice of λ is obviously crucial and the method of cross-validation is a popular method for choosing λ. The most popular choice for m is $m = 2$ yielding a *cubic spline* as the solution to (1).

While spline functions have proved to be valuable approximation tools, they also arise naturally in their own right in economics. Standard income tax functions with increasing marginal tax rates constitute a *linear spline* as do familiar 'kinked' demand curves and 'kinked' budget sets. *Quadratic splines* serve as useful ways of generating asymmetric loss functions for use in decision theory. Spline functions are also useful tools for capturing structural change. For example, a researcher may believe the relationship between two variables y and x to be locally a polynomial, but that at precise points in terms of x the relationship 'changes', not in a discontinuous fashion. Common choices for such x variables are time, age, education or income to name a few, with a nearly unlimited number of choices of candidates for y variables. An extensive reference source for the use of spline functions in economics, especially in models of structural change, is Poirier (1976).

In econometrics spline functions are most often employed to parametrize a regression function. This usage may reflect an attempt to permit structural change, or simply reflect the flexibility and good approximation properties of splines. In distributed lag analysis, spline functions have been used as natural generalizations of Almon polynomial lags. *Periodic* cubic splines have also proved useful in seasonal adjustment and in analysis of electricity load curves. In all such settings the number of knots is significantly less than the number of data points. The attractiveness of spline functions in these applications is in part due to the fact that given the knots they can be expressed as linear functions of unknown parameters, hence facilitating statistical estimation. Estimation of the knots themselves, however, is a difficult task due both to numerical and statistical complications.

In statistics spline functions are also used in many additional areas. Examples include non-parametric regression, multidimensional splines, histogram smoothing, spectral density estimation, isotonic regression and interpolation of distribution functions for which there is no closed-form analytic representation. The survey by Wegman and Wright (1983) serves as an excellent reference source for the many uses of splines in statistics.

BIBLIOGRAPHY

Poirier, D.J. 1976. *The Econometrics of Structural Change with Special Emphasis on Spline Functions*. Amsterdam: North-Holland.

Schoenberg, I.J. 1946. Contributions to the problem of approximation of equidistant data by analytic functions: Parts I and II. *Quarterly Journal of Applied Mathematics* 4, 45–99. 112–41.

Schumaker, L.L. 1981. *Spline Functions: Basic Theory*. New York: Wiley.

Wegman, E.J. and Wright, I.W. 1983. Splines in statistics. *Journal of the American Statistical Association* 78, June, 351–65.

Whittaker, E.T. 1923. On a new method of graduation. *Proceedings of the Edinburgh Mathematical Society* 41, 63–75.

Stationary Time Series

E.J. HANNAN

The concept of a stationary time series was, apparently, formalized by Khintchine in 1932. An infinite sequence $y(t)$, $t = 0, \pm 1, \ldots$, of random variables is called stationary if the joint probability law of $y(t_1), y(t_2), \ldots, y(t_n)$ is the same as that of $y(t_1 + t), \ldots, y(t_n + t)$ for any integers, $t_1, t_2, \ldots, t_n, t$ and any n. Thus the stochastic mechanism generating the sequence is not changing. In the natural sciences approximately stationary phenomena abound, but the continuing social evolution of man makes such phenomena rare in social science. Nevertheless, stationary time series models have been widely used in econometrics since they may fit the data well over periods of time that are not too long and thus may provide a basis for short-term predictions. The notions of trend, cycle, seasonal are closely related to a frequency decomposition of a series, with the trend corresponding to very low frequencies, and the spectral decomposition of a stationary series [see (2) below] is therefore of interest to economists. Finally, models have also been used where the observed series is regarded as the output of an evolving mechanism whose input is stationary.

If $\{y(t)\}$ is stationary then $E\{y(s)y(t)\}$ depends only on $t - s$. A sequence for which this is so is called weakly stationary but it is the (strict) concept of stationarity that is physically important. Khintchine (1934) obtained the Wiener–Khintchine relation (from theorems due to von Neumann and Wintner), for weakly stationary series.

$$E\{y(s)y(s+t)\} = \int_{-\pi}^{\pi} e^{it\omega} \, dF(\omega). \tag{1}$$

Here $F(\omega)$ is a distribution function (and an odd function) that distributes the total variance, $E\{y(t)^2\}$, over the frequencies $\omega \in [-\pi, \pi]$. (The frequency in oscillations per time unit is $\omega/2\pi$.) Strictly, Khintchine considered continuous time functions and Wold (1934) translated the theory into discrete time. About the same time, and independently, Wiener essentially constructed (1) from a (suitable) time function. Loosely his theory could be taken as constructing (1) from a single realization (history) of the random process, $y(t)$ when that is ergodic (see below). Corresponding to (1) there is a representation (Cramér, 1942):

$$y(t) = \int_0^\pi \{\cos t\omega \cdot d\xi(\omega) + \sin t\omega \cdot d\eta(\omega)\}, \tag{2}$$

where $\xi(\omega)$, $\eta(\omega)$ are random functions of ω with 'orthogonal increments', so that changes in these functions over non-overlapping intervals are uncorrelated. Also

$$E\{\xi(\omega_1)\eta(\omega_2)\} \equiv 0$$

and

$$E\{d\xi(\omega)^2\} = E\{d\eta(\omega)^2\}$$
$$= 2dF(\omega), \ \omega \neq 0, \pi,$$
$$E\{d\xi(0)^2\} = dF(0), \ E\{d\xi(\pi)^2\} = dF(\pi).$$

Thus $y(t)$ is represented as a linear superposition of sinusoidal oscillations with randomly determined amplitude and phase. This chaotic, uncorrelated behaviour of the 'Fourier transform', $[\xi(\omega), \eta(\omega)]$, of $y(t)$ is characteristic of stationary time series. If $F(\omega)$ jumps at ω_0 then $y(t)$ contains a periodic component at that frequency (e.g. a seasonal component) but the most relevant case is that where $F(\omega)$ is absolutely continuous (a.c.) so that $dF(\omega)$ may be replaced by $f(\omega) \, d\omega$ in (1). Then each frequency contributes only infinitesimally to (2). It is this case that is considered below.

Let $z(0)$ be some (measurable) function of the sequence $y(t)$ and $z(s)$ be the value of the function when the sequence is translated through s time units. If $E\{|z(0)|\} < \infty$, Birkhoff (1931) established the (pointwise) ergodic theorem, namely that for all such $z(t)$ the mean, $T^{-1}\Sigma_1^T z(t)$, converges almost surely. The limit will be $E\{z(0)\}$ for all such $z(0)$ if and only if $z(t) \equiv z(0)$ a.s. implies that $z(0)$ is a constant. The process is then said to be ergodic. In that case the whole stochastic structure of $y(t)$ can be discovered from one, indefinitely long, realization. If only one realization is available (the standard case) then ergodicity cannot be verified or disproved and to assert that $y(t)$ is ergodic is merely to assert that all aspects of the structure that are constant over one realization shall be treated as constants.

Kolmogoroff (1939) developed the theory for the prediction of a stationary time series, linearly from its infinite past, and Wiener also, shortly after and independently, developed much of the same theory (see Wiener (1945), p. 59, footnote). In this connection Wold (1934) showed that:

$$y(t) = \sum_0^\infty \kappa(j)\varepsilon(t-j) + v(t), \qquad \kappa(0) = 1,$$
$$\sum \kappa(j)^2 < \infty, \qquad\qquad E\{\varepsilon(s)\varepsilon(t)\} = \delta_{st}\sigma^2. \tag{3}$$

The $\varepsilon(t)$ are the linear innovations (or one step prediction errors) and $v(t)$ is purely deterministic, i.e. can be exactly predicted from its own past. Also

$$\sigma^2 = \exp\left\{ (2\pi)^{-1} \int_{-\pi}^{\pi} \log 2\pi f(\omega)\, d\omega \right\},$$

a remarkable formula due initially to Szego. If $\sigma^2 > 0$, that is $\log f(\omega)$ is integrable, then

$$f(\omega) = (\sigma^2/2\pi) \left| \sum_0^\infty \kappa(j) e^{ij\omega} \right|^2,$$

$$k(z) = \sum_0^\infty \kappa(j) z^j \neq 0, \qquad |z| < 1, \tag{4}$$

and the spectrum is said to be 'factored'. The function $k(z)$ is said to be 'outer' and is uniquely determined. This theory is important for an understanding of structure but, since the infinite past will not be available, has to be replaced by a constructive theory for practical purposes. Any $y(t)$ for $\sigma^2 > 0$, in the a.c. case [when $v(t)$ in (3) is null], may be represented as:

$$y(t) = Cx(t) + \varepsilon(t), \qquad x(t+1) = Ax(t) + B\varepsilon(t), \tag{5}$$

where $x(t)$ is an unobserved 'state' vector. If A may be taken as finite, and only then, $k(z)$ [see (4)] is a rational function of z. Then Kalman (1960) showed how the best linear predictor of $y(t+1)$, from $y(t)$, $y(t-1)$, ..., $y(1)$, could be calculated by a recursion on t, a construction that has come to be called the 'Kalman filter'.

Though for $y(t)$ ergodic the whole structure may be known from an indefinitely long realization, the statistical problem of constructing estimates of (or approximations to) aspects of that structure remains. Work as early as the 18th century is still of some relevance here. Early work was mainly concerned to represent $y(t)$ by means of finitely may sinusoids, plus a 'white noise' error term (that is a sequence whose $f(\omega)$ is constant). The central technique is the calculation of

$$w(\omega) = T^{-1/2} \sum_1^T \{ y(t) \exp it\omega \},$$

nowadays usually for $\omega_j = 2\pi j / T, j = 0, 1, \ldots, [T/2]$. However, for computational reasons this was initially computed at equal intervals of the period, $2\pi/\omega$. Thus $I(\omega) = |w(\omega)|^2$ was called the periodogram by Schuster (1851–1934). For T even [subtract $w(\pi) \cos t\pi$ when T is odd],

$$y(t) = \omega(0) + 2 + \sum_1^{T/2} \{ \cos t\omega_j \mathscr{R}[w(\omega_j)] + \sin t\omega_j \mathscr{I}[w(\omega_j)] \}, \tag{6}$$

A comparison of (6) with (2) shows the close relation of $w(\omega)$ to $\xi(\omega)$, $\eta(\omega)$. In 1965 computationally cheap methods for computing $w(\omega_j)$ were rediscovered (fast Fourier transform algorithm). Direct estimation of $f(\omega)$ through the averaging of a few values of $I(\omega_j)$ for ω_j near to ω is thus computationally feasible and has largely replaced methods based on the use of autocovariances,

$$c(j) = T^{-1} \sum_{j+1}^{T} y(t)y(t-j)$$

(see Blackman and Tukey, 1958).

A second mainstream of ideas centres on directly estimating $k(z)$. Here an important class of autoregressive (AR) models was introduced by Yule (1927), namely

$$\sum_{0}^{p} \alpha(j)y(t-j) = \varepsilon(t), \qquad \alpha(0) = 0,$$

$$\sum \alpha(j)z^j \neq 0, \qquad |z| \leqslant 1, \tag{7}$$

that puts $k(z) = [\Sigma \alpha(j)z^j]^{-1}$. Yule also introduced the equations of estimation (Yule–Walker equations)

$$\sum_{0}^{p} \hat{\alpha}_p(j)c(j-k) = \delta_{0k}\hat{\sigma}_p^2, \qquad k = 0, 1, \dots, p. \tag{8}$$

A recursion on p, due initially to Levinson (see an appendix to Wiener, 1945) enables this to be cheaply computed for a succession of p values. However, (8) is not ideal and other, closely related procedures have been introduced; for a discussion of such 'lattice' methods see Friedlander (1982). Akaike (1969) suggested that p might be chosen to minimize $\mathrm{AIC}(p) = \log \hat{\sigma}_p^2 + 2p/T$, which completes the estimation method. Box and Jenkins (1971) emphasized the case where $k(z)$ is a rational function, hoping thereby to reduce the number of parameters needed for a good approximation, as compared with (7). If A in (5) has minimal dimension p (the 'McMillan degree') then

$$\sum_{0}^{p} \alpha(j)y(t-j) = \sum_{0}^{p} \beta(j)\varepsilon(t-j),$$

$$\sum \alpha(j)z^j \neq 0, \qquad |z| \leqslant 1,$$
$$\sum \beta(j)z^j \neq 0, \qquad |z| < 1. \tag{9}$$

It is this ARMA (autoregressive-moving average) representation that Box and Jenkins used for estimation purposes. The estimation equations are non-linear and are obtained via a Gaussian likelihood for $y(t)$, $t = 1, \dots, T$. Again p may be chosen by $\mathrm{AIC}(p)$, which now is $\log \hat{\sigma}_p^2 + 2p/T$, $\hat{\sigma}_p^2$ being the estimate of $\sigma^2 = E\{\varepsilon(t)^2\}$ in (9). In practice the maximum lag on the right side in (9) might be taken as different from p so as possibly to reduce further the number of parameters needed. If $\hat{\alpha}(j)$, $\hat{\beta}(j)$ are the estimated parameters then $\hat{k}(z) = \Sigma \hat{\beta}(j)z^j / \Sigma \hat{\alpha}(j)z^j$, whence an estimate of $f(\omega)$ results [see (4)].

In a more general situation $y(t)$ might be a vector and regarded as the output of a stationary system (endogenous variables) for which a vector input of exogenous variables is also observed. The analogue of (3) would now be

$$y(t) = \sum_0^\infty K(j)\varepsilon(t-j) + \sum_0^\infty L(j)u(t-j)$$

from which an analogue of (5) would follow, namely:

$$y(t) = Cx(t) + Du(t) + \varepsilon(t),$$

$$x(t+1) = Ax(t) + Gu(t) + B\varepsilon(t), \tag{10}$$

where again $x(t)$ is an observed state vector and now $E\{\varepsilon(s)\varepsilon(t)\} = \delta_{st}\Omega$, $\Omega > 0$. If and only if $k(z) = \Sigma K(j)z^j$, $l(z) = \Sigma L(j)z^j$ are rational, may A be chosen finite and its minimal dimension will be the maximum lag in an ARMAX (ARMA plus exogenous variables) model of the form of (9), but with $u(t-j)$, $j = 1, \ldots, p$, also occurring. The problem of a unique specification of (10), or of the ARMAX representation, is the identification problem. This was considered in an econometric context in Hannan (1971) but the decisive contributions came from systems engineers who recognized the importance of the McMillan degree and constructed coordinate systems that 'name' equivalence classes of structures for systems of given degree. Some account of these ideas as well as of methods for estimating (10) are given in Hannan and Kavalieris (1984).

Many of the statistical methods begin from a Gaussian likelihood or from an approximation to it of the form (Whittle, 1951):

$$-2T^{-1} . \log \text{likelihood} = \Sigma\{\log[2\pi f(\omega_j)] + I(\omega_j)/[2\pi f(\omega_j)]\}. \tag{11}$$

The validity of the methods is much wider and extends to the case where the best linear predictor for $y(t)$ is actually the best predictor, that is, $\varepsilon(t)$ is a sequence of stationary martingale differences. However modification of this theory is commencing, both to introduce methods that are more robust than those based on a Gaussian likelihood and to deal with truly non-linear phenomena.

BIBLIOGRAPHY

A good general reference for the structure theory of stationary time series is Rozanov (1967). General treatments of this theory and of the statistical methods are in Priestley (1981). There is historical material in Wold (1934) and Doob (1953). For recent material, for example on robust methods and non-linear models, see Brillinger and Krishnaiah (1983) and Hannan, Krishnaiah and Rao (1985).

Akaike, H. 1969. Fitting autoregressive models for prediction. *Annals of the Institute of Statistical Mathematics* 21, 243–7.

Birkhoff, G.D. 1931. Proof of the ergodic theorem. *Proceedings of the National Academy of Sciences of the United States of America* 17, December, 556–600.

Blackman, R.B. and Tukey, J.W. 1958. *The Measurement of Power Spectra*. New York: Dover.

Box, G.E.P. and Jenkins, G.M. 1971. *Time Series Analysis, Forecasting and Control*. San Francisco: Holden-Day.

Brillinger, D.R. and Krishnaiah, P.R. (eds) 1983. *Handbook of Statistics 3*, Time Series in the Frequency Domain. New York: North-Holland.

Cramér, H. 1942. On harmonic analysis in certain functional spaces. *Arkiv för Matematik, Astronomi och Fysik* 28B, no. 12.

Doob, J.L. 1953. *Stochastic Processes*. New York: Wiley.

Friedlander, B. 1982. Lattice filters for adaptive processing. *Proceedings I.E.E.E.* 70, August, 830–67.

Hannan, E.J. 1971. The identification problem for multiple equation systems with moving average errors. *Econometrica* 39, September, 751–66.

Hannan, E.J. and Kalvalieris, L. 1984. Multivariate linear time series models. *Advances in Applied Probability* 16, September, 492–561.

Hannan, E.J. and Krishnaiah, P.R. and Rao, M.M. 1985. *Time Series in the Time Domain*. New York: North-Holland.

Kalman, R.E. 1960. A new approach to linear filtering and prediction problems. *Transactions of the American Society of Mechanical Engineers. Journal of Basic Engineering, Series D* 82, March, 35–45.

Khintchine, A. 1934. Korrelationstheorie de stationären stochastiischen Prozesse. *Mathematische Annalen* 109, 604–15.

Kolmogoroff, A.N. 1939. Sur l'interpolation et extrapolation des suites stationnaires. *Comptes Rendus, Académie des Sciences (Paris)* 208, June, 2043–5.

Priestley, M.B. 1981. *Spectral Analysis and Time Series*. New York: Academic Press.

Rozanov, Yu.A. 1967. *Stationary Random Processes*. San Francisco: Holden-Day.

Whittle, P. 1951. *Hypothesis Testing in Time Series Analysis*. Uppsala: Almqvist and Wiksell.

Wiener, N. 1945. *Extrapolation, Interpolation and Smoothing of Stationary Time Series*. New York: Wiley.

Wold, H. 1934. *A Study in the Analysis of Stationary Time Series*. Stockholm: Almqvist and Wiksell.

Yule, G.U. 1927. On a method of investigating periodicities in disturbed series with special reference to Woolfer's sunspot numbers. *Philosophical Transactions of the Royal Society of London. Series A* 226, 267–98.

Statistical Decision Theory

JAMES O. BERGER

Decision theory is the science of making optimal decisions in the face of uncertainty. Statistical decision theory is concerned with the making of decisions when in the presence of statistical knowledge (data) which sheds light on some of the uncertainties involved in the decision problem. The generality of these definitions is such that decision theory (dropping the qualifier 'statistical' for convenience) formally encompasses an enormous range of problems and disciplines. Any attempt at a general review of decision theory is thus doomed; all that can be done is to present a description of some of the underlying ideas.

Decision theory operates by breaking a problem down into specific components, which can be mathematically or probabilistically modelled and combined with a suitable optimality principle to determine the best decision. Section 1 describes the most useful breakdown of a decision problem – that into actions, a utility function, prior information and data. Section 2 considers the most important optimality principle for reaching a decision – the Bayes Principle. The frequentist approach to decision theory is discussed in section 3, with the Minimax Principle mentioned as a special case. Section 4 compares the various approaches.

The history of decision theory is difficult to pin down, because virtually any historical mathematically formulated decision problem could be called an example of decision theory. Also, it can be difficult to distinguish between true decision theory and formally related mathematical devices such as least squares estimation. The person who was mainly responsible for establishing decision theory as a clearly formulated science was Abraham Wald, whose work in the 1940s, culminating in his book *Statistical Decision Functions* (1950), provided the foundation of the subject. (The book does discuss some of the earlier history of decision theory.) General introductions to decision theory can be found, at an advanced level, in Blackwell and Girshick (1954) and Savage (1954); at an intermediate level in Raiffa and Schlaifer (1961), Ferguson (1967), De Groot (1970) and Berger (1985); and at a basic level in Raiffa (1968) and Winkler (1972).

1 ELEMENTS OF A DECISION PROBLEM

In a decision problem, the most basic concept is that of an action a. The set of all possible actions that can be taken will be denoted by A. Any decision problem will typically involve an unknown quantity or quantities; this unknown element will be denoted by θ.

Example 1. A company receives a shipment of parts from a supplier, and must decide whether to accept the shipment or to reject the shipment (and return it to the supplier as unsatisfactory). The two possible actions being contemplated are:

a_1: accept the shipment, a_2: reject the shipment.

Thus $A = \{a_1, a_2\}$. The uncertain quantity which is crucial to a correct decision is:

$\theta =$ the proportion of defective parts in the shipment.

Clearly action a_1 is desirable when θ is small enough, while a_2 is desirable otherwise.

The key idea in decision theory is to attempt a quantification of the gain or loss in taking possible actions. Since the gain or loss will usually depend upon θ as well as the action a taken, it is typically represented as a function of both variables. In economics this function is generally called the *utility function* and is denoted by $U(\theta, a)$. It is to be understood as the gain achieved if action a is taken and θ obtains. (The scale for measuring 'gain' will be discussed later.) In the statistical literature it is customary to talk in terms of loss instead of gain, with typical notation $L(\theta, a)$ for the loss function. Loss is just negative gain, so defining $L(\theta, a) = -U(\theta, a)$ results in effective equivalence between the two formulations (whatever maximizes utility will minimize loss).

Example 1 (cont.). The company determines its utility function to be given by:

$$U(\theta, a_1) = 1 - 10\theta, \qquad U(\theta, a_2) = -0.1.$$

To understand how these might be developed, note that if a_2 is chosen the shipment will be returned to the supplier and a new shipment sent out. This new shipment must then be processed, all of which takes time and money. The overall cost of this eventuality is determined to be 0.1 (on the scale being used). The associated utility is -0.1 (a loss is a negative gain). Note that this cost is fixed: that is, it does not depend on θ.

When a_1 is chosen, quite different considerations arise. The parts will be utilized with, say, gain of 1 if none are defective. Each defective part will cause a reduction in income by a certain amount, however, so that the true overall gain will be 1 reduced by a linear function of the proportion of defectives. $U(\theta, a_1)$ is precisely of this form. The various constants in $U(\theta, a_1)$ and $U(\theta, a_2)$ are chosen to reflect the various importance of the associated costs.

The scale chosen for a utility function turns out to be essentially unimportant, so that any convenient choice can be made. If the gain or loss is monetary, a suitable monetary unit often can provide a natural scale. Note, however, that utility functions can be defined for any type of gain or loss, not just monetary. Thus, in example 1, the use of defective parts could lead to faulty final products from the company, and affect the overall quality image or prestige of the company. Such considerations are not easily stated in monetary terms, yet can be important enough to include in the overall construction of the utility function. (For more general discussion of the construction of utility functions, see Berger, 1985.)

The other important component of a decision problem is the information available about θ. This information will often arise from several sources, substantially complicating the job of mathematical modelling. We content ourselves here with consideration of the standard statistical scenario where there are available (i) *data*, X, from a statistical experiment relating to θ; and (ii) background or *prior* information about θ, to be denoted by $\pi(\theta)$. Note that either of these components could be absent.

The data, X, is typically modelled as arising from some *probability density* $p_\theta(X)$. This, of course, is to be interpreted as the probability of the particular data value when θ obtains.

Example 1 (cont.). It is typically too expensive (or impossible) to test all parts in a shipment for defects, so that a statistical sampling plan is employed instead. This generally consists of selecting, say, n random parts from the shipment, and testing only these for defects. If X is used to denote the number of defective parts found in the tested sample, and if n is fairly small compared with the total shipment size, then it is well known that $p_\theta(X)$ is approximately the binomial density:

$$p_\theta(X) = \frac{n!}{X!(n-X)!} \theta^X (1 - \theta)^{n-X}.$$

The *prior* information about θ is typically also described by a probability density $\pi(\theta)$. This density is the probability (or mass) given to each possible value of θ in the light of beliefs as to which values of θ are most likely.

Example 1 (cont.). The company has been receiving a steady stream of shipments from this supplier and has recorded estimates of the proportion of defectives for each shipment. The records show that 30 per cent of the shipments had θ between 0.0 and 0.025, 22 per cent of the shipments had θ between 0.025 and 0.05, 15 per cent had θ between 0.05 and 0.075, 11 per cent had had θ between 0.075 and 0.10, 13 per cent had θ between 0.10 and 0.15, and the remaining 9 per cent had θ bigger than 0.15. Treating the varying θ as random, a probability density which provides a good fit to these percentages is the beta $(1,14)$ density given (for $0 \leqslant \theta \leqslant 1$) by:

$$\pi(\theta) = 14(1 - \theta)^{13}.$$

(E.g. the probability that a random θ from this density is between 0.0 and 0.025 can be calculated to be 0.30, agreeing exactly with the observed 30 per cent.) It is very reasonable to treat θ for the current shipment as a random variable from this density, which we will thus take as the prior density.

2 BAYESIAN DECISION THEORY

When θ is known, it is a trivial matter to find the optimal action; simply maximize the gain by maximizing $U(\theta, a)$ over a. When θ is unknown, the natural generalization is to first 'average' $U(\theta, a)$ over θ, and then maximize over a. The correct method of 'averaging over θ' is to determine the overall probability density of θ, to be denoted $\pi^*(\theta)$ (and to be described shortly), and then consider the *Bayesian expected* utility:

$$U^*(a) = E^{\pi^*}[U(\theta, a)] = \int U(\theta, a)\pi^*(\theta) \, d\theta.$$

(This last expression assumes that θ is a continuous variable taking values in an interval of numbers. If it can assume only one of discrete set of values, then this integral should be replaced by a sum over the possible values.) Maximizing $U^*(a)$ over a will yield the optimal *Bayes action*, to be denoted by a^*.

Example 1 (cont.). Initially, assume that no data, X, are available from a sampling inspection of the current shipment. Then the only information about θ is that contained in the prior $\pi(\theta)$; $\pi^*(\theta)$ will thus be identified with $\pi(\theta) = 14(1 - \theta)^{13}$. Calculation yields:

$$U^*(a_1) = \int_0^1 (1 - 10\theta)14(1 - \theta)^{13} \, d\theta = 0.33,$$

$$U^*(a_2) = \int_0^1 (-0.1)14(1 - \theta)^{13} \, d\theta = -0.1.$$

Since $U^*(a_1) > U^*(a_2)$, the Bayes action is a_1, to accept the shipment.

When data, X, are available, in addition to the prior information, the overall probability density π^* for θ must combine the two sources of information. This is done by *Bayes' Theorem* (from Bayes, 1763), which gives the overall density, usually called the *posterior density*, as:

$$\pi^*(\theta) = p_\theta(X) \cdot \pi(\theta)/m(X),$$

where:

$$m(X) = \int p_\theta(X)\pi(\theta) \, d\theta$$

(or a summation over θ if θ assumes only a discrete set of values) and $p_\theta(X)$ is the probability density for the experiment with the observed values of the data X inserted.

Example 1 (cont.). Suppose a sample of $n = 20$ items is tested, out of which $X = 3$ defectives are observed. Calculation gives that the posterior density of θ is:

$$\pi^*(\theta) = p_\theta(3) \cdot \pi(\theta)/m(3) = \left[\frac{20!}{3!17!} \theta^3(1 - \theta)^{17} \right] \cdot [14(1 - \theta)^{13}]/m(3)$$

$$= (185,504)\theta^3(1 - \theta)^{30},$$

which can be recognized as the beta $(4, 31)$ density. This density describes the location of θ in the light of all available information. The Bayesian expected utilities of a_1 and a_2 are thus:

$$U^*(a_1) = \int_0^1 (1 - 10\theta)\pi^*(\theta)\,d\theta = \int_0^1 (1 - 10\theta)(185{,}504)\theta^3(1 - \theta)^{30}\,d\theta = -0.14,$$

and

$$U^*(a_2) = \int_0^1 (-0.1)\pi^*(\theta)\,d\theta = -0.1.$$

Clearly a_2 has the largest expected utility, and should be the action chosen.

3 FREQUENTIST DECISION THEORY

An alternative approach to statistical decision theory arises from taking a 'long run' perspective. The idea is to imagine repeating the decision problem a large number of times, and to develop a decision strategy which will be optimal in terms of some long-run criterion. This is called the *frequentist* approach, and is essentially due to Neyman, Pearson and Wald (see Neyman and Pearson, 1933; Neyman, 1977; Wald, 1950).

To formalize the above idea, let $d(X)$ denote a *decision strategy* or *decision rule*. The notation reflects the fact that we are imagining repetitions of the decision problem which will yield possible different data X, and must therefore specify the action to be taken for any possible X. The utility of using $d(X)$ when θ obtains is thus $U[\theta, d(X)]$. The statistical literature almost exclusively works with loss functions instead of utility functions; for consistency with this literature we will thus use the loss function $L(\theta, d) = -U(\theta, d)$. (Of course, we want to minimize loss.)

The first step in a frequentist evaluation is to compute the *risk function* (expected loss over X) of d, given by:

$$R(\theta, d) = E_\theta\{L[\theta, d(X)]\} = \int L[\theta, d(X)]p_\theta(X)\,dX.$$

(Again, this integral should be a summation if X is discrete valued.) For a fixed θ this risk indicates how well $d(X)$ would perform if utilized repeatedly for data arising from the probability density $p_\theta(X)$. For various common choices of L this yields familiar statistical quantities. For instance, when L is 0 or 1, according to whether or not a correct decision is made in a two-action hypothesis testing problem, the risk becomes the 'probabilities of type I or type II error'. When L is 0 or 1, according to whether or not an interval $d(X)$ contains θ, the risk is 1 minus the 'coverage probability function' for the confidence procedure $d(X)$. When $d(X)$ is an estimate of θ and $L(\theta, d) = (\theta - d)^2$, the risk is the 'mean squared error' commonly considered in many econometric studies. (If the estimator $d(X)$ is unbiased, then this mean squared error is also the variance function for d.)

281

Example 2. Example 1, involving acceptance or rejection of this shipment, is somewhat too complicated to handle here from the frequentist perspective; we thus consider the simpler problem of merely estimating θ (the proportion of defective parts in the shipment). Assume that loss in estimation is measured by *squared error*; that is:

$$L[\theta, d(X)] = [\theta - d(X)]^2.$$

A natural estimate of θ, based on X (the number of defectives from a sample of size n), is the sample proportion of defectives $d_1(X) = X/n$. For this decision rule (or *estimator*), the risk function when X has the binomial distribution discussed earlier (so that X takes only the discrete values $0, 1, 2, \ldots, n$) is given by:

$$R(\theta, d) = \sum_{X=0}^{n} \left(\theta - \frac{X}{n}\right)^2 p_\theta(X) = \theta(1 - \theta)/n.$$

The second step of a frequentist analysis is to select some criterion for defining optimal risk functions (and hence optimal decision rules). One of the most common criteria is the *Minimax Principle*, which is based on consideration of the minimum possible risk:

$$R^*(d) = \max_\theta R(\theta, d).$$

This indicates the worst possible performance of $d(X)$ in repeated use, and hence has some appeal as a criterion based on a cautious attitude. Using this criterion, an optimal decision rule is, of course, defined to be one which minimizes $R^*(d)$, and is called a *minimax decision* rule.

Example 2 (cont.). It is easy to see that:

$$R^*(d_1) = \max_\theta R(\theta, d_1) = \max_\theta \frac{\theta(1 - \theta)}{n} = \frac{1}{4n}.$$

However, d_1 is not the minimax decision rule. Indeed, the minimax decision rule turns out to be:

$$d_2(X) = (X + \sqrt{n}/2)/(n + \sqrt{n}),$$

which has $R^*(d_2) = 1/[4(1 + \sqrt{n})^2]$ (cf. Berger, 1985, p. 354). The minimax criterion here is essentially the same as the minimax criterion in game theory. Indeed, the frequentist decision problem can be considered to be a zero-sum two-person game with the statistician as player II (choosing $d(X)$), an inimical 'nature' as player I (choosing θ), and payoff (to player I) of $R(\theta, d)$. (Of course, it is rather unnatural to assume that nature is inimical in its choice of θ.) (For further discussion of this relationship, see Berger, 1985, ch. 5.)

Minimax optimality is but one of several criteria that are used in frequentist decision theory. Another common criterion is the Invariance Principle, which calls for finding the best decision rule in the class of rules which are 'invariant' under certain mathematical transformations of the decision problem. (See Berger, 1985, ch. 6, for discussion.)

There also exist very general and elegant theorems which characterize the class of acceptable decision rules. The formal term used is 'admissible'; a decision rule, d, is *admissible* if there is no decision rule, d^*, with $R(\theta, d^*) \leq R(\theta, d)$, the inequality being strict for some θ. If such a d^* exists, then d is said to be *inadmissible*, and one has obvious cause to question its use. Very common decision rules, such as the least squares estimator in three or more dimensional normal estimation problems (with sum of squares error loss), can turn out rather astonishingly to be inadmissible, so this avenue of investigation has had a substantial impact on decision theory. A general discussion, with references can be found in Berger (1985).

4 COMPARISON OF APPROACHES

For solving a real decision problem, there is little doubt that the Bayesian approach is best. It incorporates all the available information (including the prior information, $\pi(\theta)$, which the frequentist approach ignores), and it tends to be easier than the frequentist approach by an order of magnitude. Maximizing $U^*(a)$ over all actions is generally much easier than minimizing something like $R^*(d)$ over all decision rules; the point is that, in some sense, the frequentist approach needlessly complicates the issue by forcing consideration of the right thing to do for each possible X, while the Bayesian worries only about what to do for the actual data X that are observed. There are also fundamental axiomatic developments (see, Ramsey, 1931; Savage, 1954; and Fishburn, 1981, for a general review) which show that only the Bayesian approach is consistent with plausible axioms of rational behaviour. Basically, the arguments are that situations can be constructed in which the follower of any non-Bayesian approach, say the minimax analyst, will be assured of inferior results.

Sometimes, however, decision theory is used as a formal framework for investigating the performance of statistical procedures, and then the situation is less clear. In Example 2, for instance, we used decision theory mainly as a method to formulate rigorously the problem of estimating a binomial proportion θ. If one is developing a statistical rule, $d(X)$, to be used for binomial estimation problems in general, then its repeated performance for varying X is certainly of interest. Furthermore, so the argument goes, prior information may be unavailable or inaccessible in problems where routine statistical analyses (such as estimating a binomial proportion θ) are to be performed, precluding use of the Bayesian approach.

The Bayesian reply to these arguments is that (i) optimal performance for each X alone will guarantee good performance in repeated use, negating the need to consider frequentist measures explicitly; and (ii) even when prior information is unavailable or cannot be used, a Bayesian analysis can still be performed with what are called 'non-informative' prior densities.

Example 2 (cont.). If no prior information about θ is available, one might well say that choosing $\pi(\theta) = 1$ reflects this lack of knowledge about θ. A Bayesian analysis (calculating the posterior density and choosing the action with smallest Bayesian expected squared error loss) yields, as the optimal estimate for θ when X is observed:

$$d_3(X) = (X + 1)/(n + 2).$$

This estimate is considerably more attractive than, say, the minimax rule $d_2(X)$ (see Berger, 1985, p. 375).

In practical applications of decision theory, it is the Bayesian approach which is dominant, yet the frequentist approach retains considerable appeal among theoreticians. A general consensus on the controversy appears quite remote at this time. This author sides with the Bayesian approach in the above debate, while recognizing that there are some situations in which the frequentist approach might be useful. For an extensive discussion of these issues, see Berger (1985).

BIBLIOGRAPHY

Bayes, T. 1763. An essay towards solving a problem in the doctrine of changes. *Philosophical Transactions of the Royal Society*, London 53, 370–418.

Berger, J. 1985. *Statistical Decision Theory and Bayesian Analysis*. New York: Springer-Verlag.

Blackwell, D. and Girshick, M.A. 1954. *Theory of Games and Statistical Decisions*. New York: Wiley.

De Groot, M.H. 1970. *Optimal Statistical Decisions*. New York: McGraw-Hill.

Ferguson, T.S. 1967. *Mathematical Statistics: A Decision Theoretic Approach*. New York: Academic Press.

Fishburn, P.C. 1981. Subjective expected utility: a review of normative theories. *Theory and Decision* 13, 139–99.

Neyman, J. 1977. Frequentist probability and frequentist statistics. *Synthese* 36, 97–131.

Neyman, J. and Pearson, E.S. 1933. On the problem of the most efficient tests of statistical hypotheses. *Philosophical Transactions of the Royal Society*, London, 231–289–337.

Raiffa, H. 1968. *Decision Analysis: Introductory Lectures on Choices under Uncertainty.* Reading, Mass.: Addison-Wesley.

Raiffa, H. and Schlaifer, R. 1961. *Applied Statistical Decision Theory*. Boston: Division of Research, Graduate School of Business Administration, Harvard University.

Ramsey, F.P. 1931. Truth and probability. In *The Foundations of Mathematics and Other Logical Essays*, London: Kegan, Paul, Trench and Trubner. Reprinted in *Studies in Subjective Probability*, ed. H. Kyburg and H. Smokler, New York: Wiley, 1964, 61–92.

Savage, L.J. 1954. *The Foundations of Statistics*. New York: Wiley.

Wald, A. 1950. *Statistical Decision Functions*. New York: Wiley.

Winkler, R.L. 1972. *An Introduction to Bayesian Inference and Decision*. New York: Holt, Rinehart & Winston.

Statistical Inference

D.V. LINDLEY

Deduction is the process whereby we pass from a general statement to a particular case: the reverse procedure, from the particular to the general, is variously called induction, or inference. Statistical inference is ordinarily understood to involve repetition or averaging, as when an inference is made about a population on the basis of a sample drawn from it. Economic facts are typically established by means of statistical inference. Economists construct a model of the world and deduce from it implications for the real world. These are checked against the available data, leading to some degree of support for the model. Statistical inference is concerned with how this support should be calculated.

Statistical inference incorporates a parameter θ which describes the model. In the simplest cases θ is a real number but in many models it is a set of numbers or even a function. The other basic element is the data, x, being observations made on the actual economic system. So θ corresponds to the general element and x to the particular. The model describes how the data follow from the parameter value. This is usually in the form of a probability distribution $p(x \mid \theta)$: the probability of x, given the value of θ. The problem of statistical inference is to make some statement about θ given the value of x. A simple example is provided by a model that says one variable y has linear regression on another, z, the regression line having equation $y = \alpha + \beta z$ and the parameter being the pair $(\alpha, \beta) = \theta$. Data may then be collected for several pairs (y_i, z_i), $i = 1, 2, \ldots, n$ and an inference made about θ. The probability specification will ordinarily be that, for any z, y is normally distributed about $\alpha + \beta z$ with constant variance σ^2. If σ^2 is unknown then it will need to be included with α and β in θ.

Two types of inference statement are ordinarily made about θ: estimation and testing. The main distinction being that in testing some values of θ are singled out for special consideration, whereas in estimation all values of θ are treated equally. In the regression example, the hypothesis may be made that z does not affect y in the sense that $\beta = 0$. It would then be usual to test the hypothesis $\beta = 0$. In estimation, on the other hand, $\beta = 0$ plays no special role and the

285

reasonable values of β on the basis of x are required. Estimation takes two forms, point and interval. In the former θ is estimated by a single number, the point estimate; or in the multidimensional case by a set of numbers. In the latter an interval, or region, of values of θ which are reasonably supported by the data is given. In the regression example

$$b = \sum (y_i - y_.)(z_i - z_.) \Big/ \sum (z_i - z_.)^2$$

is the least-squares point estimate of β, $y_.$ and $z_.$ being the means of the y- and z-values respectively. An interval estimate would be of the form $b \pm ts$, where s is the standard deviation evaluated from the data and t is the value obtained from Student's t-distribution. Point estimates are usually inadequate because they do not include any expression of the uncertainty that exists above the parameter: interval estimates are much to be preferred and usually, as in the regression case, start with the point estimate b and construct the interval about it. Interval estimates and tests are often related by the fact that the interval contains those parameter values which would not be judged significant were a test of that value to be carried out.

There is no general agreement on how statistical inference should be performed though, in some common situations, there is good agreement about the numerical results. It is possible to recognize three main schools named after Fisher; Neyman, Pearson and Wald (NPW); and Bayes.

The Fisherian school is the least formalized and is the one most favoured by scientists, especially those on the biological side, in medicine and agriculture. Because of its lack of a strict mathematical structure it is the hardest to describe succinctly, yet, because of this it is often the easiest to use. The name is entirely apposite since it is essentially the creation of one man, R.A. Fisher (1925, 1935). Estimation is based on the log-likelihood function $L(\theta) = \log p(x \mid \theta)$. Here $p(x \mid \theta)$, the probability of data x given parameter θ, is considered as a function of θ for the observed values of the data, now considered as fixed. A point estimate of θ is provided by the maximum likelihood value $\hat{\theta}$, that maximizes, over θ, $L(\theta)$. The precision of $\hat{\theta}$ can be found using minus the second derivative of $L(\theta)$ at $\hat{\theta}$. An interval estimate is then of the form $\hat{\theta} \pm s$, where s depends on the measure of precision. Extensions to the multidimensional case are readily available and, although cases are known where the method is unsatisfactory, it often works extremely well and is deservedly popular. In the case of normal means, maximum likelihood and least-squares estimates agree. A Fisherian test of the hypothesis that θ is equal to a specified value θ_0 is found by constructing a statistic $t(x)$ from the data x and calculating the probability, were $\theta = \theta_0$, of getting the value of $t(x)$ observed, or more extreme. This probability is called the significance level: the smaller it is, the more doubt is cast on θ having the value θ_0. The best-known example is the F-test for the equality of means in an analysis of variance. It is typical of the Fisherian approach that few rules are available for the choice of the statistic $t(x)$. His genius was enough to produce reasonable answers in important cases. Often $t(x)$ is based on a point estimate of θ.

In some ways NPW is a formalized version of Fisher's approach. It has been much developed in the United States, though even there much applied work is Fisherian and it is the theoreticians who espouse NPW. There are many good expositions: for example, Lehmann (1959, 1983). Statistical inferences are thought of as decisions about θ and the merit of a decision is expressed in terms of a loss function measuring how bad the decision is when the true value is θ. If $t(x)$ is a point estimate of the real parameter θ, squared error $\{t(x) - \theta\}^2$ is the loss function ordinarily used, the loss diminishing the nearer the estimate is to the true value. In testing, the decisions are to reject or to accept the null value θ_0 being tested. The simplest loss function is zero for a correct decision and some constant, positive value for each incorrect one. The probability of rejection of $\theta = \theta_0$ when in fact it is true is typically the significance level in Fisher's approach. Having the concept of a decision and a loss function, it becomes possible to ask the question, what is the best decision (estimate or test)? The criterion used to answer this is the expected loss, the expectation being over the data values according to the probability specification $p(x | \theta)$. Thus, for point estimate $t(x)$, the expected loss is $\int \{t(x) - \theta\}^2 p(x | \theta) \, dx$. The problem then is to choose $t(x)$ to minimize this function. There is a substantial difficulty in that this expected loss depends on θ, which is unknown. Consequently additional criteria have to be used in order to select the optimum decision. For example, the decisions may be restrained in some way, as when a point estimate is restricted to be unbiased. A basic result is that the only sensible decisions are those which arise from the following procedure. Select a probability distribution $p(\theta)$ for θ and minimize the expected loss obtained by averaging over both x and θ – in the point estimation case, $\iint \{t(x) - \theta\}^2 p(x | \theta) p(\theta) \, dx \, d\theta$. This expectation being a number, the minimization is usually possible without ambiguity. However, the choice of $p(\theta)$ remains to be made. It is important to notice that in NPW theory the distribution of θ is merely introduced as a device for producing a reasonable decision (the technical term is 'admissible') and is not necessarily held to express opinions about θ.

The third system of inference is named, quite inappropriately, after the discoverer of Bayes' theorem. Laplace was the first significant user. Inference is a passage from the special x to the general θ on the basis of a model $p(x | \theta)$ going in the opposite direction, from θ to x. In the Bayesian view, inference is similarly accomplished by a probability distribution $p(\theta | x)$ of θ, given x. The two distributions are related by Bayes' theorem, $p(\theta | x) \propto p(x | \theta) p(\theta)$, where $p(\theta)$ is a distribution for θ. NPW and Bayes are similar in their introduction of probabilities for θ. A basic difference is that the Bayesian approach recognizes $p(\theta)$ as a statement of belief about θ, and not, as does NPW, just as a technical device. With this strong statement about $p(\theta)$ both x and θ have probabilities attached and the full force of the probability calculus can be employed: in particular, to make the inference $p(\theta | x)$. Now the inference is couched, not in terms of estimates or tests, but by means of a probability distribution. If $p(\theta | x)$ is centred around $t(x)$, say as its mean, then $t(x)$ may be conveniently thought of as a point estimate of θ. If θ_0 is of special interest $p(\theta_0 | x)$ may be used as a test of the hypothesis that $\theta = \theta_0$. But the full inference is the distribution $p(\theta \,|\, x)$. Consequently, once the big step of introducing $p(\theta)$ has been made, the inference problem is solved by use of the probability calculus: no other considerations are needed. For example, typically θ is multi-dimensional $\theta = (\theta_1, \theta_2, \ldots, \theta_m)$ and only a few parameters are of interest, the remainder are called nuisance parameters. If only θ_1 matters, inferences about it are easily made by the marginal distribution $p(\theta_1 \,|\, x)$ found by integrating out the nuisance parameters from $p(\theta \,|\, x)$. The regression example above for slope β(α and σ^2 being nuisance) provides an illustration.

Until World War I, Bayesian and non-Bayesian views had alternated in popularity, but the work of R.A. Fisher was so influential that it led to an almost complete suppression of the Bayesian view, which was reinforced by the work of Neyman, Pearson and Wald. Savage (1954) renewed interest in the Bayesian approach by providing it with its axiomatic structure, following Ramsey (1931) whose original ideas had lain unappreciated. Savage was much influenced by the work of de Finetti (his most accessible work is 1974/5) who provided a new view of probability that has had considerable impact upon subsequent thinking. Today the three disciplines lie uneasily together.

The Bayesian approach is the most formalized of the three inferential methods because everything is expressed within the single framework of the probability calculus, which is itself very well formalized. It has been relatively little used largely because of the perceived difficulty of assigning a distribution to θ. An important property of this method is that it is easily extended to include decision-making. As with NPW theory, a class of decisions d is introduced together with a loss function $\ell(d, \theta)$ expressing the loss in selecting d when θ obtains, and choosing that decision d that minimizes the expected (over θ) loss $\int \ell(d, \theta) p(\theta \,|\, x) \, d\theta$, using the inference $p(\theta \,|\, x)$. (This is in contrast to the NPW approach, using the expectation over x.)

There are two basic differences between the Bayesian paradigm and the other two. These concern the logical structure, and the likelihood principle. Both the Fisherian and NPW paradigms tackle an inference problem by thinking of several, apparently sensible procedures, investigating their properties and choosing that procedure which overall has the best properties. Fisher's work on maximum likelihood and its demonstrated superiority to the method of moments provides an example. In neither of these approaches are there general procedures: for example, there is no way known of constructing an interval estimate. Within NPW, Wald did introduce the minimax principle but it is generally unsatisfactory in the inference context and has not been used in practice. Against this, the techniques that are available, like maximum likelihood and analysis of variance, are easy to use and interpret (though the interpretation is often wrong: see equations (1) and (2) below). The lack of a formal structure has enabled statisticians to extemporize and come up with valuable concepts and techniques that are of substantial practical value though sometimes with weak justifications. The Bayesian paradigm proceeds differently. It begins by laying down reasonable, elementary properties to be demanded of an inference and then, by deduction, discovers which procedures have these properties. In that sense it is the complete opposite of the Fisherian and NPW views that start with the procedures. It is the method used in other branches of mathematics where the basic properties provide the axioms for the subsequent, logical development. Though there are important variants, all the axiom systems proposed lead to the result that the only inference procedures satisfying them are those that use probability: that the only sensible inference for θ, given x, is a probability statement about θ, given x. The Bayesian position is therefore a deduction from simple requirements about our inferences. NPW comes near to recognizing this in its technical introduction of $p(\theta)$. The Fisherian view never addresses the problem.

The second difference between the Bayesian and other views involves the likelihood principle. The model provides $p(x\mid\theta)$ which, for fixed θ, is a probability for x. Considered as a function of θ for fixed x, it is called the likelihood for θ (given x). It was an important contribution of Fisher's to emphasize the distinction between the probability and likelihood aspects, and to show us, for example, in the maximum likelihood estimate, the importance of the likelihood function. However, Fisher did not consider the likelihood to be the only tool for inference. In a significance test, based on a statistic $t(x)$, he used the significance level, which is an integral over values of x giving more extreme values to t than that observed, for the tested value θ_0. Clearly this cannot be calculated from the likelihood function which holds x fixed and varies θ. NPW uses the expected (over x) loss and therefore does not use the likelihood function. On the other hand, the only feature of the data used in a Bayesian procedure is the likelihood, supplementing it with the distribution for θ. The likelihood principle says that if two data sets, x and y, have the same likelihood, then the inferences from x and y should be the same. Most statistical procedures in common use today violate the principle, but Bayesian procedures do not. The latter part of that statement is clearly true from Bayes' theorem which, in order to calculate the inference, uses only the likelihood. Here is an example of its violation when an unbiased estimate is used.

Given θ, x is a random sample from a population in which each value is either 1 or 0 with probabilities θ and $1-\theta$. In one case the sample is selected to be of size n and r if the values are found to be 1. In the second case, r is chosen and the population samples until r 1's have been observed, the total sample being of size n. In each case the likelihood is $\theta^r(1-\theta)^{n-r}$ and so, by the likelihood principle, the inferences should be the same. However, in the first case the unbiased estimate of θ based on (r, n) is the familiar r/n: in the second case it is $(r-1)/(n-1)$. Significance tests of $\theta = \frac{1}{2}$ say are different in the two cases because 'more extreme' in one case means more extreme values of r for fixed n, and in the other more extreme values of n for fixed r. There are many impressive arguments in favour of the likelihood principle, even outside the Bayesian paradigm, yet it is not accepted by most statisticians and almost all inferential procedures used today violate it: maximum likelihood estimation is the obvious exception.

There is another interesting consequence of the axiomatic, Bayesian approach leading to the probabilistic form of inference, and that is that any non-probabilistic inference will somewhere violate the basic properties set out in the axioms. Indeed, it is true that every non-Bayesian procedure has a counter-example where it behaves in an absurd fashion. In illustration let $(l(x), u(x))$ be a confidence interval for θ at level α based on data x. The precise meaning of this is that

$$p(l(x) < \theta < u(x) \,|\, \theta) = \alpha, \qquad \text{for all } \theta. \tag{1}$$

Notice that this is a probability statement about x, given θ, based on $p(x \,|\, \theta)$. In words, the probability that the random interval $(l(x), u(x))$ contains θ is α, for all given θ. It is easy to produce examples for x in which the interval is the whole line; $l(x) = -\infty$, $u(x) = +\infty$, and $\alpha = 0.95$. Here we are 95 per cent confident that θ is real. This is absurd in the case of the observed x, although it is true that for 95 per cent of x's the statement will be true. Contrast this with the Bayesian statement that

$$p(l(x) < \theta < u(x) \,|\, x) = \alpha, \qquad \text{for all } x, \tag{2}$$

based on $p(\theta \,|\, x)$. This is about θ, given x: in words, the probability is α that θ lies between $l(x)$ and $u(x)$. Clearly, with $\alpha < 1$, it could never happen that the interval is the whole real line.

A key ingredient in any form of inference is clearly probability, whose laws are well understood. But there is considerable dispute over the interpretation of probability: disputes which have practical consequences. There are two broad groups: subjective and frequentist views. In the subjective view, a probability is an expression of the subject's belief. Thus (2) expresses a belief that θ lies between the numbers $l(x)$ and $u(x)$. In the frequentist view, probabilities are related to observed frequencies. Thus (1) says that the frequency with which the interval contains θ is α. The latter are objective, in the sense that the frequencies can be objectively observed by all subjects. The great majority of statisticians today adopt the frequency view, claiming an objectivity for their methods. Most Bayesians hold to the subjective approach, claiming that economists have to express beliefs about the system they are discussing. It is undoubtedly true that many users of statistics think of the frequency statements, like (1), as belief statements, like (2). It had been thought that the two views were opposites but de Finetti showed that the frequentist view of probability is a special case of the subjective view, namely when the data are believed to be exchangeable. The values $x_1, x_2, \ldots, x_n$ are exchangeable if their probability distribution is invariant under permutation of the x's. A random sample from a population would ordinarily be judged to possess this invariance. The case mentioned earlier where each x_i is either 1 or 0, with probabilities θ and $1 - \theta$ respectively, is the standard example. Here θ is a frequency probability, or chance, about which there are beliefs $p(\theta)$ changed by the data x to new beliefs $p(\theta \,|\, x)$.

Resistance to the Bayesian approach and subjective probability has centred around the genuine difficulty of assessing beliefs, especially when there is little knowledge of the parameter. Rather than face the formidable, and perhaps impossible, task of measuring belief, statisticians have concentrated on frequentist methods, sometimes ignoring their defects. A related difficulty with the subjective approach is the lack of objectivity in the sense that two subjects may, on the basis of the same data, have different beliefs. The Bayesian response is that this reflects reality and if each economist were to express all his beliefs probabilistically, we would have a clearer appreciation of the situation; and, in any case, different beliefs come together with increasing amounts of data. This is why observational studies are so important. Economics is predominantly frequentist but does have a substantial school, particularly in econometrics, of the Bayesian persuasion. The close connection between that view and decision-making makes it more attractive to the economist than to the laboratory scientist who sees himself as acquiring knowledge, not making decisions.

Inference that is statistical, involving repetition, is naturally allied to the frequency view: whereas inference, in general, has no frequency basis. But de Finetti's observation connecting exchangeability (which is essentially a finite, frequentist property) with subjectivity shows that the Bayesian view embraces both statistical and non-statistical inference. Consequently, the subjective, Bayesian paradigm has enormous potential, encompassing almost all problems of passing from the special to the general. The guilt (corresponding to θ) of a defendant in a law court on the basis of evidence x is an example. The likelihood principle says that the only relevant features are the probabilities of the evidence on the assumptions of innocence, and of guilt. Whether this potential will be realized depends in large part on overcoming the practical difficulties of assessment of beliefs.

Statistical inference depends on a probability specification $p(x \mid \theta)$ for data x, given parameter θ. If NPW it uses, in addition, a loss function: if Bayesian it introduces an additional probability specification for θ, $p(\theta)$. An important topic studies how the inference is affected by changes in any of the specifications. The inference is said to be robust if the change has little effect on it. For example, it is usual to choose $p(x \mid \theta)$ to be normal, largely because this assumption is relatively easy to handle and leads to many, simple and powerful answers. We might ask what happens if the normal is replaced by the very similar Student's t-distribution with its rather longer tails. For the mean μ of the normal, the sample mean is, by any standard, an excellent point estimate of μ: a trimmed mean, in which a few extreme observations are discarded, is not quite as good but is still reasonable. With the t-distribution however, the situation is reversed and the trimmed mean behaves better than the sample mean. The former is more robust. In recent years a lot of work has been put into the study of robust inference procedures to replace less robust ones like least squares.

The scientist who is able to plan his experiment, either in the laboratory or in the field, has a much simpler inference problem than the economist who, almost entirely, has to rely on data that have arisen naturally instead of being planned. The planned experiment can take cognizance of factors additional to those the scientist is directly interested in. This can be done either by explicitly including them in the experiment, or by a suitable randomization procedure that has high chance of eliminating any unwanted effects. The economist is usually denied both opportunities, though sometimes extra factors can be included. The inference procedure should therefore recognize uncertainties that the laboratory experiment has eliminated. This is not always done and inference in economics remains less satisfactory than in other sciences. The concept of causation is harder to understand in economics. In the regression of y on z above, it is easy to think of z causing changes in y: but it may be that changes in y and z are both caused by related fluctuations in a third variable w. The attempt by econometricians to avoid this difficulty by including many variables has led to complexities of interpretation due to the high dimensionality of the problem.

Statistical inference is ordinarily thought of as a passage from data x to parameter θ but there is another form in which the inference is from past data x to future observations y, with no explicit reference to a parameter. This is often called prediction, and the obvious application is to time series with $x = (x_1, x_2, \ldots, x_n)$, x_i being the value of some quantity at time t_i, and $y = x_{n+1}$; so that the quantity has been observed up to time t_n and it is required to predict its value at t_{n+1}. The usual way to proceed is to model the time series in some parametric form involving θ and to infer the value of θ on the basis of x. The model will specify $p(y \mid x, \theta)$ and one possibility is to predict y using $p(y \mid x, \hat{\theta})$, where $\hat{\theta}$ is a point estimate of θ. In the Bayesian view $p(y \mid x)$ is directly available for prediction, where $p(y \mid x) = \int p(y \mid x, \theta) p(\theta \mid x) \, d\theta$, using standard probability calculations. It is arguable that all practical inference problems are of this type and that the model, and θ, are only introduced as a means of solving them.

Many statistical procedures are complicated and require extensive computations: in some cases, one does not even know how to find a procedure. One possibility is to use approximation techniques and find a procedure which loses only little information in comparison with the optimum method and yet is simple. Asymptotic methods often provide such approximations. Data often consist of a random sample, or of a time series $(x_1, x_2, \ldots, x_n)$ involving n observations. It is often possible to study the limiting behaviour as n increases without limit. For example, with random samples, the maximum likelihood estimate θ is asymptotically normally distributed with mean equal to the true value and variance σ^2/n, with σ^2 calculable in terms of the second derivative of the log-likelihood. Although this is only true as n goes to infinity, it can be used to produce a 95 per cent confidence interval for θ of the form $\theta \pm 1.96 \, \sigma/n^{1/2}$. This is then an approximation, for large n, to the exact interval. Asymptotic methods have been very successful though it is often difficult to know how fast the limit is approached and whether a particular n is large or not. Stirling's asymptotic formula is remarkably accurate for n as low as 3. Some asymptotic results are not realized until n is well into the thousands.

The present position in statistical inference is historically interesting. The bulk of practitioners use well-established methods like least squares, analysis of variance, maximum likelihood and significance tests: all broadly within the Fisherian school and chosen for their proven usefulness rather than their logical coherence. If asked about their rigorous justification most of these people would refer to ideas of the NPW type: least-squares estimates are best, linear unbiased; F-tests have high power and maximum likelihood values are asymptotically optimal. Yet these justifications are far from satisfactory: the only logically coherent system is the Bayesian one which disagrees with the NPW notions, largely because of their violation of the likelihood principle. The practitioner is most reluctant to adopt this logical approach because of the apparent impracticality of it. The impracticality is largely an illusion and current work is energetically overcoming it. So the next few decades should be interesting as the various theories get amended and one emerges triumphant, or some new ideas avoid the contradictions. Whatever happens, inference will surely remain one of the most important of subjects, simply because of the ubiquity of inference problems in all aspects of human endeavour.

BIBLIOGRAPHY

De Finetti, B. 1974–5. *Theory of Probability: a Critical Introductory Treatment.* 2 vols, London: Wiley. Translation from the 1970 Italian original by A. Machi and A. Smith.

Fisher, R.A. 1925. *Statistical Methods for Research Workers.* Edinburgh: Oliver & Boyd; 12 edn, New York: Hafner Publishing Co., 1954.

Fisher, R.A. 1935. *The Design of Experiments.* Edinburgh: Oliver & Boyd; 6th edn, New York: Hafner Publishing Co., 1953.

Lehmann, E.L. 1959. *Testing Statistical Hypotheses.* New York: Wiley.

Lehmann, E.L. 1983. *The Theory of Point Estimation.* New York: Wiley.

Ramsey, F.P. 1931. *The Foundations of Mathematics and Other Logical Essays.* London: Kegan, Paul, Trench, Trubner; New York: Humanities Press, 1950.

Savage, L.J. 1954. *The Foundations of Statistics.* New York: Wiley.

Time Series Analysis

MARC NERLOVE AND FRANCIS X. DIEBOLD

Any series of observations ordered along a single dimension, such as time, may be thought of as a time series. The emphasis in time series analysis is the study of dependence among the observations at different points in time. What distinguishes time series analysis from general multivariate analysis is precisely the temporal order imposed on the observations. Many economic variables, such as prices, sales, stocks, GNP and its components, are observed over time; in addition to being interested in the interrelationships among these variables, we are also concerned with relationships among the current and past values of one or more of them, that is, relationships over time.

The study of time series of, for example, astronomical observations predates recorded history. Early writers on economic subjects occasionally made explicit reference to astronomy as the source of their ideas. For example, in 1838 Cournot said, 'As in astronomy, it is necessary to recognize the *secular* variations which are independent of the periodic variations' (Cournot, 1838, translation 1927). Jevons (1884) remarks that his study of short-term fluctuations uses the methods of astronomy and meteorology. During the 19th century interest in, and analysis of, social and economic time series evolved independently of parallel developments in astronomy and meteorology. (See Nerlove et al., 1979, pp. 1–21, for an historical survey.)

One of the earliest methods of analysing time series thought to exhibit some form of periodicity is harmonic analysis. In this type of analysis, the time series, or some simple transformation of it, is assumed to be the result of superposition of sine and cosine waves of different frequencies. However, since summing a finite number of such strictly periodic functions always results in a perfectly periodic series, which is seldom observed in practice, it is usual to add a stochastic component, sometimes called 'noise'. Thus one is led to search for 'hidden periodicities', that is the unknown frequencies and amplitudes of sinusoidal fluctuations hidden amidst noise. The method for doing so is *periodogram analysis*, suggested by Stokes (1879) and used by Schuster (1898) to analyse sunspot data

294

and later by others, principally William Beveridge (1921, 1922), to analyse economic time series.

Spectral analysis is a modernized version of periodogram analysis modified to take account of the stochastic nature of the entire time series, not just the noise component. If it is assumed that economic time series are fully stochastic, it follows that the older technique is inappropriate to their analysis and that considerable difficulties in the interpretation of the periodograms of economic series may be encountered.

At the time when harmonic analysis proved to be inadequate for the analysis of economic and social time series, another way of characterizing such series was suggested, more or less simultaneously, by the Russian statistician and economist, Eugen Slutsky (1927), and the British statistician, G.U. Yule (1921, 1926, 1927). Slutsky and Yule showed that if we begin with a series of purely random numbers and then take sums or differences, weighted or unweighted, of such numbers, the new series so produced has many of the apparent cyclic properties that were thought at the time to characterize economic and other time series. Such sums or differences of purely random numbers and sums or differences of the resulting series are the basis for the autoregressive moving-average (ARMA) processes which are the basis for modelling many kinds of time series. There is, however, nothing incompatible with looking at time series as generated by processes of this sort and the way spectral analysis looks at them. The remainder of this article explores the complementarities of these two approaches to the analysis of economic time series.

1. BASIC THEORY

1.1 Stationarity and ergodicity of time series processes. Consider a random variable x_t, where $t \in T$, the set of integers; the infinite vector $\{x_t, t \in T\}$ is called a discrete time series. Let $T_k = \{t_1, \ldots, t_k\}$ be a subset of k elements of T; the distribution of the finite dimensional vector $\{x_t, t \in T_k\}$ is a well-defined multivariate distribution function, $F_{T_k}(\cdot)$. The time series $\{x_t, t \in T\}$ is said to be *strictly stationary* if, for any finite subset T_k of T and any integer τ, the distribution function of $\{x_t, t \in T_k + \tau\}$ is the same as the distribution function of $\{x_t, t \in T_k\}$ that is, for an arbitrary finite subset of the index set. The distribution function of the finite vector of observations on x_t is invariant with respect to the origin from which time is measured. All the unconditional moments of the distribution function, if they exist, are independent of the index t; in particular,

$$Ex_t = \mu$$

$$\gamma(\tau) = E[x_t - \mu][x_{t+\tau} - \mu], \tag{1}$$

where $\gamma(\tau)$ is the autocovariance function and depends only on the difference in indices, τ. Time-series processes for which (1) holds, but which are not necessarily strictly stationary according to the definition above, are said to be *weakly stationary, covariance stationary,* or *stationary to the second order.*

Time-series processes for which $F_{T_k}(\cdot)$ is multivariate normal for any subset T_k of T are called *Gaussian processes*. For Gaussian processes covariance or weak stationarity implies strong stationarity.

In practice, we usually observe only a finite subset of one realization of a time series (from a set of many potential realizations corresponding to drawings from $F_{T_k}(\cdot)$). The question is whether a valid inference can be made about the movements of $F_{T_k}(\cdot)$ from one such observation, for example, from the time averages of sums or sums of products of the observed values. If the process is what is known as *ergodic*, time averages of functions of the observations on the time series at $k = N$ time points converge in mean square to the corresponding expectations. (See Priestley, 1981, pp. 340–43; Doob, 1953, p. 465.) While ergodicity is a deep mathematical property of the distribution function characterizing the time series in question, its meaning for a stationary time series is essentially independence of observations far enough apart in time. Thus, for example, the series generated by $x_t = r\,e^{i(\lambda t + \phi)}$, where $r \sim N(\mu, 1)$, λ fixed, and ϕ uniformly distributed on the interval $[-\pi, \pi]$ is stationary but not ergodic.

1.2 The Wold decomposition and general linear processes. Let $\{\varepsilon_t\}$ be a time series generated by a process of independent, identically distributed random variables with zero mean and variance σ^2. (Such a series is often called 'white noise'.) The infinite, one-sided moving average (MA)

$$x_t = \sum_{j=0}^{\infty} b_j \varepsilon_{t-j}, \quad \sum_{j=0}^{\infty} b_j^2 < \infty, \quad b_0 = 1, \tag{2}$$

is also a well-defined stationary process with mean 0 and variance $\sigma^2 \Sigma_0^{\infty} b_j^2$. Processes of this form and, more generally, processes based on an infinite two-sided MA of the same form are called *linear processes*, are always ergodic, and play a key role in time series analysis (Hannan, 1970).

The importance of the process (2) is underscored by the Wold Decomposition Theorem (1938) which states that any weakly stationary process may be decomposed into two mutually uncorrelated component processes, one an infinite one-sided MA of the form (2) and the other a so-called linearly deterministic process, future values of which can be predicted exactly by some linear function of past observations. The linearly deterministic component is non-ergodic.

2. LINEAR PROCESSES IN TIME AND FREQUENCY DOMAINS

2.1 Autocovariance and autocovariance generating functions. The autocovariance function of a stationary process, defined in (1) above, or its matrix generalization for vector processes, provides the basic representation of time dependence for weakly stationary processes. For the stationary process defined in (2), it is

$$\gamma(\tau) = \sigma^2 \sum_{j=0}^{\infty} b_j b_{j+\tau}. \tag{3}$$

The autocovariance generating transform is defined as

$$g(z) = \sum_{-\infty}^{\infty} \gamma(\tau)z^{\tau} \tag{4}$$

in whatever region of the complex plane the series on the right-hand side converges. If the series $\{x_t\}$ is covariance stationary, convergence will occur in an annulus about the unit circle. The autocovariance generating transform for the one-sided MA defined in (2) is

$$g(z) = \sigma^2 B(z)B(z^{-1}), \tag{5}$$

where

$$B(z) = \sum_{k=0}^{\infty} b_k z^k.$$

If $B(z)$ has no zeros on the unit circle, the process defined in (2) is invertible and also has an infinite autoregressive (AR) representation as

$$A(L)x_t = \varepsilon_t, \tag{6}$$

where L is the lag operator such that $L^j x_t = x_{t-j}$ and $A(L) = a_0 + a_1 L + a_2 L^2 + \cdots$.

Processes having an autocovariance generating transform which is a rational function of z are the so-called autoregressive moving average (ARMA) processes. If the ARMA process is both stationary and invertible, $g(z)$ may be written.

$$G(z) = \frac{P(z)P(z^{-1})}{Q(z)Q(z^{-1})} = \sigma^2 \frac{\prod_{k=1}^{m} (1 - \beta_k z)(1 - \beta_k z^{-1})}{\prod_{j=1}^{n} (1 - \alpha_j z)(1 - \alpha_j z^{-1})} \tag{7}$$

where $|\beta_k|, |\alpha_j| < 1$, all j, k. Then

$$Q(L)x_t = P(L)\varepsilon_t, \tag{8}$$

where

$$Q(L) = \prod_{j=1}^{n} (1 - \alpha_j L) \quad \text{and} \quad P(L) = \prod_{k=1}^{m} (1 - \beta_k L),$$

is the corresponding ARMA model.

2.2 Spectral density functions. The spectral density function of a linearly non-deterministic stationary process with autocovariance generating transform (5) is proportional to the value of this function on the unit circle by a factor $1/2\pi$:

$$f(\lambda) = (1/2\pi)g(e^{i\lambda}) = (\sigma^2/2\pi)B(e^{i\lambda})B(e^{-i\lambda})$$

$$= (1/2\pi) \sum_{-\infty}^{\infty} \gamma(\tau) e^{-i\lambda\tau}, \quad -\pi \leqslant \lambda < \pi. \tag{9}$$

That is, the spectral density function is the Fourier transform of the autocovariance function.

Characterization of time series by their autocovariance functions is time-domain analysis; characterization by means of their spectral density functions is frequency domain analysis. Either represents a valid way to view the temporal interdependencies of a time series.

The spectral density function for a linearly non-deterministic, stationary, real-valued time series is a real-valued, non-negative function, symmetric about the origin, defined in the interval $[-\pi, \pi)$:

$$f(\lambda) = (1/2\pi)\left[\gamma(0) + 2\sum_{\tau=1}^{\infty} \gamma(\tau)\cos\lambda\tau\right]. \tag{10}$$

Moreover,

$$E(x_t - \mu)^2 = \int_{-\pi}^{\pi} f(\lambda)\,d\lambda, \tag{11}$$

so that the spectral density function is a frequency-band decomposition of the variance of $\{x_t\}$.

When the process generating $\{x_t\}$ is merely stationary, that is, when $\{x_t\}$ may have a linearly deterministic component, the result corresponding to (10) is

$$\gamma(\tau) = \int_{-\pi}^{\pi} e^{i\lambda\tau}\,dF(\lambda), \tag{12}$$

where $F(\lambda)$ is a distribution function (Doob, 1953, p. 488).

The autocovariance function, its generating transform and the spectral distribution function all have natural generalizations to the multivariate case, that is, where $\{x_t\}$ can be thought of as a vector of time-series processes.

The estimation and analysis of spectral density and distribution functions play an important role in all forms of time-series analysis. More detailed treatments are Doob (1953), Fishman (1969), Koopmans (1974), Fuller (1976), Nerlove et al. (1979, ch. 3) and Priestley (1981).

2.3 Unobserved components (UC) models. In the statistical literature dealing with the analysis of economic time series it is common practice to classify the types of movements that characterize a time series as trend, cyclical, seasonal and irregular. The idea that a time series may best be viewed as being composed of several unobserved components is by no means universal, but it plays a fundamental role in many applications, for example, the choice of methods for seasonal adjustment. Nerlove et al. (1979, ch. 1) review the history of the idea of unobserved components in economics from its origin early in the 19th century.

In the 1960s, Nerlove (1964, 1965, 1967) and Granger (1966) suggested that the typical spectral shape of many economic time series could be accounted for by the superposition of two or more independent components with specified properties. There are basically two approaches to the formulation of UC models:

First, Theil and Wage (1964) and Nerlove and Wage (1964), Nerlove (1967) and Grether and Nerlove (1970) choose the form of components in such a way as to replicate the typical spectral shape of the series which represents their superposition. For example, let T_t represent the trend component, C_t the cyclical, S_t the seasonal and I_t the irregular; the observed (say, monthly) series is

$$y_t = T_t + C_t + S_t + I_t,$$

where

$$T_t = a_0 + a_1 t + a_2 t^2 + \cdots + a_p t^p,$$

$$C_t = \frac{1 + \beta_1 L + \beta_2 L^2}{(1 - \alpha_1 L)(1 - \alpha_2 L)} \varepsilon_{1t},$$

$$S_t = \frac{1 + \beta_3 L + \beta_4 L^2}{1 - \gamma L^{12}} \varepsilon_{2t},$$

$$I_t = \varepsilon_{3t},$$

and ε_{1t}, ε_{2t}, and ε_{3t} are i.i.d. normal variables with variance σ_{11}, σ_{22}, and σ_{33}, respectively. This approach has been carried forward by Harvey (1984), Harvey and Peters (1984) and Harvey and Todd (1984).

Second, an alternative is to find a well-fitting ARMA model (possibly fit after differences of the original series have been taken to remove trend and, given sufficient a priori restrictions on spectral properties of the components to identify them, to derive the components from the empirical model. See Box, Hillmer and Tiao (1978), Pierce (1978, 1979), Burman (1980), Hillmer and Tiao (1982), Hillmer, Bell and Tiao (1983), Bell and Hillmer (1984), Burridge and Wallis (1984), and Maravall (1981, 1984). The basis of this procedure is the fact that every stationary UC model, or the stationary part of every UC model, has an equivalent ARMA form, the so-called canonical form of the UC model (see Nerlove and Wage, 1964; Nerlove et al., 1979, ch. 4).

3. SPECIFICATION, ESTIMATION, INFERENCE AND PREDICTION

3.1 Autocovariance and spectral density functions. Suppose we have a finite number of observations of a realization of the process generating the time series $\{x_t, t \in T\}$, say, $x_1, \ldots, x_T$. The natural way to estimate μ is by

$$\bar{x} = (1/T) \sum_{t=1}^{T} x_t. \tag{14}$$

Suppose we have done so and the sample observations in fact represent deviations from the sample mean $\bar{x}$. (This new process now has zero mean.) There are basically two ways to estimate $\gamma(\tau)$ defined in (1): the first is a biased estimate

$$c(\tau) = (1/T) \sum_{t=1}^{T-|\tau|} x_t x_{t+|\tau|},$$

$$\tau = 0, \pm 1, \ldots, \pm M, \ M \leqslant (T-1), \tag{15}$$

The second is an unbiased estimate

$$\tilde{c}(\tau) = [1/(T - |\tau|)] \sum_{1}^{T-|\tau|} x_t x_{t+|\tau|},$$

$$\tau = 0, \pm 1, \ldots, \pm M, \quad M \leqslant T - 1. \tag{16}$$

Although $c(\tau)$ is biased in finite samples, it is asymptotically unbiased. The difference between $c(\tau)$ and $\tilde{c}(\tau)$ that is important for estimation is that $c(\tau)$ is a positive definite function of τ whereas $\tilde{c}(\tau)$ is not (Parzen, 1961, p. 981). The variance and covariance of the estimated autocovariances are derived *inter alia*, by Hannan (1960), and Anderson (1971). As $T \to \infty$, both tend to zero, as the estimates are asymptotically uncorrelated and consistent. However, the variance relative to the mean does not approach zero as τ increases at the same rate as T:

$$E[c(\tau) - Ec(\tau)]^2/Ec(\tau) \to \infty \quad \text{as} \quad \tau/T \to 1. \tag{17}$$

This property accounts for the failure of the estimated autocorrelation function

$$r(\tau) = c(\tau)/c(0) \tag{18}$$

to damp down as $\tau \to \infty$ as it should for a stationary, linearly non-deterministic process (Hannan, 1960, p. 43).

The 'natural' estimator to employ for the spectral density function is that obtained by replacing $\gamma(\tau)$ in (10) by $c(\tau)$ or $\tilde{c}(\tau)$. The estimator so obtained is proportional, at each frequency, to a sample quantity called the periodogram:

$$I_T(\lambda) = (2/T) \left| \sum_{1}^{T} e^{i\lambda t} x_t \right|^2 \tag{19}$$

usually evaluated at the equispaced frequencies

$$\lambda = 2k\pi/T, \quad k = 0, 1, \ldots, [T/2] \tag{20}$$

in the interval $[0, \pi]$. Although, for a stationary, nonlinearly deterministic process, the periodogram ordinates are proportionately asymptotically unbiased estimates of the spectral densities at the corresponding frequencies, they are not consistent estimates; moreover, the correlation between adjacent periodogram ordinates tends to zero with increasing sample size. The result is that the periodogram presents a jagged appearance which is increasingly difficult to interpret as more data become available.

In order to obtain consistent estimates of the spectral density function at specific frequencies, it is common practice to weigh the periodogram ordinates over the frequency range or to form weighted averages of the autocovariances at different lags. There is a substantial literature on the subject. The weights are called a 'spectral window'. Essentially the idea is to reduce the variance of the estimate of an average spectral density around a particular frequency by averaging periodogram ordinates which are asymptotically unbiased and independently distributed estimates of the corresponding ordinates of the spectral density function. Related weights can also be applied to the estimated autocovariances which are substituted in (10); this weighting system is called a 'lag window'. Naturally the sampling properties of the spectral estimates depend on the nature of the 'window' used to obtain consistency. The literature on this topic is summarized in Priestley (1981, pp. 432–94).

3.2 ARMA models. The autocovariance function and the spectral density function for a time series represent relatively non-parametric ways of describing the data. An alternative approach is to specify and estimate an ARMA model after transforming the data to render the series stationary. This means choosing the orders of the polynomials P and Q in (7) and (8) and perhaps also specifying that one or more coefficients may be zero or placing other restrictions on P and Q. The problem then becomes that of estimating the parameters of the model.

Despite the poor statistical properties of the estimated autocovariance function and a related function called the partial autocorrelation function, these are usually used to specify the orders of the polynomials P and Q. More recently Akaike (1970, 1974) has introduced a new expression called Akaike's information criterion (AIC). This is a very general criterion, which is based on information theoretic conceptions and can be used for statistical model identification in a wide range of circumstances. When a model involving k independently estimated parameters is fit, the AIC is defined as

$$\text{AIC}(k) = -2 \log[\text{maximized likelihood}] + 2k. \tag{21}$$

The appropriate value of k is that at which AIC attains its minimum value.

Once the orders of the AR and MA components have been determined a variety of maximum-likelihood or aproximate maximum likelihood methods are available to estimate the parameters. Newbold (1974) shows that if x_t is characterized by (8) with $\varepsilon_t \overset{iid}{\sim} N(0, \sigma^2)$ then the exact likelihood function for the parameters of $P(\cdot)$ and $Q(\cdot)$ is such that the maximum-likelihood estimates of the parameters and the least-squares (LS) estimates (in general highly nonlinear) are asymptotically identical. Only in the case of a pure AR model are the LS estimates (conditional on the initial observations) linear. Various approximations have been discussed (Box and Jenkins, 1970; Granger and Newbold, 1977; Nerlove et al., 1979, pp. 121–25).

Exact maximum-likelihood estimation of ARMA models has been discussed by, *inter alia*, Newbold (1974), Anderson (1977), Ansley (1979), and Harvey (1981). Following Schweppe (1965), Harvey suggests the use of the Kalman filter (1960) to obtain the value of the exact-likelihood function numerically, which may be maximized by numerical methods. The Kalman filter approach is easily adapted to the estimation of UC models in the time domain.

An alternative to exact or approximate maximum-likelihood estimation in the time domain was suggested by Hannan (1969). Estimates may be obtained by maximizing an approximate likelihood function based on the asymptotic distribution of the periodogram ordinates defined in (19). These are asymptotically independently distributed (Brillinger, 1975, p. 95), and the random variables $2I_t(\lambda)/f(\lambda)$ have an asymptotic χ^2 distribution with two degrees of freedom

(Koopmans, 1974, pp. 260–65). This means that the asymptotic distribution of the observations, $\{x_1, \ldots, x_T\}$ is proportional to

$$\prod_{j=0}^{[T/2]} [1/f(\lambda_j)] \exp[-I(\lambda_j)/f(\lambda_j)],$$

where $\lambda_j = 2j\pi/T, j = 0, \ldots, [T/2]$, are the equi-spaced frequencies in the interval $[0, \pi]$ at which the periodogram is evaluated. (See also Nerlove et al., 1979, pp. 132–6). Since the true spectral density $f(\lambda)$ depends on the parameters characterizing the process, this asymptotic distribution may be interpreted as a likelihood function. Frequency domain methods, as these are called, may easily be applied in the case of UC models.

Whether approximate or exact maximum-likelihood estimation methods are employed, inference may be based on the usual criteria related to the likelihood function. Unfortunately, serious difficulties may be encountered in applying the asymptotic theory, since the small sample distributions of the MLE's are known to be extremely different from the limiting distributions in important cases. (See Sargan and Bhargava, 1983; Anderson and Takemura, 1984.)

3.3 Prediction and extraction. The problem of prediction is essentially the estimation of an unknown future value of the time series itself; the problem of extraction, best viewed in the context of UC models described in section 2.3 above, is to estimate the value of one of the unobserved components at a particular point in time, not necessarily in the future. Problems of trend extraction and seasonal adjustment may be viewed in this way (Grether and Nerlove, 1970). How the prediction (or extraction) problem is approached depends on whether we are assumed to have an infinite past history and, if not, whether the parameters of the process generating the time series are assumed to be known or not. In practice, of course, an infinite past history is never available, but a very long history is nearly equivalent. if the process is stationary or can be transformed to stationarity. It is usual, as well, to restrict attention to linear predictors, which involves no loss of generality if the processes considered are Gaussian and little loss if merely linear. To devise a theory of optimal prediction or extraction requires some criterion by which to measure the accuracy of a particular candidate. The most common is the minimum mean-square error (MMSE) criterion which is also the conditional expectation of the unknown quantity.

The theory of optimal prediction and extraction due to Kolmogorov (1941) and Wiener (1949) and elaborated by Whittle (1963) for discrete processes assumes a possibly infinite past history and known parameters. Consider the linear process defined by (2). Since the ε_t are i.i.d. zero mean with variance σ^2, it is apparent that the conditional expectation of x_{t+v} given the infinite past to t is

$$\hat{x}_{t+v} = b_v \varepsilon_t + b_{v+1} \varepsilon_{t-1} + \cdots. \tag{22}$$

Of course, even if the parameters $b_j, j = 0, 1, \ldots$, are assumed to be known, the series $\{\varepsilon_t\}$ is not directly observable. The ε_t's are sometimes called the *innovations* of the process, since it is easy to show that $\varepsilon_{t+1} = x_{t+1} - \hat{x}_{t+1}$ are the one-step ahead prediction errors. If the process is invertible, it has the autoregressive representation (6) and so can be expressed solely in terms of the, generally infinite, autoregression

$$\hat{x}_{t+v} = D(L)x_t,\tag{23}$$

where the generating transform of the coefficients of D is

$$D(z) = \frac{1}{B(z)}\left[\frac{B(z)}{z^v}\right]_+.\tag{24}$$

The operator $[\cdot]_+$ eliminates terms having negative powers of z. (The Wiener–Kolmogorov theory is more general than this, since $\{x_t\}$ is allowed to be any non-deterministic, stationary process.)

The problem of extraction may best be viewed in the context of multiple time series; in general we wish to 'predict' one time series $\{y_t\}$ from another related series $\{x_t\}$. It is not necessary that the series $\{y_t\}$ actually be observed as long as its relationship to an observed series $\{x_t\}$ can be described. (See Nerlove et al., 1979, ch. 5.)

The Kalman filter approach (1960) to prediction and extraction is both more special and more general than the Wiener–Kolmogorov theory: attention is restricted to finite parameters, linear processes (effectively ARMA models if the processes considered are stationary), but these processes need not be stationary. The parameters may vary with time, and we do not require an infinite past. This approach represents a powerful tool of practical time-series analysis and may be easily extended to multiple time series. A full discussion, however, requires a discussion of 'state-space representation' of time series processes and is beyond the scope of this article. (See Anderson and Moore, 1979.)

4. MULTIPLE TIME SERIES ANALYSIS

A general treatment of multiple time-series analysis is contained in Hannan (1970). The two-variable case will serve to illustrate the matter in general. Two stationary time series $\{x_t\}$ and $\{y_t\}$ are said to be jointly stationary if their joint distribution function does not depend on the origin from which time is measured. Joint stationarity implies, but is not in general implied by, weak or covariance joint stationarity; that is, $\mathrm{cov}(x_t, y_s)$ is a function of $s - t$ only. In this case the cross-covariance function is

$$\gamma_{yx}(\tau) = E[y_t - \mu_y][x_{t-\tau} - \mu_x],\tag{25}$$

where $\mu_x = Ex_t$ and $\mu_y = Ey_t$. Note that $\gamma_{yx}(\tau)$ and $\gamma_{xy}(\tau)$ are, in general, different. The cross-covariance generating function is defined as

$$g_{yx}(z) = \sum_{-\infty}^{\infty} \gamma_{yx}(\tau)z^\tau\tag{26}$$

in that region of the complex plane in which the right-hand side of (26) converges. For two jointly stationary series this occurs in an annulus containing the unit circle. In this case, the cross-spectral density function is defined as

$$f_{yx}(\lambda) = (1/2\pi)g_{yx}(e^{i\lambda}).\tag{27}$$

Since $\gamma_{yx}(\tau)$ and $\gamma_{xy}(\tau)$ are not equal, the cross-spectral density function is complex valued. The real part is called the co-spectral density and the complex part, the quadrature spectral density, and written

$$f_{yx}(\lambda) = c_{yx}(\lambda) + iq_{yx}(\lambda). \tag{28}$$

In polar form, the cross-spectral density may be written

$$f_{yx}(\lambda) = \alpha_{yx}(\lambda) \exp[i\phi_{yx}(\lambda)], \tag{29}$$

where $\alpha_{yx}(\lambda) = [c_{yx}^2(\lambda) + q_{yx}^2(\lambda)]^{1/2}$ is called the amplitude or gain, and where $\phi_{yx}(\lambda) = \arctan\{-q_{yx}(\lambda)/c_{yx}(\lambda)\}$ is called the phase. Another useful magnitude is the coherence between the two series, defined as

$$\rho_{yx}(\lambda) = \frac{|f_{yx}(\lambda)|^2}{f_{xx}(\lambda)f_{yy}(\lambda)}, \tag{30}$$

which measures the squared correlation between y and x at a frequency λ. Clearly, $\rho_{yx}(\lambda) = \rho_{xy}(\lambda)$. Estimation of cross-spectral density functions and related quantities are discussed in Priestley (1981, pp. 692–712).

The formulation of ARMA and UC models discussed earlier may easily be extended to the multivariate case by interpreting the polynomials in the lag operator as matrix polynomials and the scalar random variables as vectors. Although these models bear a superficial resemblance to the corresponding univariate ones, their structure is, in fact, much more complicated and gives rise to difficult identification problems. In the univariate case, we can formulate simple conditions under which a given covariance function identifies a unique ARMA or UC model, but in the multivariate case these conditions are no longer sufficient. Hannan (1970, 1971) gives a complete treatment. More recently state-space methods have been employed to study the structure of multivariate ARMA models (Hannan, 1976 and, especially, 1979).

5. APPLICATIONS

Time series analytic methods have many applications in economics; here we consider four: (1) Forecasting, (2) Description of seasonality and seasonal adjustment, (3) Analysis of the cyclic properties of economic time series, and (4) Dynamic econometric modelling.

5.1 Forecasting. Time-series models, together with associated methods of trend removal, such as differencing, are widely used in forecasting economic time series. In addition there is a close relationship between the forecasts generated in this way and the forecasts based on the so-called final form of an econometric model.

One of the simplest forecasting procedures is exponential smoothing based on the relationship

$$\hat{y}_{t+1,t} = (1-\theta)y_t + \theta\hat{y}_{t,t-1}, \tag{31}$$

where y_t is the observed series, $\hat{y}_{j,k}$ is the forecast of the series at time j made on the basis of information available up to time k. Muth (1960) showed that (31) gives an optimal (MMSE) forecast if the model generating the time series is $y_t - y_{t-1} = \varepsilon_t - \theta\varepsilon_{t-1}$. Time series which are stationary *after* differencing are said to be generated by autoregressive integrated moving-average (ARIMA) processes. Holt (1957) and Winters (1960) generalize the exponential smoothing approach to models containing more complex trend and seasonal components. Further generalization and proofs of optimality are contained in Theil and Wage (1964) and Nerlove and Wage (1964).

Box–Jenkins procedures (Box and Jenkins, 1970) are based on general ARIMA models of time series processes. The developments discussed in the preceding paragraph led to the more general development of UC models, which give rise to restricted ARIMA model forms (Nerlove et al., 1979).

State-space representations of these models permit the application of the Kalman filter to both estimation and forecasting. Harvey (1984) presents a unified synthesis of the various methods.

5.2 Description of seasonality and seasonal adjustment. Many economic time series exhibit fluctuations which are more or less periodic within a year or a fraction thereof. The proper treatment of seasonality, whether stochastic or deterministic, is the subject of a large literature, summarized rather selectively in Nerlove et al. (1979, ch. 1).

Spectral analysis has been used to detect the presence of seasonality (Nerlove, 1964). Deterministic seasonality, just as deterministic trend, offers no great conceptual problems but many practical ones. Stochastic seasonality is best viewed in terms of UC models (Grether and Nerlove, 1970). Appropriate UC models may be determined directly or by fitting an ARIMA model and deriving a related UC model by imposing sufficient a priori restrictions (Hillmer and Tiao, 1982; Bell and Hillmer, 1984).

5.3 Analysis of the cyclic properties of economic time series. Suppose that the time series $\{x_t\}$ is a linearly non-deterministic stationary series and that the series $\{y_t\}$ is formed from $\{x_t\}$ by the linear operator

$$y_t = \sum_{j=m}^{n} w_j x_{t-j}, \ \sum_{m}^{n} w_j^2 < \infty. \tag{32}$$

Such an operator is called a time-invariant linear filter. Analysis of the properties of such filters plays an important role in time series analysis since many methods of trend estimation or removal and seasonal adjustment may be represented or approximated by such filters. More interestingly, systems of simultaneous econometric equations can also be viewed in this manner and their dynamic stochastic properties studied by analysing the properties of approximating filters. An interesting example which combines both elements is given by Adelman (1965) who showed that the 20-year long swings in various economic series found by Kuznets (1961) may well have been the result of the trend filtering operations used in preliminary processing of the data. For a fuller treatment see Nerlove et al. (1979, pp. 53–7).

5.4 Dynamic econometric modelling. There is a close connection between multivariate time-series models and the structural, reduced and final forms of econometric models: the standard simultaneous-equations econometric model (SEM) is a specific and restricted case.

Suppose that a vector of observed variables y_t may be subdivided into two classes of variables, 'exogenous', $\{x_t\}$, and endogenous, $\{z_t\}$. A dynamic, multivariate simultaneous linear system may be written

$$\begin{bmatrix} \Psi_{11}(L) & \Psi_{12}(L) \\ 0 & \Psi_{22}(L) \end{bmatrix} \begin{pmatrix} z_t \\ x_t \end{pmatrix} = \begin{bmatrix} \Theta_{11}(L) & 0 \\ 0 & \Theta_{22}(L) \end{bmatrix} \begin{pmatrix} \varepsilon_{1t} \\ \varepsilon_{2t} \end{pmatrix} \tag{33}$$

where $\Psi_{ij}(\cdot)$ and $\Theta_{ij}(\cdot)$, $i, j = 1, 2$, are matrix polynomials in the lag operator L. Such systems are known as ARMAX models and conditions for their identification are given by Hatanaka (1975). The reduced form of the system is obtained by solving for $\{y_t\}$ in terms of $\{x_t\}$. The final form is then obtained by eliminating the lagged z's; see Zellner and Palm (1974) and Wallis (1977).

BIBLIOGRAPHY

Adelman, I. 1965. Long cycles – fact or artifact? *American Economic Review* 60, 443–63.

Akaike, H. 1970. Statistical predictor identification. *Annals of the Institute of Statistical Mathematics* 22, 203–17.

Akaike, H. 1974. A new look at the statistical model identification. *IEEE Transactions on Automatic Control* 19, 716–23.

Anderson, B.D.O. and Moore, J.D. 1979. *Optimal Filtering.* Englewood Cliffs: Prentice-Hall.

Anderson, T.W. 1971. *The Statistical Analysis of Time Series.* New York: John Wiley.

Anderson, T.W. 1977. Estimation for autoregressive moving average models in the time and frequency domains. *Annals of Statistics* 5, 842–65.

Anderson, T.W. and Takemura, A. 1984. Why do noninvertible moving averages occur? Technical Report No. 13, Department of Statistics, Stanford University.

Ansley, C.F. 1979. An algorithm for the exact likelihood of a mixed autoregressive-moving average process. *Biometrika* 66, 59–65.

Bell, W. and Hillmer, S. 1984. Issues involved with seasonal analysis of economic time series. *Journal of Business and Economic Statistics* 2, 291–349.

Beveridge, W.H. 1921. Weather and harvest cycles. *Economic Journal* 31, 429–52.

Beveridge, W.H. 1922. Wheat prices and rainfall in western Europe. *Journal of the Royal Statistical Society* 85, 412–59.

Box, G.E.P., Hillmer, S.C. and Tiao, G.C. 1978. Analysis and modeling of seasonal time series. In *Seasonal Analysis of Economic Time Series.* ed. A. Zellner, Washington, DC: US Department of Commerce, Bureau of the Census, 309–44.

Box, G.E.P. and Jenkins, G.M. 1970. *Time Series Analysis: Forecasting and Control.* San Francisco: Holden-Day.

Brillinger, D.C. 1975. *Time Series: Data Analysis and Theory.* New York: Holt.

Burman, J.P. 1980. Seasonal adjustment by signal extraction. *Journal of the Royal Statistical Society*, Series A, 143, 321–37.

Burridge, P. and Wallis, K.F. 1984. Calculating the variance of seasonally adjusted series. Working Paper, University of Warwick.

Cournot, A.A. 1838. *Researches Into the Mathematical Principles of the Theory of Wealth.* Trans. N.T. Bacon, New York: Macmillan, 1927.

Doob, J.L. 1953. *Stochastic Processes.* New York: John Wiley.

Fishman, G.S. 1969. *Spectral Methods in Econometrics.* Cambridge: Harvard University Press.

Fuller, W.A. 1976. *Introduction to Statistical Time Series.* New York: John Wiley.

Granger, C.W.J. 1966. The typical spectral shape of an economic variable. *Econometrica* 34, 150–61.

Granger, C.W.J. and Newbold, P. 1977. *Forecasting Economic Time Series,* New York: Academic Press.

Grether, D.M. and Nerlove, M. 1970. Some properties of 'optimal' seasonal adjustment. *Econometrica* 38, 682–703.

Hannan, E.J. 1960. *Time Series Analysis.* London: Methuen; New York: Wiley.

Hannan, E.J. 1969. The estimation of mixed moving average autoregressive systems. *Biometrika* 56, 223–5.

Hannan, E.J. 1970. *Multiple Time Series.* New York: John Wiley.

Hannan, E.J. 1971. The identification problem for multiple equation systems with moving average errors. *Econometrica* 39, 751–65.

Hannan, E.J. 1976. The identification and parameterization of ARMAX and state space forms. *Econometrica* 44, 713–23.

Hannan, E.J. 1979. The statistical theory of linear systems. In *Developments in Statistics,* ed. P.R. Krishnaiah, New York: Academic Press, 83–121.

Harvey, A.C. 1981a. *The Econometric Analysis of Time Series.* Oxford: Allan.

Harvey, A.C. 1981b. *Time Series Models.* Oxford: Allan: New York: Halsted Press.

Harvey, A.C. 1984. A unified view of statistical forecasting procedures. *Journal of Forecasting* 3, 245–75.

Harvey, A.C. and Peters, S. 1984. Estimation procedures for structural TSM's. Working Paper, London School of Economics.

Harvey, A.C. and Todd, P.H.J. 1984. Forecasting economic time series with structural and Box–Jenkins models: a case study (with discussion). *Journal of Business and Economic Statistics* 1, 299–315.

Hatanaka, M. 1975. On the global identification of the dynamic simultaneous equations model with stationary disturbances. *International Economic Review* 16, 545–54.

Hillmer, S.C. and Tiao, G.C. 1982. An ARIMA-model-based approach to seasonal adjustment. *Journal of the American Statistical Association* 77, 63–70.

Hillmer, S.C., Bell, W.R. and Tiao, G.C. 1983. Modeling considerations in the seasonal analysis of economic time series. In *Applied Time Series Analysis of Economic Data,* ed. A. Zellner. Washington, DC: Dept. of Commerce, Bureau of the Census, 74–100.

Holt, C.C. 1957. Forecasting seasonals and trends by exponentially weighted moving averages. ONR Research Memorandum No. 52, Carnegie Institute of Technology.

Jevons, W.S. 1884. *Investigations in Currency and Finance.* London: Macmillan; New York: A.M. Kelley, 1964.

Kalman, R.E. 1960. A new approach to linear filtering and prediction problems. *Transactions of the American Society of Mechanical Engineers. Journal of Basic Engineering,* Series D 82, 35–45.

Kolmogorov, A. 1941. Interpolation und Extrapolation von Stationären Zufäligen Folgen. *Bulletin of the Academy Science (Nauk), USSR, Mathematical Series* 5, 3–14.

Koopmans, L.H. 1974. *The Spectral Analysis of Time Series.* New York: Academic Press.

Kuznets, S. 1961. *Capital and the American Economy: Its Formation and Financing.* New York: NBER.

Maravall, A. 1981. *Desestacionalizacion y Politica Monetaria.* Economic Studies 19, Bank of Spain, Madrid.

Maravall, A. 1984. Model-based treatment of a manic depressive series. Working Paper, Bank of Spain, Madrid.

Muth, J.F. 1960. Optimal properties of exponentially weighted forecasts. *Journal of the American Statistical Association* 55, 299–305.

Nerlove, M. 1964. Spectral analysis of seasonal adjustment procedures. *Econometrica* 32, 241–86.

Nerlove, M. 1965. A comparison of a modified Hannan and the BLS seasonal adjustment filters. *Journal of the American Statistical Association* 60, 442–91.

Nerlove, M. 1967. Distributed lags and unobserved components in economic time series. In *Ten Economic Essays in the Tradition of Irving Fisher*, ed. W. Fellner, et al., 126–69, New York: John Wiley.

Nerlove, M., Grether, D.M. and Carvalho, J.L. 1979. *Analysis of Economic Time Series.* New York: Academic Press.

Nerlove, M. and Wage, S. 1964. On the optimality of adaptive forecasting. *Management Science* 10, 207–24.

Newbold, P. 1974. The exact likelihood function for a mixed autoregressive-moving average process. *Biometrika* 61(3), 423–6.

Parzen, E. 1961. An approach to time series analysis. *Annals of Mathematical Statistics* 32, 951–89.

Pierce, D.A. 1978. Seasonal adjustment when both deterministic and stochastic seasonality are present. In *Seasonal Analysis of Economic Time Series*, ed. A. Zellner, Washington, DC: Department of Commerce, Bureau of the Census, 242–80.

Pierce, D.A. 1979. Signal extraction error in nonstationary time series. *Annals of Statistics* 7, 1303–20.

Priestley, M.B. 1981. *Spectral Analysis and Time Series.* New York: Academic Press.

Sargan, J.D. and Bhargava, A. 1983. Maximum likelihood estimation of regression models with moving average errors when the root lies on the unit circle. *Econometrica* 51(3), May, 799–820.

Schuster, A. 1898. On the investigation of hidden periodicities with application to the supposed 26-day period of meteorological phenomena. *Terrestrial Magnetism and Atmospheric Electricity* [now *Journal of Geophysical Research*], 3, 13–41.

Schweppe, F.C. 1965. Evaluation of likelihood functions for Gaussian signals. *IEEE Transactions on Information Theory* 11, 61–70.

Slutsky, E. 1927. The summation of random causes as the source of cyclic processes. *Econometrica* 5, April 1937, 105–46.

Stokes, G.C. 1879. Note on searching for hidden periodicities. *Proceedings of the Royal Society* 29, 122–5.

Theil, H. and Wage, S. 1964. Some observations on adaptive forecasting. *Management Science* 10, 198–206.

Wallis, K.F. 1977. Multiple time series analysis and the final form of econometric models. *Econometrica* 45(6), September, 1481–97.

Whittle, P. 1963. *Prediction and Regulation by Linear Least-squares Methods.* London: English University Press; Princeton, N.J.: Van Nostrand.

Wiener, N. 1949. *The Extrapolation, Interpolation and Smoothing of Stationary Time Series with Engineering Applications*. New York: John Wiley.

Winters, P.R. 1960. Forecasting sales by exponentially weighted moving averages. *Management Science* 6, 324–42.

Wold, H.O. 1938. *A Study in the Analysis of Stationary Time Series*. Stockholm: Almqvist and Wiksell.

Yule, G.U. 1921. On the time-correlation problem, with special reference to the variate-difference correlation method. *Journal of the Royal Statistical Society* 84, *July*, 497–526.

Yule, G.U. 1926. Why do we sometimes get nonsense correlations between time series? A study in sampling and the nature of time series. *Journal of the Royal Statistical Society* 89, 1–64.

Yule, G.U. 1927. On a method of investigating periodicities in disturbed series with special reference to Wolfer's sunspot numbers. *Philosophical Transactions of the Royal Society of London* Series A, 226, 267–98.

Zellner, A. and Palm, F. 1974. Time series analysis and simultaneous equation econometric models. *Journal of Econometrics* 2, 17–54.

Transformation of Statistical Variables

D.R. COX

Transformations of many kinds are used in statistical method and theory including simple changes of unit of measurement to facilitate computation or understanding, and the linear transformations underlying the application and theory of multiple regression and the techniques of classical multivariate analysis. Nevertheless the word transformation in a statistical context normally brings to mind a non-linear transformation (to logs, square roots, etc.) of basic observations done with the objective of simplifying analysis and interpretation. The present article focuses on that aspect.

Mostly we discuss problems in which variation in a univariate response variable, y, is to be explained in terms of explanatory variables $x_1, \ldots, x_p$; the terminology here is self-explanatory and avoids overuse of the words dependent and independent! We consider transformations of y and/or some or all of the explanatory variables. Note that where a number of variables are of very similar kinds, it may be sensible to insist on transforming them in the same way.

A brief historical note is desirable. Until the wide availability of computers, the majority of relatively complicated statistical analyses used the method of least squares or fairly direct elaborations thereof. Particular requirements of these methods are linear representations of the expected response, constancy of variance and normality of distribution of errors. When the data manifestly do not obey one or more of these conditions, transformation of variables provides a flexible and powerful technique for recovering a situation to which well-understood methods of analysis are reasonably applicable and thus greatly extends the range of applicability of those methods. With powerful and sometimes even flexible computing facilities now commonplace, such transformations, while remaining important, are less so than they used to be, because it is now feasible to develop special models for each specific application and to implement an appropriate analysis from first principles.

310

PURPOSE OF TRANSFORMATIONS. The key assumptions of the 'classical' methods mentioned above are (a) simplicity of structure, additivity, linearity, absence of interaction; (b) constancy of variance; (c) normality of error distribution. Independence of errors is another very important assumption, needing especially careful consideration in the case of time series data, but is not particularly relevant in the present discussion.

While the relative importance of (a)–(c) depends on the context, they are listed in broadly decreasing order of importance. Linear relations are easy to specify and understand; absence of interaction, for example that important relations retain their form for different groups of data, is important not only for understanding but also as a basis for extrapolation to new groups of data.

Constancy of variance has a triple role. If the pattern of variance is of intrinsic interest, constancy of variance is a reference level for interpretation. If the effect of explanatory variables on whole distributions is of interest, constancy of variance suggests that only changes in location need be studied. Finally constancy of variance is required for various technical statistical reasons. Appreciable changes in variance vitiate standard errors and tests of significance and will lead to a general loss of efficiency; the method of weighted least squares can be used when the nature of the changes in variance is at least roughly known.

The assumption of normality of error distributions is particularly important if the ultimate objective is prediction in the tails of a distribution. Otherwise appreciable non-normality is sometimes an indication that a quite different distributional formulation is called for, sometimes a warning about the occurrence of aberrant values in the data and more broadly is a sign of potential loss of efficiency and possible failure of tests of significance.

The possibility of approximately satisfying all three requirements simultaneously is often an expression of rational optimism, to be assumed although not taken for granted.

An important aspect of any statistical analysis is the presentation of conclusions in a simple form and this may demand reinterpretation of conclusions on to the original scale of measurement.

CONSTRUCTION OF TRANSFORMATIONS. We now discuss in outline a number of techniques for choosing a suitable transformation.

The two most important techniques are probably previous experience of similar data, and the application of diagnostic checks to the analysis of untransformed data. In the latter case it may be clear that 'pulling in' either of the upper tail or of the lower tail of the data would be helpful.

To stabilize variance, a widely used technique is to establish either empirically or theoretically a relation between variance and mean. If for observations of true mean μ the variance is $v(\mu)$, then it is easy to show by local linearization that the transformation

$$y \rightarrow \int_{\theta}^{y} dx/\sqrt{v(x)}$$

311

will induce observations of approximately unit variance. A common possibility is to find $v(\mu)$ approximately of the form $a\mu^b$, often established by plotting log sample variance against log sample mean, when a line of slope b should result. This leads to a power transformation except for $b = 2$, when a log transformation is indicated. The z transformation of correlation coefficients, r,

$$r \to \tfrac{1}{2} \log\{(1 + r)/(1 - r)\}$$

is historically the first example of this argument, the relation between mean and variance being obtained theoretically.

Some simple equations expressing non-linear relations have simple linearizing transformatons, of which the most common and important is the relation

$$y = \alpha x_1^{\beta_1} x_2^{\beta_2},$$

which is linearized by taking logs of all variables. A more empirical approach, not in fact much used in practice, is to search within some family of possible transformations for one which minimizes a measure of non-linearity or interaction.

A much more formal approach to the choice of a transformation is to start with some parametric family of transformations $y \to y^{(\lambda)}$ of which the most important is normally the family of power transformations, including as a limiting case the log transformation. The unknown parameter λ indexes the transformation that is appropriate. If now it is assumed that for some unknown λ the transformed values satisfy all the standard assumptions of some special convenient model, such as the normal theory general linear model, formal methods of estimation, in particular the method of maximum likelihood, can be applied to estimate λ, to see whether there is evidence that a transformation really does improve fit, to compare the values of λ in several unrelated sets of data, and so on. The calculations are relatively simple and straightforward. The usual procedure is to choose as a scale for analysis that corresponding to a simple value of λ reasonably consistent with the data.

Transformations to normality are always possible for a single continuous distribution, because any continuous distribution can be transformed into any other. Normalizing transformations are quite widely used in theoretical arguments; their direct use in the analysis of empirical data is on the whole rather less common, essentially for the reasons outlined above.

SOME FURTHER DEVELOPMENTS. The topics outlined above have an extensive literature. Some recent points of discussion and open issues are as follows:

(i) There are no good techniques for the transformation of multivariate distributions other than component by component.

(ii) Transformation selection by methods that are robust to outliers have been discussed, although in many practical situations it is the extreme observations that carry the most information about the appropriateness of transformations and whose accommodation is particularly important.

(iii) Following the choice of a transformation estimation and interpretation of effects is usually carried out on the transformed scale as if this had been given a priori. The appropriateness and justification of this has been the subject of lively discussion.

(iv) It is possible to transform to simple models other than the standard normal ones, for example to the exponential based models so useful in the analysis of duration data.

(v) The main procedures discussed above involve an interpretation essentially in terms of the expected response on the transformed scale. An alternative approach postulates that the expected value of the response on the original scale is a suitable non-linear function of a linear combination of explanatory variables. To distinguish empirically between these formulations is likely to require a large amount of high quality data.

(vi) Methods can be developed for estimating transforming functions totally non-parametrically. Such an approach uses a great deal of computer time.

BIBLIOGRAPHY
Bartlett (1943) gives an excellent account of the early work; Box and Cox (1964) discuss the estimation of transformations via the likelihood and Bayesian methods. Butter and Verbon (1982) describe economic applications in some depth. Bickel and Doksum (1981) and Box and Cox (1982) give opposing views of estimation following a transformation.

Bartlett, M.S. 1947. The use of transformations. *Biometrics* 3, 39–52.

Bickel, P.J. and Doksum, K.A. 1981. An analysis of transformations revisited. *Journal of the American Statistical Association* 76, 296–311.

Box, G.E.P. and Cox, D.R. 1964. An analysis of transformations. *Journal of the Royal Statistical Society*, Series B 26, 211–43.

Box, G.E.P. and Cox, D.R. 1982. An analysis of transformations revisited, rebutted. *Journal of the American Statistical Association* 77, 209–10.

den Butter, F.A.G. and Verbon, H.A.A. 1982. The specification problem in regression analysis. *International Statistical Review* 50, 267–83.

Abraham Wald

E.R. WEINTRAUB

Born in Cluj, Rumania, Wald came to Vienna in 1927 to study mathematics with Karl Menger, the geometer and son of the economist Carl Menger. Menger introduced Wald to the active mathematical group in Vienna, and secured for him a position as mathematical tutor to the economist Karl Schlesinger. This led to Wald's producing the first proofs of existence for models of general equilibrium; his analysis was based on Cassel's restatement of the Walrasian model, as modified by Schlesinger's treatment of free goods. These works were published in the proceedings of Menger's mathematical colloquium, and a summary was published in the *Zeitschrift für Nationalökonomie* in 1936. These papers were remarkable for their time and, with von Neumann's paper on equilibrium in a model of an expanding economy, are the first significant contributions to the mathematical analysis of general equilibrium models in economics. Wald is the link between the early work by Walras and the later work by Kenneth Arrow, Gerard Debreu and Lionel McKenzie on the existence of competitive equilibria.

A fine mathematician, Wald was nevertheless prevented from gaining a regular academic position because of Viennese anti-semitism. Menger helped Wald secure a consultancy position with Oskar Morgenstern who directed the Institut für Konjunkturforschung, where Wald took an interest in the statistical problems that were associated with the analysis of business cycles. Wald's book on seasonal adjustment of time series was a result of his work at Morgenstern's Institut.

Wald was able to escape from Vienna when the Nazis arrived, and made his way to the United States where he initially secured a fellowship, in 1938, at the Cowles Commission which was then at Colorado Springs. When the Commission moved to Chicago, Wald obtained a position, on a Carnegie grant, as Harold Hotelling's assistant at Columbia University. He moved to a faculty post at Columbia in 1941, and was promoted to Associate Professor in 1943 and Professor in 1944.

Wald's contributions to statistics are immense. His most significant paper

314

appeared in 1939 in the *Annals of Mathematical Statistics* as 'Contributions to the theory of statistical estimation and testing hypotheses' (in Wald, 1955). This paper, written before modern decision theory was developed, contained notions of decision space, weight and risk functions, and minimax solution (based on von Neumann's 1928 paper on game theory). Wald's paper was not appreciated at the time, much as was the case with his papers on general equilibrium theory. He did not return to statistical decision theory until 1946, after von Neumann and Morgenstern had presented the theory of games.

During World War II, Wald worked with the Statistical Research Group and developed much of the theory of sequential analysis. Although he did not create the idea of taking observations sequentially, Wald did invent the sequential probability ratio test. This original material was published in 1947 after wartime restrictions were lifted.

In 1950, at the height of his powers, Wald and his wife died in a plane crash in India.

SELECTED WORKS
In 1952 *The Annals of Mathematical Statistics* devoted the first part of its Volume 23 to a memorial to Wald. Articles on Wald by Jacob Wolfowitz, Karl Menger, and Gerhard Tintner were followed by a complete bibliography of Wald's writings. Wald's professional correspondence, and papers from his Viennese days, cannot be located, though it is possible that Karl Menger's archives, currently closed to examination, may contain some material on Wald.

1934. Über die eindeutige positive Lösbarkeit der neuen Produktions gleichungen I. In *Ergebnisse eines mathematischen Kolloquiums, 1933–34*, ed. K. Menger. Trans. by W. Baumol as 'On the unique non-negative solvability of the new production equations, part I', in *Precursors in Mathematical Economics*, ed. W.J. Baumol and S.M. Goldfeld, London School of Economics Series of Reprints of Scarce Works on Political Economy No. 19, London: London School of Economics, 1968.

1935. Über die Produktionsgleichungen der ökonomischen Wertlehre II. In *Ergebnisse eines mathematischen Kolloquiums, 1934–35*, ed. K. Menger. Trans. by W. Baumol as 'On the production equations of economic value theory, part II', in *Precursors in Mathematical Economics*, ed. W.J. Baumol and S.M. Goldfeld, London School of Economics Series of Reprints of Scarce Works on Political Economy No. 19, London: London School of Economics, 1968.

1936. Über einige Gleichungssysteme der mathematischen Ökonomie. *Zeitschrift für Nationalökonomie*. Trans. by O. Eckstein as 'On some systems of equations in mathematical economics', *Econometrica* 19(4), October 1951, 368–403.

1947. *Sequential Analysis*. New York: John Wiley.

1950. *Statistical Decision Functions*. New York: John Wiley.

1955. *Selected Papers in Statistics and Probability*. New York: McGraw-Hill.

315

Wiener Process

A.G. MALLIARIS

Brownian motion is the most renowned, and historically the first stochastic process that was thoroughly investigated. It is named after the English botanist, Robert Brown who in 1827 observed that small particles immersed in a liquid exhibited ceaseless irregular motion. Brown himself mentions several precursors starting at the beginning with Leeuwenhoek (1632–1723). In 1905 Einstein, unaware of the existence of earlier investigations about Brownian motion, obtained a mathematical derivation of this process from the laws of physics. The theory of Brownian motion was further developed by several distinguished mathematical physicists until Norbert Wiener gave it a rigorous mathematical formulation in his 1918 dissertation and in later papers. This is why the Brownian motion is also called the Wiener process. For a brief history of the scientific developments of the process see Nelson (1967).

Having made these remarks we now define the process. A *Wiener process* or a *Brownian motion process*

$$\{Z(t, \omega): [0, \infty) \times \Omega \to R\}$$

is a stochastic process with index $t \in [0, \infty)$ on a probability space Ω, and mapping to the real line R, with the following properties:

(1) $Z(0, \omega) = 0$ with probability 1, that is by convention we assume that the process starts at zero.

(2) If $0 \leqslant t_0 \leqslant t_1 \leqslant \cdots \leqslant t_n$ are time points then for any real set H_i

$$P[Z(t_i) - Z(t_{t-1}) \in H_i \text{ for } i \leqslant n] = \prod_{i \leqslant n} P[Z(t_i) - Z(t_{i-1}) \in H_i].$$

This means that the increments of the process $Z(t_i) - Z(t_{i-1})$, $i \leqslant n$, are independent variables.

316

(3) For $0 \leqslant s < t$, the increment $Z(t) - Z(s)$ has distribution

$$P[Z(t) - Z(s) \in H] = (1/\sqrt{2\pi(t-s)}) \int_H \exp[-x^2/2(t-s)] \, dx.$$

This means that every increment $Z(t) - Z(s)$ is normally distributed with mean zero and variance $(t - s)$.

(4) For each $\omega \in \Omega$, $Z(t, \omega)$ is continuous in t, for $t \geqslant 0$.

Note that condition (4) can be proved mathematically using the first three conditions. Here it is added because in many applications such continuity is essential. Although the sample paths of the Wiener process are continuous, we immediately state an important theorem about their differentiability properties.

Theorem. (Non-differentiability of the Wiener process.) Let $\{Z(t), t \geqslant 0\}$ be a Wiener process in a given probability space. Then for ω outside some set of probability 0, the sample path $Z(t, \omega)$, $t \geqslant 0$, is nowhere differentiable.

Intuitively, a nowhere differentiable sample path represents the motion of a particle which at no time has a velocity. Thus, although the sample paths are continuous, this theorem suggests that they are very kinky, and their derivatives exist nowhere. The mathematical theory of the Wiener process is briefly presented in Billingsley (1979) and more extensively in Knight (1981).

The first application of Brownian motion or the Wiener process in economics was made by Louis Bachelier in his dissertation 'Théorie de la spéculation' in 1900. Cootner (1964) collects several papers and cites additional references on the application of the Wiener process in describing the random character of the stock market. In the early 1970s Merton, in a series of papers, established the use of stochastic calculus as a tool in financial economics. The Wiener process is a basic concept in stochastic calculus and its applicability in economics arises from the fact that the Wiener process can be regarded as the limit of a continuous time *random walk* as step sizes become infinitesimally small. In other words, the Wiener process can be used as the cornerstone in modelling *economic uncertainty* in continuous time. For purposes of illustration consider the stochastic differential equation

$$dX(t) = \mu(t, x) \, dt + \sigma(t, x) \, dZ(t) \tag{1}$$

which appears in the economic literature describing asset prices, rate of inflation, quantity of money or other variables. In (1), changes in the variable $X(t)$, denoted as $dX(t)$, are described as a sum of two terms: $\mu(t, x)$ which is the *expected* instantaneous change and $\sigma(t, x) \, dZ(t)$ which is the *unexpected* change. Furthermore, this unexpected change is the product of the instantaneous standard deviation $\sigma(t, x)$ and uncertainty modelled by increments in the Wiener process. See Merton (1975) for a methodological essay on continuous time modelling and Malliaris and Brock (1982) or Harrison (1985) for numerous applications of the Wiener process in economics and business.

Economists have constructed various processes based on the Wiener process. Let $\{Z(t), t \geqslant 0\}$ be a Wiener process and use it to construct a process

$\{W(t), t \geqslant 0\}$ defined by $W(t) = Z(t) + \mu t$, $t \geqslant 0$, where μ is a constant. Then we say that $\{W(t), t \geqslant 0\}$ is a *Wiener process* or *Brownian motion process with drift* and μ is called the drift parameter. In this case the only modification that occurs in the definition of a Wiener process is in property (3) where $W(t) - W(s)$ is normally distributed with mean $\mu(t - s)$ and variance $(t - s)$. Finally, let $W(t)$ be a Wiener process with drift as just defined. Consider the new process given by $Y(t) = \exp[W(t)]$, $t \geqslant 0$. Then $\{Y(t), t \geqslant 0\}$ is called a *geometric Brownian motion* or *geometric Wiener process*.

The availability of an extensive mathematical literature on the Wiener process and the economists' fundamental goal to model economic uncertainty in continuous time suggest that this process will continue to be an important tool for economic theorists.

BIBLIOGRAPHY

Billingsley, P. 1979. *Probability and Measure.* New York: John Wiley.

Cootner, P.H. 1964. *The Random Character of Stock Market Prices.* Cambridge, Mass. MIT Press.

Harrison, J.M. 1985. *Brownian Motion and Stochastic Flow Systems.* New York: John Wiley.

Knight, F.B. 1981. *Essentials of Brownian Motion and Diffusion.* Mathematical Surveys, Number 18. The American Mathematical Society, Providence, Rhode Island.

Malliaris, A.G. and Brock, W.A. 1982. *Stochastic Methods in Economics and Finance.* Amsterdam: North-Holland Publishing Company.

Merton, R.C. 1975. Theory of finance from the perspective of continuous time. *Journal of Financial and Quantitative Analysis* 10, 659–74.

Nelson, E. 1967. *Dynamical Theories of Brownian Motion.* Princeton, New Jersey: Princeton University Press.

Contributors

Irma Adelman Professor of Economics, University of California, Berkeley. Fellow, Econometric Society; Member, Social Science Assembly, National Academy of Sciences; Vice President, American Economics Association. *Theories of Economic Growth and Development* (1958); *Society, Politics and Economic Development: a quantitative approach* (1967); *Economic Growth and Social Equity in Developing Countries* (1973); *Practical Approaches to Development Planning – Korea's second five year plan* (1969); *Income Distribution Policy in Developing Countries: a case study of Korea* (1978).

F.J. Anscombe Professor, Department of Statistics, Yale University. *Computing in Statistical Science Through APL* (1981).

Kenneth J. Arrow John Kenney Professor of Economics, Professor of Operations Research, Stanford University. Nobel Memorial Prize in Economic Science (1972). 'Le role des valeurs boursieres pour la repartition la meilleure des risques', *Econometrie* (1953); 'Existence of equilibrium for a competitive economy', *Econometrica* (with G. Debreu, 1954); 'Uncertainty and the welfare economics of medical care', *American Economic Review* (1963); *Social Choice and Individual Values* (1963); *Essays in the Theory of Risk-Bearing* (1971).

Robert L. Basmann Econometric Statistician. *Advances in Econometrics* (ed., with George F. Rhodes, 1982); *The Generalized Fechner – Thurstone Direct Utility Function* (ed., 1988).

James O. Berger Richard M. Brumfield Distinguished Professor of Statistics, Purdue University. Guggenheim Fellow (1977–8); Sloan Fellow (1979–81). 'The robust Bayesian viewpoint', *Robustness in Bayesian Statistics* (ed. J. Kadane, 1984); *Statistical Decision Theory* (1985); *The Likelihood Principle: a review and generalizations* (1988); 'Analyzing data: is objectivity possible?', *American Scientist* (1988).

Soo Hong Chew Professor, Department of Economics, University of Arizona. 'A generalization of the quasilinear mean with applications to the measurement of income inequality with decision theory resolving the Allais paradox', *Econometrica* (1983); 'Risk aversion in the theory of expected utility with rank-dependent probabilities', *Journal of Economic Theory* (forthcoming).

Gregory C. Chow Professor of Economics, Princeton University. *The Chinese Economy* (1985); *Econometrics* (1983); *Econometric Analysis by Control Methods* (1981); *Demand for Automobiles in the United States: A Study in Consumer Durables* (1957); 'Tests of equality between sets of coefficients in two linear regressions', *Econometrica* (1960).

Stephen R. Cosslett Professor, Department of Economics, Ohio State University. 'Distribution – free maximum likelihood estimator of the binary choice model', *Econometrica* (1983).

D.R. Cox Warden, Nuffield College, Oxford. Fellow, Royal Society. *Theoretical Statistics* (1974); *The Theory of Stochastic Processes* (with H.D. Miller, 1965); *Survival Data* (with D. Oakes, 1979); *Point Processes* (with Valerie Isham, 1980); *Renewal Theory* (1962); *Analysis of Survival Data* (with D. Oakes, 1984).

John G. Cragg Professor of Economics, University of British Columbia. 'On the relative small-sample properties of several structural-equation estimators', *Econometrica* 35 (1967); 'Some statistical models for limited dependent variables with application to the demand for durable goods', *Econometrica* 39 (1971); *Expectations and the Valuation of Shares* (with Burton G. Malkiel, 1982); 'Estimation and testing in time-series regression models with heteroscedastic disturbances', *Journal of Econometrics* (1982); 'More efficient estimation in the prescence of heteroscedasticity of unknown form', *Econometrica* 51 (1983); 'The relationship of dividend payments to the characteristics of the earning streams of corporation' in *Prices, Competition and Equilibrium* (ed. M.H. Peston and R.E. Quaudt, 1986).

Francis X. Diebold Economist, Division of Research and Statistics, Federal Reserve Board, Washington; Lecturer, Department of Economics, University of Maryland. *Empirical Modelling of Exchange Rate Dynamics* (1988); 'Serial correlation and the combination of forecasts', *Journal of Business and Economic Statistics* (1987); 'Testing for bubbles, reflecting barriers, and other anomalies', *Journal of Economic Dynamics and Control* (1988); 'Endogenous risk in a rational-expectations portfolio-balance model of the Deutschmark/Dollar rate', *European Economic Review* (with Peter Pauly, 1988); 'The dynamics of exchange rate volatility: a multivariate latent-factor arch model', *Journal of Applied Econometrics* (1989); 'Scoring the leading indicators', *Journal of Business* (1989).

A.W.F. Edwards Reader in Mathematical Biology, University of Cambridge. *Likelihood* (1972); *Foundations of Mathematical Genetics* (1977); *Pascal's Arithmetical Triangle* (1987); 'Are Mendel's results really too close?', *Biological Review* (1986).

Giancarlo Gandolpho Professor of International Economics, Faculty of Economics and Commerce; Director of Graduate Studies, Department of Economics, University of Rome. *Mathematical Methods and Models in Economic Dynamics* (1971); *Qualitative Analysis and Economic Estimation of Continuous Time Dynamic Models* (1981); *A Disequilibrium Model of Real and Financial Accumulation in an Open Economy: theory, empirical evidence, and policy simulations* (with P.C. Padoan, 1984); *International Economics I and II* (1987); 'The Italian continuous time model: theory and empirical results', *Economic Modelling* (with P.C. Padoan, 1989).

Joseph L. Gastwirth Professor of Statistics, George Washington University. Guggenheim Fellow (1985); Fellow, American Statistical Association. *Statistical Reasoning in Law and Public Policy* (1988); 'Nonparametric tests in small unbalanced samples: application in employment discrimination cases', *Canadian Journal of Statistics* (with J.L. Wang, 1987); 'Two statistical methods for analyzing claims of employment discrimination', *Industrial and Labor Relations Review* (1984); 'Interpolation from grouped data for unimodal densities', *Econometrica* (with A. Krieger, 1984); 'Robust estimation of the Lorenz curve and Gini index', *Review of Economics and Statistics* (1972); 'On robust Procedures', *Journal of the American Statistical Association* (1966).

Clive W.J. Granger Professor of Economics, University of California, San Diego. Fellow, Econometric Society; Guggenheim Fellow (1988). *Spectral Analysis of Economics Time Series* (with M. Hatanaka, 1964). *Predictability of Stock Market Prices* (with O. Morgenstern, 1970); *Introduction to Bilinear Time Series Models* (with A. Andersen, 1978); *Forecasting in Business and Economics* (1980); *Forecasting Time Series* (with Paul Newbold, 1987).

E.J. Hannan Emeritus Professor, Australian National University. Fellow, Econometric Society, Australian Academy of Science, Academy of Social Science in Australia. *Time Series Analysis* (1960); *Group Representatives and Applied Probability* (1965); *Multiple Time Series* (1970); *The Statistical Theory of Linear Systems* (with Manfred Deistler, 1988).

A.C. Harvey Professor of Econometrics, London School of Economics. *The Econometric Analysis of Time Series Models* (1981); *Time Series Models* (1981).

Alan F. Karr Professor, Department of Mathematical Sciences, Johns Hopkins University. Fellow, Institute of Mathematical Statistics; Editor SIAM Journal on Applied Mathematics. *Point Processes and their Statistical Inference* (1986);

'Inference for thinned point processes, with application to Cox processes', *Journal of Multivariate Analysis* 16 (1985); 'State estimation for Cox processes with unknown probability law' in *Stochastic Processes Applications* (1985); 'Estimation of Palm measures of stationary point processes', *Probability Theory Related Fields* 74 (1987); 'Maximum likelihood estimation in the multiplicative intensity model, via sieves', *Annual of Statistics* 15 (1987).

T. Kloek Professor of Econometrics, Erasmus University, Rotterdam. Fellow, Econometric Society. 'Simultaneous equations estimation based on principal components of predetermined variables', *Econometrica* 28 (with L.B.M. Mennes, 1960); 'Best linear and best linear unbiased index numbers', *Econometrica* 29 (with G.M. de Wit, 1961); 'A note on a class of utility and production functions yielding everywhere differentiable demand functions', *The Review of Economic Studies* 36 (with A.P. Barten and F.B. Lempers, 1969); 'Bayesian estimates of equation system parameters: an application of integration by Monte Carlo', *Econometrica* 46 (with H.K. van Dijk, 1978); 'Inferential procedures in stable distributions for class frequency data on incomes', *Econometrica* 48 (with H.K. van Dijk, 1980); 'Dynamic adjustment when the target is nonstationary', *International Economic Review* 25 (1984).

J. Kmenta Professor of Economics and Statistics, University of Michigan. Fellow, Econometric Society, American Statistical Association. *Elements of Econometrics* (1986); *Large-Scale Macro-Econometric Models* (ed. with J.B. Ramsey, 1981); *Evaluation of Econometric Models* (ed. with J.B. Ramsey, 1980); 'Formulation and estimation of production function models', *Econometrica* 37 (with A. Zellner and J. Dreze, 1966); 'On estimation of the CES production function', *International Economic Review* 8 (1967); 'Small sample properties of alternative estimators of seemingly unrelated regressions', *Journal of the American Statistical Association* 63 (with R.F. Gilbert, 1968).

William S. Krasker Professor, Harvard University. 'Estimation in linear regression models with disparate data points', *Econometrica* (1980); 'Estimation for dirty data and flawed models', *Handbook of Econometrics* (with E. Kuh and R.E. Welsch, ed. Z. Griliches and M.D. Intriligator, 1983); 'Efficient bounded-influence regression estimation', *Journal of the American Statistical Association* (with R.E. Welsch, 1982); 'Resistant estimation for simultaneous-equations models using weighted instrumental variables', *Econometrica* (with R.E. Welsch, 1985).

Dennis V. Lindley Professor of Statistics, University College, London. *Introduction to Probability and Statistics: from a Bayesian Viewpoint* (1965); *Bayesian Statistics: a review* (1972); *Making Decisions* (1985); *New Cambridge Elementary Statistical Tables* (with W.F. Scott, 1984).

R. Duncan Luce Distinguished Professor of Social Science, Director, Irvine Research Institute in Mathematical Behavioral Science, University of California.

Distinguished Scientific Contributions Award, American Psychological Association. *Response Times* (1986); *Foundations of Measurements* Vol. I (with D.H. Krantz, P. Suppes and A. Tversky, 1971); *Steven's Handbook of Experimental Psychology* (1988); *Games and Decisions* (with H. Raiffa, 1957); 'Rank-dependent subjective-expected utility', *Journal of Risk and Uncertainty* (forthcoming).

A.G. Malliaris Walter F. Mullady Senior Professor of Economics, Graduate School of Business, Loyola University of Chicago. *Stochastic Methods in Economics and Finance* (1982); 'Asymptotic growth under uncertainty: existence and uniqueness', *Review of Economic Studies* 54 (with Fwu-Ranq Chang, 1987); 'Minimizing a quadratic payoff with monotone controls', *Mathematics of Operations Research* 12(2), (with E. N. Barron and R. Jensen, 1987); 'Ito's calculus in financial decision making', *Society of Industrial and Applied Mathematics Review* 24(4) (1983); 'Martingale methods in financial decision making', *Society of Industrial and Applied Mathematics Review* 23(4), (1981); *Differential Equations, Stability and Chaos in Dynamic Economics* (1989).

Louis Narens 'Classification of concatenation measurement structures according to scale type', *Journal of Mathematical Psychology* (with R.D. Luce, 1985); 'A general theory of ratio scalability with remarks about the measurement – theoretic concept of meaningfulness', *Theory and Decision* (1981); *Abstract Measurement Theory* (1985); 'The algebra of measurement', *Journal of Pure and Applied Algebra* (with R.D. Luce, 1976); 'How we may have been misled into believing in the interpersonal comparability of utility', *Theory and Decision* (with R.D. Luce, 1983).

Marc Nerlove Professor of Economics, University of Pennsylvania. John Bates Clark Medal, American Economic Association (1969). *Population Policy and Individual Choice: A Theoretical Analysis* (with A. Razin and E. Sadka, 1987); *Household and Economy: welfare economics of endogenous fertility* (with A. Razin and E. Sadka, 1987); *Analysis of Economic Time Series: a synthesis* (with D.M. Grether and J.L. Carvalho, 1979); *Estimation and Indentification of Cobb–Douglas Production Functions* (1965); *The Dynamics of Supply: estimation of farmers' response to price* (1958); *Distributed Lags and Demand Analysis* (1958).

William Parry Professor, Mathematics Institute, University of Warwick. 'Metric classification of ergodic nilflows and unpotent affines', *American Journal of Mathematics* 3 (1971); *Entropy and Generators in Ergodic Theory* (1969); *Topics in Ergodic Theory* (1981); 'An analogue of the prime number theorem for closed orbits of Axiom A flows', *Annals of Mathematics* 188 (with M. Pollicott, 1983).

Dale J. Poirier Professor of Economics, University of Toronto. *The Econometrics of Structural Change* (1976); 'Frequentist and subjectivist perspectives on the problems of model building in economics (with discussion)', *Journal of Economic Perspectives* 2 (1988); 'A diagnostic test for normality within the power exponential family', *Journal of Business and Economic Statistics* 4 (with Mario Tello and Stanley Zin, 1986); 'Model occurrence and model selection in panel data sets', *Journal of Econometrics* 17 (with Steven Klepper, 1981); 'Partial observability in bivariate probit models', *Journal of Econometrics* 12 (1980); 'A note on the interpretation of regression coefficients within a class of truncated distributions', *Econometrica* 46 (with Angelo Melino, 1978).

I. Richard Savage Professor of Statistics, Yale University. *Statistics: Uncertainty and Behavior* (1968).

Christopher A. Sims Professor, Department of Economics, University of Minnesota. 'A rational expectations framework for short run policy analysis' in *New Approaches to Monetary Economics* (ed. Barnett and Singleton, 1987); 'Forecasting a conditional projection using realistic prior distributions', *Econometric Review* (with T. Duan and R. Literman, 1984); 'Comparison of inter-war and post-war business cycles: monetarism reconsidered', *American Economic Review* (1980); 'Macroeconomics and reality', *Econometrica* (1980); 'Distributed log estimation when the parameter space is explicitly infinite-dimensional', *Annals of Mathematical Statisticals* (1972).

Stephen M. Stigler Professor, Department of Economics, University of Chicago. *The History of Statistics: the Measurement of Uncertainty before 1900* (1986).

E. Roy Weintraub Professor, Department of Economics, Duke University. *General Equilibrium Theory* (1974); *Microfoundations* (1979).

Halbert White Professor of Economics, University of California, San Diego. 'Using least squares to approximate unknown regression functions', *International Economic Review* (1980); 'Nonlinear regression on cross-section data', *Econometrica* (1980); 'A heteroscedasticity-consistent covariance matrix estimator and a direct test heteroskedasticity', *Econometrica* (1980); 'Consequences and detection of misspecified nonlinear regression models', *Journal of the American Statistical Association* (1981); *Asymptotic Theory for Econometricians* (1984); *A Unified Theory of Estimation and Inference for Nonlinear Dynamic Models* (with A. Ronald Gallant, 1988).

Peter Whittle Churchill Professor of the Mathematics of Operational Research, University of Cambridge. *Hypothesis Testing in Time Series Analysis* (1951); *Prediction and Regulation* (1963); *Probability* (1970); *Optimisation under Constraints* (1971); *Optimisation over Time* (2 Vols., 1982/3); *Systems in Stochastic Equilibrium* (1986).

Arnold Zellner H.G.B. Alexander Distinguished Service Professor of Economics And Statistics, Director, H.G.B. Alexander Research Foundation, Graduate School of Business, University of Chicago. Fellow, Econometric Society, American

Statistical Association. *An Introduction to Bayesian Inference in Econometrics* (1987); *Basic Issues in Econometrics* (1984); 'An efficient method of estimating seemingly unrelated regressions and tests for aggregation bias', *Journal of the American Statistical Association* (1962); 'Statistical analysis of econometric models', *Journal of the American Statistical Association* (1979); 'Bayesian Econometrics', *Econometrica* (1985); 'Science, economics and public policy', *The American Economist* (1987).